'Finally, absolutely fresh and significan̶t̶ ̶i̶n̶s̶i̶g̶h̶t̶s̶ on China! Dr. David Scharff has achieved what neither a desk-bound policy wonk nor an impression-gathering journalist could have done: given us a bottom-up portrait of China today. Drawing on interviews conducted over more than a decade as an on-site psychiatrist, he lets his subjects tell their own stories, as individuals, couples and families. And what stories they are; dramatic tales of change, trauma, and of resilience and affirmation in the lives of real men, women, and children in today's China. In every interview one feels the weight of tradition but, equally, pressures for change from the Communist Party's periodic crusades and from the country's embrace of globalization. Who knows where this complex process will lead? Dr. Scharff does not claim to have the answer, but his reality-based speculations are always wise and often brilliant.'

–S. Frederick Starr, PhD, Founding Chair of the Central Asia-Caucasus Institute and Silk Road Studies Program; Research Professor and Distinguished Fellow, American Foreign Policy Institute, Washington, DC

'For 13 years, Dr. Scharff has visited China: teaching, treating, and supervising Chinese mental health professionals while focusing on marriage, sexuality and familial relations from psychoanalytic, cultural and historical perspectives. His explorations are informed by the common humanity of the Chinese people, Chinese culture and specific historical events (e.g., the many traumata, the one child family, etc.) This book is replete with clinical examples. He considers how current changes in marital and familial relations will impact future Chinese culture. I highly recommend this wonderful book.'

–Elise Snyder, MD, is Associate Clinical Professor, Yale University; Visiting Professor, Sichuan University; and President, China American Psychoanalytic Alliance

'This book is written by a distinguished American psychoanalyst and family and couple therapist who has had extensive experiences with a number of middle-class families and couples in China. It illustrates the importance of recognizing past and present historical events and cultural elements in the effort to understand human psychology. It is most timely as we wonder how the COVID-19 pandemic will change individuals, couples and families in China and as well as in other parts of the world.'

–Vamik Volkan, MD, Emeritus Professor of Psychiatry; Author of Large Group Psychology: Racism, Societal Divisions, Narcissistic Leaders and Who We Are Now (2020)

'David Scharff, an experienced psychoanalyst and family and couples therapist, gives us a wonderful book which integrates Chinese personal and family dynamics with cultural and historical developments, including the Confucian heritage, the Cultural Revolution, the Great Leap Forward, urban migration, and the one-child policy, and their sequelae. His case material is clear, rich, personal, and fascinating. All readers interested in modern China or in comparative marital patterns should read this book.'

–Peter Loewenberg, PhD, Emeritus Professor of History and Political Psychology, UCLA; Founding Chair, International Psychoanalytical Association's China Committee

'Rapid economic and social development in China is producing opportunity for better standards of living, but also places significant stress on families. Dr. Scharff is one of the pioneers who have introduced and developed marital and family therapy in China. While training Chinese therapists, he has sought to understand Chinese families and to help them with a wide variety of difficulties. This new book brings together his valuable views and understanding of Chinese couples and families based on solid clinical experience. Both Chinese therapists and a wide variety of students of China will derive great benefit from this book.'

–Jianyin Qiu, MD, PhD, Deputy Director, Department of Medical Psychology, Jiao Tong University Medical School, Shanghai; Vice Director, Psychoanalytic Committee of the Chinese Mental Health Association

'David Scharff MD is a leading presence in the field of family therapy as practiced in China – and a pioneer in this realm, for he actually helped to build the field from the ground up by training many of China's present practitioners. In this treasury (he calls it a "treatise") Dr. Scharff shares with us years of distilled experience and reflection. He is an acute and empathetic observer, with a sensitive eye to the humanity and individuality of each case he discusses, but also a discerning sense of what may make the craft, or at least its practice, distinct and different in a Chinese setting. As a social scientist I cannot opine on the merit of his work for his fellow psychoanalysts, but I can attest that Dr. Scharff is peering at China though an exciting new lens: and that his insights will be valuable to readers well beyond the confines of his profession.'

–Nicholas Eberstadt, PhD, Henry Wendt Chair in Political Economy at the American Enterprise Institute; Senior Advisor to the National Bureau of Asian Research; Author of China's Changing Family Structure: Dimensions and Implications *(2019)*

'This book is a crystallization of an American psychoanalyst's rich experiences of training and teaching couple and family therapy in China. He not only teaches us how to help Chinese couples with impasses in their marriages through employing psychoanalytic theory and technique, but he also interprets patterns of Chinese marital and family relationships. He traces the tremendous changes that have occurred over time as well as current challenges from the multiple perspectives of society, culture, history and psychic trauma. This book speaks to the central question: "How does the history of Chinese culture influence the intimacy of family life today?" There are many Chinese translations of classical psychoanalytic books, but this is the first book to bring to hand detailed interviews of Chinese couples and families. This book will bring new insight to Chinese students and practitioners of psychotherapy and psychological counselling.'

–Yang Yunping, MD, Psychiatrist and Psychoanalyst; Member of the International Psychoanalytical Association; Senior Staff, Anding Hospital, Beijing

'David Scharff's *Marriage and Family in Modern China* brings a much-needed probe into the values, habits and practices urban Chinese bring to their marriages. Scharff's psychoanalytical framework provides a useful heuristic framework that is at times, deliciously insightful in its probing of individuals' subjective experience as it pertains to love, sex, and marital misery and bliss.'

–William Jankowiak, PhD, Professor of Anthropology at the University of Nevada, Las Vegas; Co-author of Family Life in China *(2016)*

'David Scharff is the first writer to explore Chinese families and marriages from a psychoanalytic point of view. His book offers deep understanding of the Chinese collective unconscious and of the light and dark that lurk inside Chinese families. The book is enriched by abundant case material set in historical and cultural context, providing insights essential to psychoanalytic clinicians and teachers as they work to understand the unique challenges in practicing family and marital therapy in China. Scharff's brilliant insights offer an essential guide to all mental health practitioners – Chinese and Western alike – to their clients, and to all who wish to understand the challenges facing Chinese families today.'

–Li Mengchao, MD, Psychiatrist in Private Practice, Shanghai; Associate Editor of Psychoanalysis and Psychotherapy in China

'This book asks much-needed questions on intercultural and couple and family psychoanalysis, focusing on clinical vignettes of Chinese families. Using object relations theory and drawing on his own experiences of engaging with China through teaching, Scharff's wide-ranging study explores the intersections between current and prospective social and political trends with developments inside the family. Scharff's study helps meet the growing demand for tools that address the burgeoning mental health needs of Chinese people living in the People's Republic and abroad. It looks set to become a book of choice for psychology professionals working with Chinese families who are experiencing challenges.'

–Elaine Jeffreys, PhD, Professor, University of Technology, Sydney; Author of Sex in China *(2015)*

'This immensely rich book offers profound insights into Chinese ways of life and Chinese society. Through reading detailed and often touching interviews and therapies with Chinese couples and families, the reader will learn how China's history and rapid modernization influence families and pose often complicated challenges for young people raising children. The book's insightful information about Chinese society and history gives a unique contextual background, offering profound insights for all with interest in China. The book is furthermore an excellent textbook for psychoanalytic couple and family therapy.'
–Sverre Varvin, Psychoanalyst, Professor, Oslo Metropolitan University; Chair, China Committee of the International Psychoanalytical Association; Co-editor of Psychoanalysis in China *(2014)*

'David Scharff masterfully succeeds in enriching his readers in this book that is drawn from his many years of teaching couple and family therapy in China. His skilful combination of detailed case demonstration and psychoanalytic theory offers the reader deep insight into Chinese couples and families, all against the background of a fascinating synthesis of the social–psychological history of modern China. Scharff writes from the position of a student who tries to understand the influence of Chinese culture and society on couples and families. He explores this previously unexamined area, one that is intrinsically foreign to most Westerners, without any false claims to finality. But this book offers much more than an examination of couple and family therapy in China. Set on the background of the country's long history, the reader gets an in-depth introduction into living conditions in modern China.'
–Tomas Plänkers, Psychoanalyst; Sigmund Freud Institut, Frankfurt, Germany; Consultant Member of the International Psychoanalytic Association's China committee; Editor of Landscapes of the Chinese Soul (Karnac, 2014).

'This book provides a comprehensive account of contemporary marital and family relations in China, placed in the context of China's rich traditional and varied cultures and its turbulent and ever-evolving history. It is essential reading for all who teach and supervise Chinese mental health professionals and treat Chinese individuals, couples and families. It demonstrates how important social and cultural issues produce challenges within the intimacy of the family and shows how they are addressed in the therapeutic setting.'
–Ralph E. Fishkin, D.O., Co-President, Supervising Analyst, Psychoanalytic Center of Philadelphia; Board Representative: International Psychoanalytical Association (2019–2021); Clinical Associate Professor of Psychiatry, Thomas Jefferson University

Marriage and Family in Modern China

Marriage and Family in Modern China is a groundbreaking psychoanalytic examination of how 70 years of widespread social change have transformed the intimacies of life in modern China.

The book describes the evolution of marriage and family structure, from the ancient tradition of large families preferring sons, arranged marriages and devaluation of girls, to a contemporary dominance of free-choice marriages and families that now prefer to remain small even after the ending of the One Child Policy. David Scharff uses extensive reports of his psychoanalytic interventions to demonstrate how the residue of widespread trauma suffered by Chinese families during past centuries has interacted with the effects of rapid modernization to produce new patterns of individual identity, personal ambition and family structure.

This wholly original book offers new insight into Chinese families for all those interested in psychoanalytic psychotherapy and in the intricacies of Chinese domestic life.

David E. Scharff, MD, is Co-Founder and Former Director of the International Psychotherapy Institute; Chair of the International Psychoanalytic Association's Committee on Family and Couple Psychoanalysis; Clinical Professor of Psychiatry at Georgetown University and at the Uniformed Services University of the Health Sciences, Bethesda, Maryland; and editor-in-chief of *Psychoanalysis and Psychotherapy in China*. He directs training programs in analytic couple and family therapy in Beijing and Moscow.

The Library of Couple and Family Psychoanalysis

Series Editors: Susanna Abse, Christopher Clulow, Brett Kahr, and David E. Scharff

The library consolidates and extends the work of Tavistock Relationships, and offers the best of psychoanalytically informed writing on adult partnerships and couple psychotherapy.

Marriage and Family in Modern China

A Psychoanalytic Exploration

David E. Scharff

Routledge
Taylor & Francis Group

LONDON AND NEW YORK

First published 2021
by Routledge
2 Park Square, Milton Park, Abingdon, Oxon OX14 4RN

and by Routledge
52 Vanderbilt Avenue, New York, NY 10017

Routledge is an imprint of the Taylor & Francis Group, an informa business

British Library Cataloguing-in-Publication Data
A catalogue record for this book is available from the British Library

Library of Congress Cataloging-in-Publication Data
Names: Scharff, David E., 1941- author.
Title: Marriage and family in modern China : a psychoanalytic exploration / David E. Scharff.
Description: Abingdon, Oxon ; New York, NY : Routledge, 2021.
| Series: The library of couple and family psychoanalysis series |
Includes bibliographical references and index.
Identifiers: LCCN 2020034455 (print) | LCCN 2020034456 (ebook) | ISBN
9780367569488 (hardback) | ISBN 9780367569471 (paperback) | ISBN 9781003100034 (ebook)
Subjects: LCSH: Families--China--Psychological aspects. | Marriage--China. | China--Social conditions--21st century. | China--Civilization--21st century.
Classification: LCC HQ684 .S35 2021 (print) | LCC HQ684 (ebook) | DDC 306.850951--dc23
LC record available at https://lccn.loc.gov/2020034455
LC ebook record available at https://lccn.loc.gov/2020034456

ISBN: 978-0-367-56948-8 (hbk)
ISBN: 978-0-367-56947-1 (pbk)
ISBN: 978-1-003-10003-4 (ebk)

Typeset in Garamond
by SPi Global, India

Contents

     with an Extramarital Affair   154

12   Divorce   176

PART 3
The Changing Face of Families   193

13   The Young and Changing Family   195

14   Families of Young Adolescents   229

15   Older Adolescents, Youth and Two-Child Families   249

16   A Couple Therapy   270

17   China in Light of COVID-19   287

18   A Return to Our Questions   290

     References   293
     Index   301

Figures

Series Editor's Foreword

Christopher Clulow

Love in an Age of COVID-19

As I write this Foreword, the United Kingdom, in common with countries across the world, is struggling to manage the tension between individual and collective needs generated by a global pandemic. Nowhere is the impact likely to be felt more keenly than in the love relationships that characterise family life. While everyone is vulnerable to an infection that is no respecter of boundaries, individuals can respond to this invisible threat in ways that have an impact on relationships. When threatened, the default response is usually to reach for the familiar and the known; there is not enough emotional bandwidth to engage with the unfamiliar and unknown. For couple therapists, this is the challenge: how to help balance the security of stability and continuity with the need for change.

What can psychoanalysis tell us about this tension, and will its insights hold up for people coming from diverse cultural backgrounds? Over a decade ago, David Scharff, a psychiatrist and psychoanalyst of international repute, embarked on a journey to explore these questions with Chinese psychotherapists. Coincidentally, his starting point was an invitation he and his wife Jill received to visit the city of Wuhan, the site where the current pandemic is understood to have begun. He writes almost as an anthropologist, inviting us to join him in the process of discovering ways to establish and develop relationships with fellow professionals from very different backgrounds. Crucially, these relationships have been based on mutual respect and an openness to learning. They have resulted in a book that is both highly personal and hugely enriching for the field of couple and family psychoanalysis.

'Groundbreaking' is an adjective too commonly used of publications in this field, but this book is entitled to it. In a territorial sense, the reader is invited to become acquainted with people who have grown up within a cultural and historical context very different from that in the Western world. Are these differences fundamental? Yes and no. What we learn from this book is that although we may have a predilection to focus on differences, what unites us is greater than what divides us. As we read the vivid accounts of therapy with Chinese couples and families, we cannot help but revisit the internal territory of our own beliefs and assumptions, questioning whether and in what ways we really are so different from them.

I was privileged to be a small part of this voyage of discovery when I was invited to join the faculty offering a training programme for Chinese therapists, one of a succession of programmes that have provided the source material for this book. In prospect, the most controversial part of the programme for me was the live therapy of a family, continuing over five days in front of an audience of approaching 100 therapists. This sat uneasily with my preference for the privacy of the consulting room, raising questions about the ethics and value of performing therapy publicly. I did not need to worry. Much care was taken in respecting and protecting the confidence of family members. What would not have been possible in the West, given the private nature of family relationships there, was possible and constructive in an Eastern context, where the boundary between private and public lives was more permeable.

The presenting problem in the family therapy to which I was party was depression in a late adolescent child/woman. Her tears met with sympathetic yet infantilising concern from the female members of the family and with irritation from her father. As the family dynamics emerged over five days, it became clear that her depression contained anxieties about separation and protest about control, which resonated deeply with other family members. In some ways, this was a very Western conundrum: the quest for autonomy coming into conflict with parental authority – an adolescent conflict. But she was also a channel conveying the unvoiced emotions of other family members, including those deriving from a legacy of family trauma. What at first was registered as individual frailty turned out to be a strength: the strength to challenge the functionality of keeping painful feelings private. Reformulating the symptom galvanised change in the family system, something that was discernible in a remarkably short period of time.

The experience provided me with the forceful reminder that context and meaning are inextricably interconnected; you can't have one without the other. This assertion is in line with a central tenet of couple and family psychoanalysis: inner and outer realities are both wedded to and distinguishable from each other. We cannot assume that the otherness of others is other than our otherness to ourselves, yet we also know that others really are other to us. Without knowledge of this reality, there can be no testing of reality, and without the opportunity to test our realities against those of others, there can be no development. Some of what we take for reality is rooted in assumptions formed in the past, relevant only to that time and place. But the past, as well as being another country, remains active and influential in the present. Polarising 'marriage' and 'divorce' in these contexts – buying into the false notion that a choice must be made between fusion *or* isolation, between past *or* present – offers us a definition of psychopathology. Life, at its best, involves achieving a dynamic rapprochement between our connection to ourselves and our connections with others, something that is constantly under review as we sustain our sense of ourselves while valuing the perspectives of others in the ever-changing landscape of our lives.

These ordinary challenges permeate the unconscious fabric of family life and constitute the substance of much therapeutic work with troubled relationships. Working across cultural divides can hold a mirror to the limits of our understanding and offer opportunities to extend our appreciation and acceptance of difference. For this reason, the *Library of Couple and Family Psychoanalysis* is committed to engaging with cultural diversity, for it offers a well-signed if sometimes uncomfortable route to developing the profession. I commend this book to you as a vivid account of an original, thought-provoking, 'groundbreaking' project. It is informative about the various contexts within which family life is played out in contemporary China, unusual in providing a range of verbatim illustrations of therapeutic work with families and couples, wonderfully free of therapeutic jargon and clearly a deeply important personal work. We are fortunate to be able to include it in the Series.

Christopher Clulow
Series Co-Editor
St Albans, United Kingdom

Acknowledgments

I am grateful to many collaborators whose contributions to this book imbue its pages. In particular, Fang Xin has sponsored and organized our trainings in Beijing, initially from her position in the Counseling Department of Peking University and later through her own company. Her contribution has been both generous and essential. Next in my long list of people to whom I owe so much, is Gao Jun, or as she calls herself in English, Gallant. She was our first translator, but, as a skilled clinician and serious academic, quickly became a collaborator in all our clinical encounters and teaching. Jill Savege Scharff, my wife, and Janine Wanlass, a colleague of many years, have been my most frequent collaborators and colleagues in thinking about issues of culture and the family. In a real sense, they are co-creators of this book. I have had many other valued colleagues who have come to China with us, and many Chinese colleagues who have offered generous and invaluable help, translation and substantive contributions. In particular, I wish to thank Professors Shi Qijia and Tong Jun of Wuhan Mental Health Center for their frequent facilitation of our work; Christopher Clulow, Earl Hopper, Elizabeth Palacios, Yolanda Varela, Monica Vorchheimer, Norma Caruso, Amita Sehgal, Damian McCann, Michael Stadter, Jane Prelinger, Mary Morgan and Kate Scharff, each of whom has joined us in our venture in teaching in China and contributed specifically to my understanding of Chinese families. Li Yanling has worked with us for many years and contributed the clinical material for Chapter 16 from our consultation group, which Chen Yiting translated. I am indebted to both of them. Wang Wei and Li Zhen have been steady and intelligent translators and more than that, have counseled us about China and our patients. Wang Jaiqi, currently a psychology graduate student the University of Groningen, served as a volunteer research assistant in combing the Chinese language literature on aspects of couple and family life, something I could not have done without her. My life-long friend Fred Starr, an eminent scholar of the Orient, gave critically helpful comments on how to improve the book. Jill Scharff has, in addition to sharing the work and interest in China, listened and contributed to my evolving understanding of China and the families we saw, and then read through the entire manuscript and made many helpful comments that led to its improvement. Here I want to express my loving gratitude to her for this and for her unending support.

My thanks to Phoenix Publishing House, and to Wiley, Karnac, and Routledge Publishers for permission to draw on the following of my publications:

Chapter 2 draws on a case published as Scharff, J. S. and Scharff, D. E. (2011) The impact of Chinese cultures on a marital relationship. *Special Issue: Psychoanalysis in China. International Journal of Applied Psychoanalytic Studies* 8(3):249–260. The paper is also published in Scharff, D. E. and Varvin, S. eds (2014) *Psychoanalysis in China*. London: Karnac. pp. 277–287. By kind permission of Wiley Online Publications.

Chapter 6 draws on a case I reported with Janine Wanlass in 2019 as: Brief intervention with a Chinese family of a school-refusing fourteen-year-old girl. *Couple and Family Psychoanalysis* 9(1):55–72. By kind permission of Phoenix Publishing House.

Chapter 7 recounts a case I previously published in 2017 as: Brief intervention with a Chinese couple. *Family and Couple Psychoanalysis* 7(1):81–101. By kind permission of Phoenix Publishing House.

Chapter 10 reports on a case previously published by Shi Qijia and myself in 2011 as: Cultural factors and projective identification in understanding a Chinese couple. *International Journal of Applied Psychoanalytic Studies* 8(3):207–217. It was republished in Scharff, D. E. and Varvin, S. eds (2014) *Psychoanalysis in China*. London: Karnac. pp. 288–297. By kind permission of Wiley Online Publications.

Chapter 14 reports on a family previously published by Jill Scharff and David Scharff in 2015 as: Brief intervention with a Chinese family. *Couple and Family Psychoanalysis* 5(1):57–75. This was also published in Scharff, D. E. and Varvin, S. eds (2014) *Psychoanalysis in China*. London: Karnac. pp. 31–49. By kind permission of Phoenix Publishing House.

Finally, I am grateful to Russell George, Alec Selwyn, Stewart Beale and Kate Hawes of Routledge for their facilitation in bringing this book to fruition, and to Karthik Thiruvengadam, and especially to Natalie Hamil for help in editing and production.

This book is the result of the contributions of all these colleagues as well as the those of the students of the trainings we have conducted together over the past decade, and of the generosity of the couples and families who agreed to be interviewed and to allow us to share their stories towards the goal of increased understanding of the challenges facing today's Chinese families. I owe an unending debt to them and am enormously grateful.

Part I

Marriage and Family in the Context of Contemporary China

Chapter 1

Introduction

I never imagined that I would be so involved with China. As far as I knew, China was an opaque society. What I read about it was usually in terms of China's adversarial position with regard to the United States and to our culture. But for the last dozen years, I have found myself deeply immersed in the study of what is happening with changing patterns of marriage and family life in modern China. This book sets out things I have learned in many trips to China, but unlike the now-frequent news stories about Chinese politics, international relations and economy, trade or even their struggles with environmental dangers, I have been interested in learning about relationships in China.

China has been multiply traumatized for the last 200 years. Many changes in the rules governing social life have led to a cascade of unpredictable consequences in China's highly managed society. The social engineering practiced for the last 70 years has been full of unintended consequences. For me as a psychoanalyst and family and couple therapist, the most interesting effects have concerned patterns of marriage and relationships, the shape of family life, and the consequences for the mental health of the families and of their children. Changes in these patterns derive from aspects of the widespread social changes, China's battle with poverty and its growing economy, repeated waves of trauma in China, an aging population and the shrinking workforce, all counteracted by an enormous resilience, energy, creativity and intelligence of people who work hard to adapt to every change in circumstances. When I have met Chinese colleagues and engaged with Chinese patients, I am struck both with the differences between our cultures and the commonality of human experience. This is the story of what I have learned.

This book is about the Chinese as a people and the implications of current developments for the future of China. As an outsider who cannot speak the language, I write from a perspective of profound respect for a people I have encountered using the unusual lens of a psychoanalyst who is interested in the interplay of cultural differences and personal commonalities. My lens yields pictures that have not so far been developed, pictures that are just as relevant to our emerging understanding of China as those taken from the perspective of economics, demographics or international affairs. It is my hope that the reader of this book will emerge with new, up-close and personal impressions of actual Chinese people, and that this will enhance the mutual understanding between us, not only as Western mental health professionals and our Chinese colleagues and patients, but as people from two very different cultures who seek to know and be known by each other. This seems all the more important to me as I watch the growth of an increasing wariness between our nations at the very time when our pressing international need is for increased mutuality and understanding.

In writing, I have drawn on my experience with a number of families and couples from the Chinese middle class who sought consultation for family difficulty. I believe this book offers much more than a view of how to understand these personal challenges, because every couple or family that sought our help inevitably brought elements of their entire culture and society with them to the consultations. I began my study as if focusing a kind of clinical high-powered microscope on the individuals, couples and families themselves, but I have embedded that view in a consideration of the social and cultural issues that constitute our understanding just as surely as do the clinical considerations.

Integrating this dual focus – between the microscopic view of the family and the macroscopic view of the society in which the family is embedded – offers the possibility of constructing a stereoscopic picture that links each person and family to the culture, that can show us the role of the culture in constructing individual experience and the role of the individuals and families in constructing the culture.

Four Questions

Looking from this dual perspective, four crucial questions emerge.

First, how does the history of Chinese culture influence the intimacy of family life today?

China has an ancient history – more than 2,500 years – of explicitly valuing the family as the fundamental unit of social structure, a building block in each community, which is a fundamental Confucian tenet. It depicts a defined hierarchy that extends from loyalty to the emperor, to the father, the son and the whole family, and then to the surrounding social group. The configuration of this loyalty to the family and group was challenged by the social restructuring of the Communist Party beginning in 1950, then again with the imposition of the One Child Policy 30 years later, by the opening up of society of the 1980s, and again now with the ending of the One Child Policy. We do not know how this will change Chinese families going forward, but the experiences I chronicle in this book can give us a good start towards that understanding.

Second, how do the large-scale social factors influence developments inside the family, and how will these family developments, in a reciprocal way, influence the social changes to China as a nation?

China has a history of repeated social and personal trauma dating back more than 200 years. Therefore, national trauma is a central feature of modern Chinese history, from the Opium Wars caused by the imposition of the opium trade by the Western powers from the eighteenth century into the late nineteenth century; the overthrow of the final Qing Dynasty early in the twentieth century; the fight between the Kuomintang and the Communist Party, interspersed with Japanese invasions that began at the end of the nineteenth century and continued into the first half of the twentieth century; and a combination of famine and cultural disruption from the late 1950s until the mid-1970s. And, of course, there have been large scale natural disasters such as the Tangshan, Sichuan and Yunnan earthquakes over the last 50 years that caused widespread harm in focused geographical regions.

In the midst of all this, China has been rapidly urbanizing, going from a predominantly rural society in the mid-twentieth century to a predominantly urban one now. Current internal migration and rapid urbanization, the expansion of internet-driven social connectedness and the explosive growth of what already is or will soon be the largest middle class in the world all produce disruptions to family and economic life in the transition to modernization. These changes cause further strain to families, and in turn, the family strains inevitably wash back into society. We will be examining many couples and families in detail in order to see the impact of these large-scale issues on family life.

Third, how do the current challenges facing young families and couples have an impact on emerging Chinese culture?

Many news articles focus on the growing power of internet culture and the plight of netizens everywhere. But the challenges facing Chinese families extend more importantly into the usual areas of how best to use education, plans for their own new and emerging families, the changing picture of employment from predominantly state-owned enterprises to private employment and the future in a society that will increasingly have a population top-heavy with elderly, dependent citizens. The challenges facing young people include whether to marry at all, whether and how many children to have, how to include much-needed help from grandparents in child-rearing and then, very soon, how to provide for those same grandparents as they age and are no longer self-sufficient. As we will see, these are both widespread social issues and very personal matters for families. Care of the elderly, for instance, is a problem for the young parents we have seen, and it will be even more of a problem for their children as these very couples age over the next 30 years.

Fourth, and finally, how can we help our Chinese colleagues more effectively serve the mental health needs that are currently emerging?

A major feature of this book is the detailed exploration of clinical issues and the questions they raise. It is not that I and my Western colleagues can presume to personally treat the large numbers of couples, families and individuals who seek help in China. Partly it is a sign of an increasingly mature country that more couples and families do seek help, just as this is true in the West. It is a sign of the maturation of the mental health system that it understands the needs and strives to face the challenges inherent in meeting those needs. Rather, the question is how can mental health professionals like me use an enhanced understanding of China's social system and of individual Chinese patients and families to further enable our Chinese colleagues to better serve their individual, couple and family patients who come for help, just as our patients need help in the West and just as we continually strive to enhance our understanding of patients at home?

These four overarching questions have guided me in writing this book, and I will periodically come back to them as the book documents my attempt to understand more about China through a clinical and social lens.

Coming to China

A dozen years ago, out of the blue, my wife Jill got an email from a Chinese psychologist she didn't know in Wuhan (a city neither of us had heard of) named Li Mengchao, who gives himself the English name Michael. (Many Chinese give themselves English names, which will be used in this book when they have used them with us.) Michael had read a book of hers on unconscious communication (Scharff, 1992) and wanted to know if she had written more on the subject. She sent him another article, and when he thanked her, he added that the professor who headed the hospital would be glad to invite her to Wuhan to teach. Jill does not like to travel as much as I do, but neither of us had ever been to China and she was happy to accept the invitation. I asked to accompany her, and both she and the Wuhan professor agreed. After some friendly and accommodating negotiation, Professor Shi Qijia made arrangements for us to teach over several days. He told us that students would come from across China and that they would be capable of absorbing some of our more advanced material.

Googling Wuhan, we found that it's a second-tier but large Chinese industrial city, then of eight million, the place of Chairman Mao's birth. We arrived and were ensconced in a modern hotel located a few blocks from the Wuhan Hospital for Psychotherapy, which Professor Shi directed. The hotel was located at a multi-road intersection where vehicles of all sizes and descriptions intersected, came together in a flood tide and then ebbed, leaving wave upon wave of gathering bicycles, scooters, people and cars gathering and dispersing, coming and going.

We marveled at the bicycles and motor scooters, thousands of them loaded with people and goods, including an entire household loaded on the back of a bicycle, boxes and furniture piled high, wobbling down the road. On a day when it rained, a sea of umbrellas crossed the intersection and then disappeared down the various roads. When we walked to the hospital, we passed people squatting, cooking in woks with charcoal fires on the sidewalk, sometimes just for themselves and often to sell to passersby.

On our first day, Professor Shi picked us up at the hotel and took us to the hospital, introducing us to his staff while treating us to an elaborate tea ceremony hosted by his secretary in his office, which was dominated by large chairs that looked like thrones for emperors. Professor Shi's English was excellent, as was that of some of his senior students, including Rose Wu, who was assigned to be our immediate guide and interpreter. Rose was a young psychiatrist who, like all the young adults that we met, was an only child who had been successful in her academic pursuits and now was a senior trainee at the Wuhan Hospital, which we learned was one of three of the most prestigious training grounds in China for psychiatrists and psychologists interested in psychotherapy. Dr. Tong Jun, a woman, was Head of Clinical Services and Associate Director. Dr. Tong also spoke fluent English but often with such speed and an accent that we had to work to follow. This trio was our point of contact with Chinese students and colleagues, most of whom did not speak sufficient English to communicate effectively with us, or indeed, any English at all. We, of course, spoke no Chinese, and even though we have been going to China for more than 13 years at the time of this writing, we have no capacity to communicate in Chinese. While I wish more Chinese could speak effective English, I have no room to complain given my inability to communicate effectively in any language other than English.

So, we began to teach, lecturing to a group of 70 or 80 students who had come from all around China to hear us talk about couple and family therapy, which we teach from a psychoanalytic point of view. We have done so throughout our careers in the North and South America, Europe and Australia, and we have founded training programs and an institution to house them, The International Psychotherapy Institute, based in Washington DC, with students from around the United States and overseas. Our international students came originally from Panama, but eventually included students from around the world, including, for instance, Mexico, Europe and China. That program, which we began in the 1970s, imported psychoanalytic ideas from England and Scotland. Jill, who was born and trained in Scotland, and I, who was always interested in the same group of ideas from Great Britain that she was, had each spent a year in London learning in more depth, and then, together with other colleagues, imported this school of thought to the United States.

This group of ideas is called 'Object Relations Theory,' and it is based on the idea that what motivates development from the beginning of life is the need for relationships, first between baby and parents, and then later with the widening array of people throughout the lifespan. Our particular specialty area, the one that we are most called upon to teach nationally and internationally, is the application of this school of psychoanalytic ideas to couple and family therapy, an interest that Jill and I shared from the time that we met in England in the early 1970s. It was this group of ideas that Dr. Shi asked us to teach in Wuhan. The concept of 'projective identification,' the subject of that book of Jill's that Li Mengchao wrote to her about, is a central concept, first introduced by the psychoanalyst Melanie Klein in 1946 and elaborated over the years to cover the way people communicate unconsciously to each other about their emotional life – their unconscious wishes, fears, anxieties and even inner organizations. They do so by communicating in essentially nonverbal ways that each of us is born to receive, and that each growing person then unconsciously refines as the way she receives and reacts to others, an essential skill in person-to-person emotional understanding, a life skill we all have that is essential to social communication and survival. The honing of that skill is particularly crucial for training of psychotherapists, who spend long hours developing their capacity to understand others. This will be elaborated in Chapter 3.

Accordingly, we prepared a PowerPoint slideshow to guide our teaching, beginning with the building blocks of our ideas taken from the works not only of Freud, but of such central British contributors as Ronald Fairbairn (1952), Melanie Klein (1975a, 1975b), Donald Winnicott (1971a, 1971b), John Bowlby (1958, 1969) and Wilfred Bion (1962, 1967, 1970). These psychoanalytic writers form a group whose contributions together can be called 'object relations theory.' In China, this particular orientation had a different stamp than other introductory psychoanalytic and psychodynamic programs that had been introduced some years earlier.

We quickly learned that psychoanalysis already, by 2007, had become something of a popular cult in the growing mental health world of China, and even beyond, into the academic world. Since we come from the United States, where Freud and psychoanalysis have frequently been written off as old and out-of-date theory – even pronounced dead – we were delighted to see that psychoanalysis was popular in China. Professor Shi told us that while psychoanalysis had been forbidden along with many Western ideas with the advent of the Communist Party, beginning in the 1980s, soon after the opening up of China by Deng Xiaoping in the wake of Chairman Mao's death, Chinese culture began to embrace many of the technologies and ideas of the West (Shi, 2014). The first inroads came from a group of German psychotherapists and psychoanalysts, headed by Dr. Alf Gerlach, who were funded by the German government, which has cultural projects around the world, to come to China and teach psychotherapy. They did this by offering training in psychoanalysis, behavioral therapy and family systems therapy all in one package, and by coming to China twice a year to offer this to a group of students, letting them eventually choose what branch of psychotherapy interested them most. A group of teachers from Germany had been coming to Wuhan, Shanghai and Beijing for several years before we got there, teaching in-depth for a week each in their twice-yearly visits, and offering what they called 'self-experience' to the students. A 'self-experience' consists of a couple of hours of introductory psychotherapy offered to the students by the teachers in one-on-one interviews twice a year, and was intended to introduce them to the idea of an uncovering form of psychotherapy, with the idea that they would be able to continue that exploration in the intervals between these trainings. This 'self-experience' was intended to be a beginning. For some of the students, it piqued interest and empowered them to go on later to seek a more thoroughgoing psychotherapy.

Professor Shi Qijia himself had spent a year in Ulm, Germany, an important center for psychoanalytic research, sponsored by and befriended by Horst Kaechele, one of the most renowned psychoanalytic researchers; a kind, brilliant, warm and inclusive senior figure. Many of the Chinese had been to Germany as part of the effort to bring analysis to China. I found it impressive that the Germans did all their teaching in English, in which all of the German teachers were proficient. It was not until much later, when I invited them to contribute articles to a journal that I founded, called *Psychoanalysis and Psychotherapy in China* (2015, 2016, 2020), that I understood that although their spoken English was fluent, there were numerous grammatical and vocabulary mistakes in their written English that required substantial editing. In a funny way, I was glad to see that native English speakers had something to add to the contributions the Germans (and later the Norwegians) had already made. (Since that beginning, trainings have been introduced by groups from Britain and the United States, with teachers now coming from all over the world to China and/or teaching remotely via the internet.)

Professor Shi went out of his way to introduce us to the culture of China beyond the clinical situation of the hospital. He took us to a different style of Chinese restaurant every night, including a night sitting outside the wall of an ancient building eating chicken's feet, invited us to elaborate tea ceremonies in his office and introduced us to different parts of the city including the East Lake, now brown and polluted, but in the history of China a beautiful park surrounding the lake in which Chairman Mao had swum as a young man. We were taken to a then-new museum that housed the contents of the tomb of Marshall Yu from 2,500 years ago, recently excavated to reveal intact sculptural treasures of fantastic animals, luxurious household furnishings and a complete orchestra of woodwinds, strings and percussion instruments, including a full set of 64 bells, ranging from the tiniest bell to enormous ones, all still playable. The museum had reproduced the orchestra instruments, in order to pre-serve the originals, and offered daily concerts with the reproduction orchestra playing both ancient and modern music.

In our initial visit, we were stunned by the mass energy and chaos of the street life in Wuhan, the rich and ancient cultural heritage. We hur-ried across the busy streets and strolled along the alleys past the street food vendors. The sights and smells were intoxicating, but we had been warned – no street food! We started by putting up our PowerPoint slides and talking too much, as we would back in the United States. Students listened obediently, took notes and asked no questions. We had no idea whether what we were saying went over their heads, bored them to tears or was on the mark. As time went on, we learned that this was (then) the usual response of Chinese students. For generations, they had been taught to respect their teachers highly, to act in compliance, obedience and reverence and not to question the Teacher. Psychotherapists, too, in China are thought of as Teachers, so the initial response of many patients is to be compliant and unquestioning. This leads to pent-up resentment, anger and silent misunderstanding. But in our early days in China, we did not understand these things because we were new to the culture and could not comprehend the effect of the overall culture and context in which these students had grown up – even if they were senior them-selves in their own hospitals and practices. For this first-time teaching in China, I have to say that we were culturally blind. We had brought them things they wanted to know, and we were trying to deliver them. We had no idea of the fit between what we said and what they understood or found relevant. We had been told to bring advanced material because these were advanced students, but we soon realized that those who were thought to be advanced students in China were only beginning in their exposure to our points of view. This is not to disparage the quality of Chinese intellect or desire to learn. It reflects the enormous gulf between the culture into which we were delivering psychotherapy training and what had happened there in a country where, until the early 1980s, it was forbidden to discuss Western ideas and disciplines. Our students were starting with a much earlier set of assumptions.

In addition, and probably more to the point, the students were coming from a place of very different cultural assumptions, deep structure of thought and morality, and system of education. The education they had grown up with, at least through high school, tended to be based on rote memory and obedience in a Confucian vein. University education, cer-tainly about these ideas, was in a much earlier state of development than in the West. More importantly, as I will discuss in Chapters 4 and 5, they came from a different history and set of assumptions that imbued not only their sense of shared morality and ethics of social behavior, but also their language. To put briefly what is generally known, the Chinese are organized around a group identity in which the family has precedence, and loyalty is to family – and ultimately, to the Emperor. Family and group loyalty are more important than individuation or autonomy.

We could tell from the beginning that our translators, who in the beginning were professors Shi Qijia and Tong Jun, along with Rose Wu, took much longer to say things in Chinese than we took in English. It takes about 30-50% longer to say something in Chinese. And that's not all. It's clear that the Chinese language is structured very differently, as my colleague Tomas Plänkers of the Sigmund Freud Institute in Frankfurt has written (Plänkers, 2013). Translation is difficult not only because no words are exactly equivalent to many of ours, especially the words describing concepts such as those in psychoanalysis like the unconscious or projective identification, but because it is not a language with verbal tenses. Many words mean more than one thing and are only differentiated by the intonation and harmonics of the language, and they take their meaning from the context in which they exist. Most of all, the Chinese think in a more metaphoric idiom than we do. In the West, and especially in the United States, we like to be clear and logical. To the Chinese, this seems simplistic and concrete in contrast to their preference for metaphoric ambiguity that leaves more to the imagination and to elaboration of the listener. To the Chinese, being as concrete as we like to be – or at least, as I like to be – leads them to feel that we have the linguistic capacity of children. And from my perspective now, they would not be entirely wrong. But we did not really understand any of this in the beginning, and we trundled on with our naïve hope that we would have something to offer that would be valued.

On our second day there, something happened that forms a metaphor for the overall difficulty of cultural understanding. Drs. Shi Qijia and Tong Jun had arranged for us to interview a family in a room away from the students but that would be broadcast to the students through closed-circuit television. Jill and I are used to doing this at home in teaching conditions in which we conduct live interviews with a couple, family or individual in a video studio. They are recorded and shown to our students for teaching with the knowledge and permission of the people we are interviewing that these tapes or interviews can be used for mental health teaching. I have been doing this since the beginning of my own training where, in a Harvard-run state mental hospital, there was no audio-visual equipment and no such thing as a one-way mirror in front of which we could interview patients. Instead, we interviewed individuals or families with our colleagues seated in the audience in front of us. Our experience began with faculty conducting such interviews, but quickly we as psychiatric residents would learn to conduct these interviews ourselves in front of our peers and faculty. It was useful for curing us of the jitters of performance anxiety. And now, in China, it was an asset that we were comfortable interviewing people in this kind of setting.

On this occasion, Dr. Tong Jun, as the chief of patient care, said that she had lined up a family for Jill and me to interview, but that the 16-year-old girl, who went by an English name with flair, which I will disguise here by calling her Scarlett, had refused Dr. Tong's request to be part of the interview, thereby stymying the situation. Since I had heard Scarlett spoke fluent English, I asked if I could go talk to her in her room. I walked uneasily down the hall into Scarlett's room, and saw a slender adolescent dressed provocatively sitting on her bed and staring out the window. 'Hi Scarlett,' I said. 'I'm Dr. Scharff and I'd like to interview you with your family.' 'Okay,' said Scarlett in clear English. 'No sweat!' And she marched diffidently out of her room and down the hall ahead of me.

So, we sat down with the family, and I began by asking Scarlett where she learned her English. 'Oh, watching *Desperate Housewives*,' she said. It won't be a surprise to learn that we were convinced that her reason for being in the hospital, which we might have diagnosed as hysterical psychosis or maybe just hysterical adolescence, was for flamboyant and out-of-control behavior involving a lot of provocative talk and actions both in school and with her family. In the interview, she acted seductively. She played up to me, and then, as if in compensation for ignoring Jill, told her that she was very beautiful. To demonstrate her knowledge, at one point, after we had complimented her English, she spouted a long excerpt from Khalil Gibran's *The Prophet* in English. At the end of the interview, she said she wanted to come to the United States and visit me, but it was in the middle of the interview itself that she was most deceptive. Professor Shi was there to act as our interpreter, because while Scarlett spoke English, neither her parents nor the majority of the students listening by video connection in another room spoke English. But Scarlett said she would do the interpreting for her parents. So, we learned about her parents' marriage and a particular kind of inequality in which the mother had picked a man who she felt was safe but not her equal, and how Scarlett came between them in a manipulative way. But the main thing that we learned afterwards from Dr. Shi was that Scarlett was purposefully mistranslating what we said. Consequently, it turned out that her parents really had no clue what we were saying, and that she was misrepresenting them often as well. This evidence of her misleading her parents and confusing them as a strategy, half conscious, half unconscious, seemed to be central to the picture of turmoil she caused in the family and of her own disorganized maladaptation to her adolescent world. But it was also a powerful metaphor of a mistranslation of cultures between this Chinese family and us as Westerners, and of the mistranslation in the generation gap between parents from the old world of China and Scarlett's generation: Mistranslation showed all these dimensions – between East and West, between the old and new, between old and young in an evolving world. This initial encounter still stands as a metaphor for all the difficulties we face in going to China and for the difficulties the young generation in China faces in the conflict between old and new values.

After the interview, we returned to the teaching room with the students, expecting to be able to discuss with them what we had understood of our interview of Scarlett and her family, only to find that the vocal transmission of the interview had been almost inaudible and that we had to review the whole interview, summarizing what we understood and experienced. It was then that we began to find out how rudimentary the understanding of basic psychological principles was for this group of students. What feedback we got struck us as more typical of psychologically naïve college students or beginning medical students who would have grown up in Western culture where, for educated young people, a certain amount of psychological sophistication comes with the territory. Looking back, I have to say that part of the difficulty was that we were also interpreting things with a sureness as though we were on home territory, as if embedded in a culture much the same as the one at home.

Another woman we interviewed later that week was a teacher who had been fired for being excessively harsh with her students and had then lapsed into a severe depression. Many Chinese teachers, we were told, are harsh and fail to understand their students in terms of adolescent psychology and their developmental needs. Later in the week, we heard a case presented by Rose, the trainee psychotherapist and psychiatrist, of a young man she was seeing in the hospital. This young man wanted to be a musician, but felt that his best friend had stolen a composition from him. Losing out to his friend caused him such despair that he became suicidal. Listening from the standpoint we brought as Western psychiatrists, it was possible to feel sympathy for this young man who had something valuable taken from him, but also to question whether he had told Rose the whole truth and whether what was dominant in this young man's situation was the overall sense that he had lost a vital element of his own personality that he would never be able to get back. It was only later, as I came to understand so much more about the life or death quality of competition for so many Chinese students and their parents, to hear so often about the feeling that students had to excel or were lost, that I could see that this story was a metaphor too, a metaphor for the high-stakes of educational accomplishment and the feeling that at any moment everything valuable could be lost because somebody had stolen one's place or the value of one's achievements.

By the end of this first week, we came to feel that all the young people we met were subject to enormous pressure to succeed. The ones who could rise to the challenge formed the staff of the hospital. The most vulnerable ones who could not were liable to breakdown and to becoming patients.

I will give one more anecdote from our teaching that first time in China. Professor Shi arranged for us to travel from Wuhan to Shanghai to participate in one of the first Chinese international psychotherapy congresses. We arrived there ready to give a preconference workshop on psychoanalytic family therapy. We planned to use a video interview of a couple that we had used routinely in our teaching for many years, a video of a live interview of a couple who had given us permission to use their material for this kind of teaching. However, we had not then subtitled this video as we have subsequently learned to do, and instead had a translated transcript for the translator to speak from as we played the video. We arrived in the room to prepare for giving the seminar and showed our translator this transcript. She saw the English transcript that accompanied it and began to laugh.

I asked, 'What's the joke?'

'Do you know what she has written in Chinese?' she replied. 'Your patients begin with the woman of the couple saying to you, in English, 'We have, like, three shrinks between us.' This translation says, 'We are three very small people."

At which we all began to laugh at our naïve assumption that our clinical dialogue would be understood.

When Jill and I returned to China two years later to begin teaching a regular continuous certificate course in couple therapy, one that we still teach more than ten years later, I remembered the brief encounter with this young translator, her fluency, charm, sense of humor and intelligence. Not knowing her name, I said to Jill that I wished we could somehow find her to translate for our course in Beijing. Imagine my pleasant surprise when this young woman, named Gao Jun and calling herself Gallant in English, walked in to translate for us as we began the course. We have had the good fortune of working with her ever since, as she graduated with her PhD from the program at Beijing University that sponsored our first courses and has since become an Associate Professor of Psychology at Fudan University in Shanghai, been published widely, written a book of her own and translated several others – and nevertheless, showed up for each of our trainings. Working with Gao Jun has been our particular privilege.

The setting in which we interviewed Scarlett and other patients in this first week of exposure began our cultural education, teaching us that we were trying to translate an essentially Western experience into Chinese when our experience and theirs are in many ways untranslatable. Chinese culture was and is importantly different from our at-home culture. That difference has been the subject of my interest in the years that followed during my more than 25 trips, two or three trips yearly to China starting in 2010, and in my reading about Chinese history, culture, politics, family life, marital structure, sexuality and child development. I've come to feel that to be effective in bringing a psychoanalytic way of understanding to China, I have to listen closely and, in so far as possible, immerse myself in Chinese culture in order to learn from my Chinese colleagues and our Chinese patients. That culture and psychology, different from any other that I had the privilege of previously experiencing, continues to hold my interest. I have also come to see that, as Christopher Bollas (2013) has written, much of psychoanalysis is indirectly rooted in a kind of thinking that had seeped unseen into Western thought from Buddhism, Confucianism and Hinduism, and that today, more than ever, these ways of thinking are in a global dialogue with Western thought.

This book represents my attempt to bring together a growing appreciation of the richness of Chinese culture, the structure of Chinese thought and morality, the immense trauma done to China as a country and to its people, and the resilience of a wonderful people – all as reflected in the intimacy of the family. I now count my Chinese colleagues as lifelong friends and partners in a mutual and continuing learning process.

Chapter 2

A Chinese Marriage
History, Discontinuity and Trauma

More than a decade ago, Dr. Jill Scharff and I carried out our first five-day consultation to a Chinese couple. We did many more over the ensuing years. What we learned from this first couple informed our early immersion into Chinese culture and into the problems contemporary Chinese couples face. I begin with them because this book is a record of what we have learned over these years from interviewing couples and families, supplemented by reading, supervision of Chinese therapists and consultations with colleagues in China and the West interested in the challenges facing contemporary Chinese families. This couple exemplified problems stemming from deprivation and trauma, resilience and determination, and the struggle to find each other despite their own differences. The husband came from an educated urban family that had been separated during the Cultural Revolution, while the wife came from a rural, poor farming family with quarreling and the degradation of women.

Interviews such as the one with this couple have come to form one regular element in our teaching for students, clinicians and trainers in China. We have taught workshops in Psychoanalytic Object Relations Couple and Family Therapy and several iterations of our course in Psychoanalytic Couple Therapy at the invitation of Professor Shi in Wuhan and Professor Fang Xin of Peking University in Beijing. Our hosts have always arranged for serial translation of our concepts, slides, videos and group discussions – and for therapeutic consultations with various couples and families to be observed live or on a video feed to audiences of 70–100 mental health students, clinicians and trainers. We taught our Chinese participants the Western view of relationships and unconscious dynamics. They taught us to understand Chinese couples' and families' verbal expressions, imagery and culture. This couple and our discussion with the students illustrate how much we learned from the experience and exemplifies some of the currents that couples have struggled with as they live, work and form families in China's rapidly changing culture.

This first couple we present attended a series of five couple therapy sessions. With Gao Jun, our translator, seated between me and Dr. Jill

Scharff, and the couple seated across from us, we made a semicircle facing the audience and used microphones so that we could be heard. It was unfamiliar and somewhat uncomfortable for all of us, and the necessity for serial translation slowed down the interviews, but this process provided insight for the couple, a learning experience for the audience and a powerful lesson about intimate relationships in China for us.

Dr. Hu and Mrs. Chen[1]

Session One

Married for five years, the couple now lived in a city in Hubei Province from which they had traveled for these sessions. We will call them Dr. Hu and Mrs. Chen (not their real names). Dr. Hu is a hard-working 50-year-old scientist of slight build, his hair still black, his clothes casual. Mrs. Chen is 36, a full-time mother. (In China, wives usually keep their maiden names.) She used to have a shop, which Dr. Hu asked her to give up when she married, but she refused. Once her daughter was born, she herself chose to stay home to look after their child.

Mrs. Chen began,

We can't communicate. We see things from different angles. My husband disregards my opinion and feels criticized by any disagreement. For instance, he purchased a cup for 1,000 yuan that I would not have thought worth 100 yuan. He doesn't care what I think, and he thinks I don't know anything. But I know what a cup is worth.

Dr. Hu dismissed her complaint: 'Anyway, the issue about the cup really is not a big problem. The problem is her temper.'

In the opening minutes, the husband and wife already revealed their difficulty in feeling valued and respected by each other and their difficulty in connecting. We noticed that Dr. Hu looks younger than his years but seems stern and anxious, like the father of a rowdy adolescent. Mrs. Chen, with long dark hair and warm skin tones, wearing a pretty, long peasant dress, looked as luscious as a peach, but with her dark glasses and angry tone, she seemed like an aggrieved television star. They did not seem a likely couple. Disconcertingly, both of them smiled a lot while telling of their rage at each other and their disappointment in their marriage.

Dr. Hu continued: 'She gets quickly out of control with me, her mother, her sister, and our daughter, bossing them around, demanding that they serve her.'

'No,' she objected. 'YOU treat ME like a nanny. You are always commanding me. If I disagree with you, you react coldly or give me the silent treatment. The only way to deal with you is to ignore you and go numb.'

Jill asked if there were any good feelings between them.

Mrs. Chen said, 'I feel them occasionally.'

Dr. Hu said, 'I don't want a divorce because all wives are pretty much the same: blaming, critical, and dissatisfied.'

Mrs. Chen said, 'I could find a different husband, but I would be happier on my own, as I used to be before I got married.'

I said, 'I feel confused to see you both smiling, even though you're speaking of anger and distrust, and not getting your ideas across to each other.'

Mrs. Chen said,

> This is because we grew up differently: In my family, there are lots of children. I was the youngest, and everyone took care of me. In his family, it is basically him and his mother, who still dotes on him. But he never sees her! In my family, people express their opinions directly. In his family, people don't speak up. So now, any comment from me and he feels blamed. He wants constant praise, as if I'm his adoring nanny for whom he can do no wrong.

As the interview went along, both of us felt trapped with them in a repetitive cycle in which the couple stated mutual grievances and did not want to move out of the painful present.

Having heard the word nanny again, Jill asked, 'Who took care of you as children, and how did you feel about them?'

Mrs. Chen said, 'That question isn't relevant because there is no concept of a nanny in my family. But he had a nanny for three years.'

It turned out that Mrs. Chen was talking of a nanny in adulthood, a woman who took care of Dr. Hu before his marriage and helped him entertain his students and visiting scientists.

'After we got married,' Mrs. Chen said,

> the nanny refused to work for me as the woman of the house. She served only him. She referred to him and herself as 'our family,' and I was left out. I think he was in love with the nanny.

Dr. Hu said angrily, 'This is all nonsense. She's just a nanny.'

Mrs. Chen said, 'He treated the nanny more like a wife. When I said I wanted to get rid of the nanny, he actually fell on the floor sobbing.'

Dr. Hu said to me, 'I was mad at her for mistreating the nanny and for demanding that I sack her.'

Mrs. Chen said,

I was stunned by his sobbing. I wondered, 'Why do I have to endure this?' I don't need to be married. I used to have a shop. I was happy on my own. So, I said it was her or me, but he refused to let her go. He loves the nanny more than me.

Dr. Hu said, 'I did let her go.'

To Mrs. Chen, Dr. Hu's sobbing was evidence of a deep attachment, a greater love for his nanny than for his wife. To him, it was grief over the jealous irrationality of his wife and the loss of the kind of marriage he had hoped for. Either way, it made him out to be the bad guy.

Jill suggested, 'Perhaps you were angry that this woman met your husband's needs and not yours, loving him and not you.'

Angrily, Mrs. Chen said to Jill, 'You have it wrong. I don't need anyone else to meet my husband's needs. I can take care of him myself.'

Jill replied, 'I see you're angry at me when I get something wrong.'

'No! I'm not,' said Mrs. Chen sharply. 'I am angry about the way he treated the nanny like a wife and treated me, his wife, like a nanny.'

Jill said, 'I think I understand. Of course, as the wife you want to be Number One.'

In this first session of five, we were just getting to know this couple, working at the surface of their power struggle. Our initial impression was that Mrs. Chen seemed too young and beautiful to fit with Dr. Hu, and he seemed too old and educated to fit with her. He spoke logically, which she reacted against. She spoke in bursts of emotion for which he had contempt. She rejected his dependency on the nanny, and he squashed her independence by having asked her to give up working at her shop. Each then attacked the other for hosting those parts of themselves they could not stand. She wanted to be independent, and therefore had to deny the part of herself that longed for someone to depend on. And he wanted to depend on her, and berated her for wanting to be so independent. Each of them had been a special child, and each wanted to be Number One. We experienced their angry reactions to not feeling loved and valued, and we sensed the deadness at the center of their marriage. All of this gave us a sense of the fragility of a marriage, but without yet a sense of where their marriage might fit into the context of modern Chinese marriages.

Session 2

I asked about any reactions they had to the first session. Dr. Hu replied that he had been too busy to think about it.

Mrs. Chen said, 'I was just numb. I probably try to feel nothing so as to avoid being irritated. I avoid quarreling because of our child. I try to ignore my husband and just think about my daughter.'

Interested in learning what the child might represent in their emotional life and in their marriage, Jill asked Mrs. Chen to tell us about their daughter.

Mrs. Chen replied briefly but warmly,

> Our child is four years old. She is healthy physically and mentally, and she is lovely. He wanted me to have a nanny for her, but I didn't want one. I wanted to devote all my time to the care of the child and the house.

While we were talking about their child, who seemed already to emerge as the bright spot in their marriage, I asked how things had been for them as children. This question is one we always ask in an evaluation, because it gives a glimpse into how they carry the early experiences inside that largely determine their individual psychic make-up and how they have learned to organize experiences with others.

Dr. Hu launched into a description of his life. 'My mother was a respected career woman, a woman with a brain!' (Jill silently felt that Dr. Hu was insulting his wife by comparison.) He continued, 'She could balance family and career. She's an art director now, still working.' Jill asked how Dr. Hu's mother balanced family and a career when he was a baby.

Dr. Hu responded,

> When I was three years old, I was sent to kindergarten. But when I was six, my mother, who was an intellectual and artist, one of the kind of people who were sent to a reeducation camp in the countryside, often couldn't make it home to see me. So, I was fostered by other families in the countryside.

Jill empathized, 'It must have been hard for a six-year-old to lose his mother.'

Dr. Hu objected,

> On the contrary, it was a time of freedom, sunshine and happiness. Anyway, sometimes I got to visit my mother in her camp. When I was 13, she sent for me to join her in Wuhan, to live with her and my father. I always thought he was my father, but when I turned 20, my mother told me that he was not my father. Even then, she only mentioned it because my actual biological father had been rushed to Wuhan for

hospitalization, and she wanted me to go there to meet him before it was too late. That's how I found out. I didn't know him. I didn't have time to think about the truth or what it meant. I'm just grateful for my stepfather because he treated me well and educated me. I've been very lucky.

We could see that Dr. Hu erased all conflict, curiosity and loss in a stroke of luck, the same way he had obliterated any problem about being separated from his mother at the age of six for seven years. His childhood was impinged upon by the Cultural Revolution, when intellectuals were persecuted and sent to work in the country and their children were also sent to the countryside to live with families or in peer groups with people they had not known. In this way, we saw that Dr. Hu had experienced early separation and loss of his mother, having already not known his father. He had idealized a situation of early deprivation brought on by China's upheaval during the Cultural Revolution of 1966–1976.

Jill asked Mrs. Chen to tell us more about her family's experience. Mrs. Chen said,

I am 14 years younger than he is. I was raised in a family of four children with both our parents in the countryside. My parents loved each other. My mother was hotheaded and fought with my father constantly, which I hated, but he always gave in. That ended the quarrel. He let her get her own way. I was the youngest, my father's favorite. I was spoiled by not having to do any housework. My older sister was more competent than me. So, she had to do everything, and this made her jealous of me doing nothing. When our parents were away, my sister made me do the housework and beat me if I could not do it. When my parents came home, I told them she had been doing this to me. Then they beat my sister. This made her resent me more. Being the youngest, I was too small or too slow to do the work. Even now, my sister gets anxious watching me doing housework and takes over. When I was to be married, my father said that now that I was an adult, I must learn to do housework. I said to myself that I must do what I ought to do, endure what I must endure and I have done that. I clean, I wash the clothes and I prepare the food for my husband to cook. Because the nanny was sacked, I do everything, except the actual cooking, which he does.

Jill said,

Now I understand what Mrs. Chen meant when she said they came from very different backgrounds: Dr. Hu was raised as an only child, without his mother in the early years, and dependent on others. Mrs. Chen was raised in a family of two parents and three older siblings who took care of her. This raises the question of what kind of family you as a couple want to create. Do you want your daughter, an only child like Dr. Hu, to be raised by Mrs. Chen as an at-home mother and by warring parents, like Mrs. Chen's, or divorced parents, like Dr. Hu's?

Jill added that one thing was still bothering her: 'Dr. Hu's statement that his mother was a woman with a brain, makes me wonder if he thinks that women don't usually have a brain. Do you think that Mrs. Chen has a brain?'

Dr. Hu gave a circuitous response:

I have happy memories of the Cultural Revolution. There was no loss for me. It was a wonderful time – children all playing and doing whatever they liked, no parents around to boss them. My childhood was a wonderland of playing and reading. I had books. I didn't have to go to school, so I read the classics. I learned English from reading Shakespeare. No one mistreated me. It was a time of sunshine. The unhappiness is now. I never thought about whether a woman had a brain or not. I like women; I respect them; I think they are beautiful. But after I got married, I realized women really are disappointing, just like people always said to me. Many of my women students are fine, better than the men, but after they get married, women become unreasonable. In the old days, it was thought that men had more wisdom but...

Here, I interrupted to observe that Mrs. Chen was laughing.

Mrs. Chen said, 'My husband is not answering the question to save face for me. But in fact, he calls me simpleminded and hotheaded.'

Laughing, Dr. Hu said, 'I do! And she is.'

We saw now that Dr. Hu had glorified the peer environment of his deprived childhood and perhaps was trying to save face while Mrs. Chen gave an unabashed acknowledgement of herself as a spoiled favorite, entitled to special treatment. Yet, Dr. Hu held his ground and kept the conflict going, unlike Mrs. Chen's father, who gave her mother her way to end fights. We now began to think that Dr. Hu had developed a defensive independence in reaction to the trauma of early imposed separation from his mother due to the policies of the Cultural Revolution, when his family was targeted because his mother was an intellectual and an artist. His younger wife was born after these policies had ended, and her rural family had not been in danger. (It was often true that rural families were spared during the Cultural Revolution.) The disparity in their early experiences began to explain his longing for a mother/nanny to offer what he had missed of ordinary mothering in his early years. In this way, the national trauma of the Cultural Revolution had played a major role in his early maternal deprivation, while Mrs. Chen's early favored treatment in a rural family had played a role in her expectation of being pampered.

Session 3

Dr. Hu arrived in an American college shirt, and Mrs. Chen in her dark glasses, which she explained she wore for protection. When Jill tried to explore what she needed protection from, she snapped back, 'From the sun. It has no other meaning.' Jill felt shut down by Mrs. Chen, as she felt had previously.

Dr. Hu said, 'It was good to talk last time. There used to be groups for talking, like the political meetings or the women's union where they would make you talk.' He continued sadly, 'Now no one has a place to talk anymore.'

Mrs. Chen said dismissively, 'I never experienced those times.'

I said, 'Perhaps this large group of the audience in front of us feels like a large political association meeting, and we're making you talk.'

Dr. Hu laughed in recognition, and then observed thoughtfully, 'You do raise a lot of questions.'

Jill said to Dr. Hu, 'Indeed, it might be hard to talk with strangers like us before a group this size, but I've noticed that you are a man who makes the most of bad situations.' Dr. Hu nodded. Jill continued, 'With no mother at hand, you found a foster family. With no wife, you found a nanny.' Dr. Hu interrupted, 'Actually, I didn't have a foster family. I lived at school in a crowd of kids in a wonderland of play and fun. There was no homework, and no standard education.'

Jill asked him, 'Then how did you catch up and earn a PhD?'

Dr. Hu replied,

Everyone was at the same place, and we all started studying as soon as exams opened up. Having been in the Red Guard, I could have been a good politician, farmer or student. I learned English from my mother, became a good student, got good marks and went on from there.

(We noted that Dr. Hu now said in passing that he was also in the Red Guard, part of the gangs of anarchic young people who roamed the countryside picking targets to bully and abuse. This, too, must have had an effect on his further development.)

Jill asked Mrs. Chen to imagine Dr. Hu's childhood, so different from what Mrs. Chen experienced in rural China half a generation later.

Mrs. Chen said curtly, 'I know the story.' More compassionately, she added,

Of course it must have been difficult for him then, but he is a successful researcher and a good communicator, at least with other people, and so he looks normal. I know that the children of many parents who were sent to the camps have ended up in jail. But he is too disciplined of a person to end up like that.

She cut off any further discussion, saying, 'To me, it was simply a fact, and nothing I ever thought about. It's just what he experienced

Now speaking from our experience that both of them often shut down our inquiries, I said to them both,

I feel that when Jill or I offer a comment, we are sometimes rebuffed. I believe that you shut us down to protect yourselves from hurt that you fear we might cause you and that you might cause each other. You shut off communication to protect yourselves from rage and sadness, but then, in a paradoxical way, it only causes more rage and sadness. You, Dr. Hu, turn off your feelings, try to make the best of it and try to sound grateful, to your mother and to the nanny who meant so much to you.

Dr. Hu brushed off my expression of empathy saying, 'I'm fine without them.'

I turned to Mrs. Chen, 'Your family was together in a loving, stable situation. Even if your parents yelled, you expected it.'

Mrs. Chen said, 'But I didn't like the yelling, and they yelled a lot.'

Jill said it was sad for Mrs. Chen, who didn't like the yelling, that she had found herself yelling like her mother.

Mrs. Chen said, 'I don't want a marriage like that. I don't want quarrels. That's why I'd rather be divorced.'

I said to Mrs. Chen,

You were a special child, treated as the favorite who didn't have to work. It was extremely painful to feel that your husband had a special place for the nanny, but not for you. As a wife, you found yourself in a jealous position, more like your sister's situation than your own usual position as the favorite.

Mrs. Chen corrected me: 'The situation is not comparable because we were sisters in a family, whereas in marriage, I am the wife. I don't feel anything like my sister.' And they were back on the cycle of the nanny trauma and loss. When Jill asked about any previous relationships that might illuminate the significance of the nanny, we learned that Mrs. Chen had previously been with a man who had an affair, while Dr. Hu had an unconsummated first marriage.

Dr. Hu said, 'With my first wife, we wanted to have sex, but couldn't do it. Since then, I have had a series of relationships that were eventually disappointing.' Rather grandly he said, 'Like the novelist said, 'Women are beautiful goddesses. They are sacred.' I adore them. That's what I was always searching for. Then I got her!'

Mrs. Chen was laughing uncontrollably. It wasn't clear if she was laughing at him, or laughing in pleasure at his experiences, so Jill enquired.

Mrs. Chen said, 'I'm laughing because it is so lovely to hear him talk like that!' Mrs. Chen's laughing became quite hysterical, more like crying.

Jill said to her, 'I see you smiling, but crying through your smiles, because it's hard for you to hear his love.'

'It never occurred to me that someone of his age could sound so romantic, much too romantic for a man of his age.'

We have come to understand that intimacy and passion are traditionally less important in modern Asian marriages than in modern Western marriages (Chen and Li 2007). But we were struck that Mrs. Chen seemed taken aback to find romance in an older man she had married for his stability and fidelity, not for sex. Like most Chinese individuals, Dr. Hu and Mrs. Chen grew up valuing social harmony (Greenfield, Keller, Fuligni and Maynard, 2003). However, now, Dr. Hu chose to be remote from his family and Mrs. Chen preferred being on her own. Yet, they were both deeply distressed by the lack of harmony in their home together.

Session 4

The couple arrived for the fourth session, Mrs. Chen without her dark glasses, and both looking more relaxed. They said that things had been going better since talking to us, and that Mrs. Chen was yelling less. But the atmosphere changed suddenly when Dr. Hu contradicted himself and said that he hadn't seen any difference because he still lives in fear of her devil-side coming out.

We felt puzzled, thrown off by this reversal. Jill felt shut down again and had to deal with feeling hopeless about the couple.

Mrs. Chen said, 'This devil stuff is nonsense. My behavior is quite normal. You're the one who is peculiar.'

Dr. Hu said, 'Say whatever you want about me. It's okay we're different.' To us, he said. 'She thinks we don't fit, but I think we're a match.'

Jill asked how they matched at the time of their marriage.

Mrs. Chen explained,

We were introduced by a matchmaker. We lived in different areas and spent hardly any time together. We were different, a businesswoman and a scientist, but both of us were older and looking to marry. I chose him because he was reliable, not a man who would have affairs. I wasn't swept off my feet. It was a practical choice.

For Dr. Hu, the choice had a different basis. 'She was straightforward, easy to read, good-looking,' he said. 'She helped me through a nasty surgery, even though it was dirty work. That's when I realized that this is a woman I could live with.'

I summarized that for Mrs. Chen, it was a practical choice of a man who would be faithful, loyal, successful and undemanding, while for Dr. Hu, it was a choice of a beautiful young woman who would look after him, even if it was difficult. Jill reminded them that yesterday Mrs. Chen had said that once married, she had found to her surprise that he was too romantic for his years. Perhaps she was also surprised by his sexual desire. Mrs. Chen looked puzzled, as if the translation hadn't made sense. Dr. Hu looked blank.

Jill continued, 'Yesterday, you found Dr. Hu capable of more than you expect from a man of his age in terms of romance – and perhaps of sexual desire.'

Mrs. Chen looked uncomfortable.

Dr. Hu said,

After a few months of marriage, sex stopped going well. I work hard and I feel tired. There were so many quarrels the first year that I felt stunned and angry and did not have much desire. I was worried and got advice that I needed to have a child to save my marriage.

Mrs. Chen agreed, 'Without the child, we would be divorced.'

Dr. Hu said, 'I love children. I was thrilled to have a child. I even gave up a special scientific meeting where I would have presented my work so that I could be present at the birth.'

Mrs. Chen said again, 'Our daughter eases our relationship. We agree never to quarrel in front of her because that would upset her, like it upset me when my parents quarreled. I don't want her to feel awful like I did.'

We now heard more about how much Mrs. Chen's parents had fought. I acknowledged that Mrs. Chen's parents' anger had been deeply upsetting to her, and that she and Dr. Hu did not want to expose their couple anger to their daughter, who was the light of their lives. They worked well as parents, but sadly, not as husband

and wife. Mrs. Chen said that her child loves her father and mother equally. I responded, 'Your daughter loves the two of you, and she wants the two of you to be together. She gets the best of you as parents, and you as a couple only get what's left over once she's asleep.'

Dr. Hu said, 'When my wife is in bed by 10 pm, that's when we talk. But it's always about divorce, and then I have to go to work in the morning.'

I said, 'During the day with your daughter, sunshine reigns, but during the night, things get frightening. Talking of night makes me wonder about your dreams.'

Dr. Hu said, 'I have not remembered any dreams since I got married. I used to feel weak and had lots of dreams, but since marriage I feel strong, and I have no more sweating, dizziness or dreams.'

Mrs. Chen said,

> I used to dream a lot, but I don't remember dreams now. There's a dream I always used to have – of being in a river with big and little fish. All the fish were colorful and fat. I could only catch a little fish.

When I asked if anything occurred to Mrs. Chen about the dream, she said,

> I don't have any ideas about the dream, except that I always wondered why I always caught only little fish. My friends said that the dream might mean I would win something in the lottery, a fat fish being a bigger win than a thin fish, but a big fish would be too much to eat. A small fish is enough for me.

I asked, 'When you 'caught' your husband, did you think of your catch as a big fish or a small fish?'

Mrs. Chen said, 'It never occurred to me.'

Dr. Hu said, 'In my view, a dream is not related to real life. It's child's play.'

Again, we felt rebuffed, our exploration shut down. The couple was capable of dreaming and of metaphor, but in the interview, they shut down that capacity to avoid knowledge and pain, and they returned to more concrete matters, closing us out of shared understanding in more depth. We noticed that they were inhibited in discussing sexuality, although some of that reluctance might well be due to reticence in front of an audience and with us, whom they hardly knew. But we could see that that their marriage was tenuously based on gratitude and respect rather than love, but their sense of gratitude and respect was attacked by their disappointment and anger. Dr. Hu appreciated his wife's devotion to him during his illness. Mrs. Chen valued his treatment of her parents, which was always respectful and generous, and his academic achievement. They were grateful for each other's devotion to their child, and as adult children, Mrs. Chen encouraged Dr. Hu to be more connected to his family and values the way he was good to her family. They both respected the ideal of being a family with a child, but they did not seem to respect each other. Mrs. Chen admired her husband as a scientist, but not as a husband or a son, and he did not respect her as a businesswoman or wife. Now we began to see the way that mutual disappointment, born out of very different hopes of each other, had sowed the seeds of discontent within their marriage, which was now held together almost solely by their shared love of their child.

Mrs. Chen's dream seems to capture the problem of their marriage for each of them: they each thought that they had captured a 'big fish' in finding the other, but now found, in their disappointment, that they caught only a 'little fish.'

Session 5

The fifth session opened with their expressions of gratitude for the space to think about the implications of their lives as children without getting angry.

Dr. Hu said, 'For instance, I heard that I am too romantic, and you made space for me to listen and wonder if what I did was wrong.'

Mrs. Chen said, 'He is an old man, and according to Chinese tradition he should have an old heart, but he has a young heart.'

Jill said, 'Dr. Hu has a romantic view of women, but does he show you as his wife that he cherishes you every day?'

Mrs. Chen said, 'He's cold. He doesn't cherish the relationship, or his own mother. According to Chinese tradition, relatives are supposed to be close, but he keeps his distance.'

Jill said that, as a young boy, Dr. Hu was very close to his mother, and she was taken away from him. He had to do the best he could without her by teaching himself that it is safer to love at a distance. That was unlike the childhood experience of Mrs. Chen, who had her parents every day, but they were quarreling, which is how they stayed close, and that might be one reason why now Mrs. Chen quarrels with Dr. Hu.

Wiping away a tear as he heard this, Dr. Hu said,

> You are right, but I can't accept her way of loving me... always being harsh to me, always criticizing and suppressing me. According to Chinese tradition, you shouldn't treat a person that way if you don't want to be treated that way yourself. Speaking harshly is her family way, not mine.

Mrs. Chen said, 'Yes, our family is like that...loud, joking. He can't accept a joke. If I say something teasing, he thinks I'm criticizing him.'

Dr. Hu said, 'My wife and I have different backgrounds, educational levels and sensibilities. My mother's way is that we should not be entangled. Chinese are too entangled.'

Dr. Hu had been taught that the relatives should deal in reason, not feelings, but Mrs. Chen dealt mainly in feelings and was annoyed by him being so rational, which to her seemed cold and inconsiderate. Mrs. Chen responded to dream work, but Dr. Hu brushed it aside. Nevertheless, he would find a moment of access to expressing deeper feelings by the end of the interview. Each of them respected his or her own family's way of behaving, but they were in conflict about which model to follow. Each valued having a family, but as a couple, they were now too focused on their child to the neglect of each other. Their intimate connection had come to be mainly displayed through quarreling, not through affection and sexuality.

Dr. Hu and Mrs. Chen had a free-choice marriage, but one based on the ideal of *enqing*, not of romance. *Enqing* refers to respect, appreciation, gratitude and admiration for the fulfillment of spousal and filial duty (Li and Chen, 2002; Chen and Li, 2007). In Asian culture, *enqing* has been shown to secure marital satisfaction more reliably than intimacy based on attraction and romantic love (Ng, Peluso and Smith 2010). Divorce has become increasingly common in China, but it still creates a great deal of shame.

As we moved to end the session, the Dr. Hu said passionately and tearfully to Mrs. Chen, 'I do not betray you: I stay with you. My commitment is a true expression of feeling.' We felt moved by his sudden access to feelings only at the moment of our ending.

These sessions revealed much of what Dr. Hu and Mrs. Chen wanted in their marriage – Mrs. Chen wanted access to Dr. Hu's feelings and vulnerability. Dr. Hu wanted his rationality to prevail over her emotionality. We saw how she became either angry or numb to avoid painful communication. They told us how they each projected their goodness into their daughter, the only person with whom they could love and feel loved. With them, we were able to explore the impact of recent Chinese history and the differences between each of their cultures on their expectations and behaviors. Dr. Hu was born during the Cultural Revolution and had no school to go to and no mother to turn to, whereas Mrs. Chen's generation did not experience that deprivation and separation. Dr. Hu was the only child in an intellectual family, while Mrs. Chen was one of four siblings in an agricultural family. Together, they had one child. Because they live in a city and Dr. Hu has a university job, they must follow the official One Child Policy. This was our first exposure to the dictates of social policy in China, so unfamiliar to those from Western countries. I will return to that topic in Chapter 4.

Having said good-bye, we shook hands, except that Dr. Hu walked past Jill, not even looking at her. She felt that Dr. Hu was giving her the cold shoulder for leaving him. She felt it as pain in her heart, resonating with the pain in his own life that could not find with an open expression.

In this way, it was only at the moment of parting that the trauma of Dr. Hu's early abandonment by his mother was vividly conveyed to us by giving us the pain that he must have felt at his mother's absence in his early life. At this moment, we could really feel, and therefore understand more fully from inside a shared experience, how his pain must reach his wife, who, because of her own insecurities, refuses to contain the pain and gets rid of it by quarreling instead. It was sad to us that the trauma could only be fully communicated when there was no more time for metabolizing it, for feeding back to them what we could now understand. We ended the encounter with this couple knowing that we could not accomplish the level of change that Dr. Hu and Mrs. Chen needed, and that, to get that kind of help, they would have to continue their conversation with a local therapist.

We learned a great deal from Dr. Hu and Mrs. Chen, about their marriage specifically, and about understanding them as a couple in the Chinese context of their life. In this way, they helped us begin to understand the situation of marriage and of young families in contemporary China. Dr. Hu and Mrs. Chen come from different areas of society and from the vastly different eras that were formed by the end of the Cultural Revolution. Coming from the countryside, Mrs. Chen's family suffered no loss or cultural trauma. Coming from academia, Dr. Hu's mother was sent to the countryside for reeducation, and he was sent to a situation apparently without functional foster parents and was separated from his mother for years. Dr. Hu and his family suffered huge losses and trauma, which he preferred to deny. Instead, Dr. Hu identified with the ideals of the 'Days of Sunshine' culture of his childhood, rational communication and acceptance of separateness, whereas Mrs. Chen identified with the ideal of plain-speaking, emotional communication and family solidarity. Dr. Hu identified with the value of academic research despite its official suppression in his childhood, while Mrs. Chen, as a previously success-ful small-business woman, identified with business and no longer with rural agriculture. By the 1980s, when Dr. Hu was in university, Chinese society still devalued business but valued knowledge. Intellectuals, who had been relegated to reeducation and manual work during the Cultural Revolution, were respected once more. By the early 2000s, as China zoomed ahead in commerce, business was highly valued but not wholly respected.

Theoretically, the culture in which people are raised is represented internally in an area of the mind that has been called 'the social uncon-scious' (Foulkes, 1964; Hopper, 2003). The social unconscious is a con-stellation of social, cultural and communicational arrangements of which people remain unaware because they do not consciously consider the social forcefields in which they live any more than we consider the air we breathe. They may discuss the cultural issues, but also may not admit to what they know, or may not accept the impact of social issues in order to avoid feeling helpless in the face of influences too sweeping to con-trol. These forces have external sway – they form the link with the cul-ture, but even more importantly for our purposes in this book, they hold sway unconsciously, internally, determining a great deal of how people behave externally and, in marriage and families, with each other. A cou-ple cannot clearly see the effect on themselves of the social unconscious, of all the early and current influences, whether they be ordinary or trau-matic. In the wake of trauma and disruption, they simply feel angry, misunderstood and afraid. With the social unconscious functioning partly to keep social forces out of awareness, some people may blindly accept their circumstances as normal, some develop symptoms of mental or physical stress they cannot explain and some experience relationship difficulties. Dr. Hu and Mrs. Chen enjoyed good physical health, but in their current lives, they experienced the effects of their early social expe-rience in differing Chinese subcultures unconsciously, and specifically they did so in terms of conflict in their relationship. Even though our time with Dr. Hu and Mrs. Chen may have made them partly aware of some of the social, economic, cultural and political constraints in their couple's foundation matrix, it is unlikely that they would have felt empowered to change the pattern of their interaction without more therapy – which they may or may not have agreed to.

This couple's narrative and their way of relating to us taught us a num-ber of things about how both social change and personal dynamic fac-tors interacted for them, as present and past collided in their marital relationship. In this way, our encounter with them addressed each of the four questions we were just beginning to have as we began to know more about China and that I posed in the opening chapter of this book. First, we could begin to see how the historical Chinese culture of deference to men was expressed in this family, how it had shaped the wife's development and how it had been disrupted for the husband. Second, we saw a vivid example of how the social factors of the Cultural Revolution, of the wife's move from a rural family to an urban setting and the changing picture of how marriages are formed all contributed to shaping their marriage. Third, we saw how the challenge to this family and families like them might further shape Chinese society in the event of marital failures and divorce, or to shape things yet differently if they found a way to stay together. And fourth, we began to get an early taste of the clinical challenges facing therapists who would be called on to help such families. It was sad for us that what we learned from this couple might not, in itself, be enough to solve their own marital dilemma.

Note

1 This couple has been previously reported in Scharff, J. S. and Scharff, D, E. (2011) The impact of Chinese cultures on a marital relationship. *Special Issue: Psychoanalysis in China. International Journal of Applied Psychoanalytic Studies,* 8(3):249–260, and in D. E. Scharff and S. Varvin eds (2014) *Psychoanalysis in China.* London: Karnac. pp. 277–287. By Permission.

Chapter 3

An Introduction to Psychoanalytic Understanding of Families and Couples

Some of the terms and our way of working with the couple presented in the previous chapter will be unfamiliar to readers who are not steeped in psychological and psychoanalytic thinking and terminology, so before going further, I want to summarize some of the most fundamental ideas. Through my whole career, I have applied psychoanalytic thinking to the study and treatment of families and couples (Scharff, 1982; Scharff and Scharff, 1987, 1991). I brought this same lens to studying in China, even though a more comprehensive intercultural study also requires understanding from other disciplines, including history, culture and gender studies, sociology and demography, to name a few.

For the reader not already familiar with psychoanalytic thought, or unfamiliar with the branch of psychoanalysis known as 'object relations theory,' I will introduce a few ideas and terms that are essential to my investigations of the couples and families whose stories and interviews populate these pages. A more complete introduction is provided in *The Primer of Object Relations* by Jill Savege Scharff and myself, published in 2005 and available in English and Chinese.

The psychoanalytic study of the mind, beginning with Freud, valued the role of unconscious processes that underpin daily life and that write our dreams. Freud's own study was intensely individual, even though his famous case histories are replete with descriptions of patients' families, almost all as reported by the patients themselves. He only knew the parents of his patients directly in a few cases, and therefore did not develop an understanding of the intersection of minds and of unconscious communication in family life.

Psychic Organization

Beginning in 1940, W. R. D. Fairbairn rewrote the basic tenets of psychoanalysis with his developments published in 1952 as *An Object Relations Theory of the Personality*. In this work, he described how the need of each person, from the beginning of life, is to relate to others, and that the mind is formed by taking in, or *introjecting*, the experiences of these relationships. He then developed a theory of mental structure that he called *the endopsychic situation* that consisted of a central ego or self that relates to others in reasonable proportion, with an innate pull towards relationships and a sense of limits that allows persons to be themselves. He posited two poles of personality, however, that represent painful relating: the *rejecting object constellation*, consisting of internal organizations representing relationships of the *self* or *ego* with neglectful or persecuting people, installed in the mind by what are called *internal rejecting objects*; and the *exciting object constellation*, representing relationships of the self with *exciting objects*, that is with people who were excessively exciting of need. It is easy enough to envisage a persecuting or neglectful internal mother or father, the so-called *rejecting objects*, but *exciting objects* are a bit less intuitive. Think of the *excessively exciting object* as an internalized mother who tantalizes her child with offers that cannot be satisfied, 'I'll give you candy; oh, no I won't.' The child who is treated in this way craves things she cannot have (Fairbairn, 1952).

Both these painful extremes of relating are *split off* from central experience and *repressed*, that is, buried in the unconscious because they are too painful to be borne in consciousness. They do not disappear; they are just buried and can be retrieved under certain circumstances, and in addition, they continue to operate and to organize the mind from the unconscious – from a position, as it were, under water.

One important addition: In cases of traumatic development, and with the operation of dissociation that is more complete than normal repression, extremely painful experiences may be more deeply split-off and buried in a kind of *psychological capsule* that guards this internal memory from being experienced. However, if and when these capsules burst, then the memory of extremely painful experience may burst to the surface and take over in painful and pathological ways. This possibility is relevant to many of the people I saw in China because their personal and national trauma may have been too painful to keep in mind (Plaenkers, 2010, 2014a; Scharff and Scharff, 1994).

Unconscious Communication: Projective and Introjective Communication

In order to understand how couples and families communicate in depth, we also require a theory of unconscious emotional communication. Unconscious communication always rides 'piggyback' on conscious communication, but it is conveyed by all the nonverbal channels, including tone and rhythm of voice, body posture, smell, facial gesture and movement of the eyes. We decode emotional communication ten times faster than verbal, conscious communication because we all need to know how other people feel. That information is vital to our survival and well-being, and because of this, we are built fundamentally to read other people's minds (Scharff, 1992; Scharff and Scharff, 2011). We now know that all mammals are possessed of 'mirror neurons' that record the actions of others in our minds, and that the mirror neuron system ramifies to represent others' emotional experience in our own minds (Gallese, 2003, 2012).

This neuroscience finding needs a psychological counterpart in theory, which was developed in 1946 by another pioneer of object relations theory, Melanie Klein. She described the way an infant, suffering from an excess of aggression, would offload that dangerous mental state through *projective identification*. In this mode, the child would unconsciously, psychologically inject that part of her mind into her mother, who would then, also unconsciously, take in the child's mental experience through the mother's *introjective identification*. In this process, the child communicated to the mother the child's anger, anguish, anxiety and longing, and by taking these states of mind in, the mother could understand her child from the inside. This happens because the mother allows the child's experience to rumble around inside her mind, connect with relevant parts of her own experience, intuitively understand it and then feed it back to the child attended by less anxiety and more understanding (Scharff, 1992).

Another theorist, Wilfred Bion (1970), called this function of the mother's mental process her *reverie*, likening it to dream processes and emphasizing that this goes on largely out of awareness. In this process, the parent's mind becomes a *container* for the child's anxieties, where the contents and organization of the child's mind are the *contained* matter. The parent holds it in mind and makes sense of it. Then it is no longer so threatening to the child. Then the mother projects this improved content and structure back to the child, who now takes in the matured content and organization. This process repeats infinitely between them, and thereby forms an interactive crucible in which the child's mind grows. Mind, therefore, is a product of the interaction of projective and introjective identification. These processes are, of course, subject to distortions, failures and neglect. For instance, a disturbed parent may fail to contain the child's anxieties and instead impose her own anxieties or traumas onto and into the child, and these failures are a major object of clinical study and interpretation.

The Psychosomatic Partnership and Transitional Phenomena

Donald Winnicott, a pediatrician and psychoanalyst, contributed to our understanding by drawing on his close study of the mother-infant experience. He saw that all psychological life began in a body-and-mind partnership between baby and mother, which he called a *psychosomatic partnership*. This is a particularly useful idea when we study issues at the interface of body and emotion, and this includes both eating disorders and sexual problems, where the body expresses ideas and feelings that are hidden from the mind. Winnicott also described the way that children develop a transitional zone in play with their parents, a zone in which they play with what is inside their minds through the use of *transitional objects* and *transitional phenomena*, exemplified by a teddy bear or blanket that the child treats both as an object in the outer world, and at the same time, as though it were part of the child's mind. Think of imaginary friends to whom the child speaks and who speak for the child. In doing this, Winnicott also emphasized the importance of the *ability to play* and of the function of play in the development both of mind and of relationships. This becomes specifically important when we see children, who in normality express themselves mostly through play and for whom an inability to play is a serious problem (Winnicott, 1971a, 1971b).

The Concept of the Link

Finally, I include the ideas of Enrique Pichon Rivière, an Argentinian analyst who was the first to describe group and family therapy. Among his important concepts is that of the *link*. The *link* expresses the living relationship between two individuals, between individuals in a family or group, the connection to past and future generations, and the connection to the extended family, community and larger society. It is a complex and interactive construction, with both conscious and unconscious elements (Losso et al., 2017; Scharff, 2016; Scharff et al., 2017).

The central feature of the link is that while each person contributes to it, the link itself continuously contributes to organizing and reorganizing that person. That is to say, we are all both subjects and authors of the link. We are born into links (that is, relationships with others), we live in links, breathing them in unknowingly like the air we live in or as fish take in the water in which they swim, and we continuously contribute to our links with others. So, we participate in organizing links, and the links constantly act both to confirm and to modify us.

Links have three areas: the mind, the body and action. The mind itself, in the way that Fairbairn described, is made up of inner links between self and internal objects, and these inner constellations mirror our external links or relationships. The body is also built to express links because all emotions are expressed in bodily states. Emotion itself is a bodily state built on neural and hormonal changes. Finally, our actions and interactions with others, including our speech actions, always express the link.

The link also has two axes. The *horizontal axis* connects us to our partners, families, village, society and culture – all in the present. The *vertical axis* connects us to our forebears and our children, to the past and future of our intimate relations and culture.

Employing concepts of the link allows us to see that in family and couple therapy, observational settings that this book is built on, it is not only unconscious communication that matters. Real-time interactions and discussions matter equally and equally influence our minds. The concept of the link is a foundational idea for group and family therapy, and it gives us the basis for psychoanalytic theorizing about conscious as well as unconscious communication and interaction. It also provides better theory for the study of how we locate ourselves within culture and history, and this too is central to the story of a changing China and for the issues that present in the midst of China's culture shift.

Child and Individual Development

Many disciplines, including psychoanalysis, have contributed to our understanding of child and individual development. It is essential to have a working understanding of the processes of both individual and family growth and maturation, from the beginning of life through old age. In the pre-school years, there is sexualization of development, which is then de-emphasized in the elementary school years when skill and language acquisition take prominence. In adolescence, there is re-sexualization and rapid expansion of the abstract thinking of adolescence. In adulthood, sexuality and intimacy build towards procreativity and raising a family. Ultimately, a couple deals with the phases of aging and approaching death. (I have contributed to this literature, especially in my book *The Sexual Relationship* that traces sexual development from childhood through old age, and further in *Object Relations Family Therapy*, written with Jill Scharff [Scharff, 1982, 1998; Scharff and Scharff, 1987].) John Bowlby's groundbreaking study of the earliest attachments between young children and their mothers, which led to descriptions of secure, insecure and disorganized attachments, gave developmentalists a framework to study the role of early object relations throughout the life cycle (Bowlby, 1958, 1969). All of these contributions, and many others, are relevant to our study of Chinese couples and families. However, even if the scientific details concerning individual and family development are not familiar to the reader, general concepts will be. All that I think is necessary in this brief introduction is to say that the study of individual development, and familiarity with many of the details of development, is stock-in-trade for psychotherapists and analysts. You will see allusions to these concepts throughout the presentations of cases of this book.

Transference and Countertransference in Psychotherapy

I will often refer to the concepts of *transference* and *countertransference* in the clinical examples that follow. So, it is important to know that we define transference as *the way the patient or family brings old ways of relating to the new setting of psychotherapy.* Because all people do this in all interpersonal encounters, transference in the specialized setting of psychotherapy becomes a crucial source of information about our patients' ways of doing business in relationships. Transference includes the unconscious communication of mental states and ways of relating, so the analysis of a couple, family or individual's transference to us is a crucial source of our assessments. Understanding transference informs our interpretations to our patients about what we are coming to understand in our work with them. Using transference is a central mode in our work. Patients may, of course, correct our understanding, and we value the collaboration that allows them to do so.

A central tool in this process is the therapist's *countertransference.* A thorough discussion of this concept is well beyond our needs here. Suffice it to say that I define countertransference in a working way *as the therapist's emotional reaction to the patient and to the patient's transference.* While it is certainly true that a therapist may react to a patient because of internal issues of the therapist herself, the training and personal treatment that each therapist must have is designed to minimize interference from the therapist's own personal issues and to educate her about how to make therapeutic use of her emotional reactions, all geared towards facilitating a better understanding of the patient, couple or family's emotional life and their links with others. You will see many examples of our use of countertransference in what follows.

Finally, we use *interpretation* of what we understand as the fundamental way of interacting with couples and families. I use the word 'interpretation' to include the *full range of ways that we speak to our patients about what we are coming to understand,* including describing inconsistencies in what they say, connecting things that belong together while patients are trying to keep them apart and the underlying unconscious reasons for conducting life's business in self-defeating ways. Our interpretations are always given in the service of increasing mutual understanding, which is the foundation of care and growth.

You will see that I employ all these concepts in the encounters with Chinese couples and families that form the heart of this book. I use them whenever I work clinically, East or West. They are both my research tools and my means of working to help the families and couples I see in China and at home. This chapter specifically outlines a few of the most fundamental elements of the clinical lens through which I have sought to understand the families we interviewed, and therefore most directly pertains to the fourth question I posed in the opening chapter: how to best understand and serve Chinese families clinically, and therefore, how to teach Chinese clinicians about their needs. However, it also gives an introduction to the way I understand families in general, in order to connect that understanding to the larger social issues that are posed in the other questions we consider throughout the book.

Chapter 4

The Hidden Chinese Revolution

Hidden in plain sight, revolutionary changes have been happening in China for the last 70 years. This contemporary revolution made its start during the modern history of China that is more familiar. As one of the oldest continuous cultures in the world, China carries a deep structure of thought and morality that descends from its millennia of recorded and unrecorded history. We can take our start in the relevant part of the social history of China by recalling that 'women counted for nothing,' to quote Professor Tong Jun (2016). Traditional Han Chinese women had bound feet, which rendered it almost impossible for them to walk, confined them to the house and enforced their subservience to their husbands as masters. Men of some wealth could have concubines, so some women were further without rights in this particular way. The historical reports of politically powerful concubines do not contradict the fact that concubines were effectively enslaved. Wives were generally expected to move into the households of their husbands, where they were subservient not only to the husbands but to their mothers-in-law, who frequently dominated and tyrannized them. They could not gain real power unless and until they had a son, and then could eventually control the family through the son and his potential wife. Women were a great disappointment to their husbands and families if they did not bear sons (Jankowiak and Moore, 2017).

All of this changed radically with the Communist Party's victory over the Kuomintang in 1949. In the ensuing years, a great deal of social trauma and social disruption was brought about by the disastrous consequences of the Great Leap Forward and the largest famine in human history, in which 30–45 million people died (Becker, 1996; Yang Jisheng, 2008). Mao Zedong oversaw the collectivization of farms and the melting down of families' cooking utensils to make peasant steel for factories, steel that was of such low grade that the resulting equipment was not functional. The party arrogated jurisdiction over who could marry and divorce. Sex went from being a prerogative of men and duty of women, to being discouraged except for the purposes of procreation (more on this and refinements to the story in Chapter 9).

For the next 25 years, marital and family loyalties were subservient to loyalty to the party and the country. Obeisance was owed to Chairman Mao, just as under the Confucian ethnic it was owed to the Emperor during the 2,500 years of the Chinese dynasties. This radical change broke with millennia of the tradition of family structure, in which Chinese hoped to have large families dominated by the men, the father and the son, both in rural areas where large families were needed for farming, and in the cities where the eldest son was the successor of business ventures. Even in intellectual and mercantile families, large families were the hope and the rule. Mao substituted obedience to the party and onto himself, redirecting the ancient tradition of obedience to the Emperor and the father. This radical change co-opted the Confucian chain that went from the Emperor to the father to the son, and, in that Confucian morality, taught that in a reciprocal way, the emperor and the father were instructed to be beneficent caretakers of their people and their families. Just as the Emperor had an obligation (often neglected) to care for his country and his flock, the father and the oldest son had an obligation to care for their family, women and girls included. However, in practice, this reciprocal obligation could be ignored without significant consequence. Fathers and husbands frequently imposed their authority physically. There has been a good deal of domestic physical abuse in China. In 2005, the American Public Health Association reported that one in five women had been abused domestically in China (Liu and Chan, 1999; Wikipedia, 2019; Xu, 1997). It is not as though male domination and physical abuse did not also exist in the West, where women had few rights until late in the nineteenth century, but the new balance began to be possible in the West perhaps 100 years before this happened in China.

One unintended positive consequence of the new communist dictates about the family was that women were more highly valued than they had ever been before in China's history. Mao famously said, 'Women hold up half the sky!' While this seemed on the surface to be egalitarian and to offer new possibilities for women, in practice this was truer in the area of work than it was in the sphere of family and marriage. Nevertheless, there were significant ways in which the dawn of the communist era was good for women, who now were at least equal in work and in other unintended ways, and equal sexually even though sex was generally frowned on for everyone. Of course, there was a significant but unwritten set of sexual exceptions for Chinese Communist Party (CCP) leaders, for whom there was a great deal of sex in just the kind of way that was forbidden for everybody else. That this was true for Mao has been extensively documented by his personal physician, Dr. Liu Zhisui, who, in a biography published only in the West, described the licentious way of life of his later years (Li Zhisui, 1994). The path of change for women during these generations has been documented by Jung Chang in her 1992 book, *Wild Swans: Three Daughters of China*, which vividly portrays the transformation of opportunities for women from her grandmother's life as a concubine, to her mother's travails under the early days of communism, to her own emergence and emigration (Jung Chang, 1992). As we shall see, however, transformation of the Chinese family and of opportunities for women have continued at a gallop since the periods covered by her book.

How the One Child Policy Struck at the Heart of Chinese Tradition

Then came the One Child Policy. Dictated in the late 1970s after the death of Mao, it was designed by a nuclear engineer based on the numerical calculations that if every family only had one child, population growth could be controlled. Presumably, policymakers turned to an engineer to design this policy because there were no social scientists available because of the Cultural Revolution. The purging of intellectual endeavors and fields, especially during the Cultural Revolution from 1966 to 1976, when academics, privileged landowning farmers and people of wealth were stripped of money, power and position and sent to the countryside for 'reeducation,' resulted in a disastrous national depletion of intellectual and leadership resources. This situation is conveyed in the book and movie, *Balzac and the Little Chinese Seamstress* (Dai Sijie, 2001). Much of the change that occurred in China in this era answered to the laws of unintended consequences. If sex were no longer to be for procreation because everybody was allowed only one child, then sex had to be for something else, and in this sense, women once again became more equal to men. Although romantic aspects of sex were forbidden throughout Chairman Mao's tenure, an underground grew up with a series of underground letters called 'The Left-Behind Love Letters.' While these were denounced and forbidden, they nevertheless circulated widely but surreptitiously. Later, another series of letters, this time facilitated by the newly growing internet, also raised the possibility of enjoyable female sexuality. As a result, women began to feel that they had a right to sexual enjoyment just as men did. The One Child Policy enhanced the possibility of sexual enjoyment, both for married couples and eventually for young couples before marriage or without marriage (Jeffreys, 2009; Jeffreys and Yu 2015; Zhang, 2011; more about this in Chapter 9).

Of course, it has always been true that if men were having affairs outside of marriage, there had to be women involved. (In this narrative, I am not considering the minority situation of homosexuality, which was forbidden and not reported on in China until recently, but is now emerging from the shadows, much as it has in the West over the past 50 years.) Consequently, the family pattern for middle-class and urban Chinese families changed radically. The laws and penalties dictating the one child family were enforced quite strictly in the cities, often through draconian actions like forced abortion (Wong, 2012). However, in the countryside, enforcement was uneven, with recognition that farm families often needed more than one child. Nevertheless, when it was enforced, it could be done in severe ways. If a peasant family had a girl first, they were often allowed to have a second child. It was also a consideration if a man had a second wife; she would be allowed to have a child. Minority populations were also exempted. Overall, the one child policy was enforced more strictly in urban settings, but was indeed responsible for reducing the rate of growth in the population significantly. Many families longed for a second child but did not pursue their wish because penalties were quite severe. One could lose his or her job, or lose stature within or outside the Communist Party, while the second child would be denied education and healthcare. Probably the most significant impediment to larger families was the social stigma that quickly came to be applied to families who dared to buck the government's policy. In this way, in families with official positions, it was both forbidden and impolitic to have more than one child.

It is not clear that this policy was necessary for population control, since China's birthrate had been declining even before the imposition of the One Child Policy, but the policy became the law of the land and helped to control population size – but with a raft of unintended consequences that we shall be investigating. Although the CCP has recently ended the One Child Policy and is now urging young people to have more children for the sake of the country, there are serious indications that the birth rate will not rise significantly and will be likely to remain below the rate of population replacement. Birth rates have fallen in all developed countries, and China is now a developed country. Children are expensive in terms of education and health care. Both parents are often working, and childcare often falls to the grandparents, as has been traditional in China in any case. And contemporary young adults often want small families or even do not wish to have children or even to marry (Ye and Feng, 2000).

Under the headline, 'Hey, People's Daily – leave my womb alone!' Jeremy Goldkorn of the American China-watching website *SupChina* reported on a backlash against the government's new policy of urging more children. The People's Daily printed,

a recent commentary (in Chinese)... which urges citizens to reproduce because China's falling birth rate makes having children 'not just a family matter but also a national issue.' The piece dismisses people who don't want children as choosing a 'passive way to dealing with the stresses of modern life.'

This has inspired massive pushback. Goldkorn reported,

> One Weibo user wrote: 'It's true that having children is a national issue, but it's more of a family matter. A country can't regulate what happens in people's bedrooms, let alone in such an arbitrary way. When you don't want children, you force people to get sterilized. When you want more, you urge us to give birth. What do you think I am?'

In response to disappointing rise in birth rates since the easing of the One Child Policy,

> The government's new interest in women having more rather than fewer children has sparked intense debate on Chinese social media. The conversation largely centers on why state media always uses a denunciatory and paternalistic tone when covering the topic, blaming families unwilling to have more children for being selfish, and objectifying women as mere tools for reproduction.
> (Goldkorn, *SupChina*, August 7, 2018)

There are also groups that have suffered disastrous consequences of the One Child Policy: Thirteen million children, almost 1% of the Chinese population, make up a group of undocumented and illegal 'second children' whose parents cannot afford the fine involved in registering them. While the parents are often punished through lack of employment, the children are uneducated and without medical care, have difficulty finding a job and when, as adults, they have children, they face the same problem for that second generation of undocumented children (Liu and Chen, 2016).

There are more than a million couples whose only child has died, leaving them with emotional and financial despair. These child-widowed parents despair for their future, because in a country with no social safety net and no child to take care of them in their advancing age, there is little hope that they can survive above the poverty line (Kim, Kyung-Hoon, 2015; Yuan Ye, 2012).

Chinese families have traditionally favored sons, looking to their sons, and especially the oldest son, to carry on the family name, the family farm or the family business. There is also an emotional investment in this tradition. Only children and especially sons carry the family's future with them, endowing a sense of immortality. One generation honors the tombs of its forebears, thus keeping their memory alive. The One Child Policy did more than attempt to control the increase of China's population. Much has been written about families' intense investment in their only child, spoiling them while at the same time loading them up with the full burden of hopes for the future. Emotionally, the One Child Policy amputated the branches of the family tree that would traditionally carry families' hopes for their future. By restricting the number of children that a family could have, the policy struck at the heart of the tradition of investing in children, for now, only one child could carry that burden for each family, and in the current generation, we see just how burdened many of those only children feel.

With the end of the Communist Party's exercise of control about who could marry, the age-old tradition of negotiated marriages, often decided by the parents or through the use of matchmakers, quickly began to wane. In the place of the age-old tradition of deference to parental influence, forms of 'free-choice' marriage evolved. Marriage might now follow from romantic involvement, based on Western models. Or, for instance, it might be based on more practical decisions about who would make a good spouse, for instance, choosing somebody who had done well at school and could be expected to be a good earner, or somebody who was kind to his or her parents and therefore could be expected to be kind in marriage.

In the West, we have more than 200 years of evolution to free-choice marriage, thereby giving young people some sense of tradition in which they can learn to make more or less appropriate matches, supported by the romantic literature and the teachings of various religious and ethical traditions. There is no such depth of tradition in China. We can no longer say that the method of choosing spouses in the West is all that good, considering our 50% divorce rate and the incidence of spousal abuse, poorly executed marriages and strains on children. But the West does have a tradition that gives a fair amount of moral support and contains social structures that offer practical support to the institution of marriage. Without saying that this is adequate, we can say that it is better than nothing and that it can often help ill-conceived marriages or those many marriages that experience crises. For those marriages that take advantage of the existing resources, there is an adequate network of social support.

In significant ways, such structures do not exist in China. The history of marriage and family life in China was that couples were contained by their extended family group to which they owed their loyalty. Practical considerations outweighed romantic interests. Indeed, this underlies the whole difference in ethical and moral structure of each individual in China. Where in the West there is a celebration of individuation and individual autonomy, in China there is an ethic of putting personal interests second to the interests of the group and the family. Without saying whether this is better or worse, we can say it is definitely different. It is also tied to the difference between a culture in the West where guilt often motivates an individual to behave better, while in China shame in front of the group – 'loss of face' is the term with most resonance – is most often the motivating factor for conformity to group and family norms. We will discuss the operation of shame in China in the next chapter.

With the end of large families, these deep moral structures have been called into question. It is not just that the nuclear family is now reduced to three instead of the previous larger group, but also this has meant a sudden thinning of kinship structures (Verdery, 2019). If a couple has only one child, and if that couple are themselves only children, then there are fewer cousins as there would have been in previous generations. If there are two generations of only children, then there are no first cousins. Consequently, the whole family network is thinner, offering less family resources to individuals in that network. Eberstadt (2019) reports that, to his awareness, there is no research on mapping out the dimensions or examining the implications of the now unavoidable atrophy of the extended family and its kinship network, or the equally unavoidable rise of a 'new family type' in China.

Another unintended consequence is what happens to grandparents. Grandparents have always been involved in the care of their children's children in China, but now grandparents can only look to their one grandchild, usually shared with, or in rivalry with another set of grandparents. The older generation now often exerts a great deal of pressure on their adult children to have children because there remains the feeling that their life is meaningless without continuity of the generations. These days, we see young married people coming under enormous pressure from their parents for two reasons. Because there is no effective social safety net and no system of social security in an organized and regular way, young adults expect they will have to take care of their parents financially and emotionally as they age. The government has even mandated that they do. This means a couple is likely to have four aging parents on their backs, and perhaps grandparents as well. In addition, these middle-aged or elderly parents are likely to pressure the young adults to have children, even if the young people do not want to or are not ready. And as young people get married later and are more hesitant about having children, these potential grandparents become more and more frustrated and depressed.

When such young married couples do have children, they may well turn to their parents for childcare, often having the elder parents live with or near them. This proximity is referred to as 'one hot soup,' meaning that soup can be carried by the older generation to the younger household while still hot. Such arrangements honor the longstanding tradition of extended families. However, these young couples are also apt to be annoyed or downright angry with their parents' interference, while the older generation often feels the ground has been stripped from beneath its feet, left in the cold as grandparents because they had always expected they would be able to control what happened with the young grandchildren. Some of the families we will meet later illustrate problems that come from such situations.

The problem is not only about what happens in a battle about who is going to influence the children. The younger generation in China has been raised with a great deal of parental ambivalence about how the new generation should behave. Parents of current young adults began to understand many years ago that these children had to be out for themselves and entrepreneurial in order to survive and succeed. As anthropologist Vanessa Fong has written (2007), this new understanding was in conflict with the old values. Fong was able to document how parents of children in the last 20 years gave mixed messages about whether children should remain loyal to their family or should go out and make it for themselves. Since these families only had one child, it was empowering to the girls (Fong, 2002), but the children also unconsciously absorbed their parents' conflicts. This legacy has carried forward, posing a quality of shame and guilt about letting the family down, and, at the same time, carrying a fear of 'not making it' in an increasingly competitive world.

I have already discussed how the One Child Policy fundamentally altered family structure and goals. Even in the countryside where a second child was often allowed, there was a shift from very large families to much smaller ones of perhaps two children. This inevitably changed the hierarchy of the Confucian model of the family, with deference to the father and then to the oldest son. Indeed, daughters were counted as a loss to the family because at the point of marriage, they would move to their husband's family where they became the lowest person on the totem pole until and unless they were lucky enough to have a son, at which point she could gain power when her son married and she could then control his wife and family.

Among the demographic issues generated by the One Child Policy, another obvious one is the excess of young males over females. The population of births was significantly distorted over the past generation, so that the ratio of boys to girls has risen from the usual biological norm of approximately 101 boys to 100 girls, to as high as 120 boys to 100 girls overall. In certain provinces, the ratio of boys to girls has apparently exceeded 130/100, and in not a few places, it has exceeded 150/100 (Eberstadt, 2019). In practical terms, this means there are a significant number of unmarriageable 'leftover' men, especially in the rural areas, where for a man not to marry has been considered a social catastrophe. Urban men can seek a country wife, but a country man cannot expect to interest a more educated urban wife. As a result, bride prices have risen in the countryside, and even widows and divorcees have been considered marriageable, which they were not in the past. There is an interesting coda to these changes: If a family does have two sons, the bride price for the first will be higher, because the bride's family understands that future resources will go not to the newlywed couple, but to financing a marriage for the second son (Eberstadt, 2019).

There have been exceptions to the One Child Policy, for instance for minorities or rural families that are allowed to have a second child (or occasionally a third) if the first is a girl, or more than one child is needed to help farm, and there are many families that have evaded the stricture or paid the penalty fee. But there are reports of many other instances where the One Child Policy has been enforced in draconian ways both in the country and the city, with forced abortion, or in which families have given up infant daughters for international adoption in hopes of having a son. The father of one urban family with two teenaged daughters demurred when I asked him how it had been possible to have two children. He signaled that it was better not to discuss this directly because it was a sensitive topic. He simply said, 'There are ways.' I have also seen cases in which a family of means went abroad specifically in order to have a second child, since that was legal. If such a child thereby is given citizenship in another country by place of birth, such a child is not recognized as Chinese and has no access to government-provided health care and education.

There have been dire predictions about this situation, since in a number of Western countries, the index of unmarried men has correlated with propensities for lawlessness or revolution. However, because of a long history of favoring male births and of infanticide or the adopting out of girls, China also has long history of a preponderance of men. Therefore, the social implications of the gender imbalance are not yet clear (Eberstadt, 2019). There certainly is a shortage of women in a country that does not favor in-migration of wives from abroad, although there is now a small underground practice of importing brides from other Asian countries (Gannon, 2019; Yen Duong, 2018). The mental health implications of this situation, as with many other distortions of the population, are far from clear.

Another changing population trend comes from the large-scale internal migration from the rural areas into the cities. Chinese state policy sponsors this migration, accompanied by the expansion of urban areas and construction of new cities of over a million people at an immense rate. The plight of internal migrants who cannot obtain a new urban *hukou* or residence permit is great. Their rights remain tied to their hukou in the country towns from which they have emigrated. The government most often refuses to grant hukous in the new place of residence. Their work is needed, but they exist in grey zone. This means that in their new city, they have no right to education for their children, no right to medical care for themselves and no political rights. This lack of rights and opportunity extends to the next generation of their children and grandchildren who are effectively stateless and ineligible for education or medical care. Even when some families of those without hukous have managed to find schools expressly for their hukou-less children, the government has closed some of their underground schools without explanation, magnifying the situation in which education is denied to those children. The number of these children without rights makes up 1% of China's population, and while China has recently moved to grant more hukous to such migrants, this leniency seems as yet to apply to small numbers (*News China*, June 1, 2019).

Another aspect of the overall situation involves the fact that there is an inadequate government-sponsored social security safety net, so that a large percentage of the aged in an aging population is inadequately protected. As of 2017, less than two thirds of China's working-age population were covered by any pension schema, and only about one third of urban migrants were covered. In rural areas, the pension plans only offered 'basic benefits' of 70 RMB per month (about $10 US) for those retirees who qualified (Eberstadt, 2019). The government has regularly claimed that it was on track to do better, but that is a work in progress (*The Economist*, August 11, 2012).

Children grow up with two parents and as many as four grandparents, all six of them valuing and spoiling the child. The child who is the product of this social structure has been popularly called the 'six pocket child,' a term that underlines the way the new social structure promotes a tendency for families to indulge and spoil their special child on whom rests all their hopes for the future, a future that formerly could be vested in several children. It has become increasingly evident, however, that these valued children will pay a social and economic price for being only children: They will face the responsibility of supporting their parents and grandparents financially and practically in their dependent old age. The demographics of the workforce for the next 20 years are already set until 2040, because all of those workers are already born (Eberstadt, 2019). It is clear, therefore, that there will be an enormous and increasingly elderly population and a seriously diminished workforce that must support them either through direct transfer of wealth within families, or through government-sponsored wealth transfer of a kind that happens through pension systems and social security in the West, but that largely does not exist in today's China (Wang Feng et al., 2019). No one yet knows what this will mean for these three generations of the elderly, working-age adults and dependent children when these children are themselves middle-aged 30–50 years from now, because the one-child social experiment has never been done before. Even as the Western press writes about the economic and military rise of China, and explores its environmental and political issues, there is little public mention of what these demographic facts might mean for China's future economic development.

Paradoxically, the unintended consequences of these demographic changes are quite positive for women. If a family only has one child, its girl is most often as special as a boy would have been. This has elevated the standing of women. There are exceptions in families in which the parents never let the girl forget she is not a boy, or in which she is unconsciously shaped to act as the family's boy. But in general, girls have come to be highly valued. In addition, since boys are excessively numerous, young women are now in the position of having their choice of men and are less likely to put up with those they refer to as the 'spoiled princelings' who were a regular product of past Chinese upbringing. And it remains true that girls are often better to their parents than boys. At least, this is the impression in the West, and it seems anecdotally true in China too. This often means that, while some families without sons continue to feel that as a bitter loss, in general, girls are often, or even usually, highly treasured these days in ways that they would not have been formerly. However, many young people feel burdened by obligations to their families, and are not sure either that they want to get married or have children, or that they will be up to supporting the obligation to their parents emotionally and financially.

There are other factors relevant to family structure and to risks for enormous strain for young adults. These factors are different for the rural families than they are for urban families, and enormously different for laboring or peasant families in the country or city than for educated families. There is less and less work and opportunity for rural young people. The enormous internal migration to the cities is supported by government pressure to bring people off the land and into the cities, and by the government's project of building many new cities. As young individuals and couples come into the cities in order to find work, they are likely to leave their child or children behind with parents or relatives if they can, but often with other people if there is no available relative. There is no place for their children in the city. These children, called 'left-behind children,' are often at risk.

In large cities like Shenzhen, an economic engine of modern China in a special economic zone created by the government, there is an enormous need for workers, who live often in cramped quarters and work long hours without essential rights. If they have left their children behind, they may visit them once or twice a year, often in the time of the Spring Festival. There is a large-scale movement of people at the time of the Spring Festival in late winter. One such family is portrayed poignantly in the Chinese film *Last Train Home*, a chilling documentary of a couple working themselves to the bone in a large city, experiencing a harrowing journey in the overcrowded trains and mass migration of the Spring Festival, only to get home and find that their adolescent children want nothing to do with them and are, in any event, out of control and at great risk. At the end of their brief home stay, the couple leaves, dispirited about what they have met at home and about the lack of filial feeling on the part of their two adolescent children (Lixin Fan, 2009).

In 2015, The Chinese government turned to a two-child policy, even in addition to the preexisting policy that when two only-children married, they were already entitled to have two children. However, the government has relaxed its policy at a time when China, as a rapidly developing country, has joined other developed countries in that young couples no longer wish to have large families. So, although China has ended its One Child stricture and perhaps is on the verge of relaxing all controls on the size of family, young couples now feel that children are too expensive. They would rather funnel their resources into their one child than into large families.

The early result is a birth rate far below what the government had hoped to achieve in relaxing the One Child Policy. It looks doubtful that the new policy will result in a substantial enlargement of the young population or the workforce. China's birth rate is often rated as the lowest in the world at 1.6 children per woman, much below the 2.1 children per woman needed to maintain an even population, even after the government has eliminated the One Child Policy. However, the end of the policy, and now the government's recent policy of encouraging more children, has meant that many couples who formerly despaired of having a second or even a third child are now trying, but many of these are in the later childbearing years. There has been a surge in the use of fertility clinics for such services, such as In Vitro Fertilization (IVF), both in China and abroad, so that for those who can afford it, fertility tourism has flourished. Even though it looks as though this will not be enough to provide for stable population, it is an important phenomenon in China as elsewhere in the world (Blain, 2018).

Consequently, China is faced with a rapidly aging population and a shrinking workforce that will be insufficient to finance the population economically in the coming decades. The magnitude of this problem is much larger than it is in Western countries, where there are also shrinking birth rates, but not to such a drastic extent. In addition, many Western countries, benefiting from immigration from poorer countries, can import labor and talent. China has no significant inward immigration from abroad. The result is what looks to become a demographic crisis of major proportions (Eberstadt, 2019). This too will have implications for mental health, hitting the poor more drastically than it will the relatively well-off middle and upper-middle class populations.

All of these factors, in varying combinations, come into play when we see couples and families clinically in China. As in any evolving country and culture, the deep structure of old traditions and legacies is always in an evolving relationship to the demands of modern life. This is certainly true in the United States, Europe and South America, but it is especially true in China, where the disruptions to tradition were sudden and traumatic and where social engineering took place on an unprecedented scale with the advent of the Communist Party's control of social life in 1949. More destruction, in a completely different direction, occurred with the imposition of the One Child Policy in the early 1980s, with the economic pressures that have recently driven people off the land and into the cities, and again with the change in orientation to the size of families, which has come about with the increasing wealth and well-being of the Chinese population and with the ending of the One Child Policy. In considering many aspects of couple and family life in modern China, we will see over and over again how these factors play out in complex and often puzzling ways – puzzling to us as clinicians, and puzzling to the couples and families as they attempt to deal with their rapidly changing culture, which in many ways has lost its traditional moorings.

To date, there has there been no discussion in psychoanalytic and psychotherapeutic literature of the psychological implications for individuals and families regarding these changes. Analysts and therapists tend to focus on the individual patients and families in their offices, ignoring the impact of large social trends on the well-being of the families and patients of the future. Psychotherapists tend to leave such thinking to policy people. But these demographic factors in China are going to have a major impact on the individuals and families who seek our help, and in the future, those who seek the help of clinicians who are currently our students.

We need to have a sense of these macroscopic issues in order to understand our questions about how they have an impact on the families and individuals we see. We have that kind of knowledge more at home in the West, where we absorb it through reading newspapers and seeing television news. We need comparable understanding about China because ultimately, social distress translates into personal distress. We and the next generation of Chinese therapists will be tasked with helping the families to pick up the pieces!

Chapter 5

Changing Values in Contemporary China

In convincing papers, several leaders in Chinese mental health have said that as psychoanalysis comes to China, it will be modified to take on Chinese characteristics. Analysis will not remain a pure Western development in the way we now know it. Cultural factors must inevitably modify analysis, and no one knows yet what Chinese psychoanalysis will look like 50 years from now (Yang Yunping, 2011; Zhong Jie, 2014), or indeed how it might in turn modify worldwide analytic thinking and practice.

While editing a journal issue on psychoanalysis and psychoanalytic psychotherapy in China (D. Scharff, 2011), and working with Sverre Varvin on the book *Psychoanalysis in China* (Scharff and Varvin, 2014), it became evident that Chinese contributors, and indeed Chinese clinicians, all wanted their Western psychotherapy teachers to understand how Chinese culture plays a major role in its encounter with psychoanalysis. For some Western contributors, the introduction of analytic therapies and their teaching seemed a rather straightforward matter. As one American colleague put it, 'The Chinese want to know how to do analytic therapy and we want to teach them. The problems they encounter in learning analytic therapy are not really different than for our Western students.' The problem is that most Chinese contributors do not see things that way. Several have made the point that Westerners needed to understand some fundamental things about China and the Chinese, and they have labored to help us.

I first encountered a vivid description of this problem at a Beijing Congress of the International Psychoanalytic Association in 2010 when I heard a paper by Dr. Zhong Jie (2011), an advanced candidate in the first IPA training and a firm advocate of analysis. He described vividly his encounter in his Beijing practice with a psychotherapy patient who posed one of the questions about how analytic ways of thinking fit with the Chinese mentality when she announced that she was terminating psychotherapy because she felt it was going to pull her away from her family by moving her towards an individualism that made her extremely uncomfortable with its opposition to her family loyalties. Dr. Zhong felt deeply the tension in this woman's assertion. What could be his answer to this challenge? In the end, he had to say that he did not know. In hearing his moving paper, and in conversation with him, I sensed that he felt this was a quandary not only for his patient, but also for himself.

To understand this problem, which I have come to believe is central to Westerners teaching or seeing patients in China, we need to understand that the philosophical underpinnings of culture for the large majority of Chinese – who are 95% Han Chinese – are radically different from the philosophical assumptions of the West. Psychoanalysis, which is quintessentially a Western invention, is rooted in Plato, Aristotle and the Judeo-Christian tradition. In the evolution of this tradition, we strive for an individual development that is not based primarily on family loyalty and filial duty. Western religious loyalty to God, or the Greco-Roman callings to moral standards and virtues, constitutes a body of principles towards which individual men and women strive. We are more or less on our own as individuals in moral or religious development, supported, however, by a rich and elaborated culture that delivers these principles through family influence and through social, educational and religious institutions. In Western tradition, an individual is often in a competitive position in regard to others, and in support of striving for individual betterment and autonomy that pulls the person away from being subservient to family, even when valuing the family. It is not that relationships are unimportant. Modern object relations theory, for instance, stresses the importance of relationships throughout life, but it also promotes an autonomy that is foreign to traditional Chinese thought. The lessons for psychoanalysts and psychotherapists also apply to any other field in which people are trying to understand the roots of Chinese thought.

Confucian and Related Values

In China, Confucian, Daoist and Buddhist traditions still hold sway despite the attacks on them during the Maoist period. The most pervasive tradition is the Confucian morality of loyalty to the emperor, the father, the oldest son and the family. Chinese people think of themselves as members of groups – the national group, the family group and the work group. The idea of putting one's own interests ahead of these loyalties goes against the bone. Although things are changing now, the idea of individualism has historically been foreign to the Chinese, and the pull of psychoanalysis towards individuation and autonomy still grates on the sensibility of many Chinese. There is a sense of personal humility and submission to the will of the emperor, leader, father and family built into Chinese sensibility. While Mao and the entire Communist development of the New China destroyed many of the structures of 2,500 years of imperial tradition, this sense of family and group loyalty was not so much destroyed as modified and made use of by Mao. In a real sense, Mao was the latest of the emperors. He put national cohesion ahead of individual rights, as did the emperors. When he promulgated a series of mandates, loyalty to him and to the party ranked ahead of family or personal loyalty. Loyalty to the family was, by party ideology, superseded by loyalty to the work group and to Chairman Mao himself, but what stayed the same underneath this change was that group loyalty, now to the work group, was still valued more than individual accomplishment or individual rights (Yang Yunping, 2011; Lin Tao, 2014; Shi Qijia, 2014). Recently, the direction of the Chinese Communist Party (CCP) has returned to this ideology, urging loyalty to the country and to the values and leadership of its president.

Other Chinese psychologists have added to the view of the Chinese cultural and social mores that underlie psychic organization. The Daoist contribution of fitting in with nature and urging a certain kind of passivity and adaptability to circumstances adds to the Buddhist contribution of the 'middle way' that urges restraint of overt aggression in individual striving. This fits with the balance of Yin and Yang that urges a balancing of forces rather than choosing one dominant position (Li Ming, 2014). Reading of these elements of Chinese character has helped me understand the surface of balance and insistence on deference to authority that has marked the experience of many Western colleagues in their encounters with Chinese students. A few years ago, many psychoanalysts teaching and supervising in China reported encountering the kind of 'unquestioning respect' in their Chinese students that made it impossible for students to criticize their Western teachers, or even to venture their own opinions in class (Haag, 2014; Gullestad, 2014). Psychotherapy teachers first coming to China, and then newly minted Chinese therapists themselves, were revered as teachers, so it was an alien idea for students to complain or to disagree, or for a patient to either complain to her therapist or to voice negative transferential ideas.

We came to understand that students' deference towards us as teachers, and of patients' deference towards therapists whom they saw as teachers, was based on deeply held values, not a lack of gumption. Over several years, as our teaching and our therapies welcomed questions and encouraged disagreement, we were inserting a fundamentally Western attitude that bucked 2,500 years of tradition and culture deeply embedded in the Chinese psyche. Other forces of social change supported this increased social assertiveness as well. So, most of us noticed that during the last 15 years, the attitudes of our students have changed fundamentally. Now we encounter as much probing and questioning in our students as that which we encourage in our home cultures. And, over time, I have also experienced couples and families to be less reverential and more open to exploration, including an increased capacity both to disagree with our interpretations and to work with them. In these ways, our Chinese students and patients are both becoming more like students and patients at home.

Or, perhaps it is equally important, as we come to understand Chinese culture better from inside our growing experience, that we hit the right notes more often and that enables our students and patients to feel more at home with us. I would like to think that this is a factor in growing mutual understanding.

Changes in Chinese Individual Personality Structure in a Changing World

China under the liberalizing influence of new economic, migratory and social policies is experiencing an evolution of social character that runs paradoxically in the opposite direction from much of what I have been describing. While the West has various brands of individualism that are consonant with democratic governance and the responsibility of the individual, rising individualism in China has been called 'the rise of the incomplete and uncivil individual,' who is partly driven by a notion of being out for himself and has, at the same time, a sense of consumer rights supported by government-sponsored entrepreneurism. This creates a kind of self-centered, opportunistic or consumer individualism that runs counter to the old emphasis on group and family loyalty (Yan Yunxiang, 2010). Because the government decides what is politically allowable, there is not a general ethos of individual social responsibility to rein in self-interest (Hansen and Svarverud, 2010). There are conflicts intrinsic to these results. On the one hand, self-interest and the empowering of individual personality are more likely to develop, and on the other, self-interest and self-promotion pull against loyalty to family and group, creating psychic conflict. It may also be that the rise of individual narcissism in China is partly influenced by seeing models of self-serving individualism portrayed in Western media that are so popular in China. It would not be the first time that the West had provided models to the rest of the world that were not entirely beneficial.

Another important problem emerged as I worked with and learned from young therapists. As I interviewed patients from wards and outpatient departments, I came to feel that both young patients and young therapists were often living in the same world of overwhelming pressure to succeed for their parents. In both cases, their parents came from that traumatized generation of the Cultural Revolution and the Great Leap Forward that I will discuss in the next chapter, and these parents had often been deprived of education and opportunity. So, the temptation had been enormous to project into their only child all the hope and ambition denied to them. In a simplified way, as I said earlier, we might say that the children who could stand the pressure and survive had become the doctors and psychologists, while the most vulnerable of those who could not take the pressure suffered breakdowns and became patients.

With evolution towards new standards of morality in China, both national personality and individual conflict are in flux. Vanessa Fong (2007) documented the way that this conflict starts in the mind of parents who want their children to maintain the old values of family loyalty but who also fear that if the child does not exhibit more individual drive and ambition, he or she will be left behind. The result is the rapid and unpredictable alternation of conflicting messages to the child, who then internalizes the parent's conflict. In times of cultural transition, it is always more difficult for a person to know exactly where to stand (Kleinman et al., 2011).

There are clear implications for analysts and therapists treating Chinese patients. I mentioned above that Chinese therapists themselves feel conflicted by the tensions of changing morality, but since Chinese therapists themselves are embedded in the rapidly changing culture, their own value structure itself is also under pressure to evolve under the influence of social change. In a way, this is not so different from the situation for Western therapists, who have had to adapt to changing ideas about gender and sexuality, homosexuality, the shape of families and ever-changing youth culture over the last 50 or more years. A Chinese therapist's non-biased, ethical stance is also challenged by the implicit morality in psychoanalysis that promotes individuation, self-actualization, sexual freedom of expression and freedom from the constraints of family loyalty that has long been the backbone of Chinese morality. Not that either Western or Chinese culture can be said to entirely live up to the ideals they espouse, but these differences nevertheless guide aspects of development. These are complex matters for any analytic therapist working and teaching about family and couple health in China.

Women in China

The change in values also applies to attitudes about women and daughters. We have seen that China's long history of male dominance was perhaps nowhere better illustrated than in the practice of foot binding that meant that women could barely walk. There were other practices that underscored the general situation in which, in effect, 'a woman is nothing' (Tong Jun, 2016). Brides went to the homes of their husbands where they lived under the rule of their husbands and mothers-in-law, while their husbands answered to their own fathers and mothers. Men, if they could afford it, were free to have concubines, who also had no rights, even though the history of China is replete with stories of powerful concubines and wives. For instance, the Dowager Empress Ci Xi, at the end of the Qing Dynasty in the late the late-nineteenth century, wielded enormous power, a notable exception to the power of the male emperor and of patriarchs (Jung Chang, 2013).

All this began to change with the assumption of power by the Communist Party. I have quoted Mao's famous declaration, 'women hold up half the sky,' an upholding of the value of women that applied more to their value in the workforce than to other rights. In any event, both men and women owed obedience to the Party, which thereby markedly diminished the place of the family in the code of moral allegiance. However, as the One Child Policy took effect, families in general came to value their Only Daughter highly. Despite the many cases in which the old values held steady and the parents resented a girl for not being a boy, most families have come to value their girl highly as their hope for the future, much as boys alone held this place in Chinese family hopes in the past (Fong, 2002). Women have also done well in the workplace, but, as in other places in the world, still do not hold a significant share of the highest executive or political positions.

Nevertheless, there continues to be more than a residual preference for boys. It is not uncommon for the insistence on a couple having a son comes to the fore of marital discord. Shi Qijia and Jill Scharff (2008) describe a marriage in which preference for a son drove the couple's marital disharmony, while also illustrating some of the changing issues for women.[1] They tell the following story.

In one session, Mr. Wang, the husband, had been driving excessively fast, frightening his wife. It was one of many expressions of his anger with her. Their only child was a girl, and Mrs. Wang now refused to have a second child, even though, as a minority Uyghur woman from Xinjiang, she was legally entitled to an exception to the One Child Policy. The authors wrote that Mr. Wang's greatest wish was for a son because of his enduring belief in the need for a son to carry his family name and legacy, and that failing in this duty was an offence to filial piety. He felt his wife could not love him if she could not agree to have a son.

Mr. Wang said, 'The reality is I want a son. I talked to her so many times ... She said only when she could accept a child psychologically would she be able to get pregnant. But she is past 35, too old already! Besides, my oldest brother had a son just last month when he was 46. His daughter is 13 years old, and now he has a one-month-old son. My second older brother has two sons.... I believe in Buddhism. If you don't have a son, you disappear from the family tree. I am working on the Wang family's genogram. Where you only have daughters and no sons, the family line is discontinued. I am afraid that after I die, my gravesite would be very lonely. No one would come mourn me. I only have a daughter, and when she is married, she will belong to another family. She won't be able to come back often to worship me.... I feel I would be so lonely without a son. I would be a lonely soul and a wild ghost. I want to plan for the future when I am dead. However, she does not understand.

'She scoffs at my idea and at my pain: 'Want another child? A child is only a toy. One child is fine.' Financially we can afford a second child, but she just won't even consider it. I guess it means, first of all, she does not love me much; secondly, she cares too much about how she looks; third, to be fair, she is busy working. But I still feel, however busy she is, getting pregnant and having another child only takes a year. In fact, her mother also supports her having a second child. But she just refuses.'

When the therapist asked Mrs. Wang if she could still have another child, she replied,

> I am not ready psychologically. I cannot accept another child for now, because my last pregnancy was not an easy one. I vomited from the beginning to the last minute. This whole process was so painful. When I was pregnant, I cried every day. I told him I did not want to live... So, I am always terrified of having a child.

Mr. Wang emphasized the devastating effect of her reluctance on him. He said, 'Once we went on a business trip and she said, 'Husband, please do not expect me to give you a son in this life.' In that moment, my heart sank to the bottom. I felt so bad that I would rather crash on the highway and die.' Turning to Mrs. Wang, he added, 'Let us die. There is nothing worth living for. You and I might as well die together.' Turning back to the therapist, he explained, 'I wanted to die. But she was not aware of my feelings. I wanted to crash our car into the curb and die.' Turning toward Mrs. Wang, he said, 'You know, that's how I felt.'
(Shi and J. Scharff, 2008, pp. 312–313)

In this excerpt, we see the way that, for this man, the sense of his honor, the filial duty to keep his branch of his family name from going extinct and the sense of himself as a lonely ghost drive his desperation and his depression. His sense of futility clashes with his wife's determination not to have a second child, in this case, at least on the surface, because of fear of another pregnancy. The idea that women should not be slaves to childrearing has become more prominent over time, and this may clash either with the wishes of their husbands or with the demands of their parents and in-laws.

Masculinity and Femininity in China[2]

Traditionally, the concepts of yin and yang, which also refer to masculinity and femininity, were interrelated and only existed in the presence and mutual influence of each other. In Chinese medicine, all men and women contain both elements, rather like Freud's concept of inherent bisexuality. However, the meanings of yin and yang are not fixed, but are more understood as dynamic flows of energy.

This notion of elemental equality and wholeness contrasts with the treatment of women as very different than men. Chastity was a requirement for women, although men, too, were discouraged from frivolous sex, which was morally held to be only for procreation. The categorization of men and women supported a larger idea of the ideal family structure (Wang Huan, 2020).

Women were both valued and suppressed. While women were always inferior in status and role, femininity was idealized. In ancient China, there was no character for 'woman' but only for 'daughter,' 'wife' and 'mother.' A woman had no identity before marriage, when she became the property of her husband's family. However, a woman had a powerful role in that marital family, for the regulation and harmony of families was [her] responsibility (Mann, 1991, pp. 208–209, quoted in Wang Huan, 2020). Since the family was the basic social unit of society, women held a central social role.

At the same time, for the most part, women were oppressed. They were not supposed to leave home unaccompanied before marriage and were limited to the house afterwards because of men's unconscious fears of destructive female powers. Chinese men were supposed to look after the well-being of the women and the entire family, but the execution of this duty was in the men's hands. Sexual pleasure and aggression were frowned upon, while the mother-son relationship was the most important organizer of the family. Other close relationships between men and women were not encouraged, either in the family or in society generally– although it was acceptable, for those who could afford it, to keep concubines. This polarity does not consider the meaning of sexuality for womanhood in a society where concubinage and foot-binding were commonly practiced, contributing to a view of women as chaste and sexually appealing to men, but also subservient and unable to walk far from home, and were therefore raised to be in the service of men generally. Chastity was prized because an 'unvirtuous, unfeminine woman' would damage men's masculinity and damage the order of things that depended on men (Mann, 2011, p. 124, quoted in Wang Huan, 2020).

Wang Huan notes,

> [Foot binding] was a bond to femininity in women. It restricted women's strength, limited their freedom of movement, gave them no choice but to remain in the family and loyal to their husbands, and most importantly, it cut off their connection with the earth, the source of feminine power. Behind this restriction and institutionalized torture, there was implicit the power of femininity and the masculine fear of such power.
>
> (Wang Huan, 2020, p. 6)

Thus, women in ancient China were idealized, and therefore their powers had to be channeled into service of the state but behind this laymen's fear of women's strength. However, while concubines and even wives were in many ways men's property, part of the social difference can be understood to be a class difference. When women came from an equal social class to that of their husbands, many of them retained property and rights, and there are many examples of powerful women in Chinese history, as women were able to negotiate their way to power – most famously, in modern history, as I have already noted, in the case of the Dowager Empress Ci Xi who ruled from behind a screen next to her weak son in the last phase of the Qin Dynasty (Ma, 2009, p. 55 quoted in Wang Huan, 2020, p. 9).

Men in China were empowered and could have several sexual partners, including other men because homosexuality was either sanctioned or tolerated, but at the same time they were given the message that they were also bound by social rules in which sex was discouraged morally, and each man was responsible for his role in the family and the wider social group. He was supposed to be an obedient child to his family, to authority and to his mother. Fathers were expected to be distant from their sons, leaving the son's upbringing and education to the mother. In this way, the mother-son was the most influential relationship. Being the mother of a son brought power and prestige to the woman who had, until then, been disempowered.

For men, brotherhood with other men took the place that close heterosexual relationships partly occupy in the West, at least in modern times. There was a belief that this important relationship would be dangerously undermined by romantic or sexual relationships with women (Yi, 1998, pp. 1–18, quoted in Wang, 2020). And there was, in the nineteenth century, a skewing of sex distribution because of widespread infanticide and son-preference so that while almost 100% of females married, as much as 20% of men did not (Ng et al., 2010, pp. 4–5, quoted in Wang, 2020). Unmarried men had a high risk of becoming bandits, and therefore encouraging them to be attached to their mothers benefitted society (Owenby, 2002, quoted in Wang Huan, 2020).

The period of the Opening Up of China since the late 1970s, the empowerment of women in the work force and then the implementation of the One Child Policy have gradually led to changing concepts of the roles of women, while the role of men has continued to stress their responsibility for carrying the major financial burden. Men have continued to have more sexual license, but as women have begun to claim sexual rights, including the right to pleasure for themselves, there is movement towards social equality. As in the West, there is more gender equality, and so the underlying concepts of masculinity and femininity are also in flux (Jeffreys and Yu, 2015).

Until recently, therefore, concepts of masculinity and femininity have operated in the service of society and of politics. But, as we shall see in a later discussion of changing views on sexuality in China, the period of Opening Up has brought radical differences to the roles and relative equality of women and men, producing a generation of relatively empowered women, a development also in parallel with the general development of a new individualism. In this way, a new ethic of mutuality has grown rapidly, one with many unintended consequences that have affected both the structure of families and the accompanying social ethic. There is a new ethic of feminine strength and equality for public entertainers and businesswomen, for women in academia and for women in every walk of life in ways that were unheard of 100 years ago. One puzzling question that remains is what will happen to the highest levels of Chinese leadership. Traditionally, leadership would pass to the eldest sons or close male family members of leaders, but this generation of leaders have, I have heard informally, mainly 'Only Daughters' and few cousins. Will these daughters inherit their fathers' Party status? Current photographs of groups of Chinese political leaders show few women. Will this picture change as it has in the West?

Shame and Loss of Face

It is almost a cliché, but true nevertheless, that shame is the most power-ful motivational emotion in Chinese culture, based as it is on loyalty to the group. Where guilt takes its power from concern for causing hurt to others, shame is the humiliation of disapproval by others. Gradations of shame and humiliation are many and subtle in China, and understanding shame is indeed crucial to working clinically with individuals, couples and families there.

In a recent article, Gao Jun and Michael Stadter describe models that focus on the self-centered quality of guilt and the other-centered quality of shame in both Western and Chinese cultures (Stadter and Gao, 2020). Since the Chinese have a predominantly interdependent model of self, compared to Westerners' independent model of self, Chinese are more interested than Westerners in the judgment of others as a source of self-esteem. It is less well-understood is that the Chinese also tend to view shame in a posi-tive light because it is a building block for interpersonal relations, and therefore Chinese people tend to feel less shame when feeling shamed.

Stadter and Gao write:

> Shame is more likely to be elicited if a person's mistakes or inadequacies are revealed to others and therefore this person believes others may have nega-tive evaluations of him/her. Instead, if a person perceives that his/her mistakes or inadequacies may cause harm or pain to others, he/she is more likely to feel guilt.
>
> [W]hen they felt ashamed, Chinese participants seem to be less likely to actually withdraw from shameful situations because they fear further expo-sure of their failures or mistakes. They are more likely to engage in a 'mental retreat,' and at the same time, they might try to cover up for what already hap-pened and/or to pretend that they are not much affected ... to still maintain interpersonal engagement.
>
> (Stadter and Jun, 2020)

Stadter and Gao emphasize that Chinese individuals, when shamed, are more likely to attempt to repair the situation interpersonally by seeking social support and demonstrating their efforts at repair of their damaged self-identity through gaining reassurance from others that they are still acceptable to the group.

> Chinese are more likely to feel vicarious shame or guilt when someone they are connected to commits a shameful act. This also suggests that when Chinese individuals act shamefully, they might be more likely to be troubled by the vicarious shame or guilt their family/friends/country may feel due to their negative acts.
>
> (Stadter and Jun, 2020)

In both China and the West, people often feel shame about coming to therapy, making them avoidant of therapy altogether. Once in therapy, shame about many topics (for instance, illegal or shameful acts, sex) may impede discussion. Interpretations the therapist perceives to be accurate may be rebuffed because of the shame these interpretations induce. Shame is likely to be mirrored in therapists' countertransference, where it needs to be tolerated in order to enable the therapist to understand the projection of the feeling of shame from the patient into the therapist (Stadter and Jun, 2020).

'Loss of Face' versus 'Humiliation'

The most effective way of discussing shame clinically in China usually does not involve using the words 'shame,' 'embarrassment' or 'humiliation.' Using these words in talking with couples and families often draws blank stares of nonrecognition. In contrast, the phrase 'loss of face' gets immediate recognition and response. In a previously published commentary on a case of mine with Clover's family that is also presented in Chapter 14, Gao Jun, an Associate Professor of Psychology who was also our translator for the case, discussed the differences between 'humiliation' and 'loss of face.' In that encounter, I had said to the mother that she was 'humiliated' by discovering that her fellow teachers knew about her daughter's difficulties while she did not. This statement drew a blank, but when I changed the wording to say that she had experienced 'loss of face,' she immediately agreed.

Gao Jun writes,

> What is the difference between humiliation and losing face? Why did the mother find it hard to accept the word 'humiliation?' ... [T]he two concepts are both from the same family of emotions, namely shame ... . [T]here are many Chinese words to differentiate aspects of shameful intense negative

feeling about one's self. The Chinese translation of the word humiliation is '耻辱 (Chi-ru)' … [indicating] a situation in which a person feels that because of his/her wrongdoing – usually severe moral transgressions or major personal failures – he/she is looked down upon by others. The contempt and disgust implied in this word is strong, and the consequence can be fatal: He/she may lose reputation and respect from others completely, and may even run the danger of being expelled by his/her group. The word 'humiliation' may also indicate a strong sense of aggression from others. The image of a bad, disgusting self is forced upon the person by others, either in reality or in one's imagination.

On the other hand, the phrase 'losing face' is far less negative and painful compared to the word 'humiliation.' There are two differing translations for the phrase 'loss of face.' One is '丢面子 (diu mian zi)' and the other is '丢脸 (diu lian).' There is a subtle but important difference between the two. The meaning of the first (diu mian zi) is similar to the English word embarrassment, usually indicating a social inadequacy or mistake that one makes in front of others, and indicates that these faults or inadequacies do not fit for the status or the role one occupies in his/her social network. The second (diu lian) is more negative in the sense that it indicates a more severe social inadequacy or even a moral transgression.

Another difference between 'humiliation' and 'losing face' concerns the personal reaction toward these shameful experiences. In Chinese, we have phrases such as 'earn face' or 'win back your face,' indicating that if a person tries to repair his/her wrongdoings afterward or correct his/her social inadequacy, he/she can restore his/her reputation and be accepted once more as a worthy member of the group. In this sense, when a Chinese person feels or is told that he/she has lost face, he/she is usually quite motivated to get it back. However, it is far more difficult to 'wash away your humiliation with others' blood.' Besides, to get rid of your humiliation also implies quite a lot of aggression towards those people who made you feel humiliated.

(Gao Jun, 2015, p. 52)

Working through Translation

All of my work with families and couples in China, as well as all of the teaching that my English-speaking colleagues and I have done there, has to be conducted through translation. We have been fortunate that our principal translators, Gao Jun and Li Zhen, and more recently Chang Wie, have had both excellent English and training in psychology and psychotherapy, which enabled them not only to translate our lectures and clinical interviews, but to fill us in regularly on those aspects of language and culture that do not translate easily. The Chinese language is so different from English or the Latin languages that exact translation is often impossible. Chinese takes longer to say the same thing, has no tenses and is much more metaphorical in its structure. Tomas Plaenkers (2014b) has written about the considerable difficulty of translating Freud's works and psychoanalysis in general into Chinese, something that has been more difficult until lately because the translations of Freud into Chinese were, until now, all done from the English *Standard Edition* of Freud, and that edition already introduced errors, idiosyncrasies and new meanings into the English-language understanding of Freud. Recently, Plaenkers and his colleagues have sponsored a project to translate Freud directly from the German originals into Chinese, which should provide more accuracy in Chinese concerning Freud's original meanings and inuendoes, but will also introduce gaps between the understanding of the English-speaking teachers (since virtually all the teaching by Westerners is in English) and Chinese students. My colleague Lin Tao (2014) has written about the difficulties in translating cultures. In a recent unpublished paper called 'Language in learning psychoanalysis: an obstacle or a bridge?', he has written about the difficulty for him, as an analyst trained in China by Western analysts but treating Chinese patients in Chinese, concluding that

> though English ... can be a bridge for communication, it can also be an obstacle to deeper understanding of psychoanalysis in the early stage of studying psychoanalysis when psychoanalytic experience was not enough. It can create misunderstanding or even blind spots in communication.
>
> (Lin Tao, 2020, personal communication)

Lin Tao describes how more thorough training enabled him to develop a psychoanalytic mind that could both bridge the inbuilt obstacles and take advantage of them in order to develop a depth of understanding, but this effort at translation at many levels requires both training and constant work (Lin Tao, 2020, personal communication). That is the kind of thinking that each of us who teaches in China has to carry out every day as we translate concepts and understanding between Chinese and Western experience.

The Larger Context of Psychotherapy in China

At the close of this chapter, let me say a few additional words about the context of our psychotherapeutic encounters with China within the much larger world of business, legal and diplomatic interchange. Most Western press coverage concerning China focuses on differences in governance, diplomacy and business, with an increasing degree of mutual national suspicion, much of it driven by rival political and economic ambitions, but equally often due to poor Western understanding of the operation of Chinese character in these spheres. Government officials, lawyers, business people and academics who visited China during the early days of Chinese Opening Up in the 1970s and 1980s have told me about dramatic differences from encounters nowadays. Chinese diplomacy and state control of business were always so different from our Western models that they were all but impossible for Westerners to understand (Solomon, 1971). These have changed beyond recognition in one generation, and they are still evolving ever more rapidly. Studies of diplomatic styles a few years ago emphasized how differently the Chinese thought diplomatically. In negotiations, the Chinese are apt to stress the centrality of 'friendship,' one of the most valued of Confucian ideals and the only one that is not hierarchical. But the Chinese expect a lot from their friends and are apt to use the bond of friendship to pressure for advantage (Solomon, 1999). Americans with business experience in China feel that there are large differences in conduct based on Chinese and Western history. In China, with its Confucian past, rules governing conduct are based on adherence to rulers – the emperor in the past, and today, the Party – while in the United States and Europe, the rule of law is supreme and the government itself is subject to law. Put simply, as it was paraphrased by a friend, the difference is that 'The West has the rule of law; The Chinese have the law of the ruler' (Jack Pirozzolo, personal communication, 2011). This statement may be overly idealizing of the West, particularly in 2020, but it is the ideology the West aspires to and is morally guided by – an ideology not in place in China. This cultural and historic difference makes it difficult for Western business interests to understand the Chinese legal system and ways of doing business. Chinese business relationships are often understood by Westerners as implying amorality without understanding that Chinese behavior stems from old precepts of Confucian negotiating tactics. And, after all, in the West, we have our own tradition of pressing for personal advantage in business and diplomacy that can be seen by others as ruthless, as spelled out, for instance, in 1515 in Machiavelli's *The Prince*. Nevertheless, Chinese colleagues have said to me recently that in China, there is an understanding that the value of a legal contract may change if subsequent opportunity offers greater financial or practical advantage, or if official orders are received from above. While this may be seen as a matter of the ambition of the current Chinese state and its state-owned businesses, much of this attitude is rooted in older traditions.

Conclusions

In this chapter, I have outlined several ways that understanding the values, ideologies and moral underpinnings of Chinese character constitute a deep structure of the Chinese mind that should always be in the minds of all those, including therapists, who wish to understand the efforts, struggles and resilience of Chinese families and couples. Despite the many changes being wrought in the Chinese situation, Chinese couples and families still carry an inheritance of their unique culture and values, which continues to steer their contemporary function.

Change in China is occurring at such a rapid pace and in so many spheres that no one knows where it will go. It is a privilege for psychotherapists and psychoanalysts that the distrust that often characterizes political, diplomatic, business and legal relationships between Westerners and the Chinese does not apply to relationships with our mental health colleagues. In our sphere of operation, they are not competing with us. They are our partners. They want to learn from us, but they also need for us to learn from and about them at the same time. The factors I have discussed about Chinese culture, as well as the factors of history, of male and female identity and of family structure are among the many things we need to be aware of as we join impressive Chinese colleagues in bringing Chinese and Western experience together towards a new synthesis – family and couple therapy, group therapy, psychotherapy and psychoanalysis with Chinese characteristics. If we do not let our enthusiasm blind us, and if we are open to the possibility of contributing something based equally on our Western experience and on China's millennia of culture and sophistication, something new and exciting for human development lies over the Eastern horizon.

Notes

1 This case was previously published in 2008 in *The International Journal of Applied Psychoanalytic Studies* as: Social change, intercultural conflict, and marital dynamics in a Chinese marriage in brief concurrent individual and couple therapy. 5(4):302–321. By permission of the journal.
2 I am grateful to Wang Huan (2020) for her recent paper on concepts of masculinity and femininity in China, from which I borrow extensively in this discussion.

Chapter 6

Trauma, Resilience and the Family

The extensive psychodynamic and psychological literature on the effects of social and individual trauma that has developed over the last 100 years begins perhaps with Freud's development of the theory of sexual trauma within families (Freud and Breuer, 1893–1895), and later his positing of the death instinct in the shadow of the First World War (Freud, 1920). Fairbairn, who saw clinical examples both of sexual abuse and war trauma, developed further theories on the origin of developmental trauma based on early separation and the continuing need for early dependent relationships (Fairbairn, 1952; Scharff and Birtles, 1994). John Bowlby's attachment paradigm was based on the trauma to early relationships of early separation and inadequate mothering (Bowlby, 1969). But it was only in the last 50 years that a more focused trauma literature developed, with foci both on developmental trauma of childhood deprivation and physical and sexual abuse, and on the trauma of war or other adult traumata. (Davies and Frawley, 1994; Van der Kolk, 2014) Jill Scharff and I have written about the effects of physical and sexual trauma on development (Scharff and Scharff, 1994), contributing to a large literature on this topic, while the study of war trauma and the growing understanding of Post-Traumatic Stress Disorder (PTSD) has enabled professionals to understand and treat many traumatic states of adulthood (Van der Kolk, 2014).

We do not have much in the way of direct study of Chinese trauma, unlike the many studies of the Holocaust and its sequelae in subsequent generations (Brenner, 2019). Tomas Plaenkers' 2010 book, *Landscapes of the Chinese Soul: The Enduring Presence of the Cultural Revolution*, presented both the context of social trauma in China in the decade from 1966 to 1976 and its sequelae through the presentation of an intensive qualitative research project on direct victims and their children. He and his colleagues have demonstrated how the direct trauma to one generation was transmitted to the children through communication of attitudes of fear and anger, and through physical and verbal violence (Plaenkers, 2010, 2011).

Trauma comes in many forms. There is the trauma of war, the devastation of natural disasters, personal tragic accidents. Then there is a separate second category of developmental trauma, the consequence of loss or absence of parents or caregivers in early life, neglect by caregivers because of illness or depression, physical and sexual abuse or deprivation to the entire family that includes young children. All these are relevant to the ability of the adult survivors of traumata to form secure bonds in marriage and later to convey a sense of safety to their own child or children. In any society, these elements interact, so developmental trauma has the potential to exacerbate damage caused by later childhood or adult trauma, and on the other hand, social trauma makes it more likely that children will face varieties of developmental trauma. For instance, in a time of war or starvation, domestic examples of trauma are often caused by the wider social situation and are magnified by the traumatic context. In this chapter, we will examine the major two levels of trauma, the social and the domestic, and see how the wider level of social trauma has an impact on the intimacy of developmental trauma. In this way, we will be addressing the questions I posed in the opening chapter about the intersection of social forces and family vulnerability.

Social Trauma

China as a country and as a culture has been frequently traumatized for much of the last 200 years. The Opium Wars (known as the Anglo-French Wars in China) from 1839 to 1842 and again from 1856 to 1860 were perpetrated by Western powers in order to impose the opium trade on China during the Qing Dynasty in exchange for silver and the right to trade. Western powers forced China to open its ports to trade and created treaty zones in Shanghai and Canton, wrested control of Hong Kong from China for 99 years and contributed to the weakening of the Qing Dynasty, although it was also weakened by domestic rebellions. Later in the nineteenth century, and again in the twentieth century, there were invasions by the Japanese. Then in the first part of the twentieth century came the fall of the Qing Dynasty, followed by almost a half-century of brutal struggle between the Chang Kai-shek's Kuomintang and the Chinese Communist Party (CCP) for control. During the particularly brutal Japanese occupation before and during World War II, the Kuomintang and CCP joined forces, but resumed their struggle against each other immediately after Japan's defeat.

All these forces have imposed elements of trauma on Chinese society to varying degrees depending on location within the country and which segments of the population were affected. Then, in 1949, Mao Zedong and the CCP assumed control of China, while Chiang Kai-shek and his forces fled to Taiwan. From 1958 to 1962, the CCP introduced the 'Great Leap Forward.' Its policies of rural agricultural collectivization and homespun industrialization produced the largest famine in human history in which 35 to 45 million people died, as well as industrial collapse, but this was largely hidden from view by the historical silence that followed it (Becker, 1996; Yang Jisheng, 2008).

Again in 1966, Mao, worried about losing his grip on leadership, unleashed the Cultural Revolution, a time of national and individual trauma in which youthful gangs of the Red Guard roamed the country causing chaos, attacking leaders, academics and landowners (Chang and Halliday, 2005). The ghosts of this most recent national trauma continue to haunt China and its families, but because people have been discouraged from discussing it, it has passed from the directly traumatized generation to current young generation without dialogue or understanding, still taking its toll on young families in ways they do not understand (Plaenkers, 2014a). It is been my experience in conducting clinical interviews and interventions with couples and families in China that people generally have little patience, and likely some fear, about discussing these past traumas that have beset them or their families. Partly this reluctance is in line with government policy that discourages discussion of the Cultural Revolution or the traumas of the Great Leap Forward. The government also downplays the trauma involved in natural disasters, such as the Tangshan earthquake of 1976 that killed 240,000, the 2008 Sichuan earthquake that killed 90,000 people including 5,300 children and the 2014 Yunnan earthquake, which had a smaller death toll but nevertheless left thousands homeless. One of the tragedies of these natural disasters is the number of families that lost their only child. Governmental censorship and general discouragement of news sources describing the devastation occurs because of the blame the government risks concerning such things as shoddy construction of schools and apartment blocks, and because of questions about the quality of emergency response. While Germany has encouraged a thorough airing of the trauma of the Holocaust and Second World War, with the effect of healing a great deal of the scarring that had followed and a national policy of rapprochement with the Jews of Israel, and while South Africa has established a Truth and Reconciliation Commission beginning in 1996, China has taken an opposite tack. The consequence is that trauma is in the deep structure of Chinese experience, but it is not understood and so operates unconsciously (Scharff, 2014).

Beginning in 1949, the CCP controlled marriages and divorces, wiping out the previous patterns of arranged or negotiated marriages controlled by the families themselves. With Mao's death in 1976, and the ensuing demise of the Gang of Four, Deng Xiaoping began the great Opening Up. Suddenly the family, too, was out from under the day-to-day control of the Communist Party, but by now the ethic of the family had been cast adrift by a generation of changes in the family as a central institution. The Chinese population simply did not know what to make of newly emerging family structures, which briefly resumed operating with the traditional idea of large families, but shortly came under the new 'One Child Policy' that dictated small, one-child families – perhaps the largest social engineering experiment ever conducted (Mei Fong, 2016). The Confucian ethic had quickly come back because there was nothing else gestating in the Chinese mind. But this time, it was contested emotionally. And because the government under Deng Xiaoping urged people to develop economically, families and individuals quickly became entrepreneurial, out for themselves, leading quickly to what might be called a new consumer individualism (Yang, 2011). However, this new direction for family and individual development was put in place without any processing of the previous traumatic attacks on family organization. This policy also led to uneven but often draconian enforcement in rural areas. Any second children who were unable to register legally or pay the fine to do so remained undocumented and without rights to education, health care or legal employment. There are approximately 13 million such children, an astonishing 1% of China's overall population (Yuan Ye, 2012).

Poverty also has a traumatizing effect on the population, often interwoven with alcoholism and domestic violence. Denigration of women and dominance by husbands of their wives and children, often accompanied by excessive physical discipline or abuse, leaves marks on many individuals, often resulting in the passing to succeeding generations a behavior that continues to leave its mark (Meng Liu and Cecilia Chan, 1999). I hear about the struggles in rural families that have moved to the city and away from the rural settings in which they grew up. These rural families, most commonly farming families, are larger and poorer. They struggle with economic deprivation, especially for those children who grew up in the wake of the Cultural Revolution, and this poverty itself imposes trauma on the families (Yang Yunping, 2014). Once in the cities, these internal migrants usually live without a *hukou* or residency registration, meaning that their citizenship rights to education, social services and health care reside in their rural home setting and do not transfer to the city. As we discussed previously, they, and any children they have, are thus without rights and services, and their children's children are also without rights (Liu and Chen, 2016).

When I interview families and couples, I am used to the reports of trauma to previous generations being vague. Parents or grandparents who were traumatized are reluctant to speak about this phase of their lives, and in consequence, succeeding generations, although they feel the impact of their parents' anxieties, know nothing about the source of their fears.

An important paper by Arthur and Joan Kleinman, medical anthropologists who focused on China for many years, explores the incorporation of the social body into the physical body, extending Freud's early discussion of conversion of mental trauma into bodily symptomatology.

Their theoretical examination of how collective experience is incorporated into individual experience focuses on how undiscussable national traumatic situations of the kind that China has experienced are expressed in individual bodily symptoms, and that is how 'culture infolds in the body (and, reciprocally, how bodily processes outfold into social space)' (Kleinman and Kleinman, 1994, pp. 710–711). They explore how trauma and the turmoil of social breakdown are remembered and cross over into inner space and then cross back over into social space, shared across persons and even classes of persons. They particularly focus on the way the body remembers things that are not or cannot be consciously remembered or discussed, so that bodily memory, biography and social history merge. They discuss particularly three paradigmatic symptoms – dizziness or vertigo, exhaustion and pain. These create interpersonal expressions of suffering when the bodily complaints are expressed and then create social distress and shared criticism when experienced in the family or the social group. This is not, they stress, a case of what psychiatrists call 'secondary gain,' a situation of using suffering to gain interpersonal advantage. Instead, they argue,

these symptoms themselves need to be seen as forms of mediation and transformation through which interpersonal processes constitute the moral core of local worlds (here [in China], work and family units). Symptoms of social suffering and the transformations they undergo are the cultural forms of lived experience. They are lived memories. They bridge social institution and the body-self as the transpersonal moral-somatic medium of local worlds … That is to say, bodies transformed by political processes not only represent those processes, they experience them as the lived memory of transformed worlds.
(Kleinman and Kleinman, pp. 716–717)

The Kleinmans' exposition does not explicitly mention the family, but their discussion fits precisely with our notion that the family is the body that lies between the individual and the wider society and culture, representing the culture to the members of the family and representing the individual family members to the culture, operating thereby as the transforming group between these two social realms.

Nicole's Family

One family illustrated some of the elements of the transmission of trauma, with massive effects on the development of their 14-year-old girl, including the transformation of social trauma from previous generations into the body of the symptomatic child, the depression of her mother and the alcoholism of her father.

Nicole, a pretty, obese 14-year-old girl, was brought to see me and my colleague Janine Wanlass by her mother and father because she had stopped going to school, been diagnosed as both psychotic and depressed, and was now staying in her room, hearing voices, feeling suicidal and fighting with her parents.

But what we heard directly from Nicole made striking sense and seemed not the slightest bit psychotic. She said that her parents fought every evening, and that her father was out most nights drinking while she stayed home alone with her mother. It became clear to us that she was staying home from school in order to protect her mother from her father. When he returned home, his wife would turn him away, sending him in a drunken state to talk to Nicole, whom he would beg for understanding.

It turned out that this man had lost quite a lot of money through lending to business partners in obscure and presumably shady deals, and he had not been paid back. He had previously held a government job. He vaguely hinted it was in defense or intelligence, but he had quit that job, or perhaps had been dismissed, in order to go into private business. He declared that his nights out drinking were an essential element of conducting business, and that although it seemed clear to us that his alcohol consumption was at a symptomatic level, he was in no way going to give up drinking because, he said, 'It's my hobby.' It occurred to us that women and sex were likely to be involved in these gatherings, since they commonly are in Chinese business dinner settings.

Nicole's mother, feeling constantly disappointed, bullied and upset by her husband, turned him over to Nicole to get him off her own back and to mollify him. Nicole's mother was the younger and less favored of two daughters, and was not particularly successful in school. We got a sense of her childhood as one of feeling unfavored, neglected and treated harshly – that is, of developmental trauma that included family mistreatment and deprivation. She had left the rural area in which she grew up and was working in a low-level clerical job in the city when she seized on her husband because she thought he had been given a book as a prize at his work. This said to her that he was intelligent, even although he was drunk and acted inappropriately when she first met him. Marrying him offered a way of establishing a family when she had little self-esteem and was afraid that she would never meet anyone.

Nicole's father's confusing history was relevant to our discussion of the impact of social trauma. He initially said that his two older brothers had been in the Army and had thereby escaped the ravages of the Cultural Revolution. He was stubbornly vague about whether the family had been under pressure during the Cultural Revolution, leading me to believe that there had been incidents for his family and older brothers because later in our sessions, he implied that one of the brothers may have been targeted for abuse. (When these things occurred, entire families were often shamed and attacked for harboring someone deemed to be an enemy of the revolution.) It began to seem to us that although the history was obscured by his confusion, it was likely that his family had been affected, or at least that they had lived in constant fear that they would be attacked. He was clearer that his family lived in the area of the Tangshan earthquake of 1976, which had affected them directly.

This man's alcoholism seemed to represent the legacy of poverty during his development, his family being under pressure when he was a young child from the political currents and threats of the Cultural Revolution and the impact of the devastation to the Tangshan area in which his family lived.

All of this figured into the complex picture in which his behavior in the family traumatized both his wife and his child. We could understand the voices Nicole heard as the echo in her head of her parents' fights, as she sought desperately to think of ways that she could save her mother from the importunities of her father. She said to us, 'I don't need to go back to school. If my mother leaves my father, I can go out and support my mother and myself easily.' Nicole had no skills, and so it occurred to us that the only means of support she could actually supply would have been prostitution, echoing an unconscious fantasy she may have had about her father's nightly sexual activities, because such fantasies may abound in children *as fantasies*, even in the absence of direct knowledge about facts.

Nicole's so-called psychosis, dropping out of school, her depression and the way that she ate in order to protect herself against becoming a sexual adolescent all bore a relationship to the transmission of both the developmental trauma of her mother and the combination of cultural and personal trauma that her father brought into the family, both parents carrying legacies of confused but traumatic family histories without conveying them through direct narrative. This family combined the effects of national social trauma with the way that large-scale trauma led to a legacy of developmental trauma for its members, and this legacy was in the process of being carried on by the couple's child.

Mr. Wu and Mrs. Liu

Another a distressed couple, Mr. Wu, the husband, and Mrs. Liu, the wife, whom I interviewed for five sessions also together with Janine Wanlass, came to us because of recurring fights. However, from the beginning it was clear that this couple loved each other and were suffering from the emergence, as if from nowhere, of the wife's distress. Her husband would try to comfort her to no avail. We saw soon that the wife carried emotion for both of them while the husband would try to calm the waters, suppressing his wife's anxiety. When Mr. Wu tried to quiet her, Mrs. Liu was more likely to erupt angrily at him. Both the couple and their therapist had identified the wife as the problem, and as you will see in our interviews, the focus stays mainly on her until the last session, even though we always intend to talk with both members of the couple in fairly equal measure.

The story quickly emerged that Mrs. Liu was frightened a great deal of the time. The example she gave was about her worries for her five-year-old son. She was very upset that his teacher had left the school without a replacement for her class. When her husband had tried to reassure her that the school would provide an adequate substitute, she grew agitated and then angry.

In order to understand the origins of her particular worry, we asked about their backgrounds growing up. Mr. Wu had grown up in a calm rural family of gentle farming people, while Mrs. Liu had grown up in the city with intellectual parents who bickered constantly. This brief description seemed to shed light on their different styles, but did not seem like an adequate explanation. We could infer more from the way that Mrs. Liu had given the example of the son's missing teacher, implying that a missing caretaker was involved in her own worries.

In the second session, we learned more: Mrs. Liu, a successful professional, had quit her job to stay home with their son when he was born, losing her source of professional self-esteem. Then, two years later, Mr. Wu had made a bad business decision and lost a good deal of money. Even though he had since recouped the loss and done even better financially, she still carried the worry from that setback and would frequently throw it up to him. She no longer trusted his judgment and worried about the family's security and about whether or not they would be able to provide for their son.

Following the path of this loss in the third session led to uncovering more significant elements of her developmental trauma that had occurred when she was her son's age.

Mrs. Liu began,

> Before this, I'd just leave the financial matters up to him. I had some concerns about investments, and I would tell him I was concerned, but I would accept whatever he decided. I would trust his judgment. But after this, I had a difficult time.

Mr. Wu said, 'Well, we had a setback, but generally my decisions are very good. Even in this instance, I made the money back in a year, and we're fine now. We've got a good family life. It was only a temporary setback, not a reason for continued worry.'

Mrs. Liu said,

> He's able to be okay, but I can't trust him any longer. I can't let go of what happened, and I worry that it will happen again. So, I don't trust his decisions like I did before. I question him. I do not assume that he knows what is best. I get very angry with him when he will not consider my opinion. I state it, but he just makes the decision anyway. He just proceeds with his idea, even when I protest. It's upsetting to me. It makes me angry, and I can't control it. I no longer trust him.

Looking for the object relations history of this reaction, I asked Mrs. Liu, 'So, who else has let you down like this in the past?'

Mrs. Liu replied,

> I guess I would say my father. When I was young, my parents argued a lot. When I was four years old, one day, my father took me to my grandparents' home in the countryside. He told me that we were just going for an overnight visit, but I had the feeling something was wrong. I was afraid that he would leave me there, even though he said he wouldn't. I was upset, I cried, I told him I wanted to go back home. That night, I even tried to hold onto the bed and to my father, because that way I would know if he got up to leave. I was so worried that he would go. But I fell asleep and couldn't keep him there. When I woke up, he was gone. He left me there for a long time, and that made me very upset back then. (Mrs. Liu was crying now.)

I noticed she was upset by it even now, and I wondered where her mother had been.

Mrs. Liu said,

> My mother was having a difficult time. I found out later from my mother that my parents weren't getting along. They were considering a divorce

and fighting a lot. My father thought it would be best if I lived with my grandparents for a time. My mother did not agree with this. She thought it wasn't a good idea, but my father took me there anyway.

Janine commented, 'So, your mother said no, but your father didn't listen.'

Mrs. Liu agreed, 'Yes, that's right. What she said did not matter.'

(Here we note the parallel: the wife protesting, the husband ignoring her concerns.)

I asked, 'Did you ever go back to living with your parents?'

Mrs. Liu answered,

Only when I was a teenager, about 16. None of us children lived with my parents. I have two brothers, one older, one younger. The older one, he lived with my mother's parents. The younger one lived with my father's parents in the countryside. It's not unusual in China for children to live with their grandparents. This is a normal part of Chinese culture.

I said, 'I understand that it's a normal occurrence in China. I'm wondering how you how you felt about it, if you felt that something was wrong.'

Mrs. Liu said, 'No, it didn't seem okay to me. I didn't feel okay. I felt upset about it.'

Turning to Mr. Liu, Janine asked, 'Did you know about this? This difficult time your wife is talking about?'

Mr. Wu said,

Yes. Well, I didn't know about it at first, but since my wife started therapy, I've learned a lot about her past, the things that upset her. So, in the past year, she's told me a lot about these kinds of things. So yes, I know about it now.

Mrs. Liu explained, 'In my therapy, I talk about all this. I understand just how upset I was about being left with my grandparents when I wanted to be with my parents, missing my mother.'

Janine observed, 'Hearing you talk about being left at your grandparents, feeling abandoned, helps me understand why you would be so upset about your son's teacher disappearing.'

Mrs. Liu acknowledged,

Yes, it's a similar thing. I don't wish any children to be left without proper care. I feel sympathetic to children, probably because of my own past. I think now I also realize that these things have an effect on my

relationships as an adult, on my marriage. I've got a better understanding
of that now since we've been talking here, too.

By this point in getting to know this couple, we began to see
how the developmental trauma affected their current life. It is
true that it is common in Chinese culture for children to live with
their grandparents, but that is not a safeguard against the children sorely missing their actual parents. We can now also see
that Mrs. Liu grew up with a depressed mother whose voice did
not matter in the care and even the disposition of her child. Mrs.
Liu also felt betrayed and abandoned by her father, who had
promised not to leave her. The theme of the abandoning mother
showed up also in the way she related to us as a couple interviewing them as a couple, because she would ignore Janine as
well as Gao Jun, our female translator, in favor of relating to me,
hoping for understanding but wary that I would not be reliable.
We could see her anger erupting not only in her angry outbursts
at her husband, but also in her overly strict disciplining of her
treasured son, a pattern we commonly see in China of parents
who are harsh with and demanding of their children out of fear
for the consequences in the future if the children fail to perform
at a high level. These are the ways Mrs. Liu's developmental
trauma from living with angry parents, and then having to live
without them, had become embedded in her personality and
now lived out with her own child.

Mr. Wu's childhood now emerged as less serene than he originally
implied. He was the bright son, a country farming family's hope for
the future, sent away from the family to learn from others. He had
to learn not to be upset and to do things on his own without tan-
gible support. As a consequence, he learned to suppress his emotions and calm the waters, to be independent even when he longed
not to be, at the expense of acknowledging upset or a longing for
parental emotional support. In this way, he missed out on being a
child in the early years. He is still the caretaker, responsible for
everyone. So, when his wife is now upset, it becomes a matter of
urgency for him to suppress her emotionally, which then upsets her
more.

In the next session, we heard more about Mrs. Liu's concerns. The
children are left in the schoolyard without a security guard, and she
fears they might be kidnapped. Although the couple worked out a
plan to compensate for the missing guard, she remained fearful and
untrusting of their solution. She knows her husband is trying to
help, but she cannot trust that it will be enough.

Mrs. Liu regretted,

I don't think I'm very good at conveying what the problem is. I think my husband would like to help, but he doesn't understand. I get very impatient with him. When I'm in a mood, I can't see that he is trying to help. I can only be upset and push him away. Sometimes, he wants to help, but I can't allow it. It's like he wants to give me a whole cake, but I can't eat that much. I wish he would feed me in small bites, but he wants me to have the whole cake.

I remarked, 'You can only take in so much.'
Mrs. Liu agreed,

Yes, and when he tries to help me, I feel he's interfering. It only makes me more upset. Then I shout at him that I want a divorce. It's not a threat. I feel it at the time. I think he's very stupid, and I don't want him near me. I say mean things to him.

Janine said, 'What you say to him, calling him stupid, foolish – that's really some of the feeling you have about yourself.'
Mrs. Liu denied that interpretation, 'No. They're words directed at him. I'm very angry at these times. I'm not rational. I want to divorce him right then.'
Mr. Wu tells us that he doesn't ever think his wife really wants divorce, but he has learned to keep quiet and minimize the upsets. But he remains frustrated because there are so many things he cannot solve.
Mr. Wu said,

When she gets upset, I try to fix the upset as quickly as possible, to find whatever she cannot find so she will calm down. But sometimes, she asks me things she already knows the answer to. For example, she asks me to find my son's shirt. She knows where it is, she knows the answer to the problem, but she won't tell me. (Mrs. Liu laughs.)

I said, 'You feel she sets you up.'
Mr. Wu said,

Also, I think she feels so badly because she has no work, no purpose. She gave up her job when she had our son. Now she cannot achieve in the same way. She's a smart, capable woman, but she has lost that view of herself.

Janine segued back to her earlier point. 'Your husband sees many strengths in you. I wonder if that isn't part of your attraction to him, that he can see the good in you that's so hard for you to find.'

Mrs. Liu deflected the comment again:

No. I think I chose him for his good character. He understands me better now than he used to, but I can't think of this when I'm in a mood. Then anything he says makes me mad, and I can't be rational. I know it's my fault. I try not to blame myself, because that only makes me feel worse. I know I should manage it.

Janine said, 'When you're upset, you feel like a child.'

This time Mrs. Liu agreed:

Yes, that's right. I feel like an out of control child. You know, I think I'm usually quite a good mother. When my son acts up, I can put him away until he can be in control. He has learned to do this. He's a good boy, well behaved. But I can't do this for myself. It's like I have only one leg. I can't walk or manage on my own. I can't listen. I can do nothing but feel angry with my son. I wish I could be more like my husband. I mean, it's not like I think he's God, but I wish I could be like him, to have better control, to be better, but I can't.

I followed up on Janine's earlier comments that Mrs. Liu had fended off.

You have so many bad feelings about yourself. It's not that you're a bad person, but it feels bad inside you. But it's complicated, isn't it? When you feel so bad, you want a divorce. But part of the reason you say all these terrible things, part of the reason you push him away, is that you want to protect him. You think you're so bad that he really deserves someone better, so if you divorced him, he would have a better life.

Mrs. Liu agreed.

I said,

It's not danger out there that's the real problem. I think you're worried about the danger inside, about being kidnapped by the bad part inside you, a bad part of yourself and you want to spare your husband from it by sending him away. In one sense, you're desperately hoping that your husband can see that part of you and stay even though he knows your bad self. You need him to stand it and to stay anyway, but it's really a tough problem.

> You do things that hurt him, but you also do them to try to protect him from what you feel is the bad inside you that could damage you both. So then, although he wants to help you, you don't know how to let him do it.

Part of the enduring legacy of the trauma of Mrs. Liu's childhood abandonment comes from the fact that when children feel something bad has happened, they feel it must be because they themselves have been bad. In that way, they can preserve the parents as good but punishing or abandoning the child because of the child's own badness (Fairbairn, 1943). Mrs. Liu carries that legacy within and lives it out by trying to show her husband her own badness, while at the same time trying to protect him from being hurt by her bad self. She also fears she will damage their child because of her bad self, and she projects that fear onto the outer world.

We now understood that both Mr. Wu and Mrs. Liu unconsciously shared an internal psychic organization that stemmed from the way each of them had, in effect, had been abandoned by their parents, but that they had adopted opposite solutions in the organization of their personalities. Nevertheless, that inner fear of abandonment was a shared unconscious anxiety, so the two of them cooperated unconsciously to locate the problem in her and try to solve it in her as well. In this way, Mr. Wu is preserved as the potential hero who can save them both, but the burden is a heavy one and each time, he finds that it doesn't work. I reminded us that he had also been the great hope for his family and his village. That burden has always been a heavy one.

In our last session together, Mr. Wu stepped forward, speaking for the first time in an undefended and open way.

Mr. Wu said,

> I want to speak about deep feelings of my own that I haven't expressed. Last night we talked meaningfully about things between us. I've been hurt by what has happened between us. My wife is a good person, but when she's in a mood, she does things that are very hurtful. Then I see a side of myself I don't recognize. I think of myself as a strong person, but I'm not strong some of these times. I cry and can't stop when she says these hurtful things to me. I feel the tears, but when I don't recognize myself I even go to the mirror to check if it's me. But when I cry, this only makes my wife angrier, and she says more hurtful things. But really, my wife is a kind person, just like I'm a kind person. But in these times, she can't stop her anger towards me. When she says she wants a divorce, I say okay, let's divorce, not because I want a divorce, but because whether I argue or stay quiet, it doesn't stop. This hurts me very much, so I cry.

Mr. Wu then speaks about all the things he loves in his wife, including her willingness to address her difficulties. He proudly heralds her professional accomplishments, which are still accruing even although she has given up regular employment, and he does so in English to make certain we understand. He says that English is a language his wife speaks better than he does, a way in which he is not the all-knowing prince. His speech about his wife is loving and touching. After this, we suggest that he is also depressed and could benefit from treatment, and he readily agrees. As this session proceeds, Mrs. Liu also can see her husband's vulnerability, and she comments that having always to be strong must be difficult for him, too.

In this brief intervention, a couple came to understand some of the roots of their distress as lying in their shared histories of loss and abandonment. Although they had different ways of adapting to these losses in the growth of their personalities, the overlap of the unconscious legacy of traumatic loss organized their relationship, both in its strengths and in its shared vulnerabilities. For Mrs. Liu, her husband offered a reliable, strong support of the kind she had longed for all her life. However, at the first sign of her husband's weakness, her confidence was shaken irreparably – at least until both individual and couple intervention could begin to repair some of the holes in her self-confidence and damage to her self-worth.

For Mr. Wu, the early losses of leaving home were accompanied by the projection of his family's idealization of him, and this interacted with the way the family pinned its hopes for the family's future on him. This resulted in his developing a veneer of competence and independence that covered an unacknowledged depression and emptiness. Through the emotional connection in his worried wife, he found in her a damaged soul that represented his own damage as well as hers. He had spent much of their relationship trying repair himself vicariously through his care for her. With intervention, each of them could begin to take these matters back into themselves, leaving their marriage and their care for their son less burdened.

The Couple's Developmental Trauma

This couple has apparently not been directly touched by the historical issues of national Chinese conflict or trauma, so they allow us to see how more personal developmental loss affects them. It is true that an aspect of Chinese culture is prominent in their shared histories – the tradition of sending children away from their parents to live with grandparents at young ages, or to leave home for educational opportunities. This pattern shows up over and over again in the histories of couples and families we have seen, and it is invariably connected with a chronic sense of loss and a lack of direct parental care. When we look back to the first example of this book, of the older academic and his young country wife, we can see that his story too was marked by being separated from his mother when she was sent to the countryside for reeducation, and as a consequence, he was sent to the country to be raised in a parentless peer group. In that case, the cause of the early separation was the national trauma of the Cultural Revolution, and the separation was more severe in there being no family presence at all, resulting in a hunger for a mother substitute, and yet also in his developing, a way of keeping himself distant. In the case of Mrs. Liu, even though there was no history of social trauma of the widespread catastrophic kind, the effect of early separation, even although it is culturally sanctioned, has nevertheless marked her personality and resulted in difficulties in a different, more actively fearful way.

There is another potential effect of the trauma of early separation that this couple grew up with. Psychoanalysis has taught us a good deal about the effects of early trauma. Recent work has also highlighted the fact that trauma experienced in one generation is likely to be passed on to succeeding generations. I alluded to this in the introductory section of this chapter, seen in Plaenkers' research on the way that children of victims of the Cultural Revolution tended to suffer from the distortions in their parents' lives as a result of those traumas. Writing by Pichon Rivière (Scharff et al., 2017; Losso et al., 2017) and Haydee Faimberg (2005) for instance, has shown clearly that trauma to one generation, if unmitigated by growth (which may well be facilitated by psychotherapy) will pass down through future generations. The son of Mrs. Liu and Mr. Wu would be vulnerable to being strongly affected by his parents' struggles in the wake of their early losses. His mother's temper and emotional lability, and her often overly strict discipline, and his father's emotional withdrawal and depression could easily convey the sense of damage to the child, who could not then know the sources of his parents' anguish, but would feel its effects nevertheless. Because of this, anything that parents do to mitigate their individual suffering and to improve their function as a parental couple will work to their child's developmental advantage. This is among the reasons that it is important for parents to know the sources of their inherited sense of loss and deprivation, because having a narrative about loss and trauma, whether in one's own generation or in previous generations, works to demystify the traumas, to enhance understanding and to mitigate lingering traumatic consequences.

Resilience

While I have dwelt on the vicissitudes of trauma in China, I must add that it is also clear that there is inherent resilience in Chinese society and in the majority of Chinese individuals and families. In most of the families, couples and individuals I have interviewed, the quality of this resilience is impressive. We count on finding a capacity for resilience in all the patients we see, and if it is not there in some fashion, our job is impossible. That quality was badly missing in Nicole's father, whose destructiveness hampered the family and got in her way. Nevertheless, we could feel a quality of determination in Nicole herself that left us with the feeling that she just might find a way to grow despite her parents' pattern of relating. In the case of Mr. Wu and Mrs. Liu, the quality of care for each other and their determination to find the good in each other formed a powerful partnership for growth and allowed us to feel optimistic for them and for their whole family. It has been true for the large majority of Chinese couples and families we have seen over many years: Despite large or small handicapping psychological conditions, an admirable innate resilience shines through. China's hope will rely on the innate resilience of its people.

It was Gao Jun who first alerted me to the need to focus not only on the elements of trauma of the kind that I have described in this chapter, but also on the resilience of our patients. Because the sample of families and couples I have studied is drawn from those who ask for help, they are, by their own definition, in difficulty of one kind or another. Sometimes the impairment we see is severe, but often it is not, representing rather adjustment difficulties in the light of challenging circumstances.

As a country, China's story is one of incredible resilience. Having experienced trauma and change frequently over the past two centuries, its story since 1980 is its rapid rise to claim the second largest economy and to have developed an increasingly dominant business culture worldwide. As this continues, Chinese ideas become more influential, even if at times conflictual, in its increasing sphere of influence.

The resilience that matters to the focus of this book is, however, the fine-grained resilience of individuals, couples and families. This level of resilience has been well-studied during the past 30 or more years in children, adolescents and adults, in situations of poverty, disaster and wartime (Chicchetti and Rogosch, 1997; Kelly and Emery, 2003; Yates et al., 2003; Benard, 2004; Rutter, 2008; Wolin and Wolin, 2010; American Psychological Association, 2014). These studies show that the ability to relate, the availability of human and environmental support, and an inborn gift for the grit to persevere all contribute to an individual or a family's ability to overcome adversity. One comparison of Chinese and Western studies of resilience showed agreement about the essential elements necessary to overcome adversity (Ping Wang et al., 2014)

Even though the examples that form the heart of this book are drawn from couples and families seeking help, with only a couple of exceptions, such as Nicole's parents, they also demonstrate that these families possess inherent resilience. Psychotherapy, in both the East and the

West, relies on our patients' capacity for resilience. That is something we can facilitate but cannot implant. The couples and families we saw, even most of the ones that initially seemed reluctant to change, would regularly surprise us when their capacities for repair emerged during our brief five-day encounters. When I use the word 'surprise,' I do not mean that I began by thinking they could not find the strength to grow. I mean surprise in the sense that we never know just where that capacity will come from or how it will show up. We simply carry an innate faith that it will, and we are almost always rewarded with demonstrations of the richness of the human spirit. That surprise buoys our confidence in the work we do both at home and in China.

Part 2

Marriage in China Today

Chapter 7

Marriage in China
Strengths and Vulnerabilities

I will begin with an overview of marriage in China, but the heart of this book is in the close-study clinical examples that follow. By embedding these clinical vignettes in a summary of social changes and the evolution of social policy, I intend to further explore my opening questions about how large-scale social factors interact with intimate couple life and shape challenges that couples face. These examples also describe how my colleagues and I work to understand clinical challenges couples have brought to us, and therefore addresses the question of how to help clinicians in their future work.

To begin, let us ask what love is in China, a question I raise at the outset because the definition of love – although infrequently discussed in psychoanalytic circles – has been discussed by notable theoreticians such as Otto Kernberg (1995), who ties it to capacity for trust, for selflessness and for sexual interest.

But in China, marriages over the millennia were formed not on these bases, but rather in more practical terms of the best interests of the family. Thinking about this problem, of what love has to do with marriage, brings me to the point of saying that in the West, with the almost exclusive idea of marriage as a matching of romantic and sexual interests, we exercise a point of view steeped in the language of individual autonomy and of personal interests that complement the self. From this vantage point, love is seeking someone who will enhance our own life and self-interest, and for whom, at the same time, we can enhance their self-interest and their life. Then the problems of loving in couples flow from issues these areas.

However, in China, the deep and ancient tradition of how couples form is steeped in loyalty to the family, the group and the emperor. Therefore, in marriage, loyalty to the family, overseen by the father's official authority and the mother's unofficial but definite power, comes first. Women were physically ceded to their husband's families under the thumb not only of their husband but their husband's mothers. However strange this seems to the modern Western mentality, it has had a socially organizing effect over a long time, and we must assume that it served a teleological purpose, ensuring the propagation and maintenance of the social order.

In their comprehensive study *Family Life in China*, Jankowiak and Moore (2017) write:

> The arranged marriages that were a hallmark of the traditional family system in China were supported ideologically by the Confucian value system, but were also reinforced by the economic control that most parents exercised over their offspring's future prospects. In agricultural societies (which is what traditional China was), control over inheritable land gives the senior generation a great deal of leverage over their offspring. This leverage is somewhat reduced when young people are exposed to urban environments where economic opportunities are more varied and less inheritance-dependent then they are in the countryside. But even in urban environments, the pervasive Confucian ideology that empowered males and elders, backed up by a legal apparatus that stood ready to enforce its precepts, meant that young people generally had to defer to their parents in matters of marriage. And parents of course considered it only right that they should control their children's marriages, given the importance of such matters in ensuring the economic viability of the household and the continuation of the patrilineal family line. In this ethos, personal sacrifice is expected for the sake of the family's well-being. Spouses' personal feelings toward each other are comparatively unimportant when it comes to loyalty, cooperation, and harmony within the larger kinship unit. In this setting marriage is never just between just two people but involves a wider set of interested actors whose behavior was strongly shaped by their views of the family's interest as a corporate entity.
>
> (pp. 74–75)

Throughout human history, arranged marriages have clearly had advantages, even though they now have a bad name in the West where they do not work so well. Individuals and families emigrating from the Asia to the West may try to maintain the custom of arranged marriages for a generation, but their acculturated children migrate emotionally to Western ways that include practices of arranging intimate partnerships based on free-choice and romantic attraction.

In the setting of Chinese arranged marriages, what was expected was that the bride should be a cooperative hard-working member of her new home without upsetting their sense of harmony and the household's viability, including a good working relationship with her new mother-in-law. For this reason, if the husband doted too much on his bride, that would challenge the power his mother had over her. In this way, although many households became harmonious, the relationship between daughter-in-law and mother-in-law was frequently a vulnerable fault line (Jankowiak and Moore, 2017, p. 75).

This harkens back to an earlier discussion in Chapter 2 about the tradition of *enqing*, which refers to marital bonds built on mutual respect, appreciation, gratitude and admiration for the fulfillment of spousal and filial duty (Li and Chen 2002, Chen and Li 2007). In Asian cultures, *enqing*, which encompasses the expectations delineated by Jankowiak and Moore, has been shown to be more important than romantic love or intimacy for the long-term satisfaction of marriages (Ng, Peluso, and Smith 2010). *Enqing*, not romantic love, promotes the harmony and cooperation that cements relationships within the larger family. Love for a spouse, therefore, becomes secondary to a mother's emotional tie to her child, especially if that child is a boy.

But, as we have seen, Chinese life has been changing rapidly. Vanessa Fong's (2007) studies on the changes and the conflicts this leads to in the minds of families have helped us to understand the evolution of loyalties from exclusive allegiance to the family group, to being more individuated and out for oneself. There is a comparable and related evolution from family-based negotiated marriages towards free-choice marriage.

Jankowiak and Moore (2017) write that concepts of romantic love have existed in China more than 3,000 years, as testified to by ancient poetry, and were presented elaborately in thirteenth-century novels as *Story of the Western Chamber*, and the eighteenth-century *Dream of the Red Mansion*. The recent Western contribution to China is less a revolutionary set of romantic possibilities than the articulation of new examples and symbols of love. This, adding to the further decline of traditional patriarchal structures, has presented young people with opportunities to do 'what they were inclined to do anyway, and follow their attractions' (ibid, p. 84).

The Chinese May Fourth Movement of 1919 made romantic love a viable option, and by the 1940s, arranged marriages were already the exception in the cities, while change came more slowly and with more family conflict in the countryside. The Communist Party's marriage law of 1950 was designed to equalize the situation between men and women so that men could no longer dominate their wives as they had under the Confucian ethic. That reform empowered women, but the partnerships the CCP promoted were principally ones of utility and service to the Party. The Marriage Act of 1950 resulted in an unprecedented rise in the divorce rate, with most of the divorces initiated by women trapped in disagreeable marriages. After a spate of these divorces by the mid-1950s, the divorce rate dropped to the previous low level. During this time the ability of parents to force unwanted marriages evaporated, although parents continued to exercise informal power, especially through harsh negative treatment of unwanted prospective sons- or daughters-in-law.

We shall later see that this power has not entirely disappeared, as evidenced through the recent phenomenon of 'parent-driven divorce' (see Chapter 12).

During the years of Mao's oversight, young people's ability to choose whom to marry flourished, although within the control of the working units. This empowered women, but with quite a lot of pushback from the males who overwhelmingly controlled the cadres from which couples were required to obtain permission to marry or divorce. Then, during the anarchy of the Cultural Revolution, young people were freer still to wander and to date. But only in the mid-1990s, with the rise in wealth, the development of opportunities for leisure in cities and the maturation of a generation of only-child young adults who had a new awareness of patterns of dating imported from the West, was it that free-choice marriages came fully into prominence (Jankowiak and Moore, 2017). Even so, parents continue to have urgent hopes for their children, as evidenced even today in the so-called 'marriage markets' in large cities, in which mothers – mostly of boys – gather in public places holding umbrellas and posters with a caption highlighting the virtues of their only child, hoping to match up with another mother seeking an eligible mate for her child.

How Do People Get Married Now?

In 2014, Deborah Davis wrote:

> Over the past three decades, a distinctly post-socialist form of marriage with high rates of divorce as well as rising rates of marriage and remarriage has emerged as the result of a 'triple turn' by the party-state in regard to the institution of marriage: a 'turn toward' marriage as a voluntary contract, a 'turn away' from close surveillance of sexual relationships, and a 'turn away' from protection of communal property. The one-child policy runs against these three prevailing 'turns' toward privatization, but to date this contradiction has been muted by a de facto distinction between (strong) control over reproduction and (weak) control over sexual relationships.
>
> (p. 551)

Jankowiak and Moore (2015) provide a sociological overview that sets the context in which our individual couples have sought their partnerships. Today, Chinese young adults are delaying marriage to ages previously unknown, making their parents, who are anxious for grandchildren and for the continuation of the family line, extremely unhappy. One young Chinese woman told me that she stopped speaking to her mother because the only real conversation her mother ever wanted to have was about when the young woman would have a child. But not only are Chinese women delaying marriage, many now say that they do not want to get married or have children at all. Pressured by their parents to have children, some comply but then give the child over to their parents to raise (*News China*, January 2017).

Jankowiak and Li (2018) write:

> Whenever the love bond becomes a culture's dominant ideal and preferred practice, patriarchal values that highlighted the superiority of senior men and women over their offspring, and in a more localized context, a husband's preeminence over his wife, can no longer prosper, much less thrive. Current changes show that urban Chinese society is heading in this direction.
>
> (p. 185)

Their research confirms the shift in courtship patterns and marriages from ones based on ethics of duty to ones based on the expectation of emotional intimacy and equality. It is not that parental influence is altogether gone: Young people are under pressure to break up if their parents are strongly against a potential union, and as we shall see later, parental pressure may even precipitate divorce. Nevertheless, in general parental control is less honored and less a matter for the formation of and maintenance of marriages. Over the last 40 years, there has been a sea change:

> For today's younger generation, marital life is no longer organized around a husband's willingness to provide and a wife's willingness to be obedient to her husband and senior in-laws, but instead is based on shared empathy and mutual respect, alongside other reciprocal processes such as consideration, cooperation and compromise.
>
> (Jankowiak and Li, 2018, p. 193)

Now young people are essentially free to choose their own partners. Although living together without marriage happens frequently now, until recently it had been an option less exercised in China than in the West.

With free-choice marriage, the dominant option among educated and middle-class young adults, and even in the rural areas, there is a new variety in how choices are made. Among the couples we have seen, the capacity for judgment seems more to be hit-and-miss than in the West. The accuracy of partner choice is not that good worldwide, since divorce rates hover around 50% in the West, but the West does have a tradition of romantic-choice marriage that dates back perhaps 200 years. Over this time, there has been an accumulation of experience, encoded in family lore, popular literature, religious teaching, television and the culture in general that offers some guidance. I have the impression that in China, with the relative novelty of free-choice marriage, the criteria that young people apply in choosing partners is even more scattershot. Couples will say, for instance, that a prospective partner seemed to be intelligent or a good earner, or to come from a higher social class. Or a man will comment on the beauty of his fiancé or wife as her chief quality. It is not that these criteria are not used in the West. Of course they are! But I have the continuing impression there is more in-dwelling capacity to find the elements of unconscious fit that determine the long-term quality of marriage. However, the influence of the family has not vanished in China. So, it is still also common for young people to have their parents in mind when considering the prospect of relationships between them and prospective spouses.

Henry Dicks, in his ground-breaking book *Marital Tensions* (1967), noted that marriage as a social institution is the expression of 'the culture's aspiration to ensure the stability, security and dignity of relational needs' between couples and their children. It is also a system of interpersonal relations that blends two people into one and relies on an overall positive balance. Dicks described three major levels or subsystems of marital fit: (1) sociocultural values and norms; (2) conscious judgments and expectations, the area of expectations partners have of each other for role performance; and (3) positive and negative unconscious forces for a marriage to be happy or healthy. The net balance has to be positive. It is this last subsystem that largely determines the felt quality of a marriage for the couple, and the sense of integrity or dissatisfaction for the self and the other (Dicks, 1967, pp. 129–133).

It is unlikely that a couple will be able to assess the unconscious elements of their partnership without an extended period of trying out what they are like together, which now is commonly undertaken in the West, as partners usually spend time getting to know each other slowly, usually by living together before marrying. A common exception applies for those couples whose religious beliefs exclude this possibility.

It is my impression, and therefore subject to disagreement, that young Chinese couples have, until relatively recently, allowed less space and time for this process of testing out their unconscious fit, the mutuality and comfort of their everyday projections and projective identifications with each other, and have been more likely to jump to choices based on surface qualities. This may change over time, but so far, the relative lack of examples in Chinese culture does not seem to support this, so that it is still in the process of being imported from Western cultural examples. The example of the older academic husband and the younger country wife in Chapter 2 is a good example of this. He chose her because she was young and beautiful, and, as we conjectured, represented the mother of his youth from whom he was separated during the Cultural Revolution. To the wife, he represented an older father figure, accomplished and established but who, in her way of thinking, was too old to make romantic or sexual demands. She expected him to take care of the family economically and to leave her to raise their child, while he expected her to be a kind of mother or 'nanny' to him. As a result, both were disappointed and angry, and turned instead to their child, who could take and receive their individual affection.

Domestic Violence and Abuse

The traditional patriarchal structure of the Chinese family meant that for most of Chinese history, husbands could abuse their authority and their wives with considerable impunity. Wife-beating was a regular practice acceptable for asserting male dominance (Gilmartin, 1990). This practice was countered in the 1980s, as the China's increasing openness and changed political climate led to new efforts to combat domestic abuse of women (Tang and Lai, 2008). The World Conference on Women, hosted in China in 1995, further increased this discussion and added pressure to change practices about abuse (Zhang, 2009).

In many families under strain, quarreling can lead eventually to violence. A Chinese nationwide survey found that in adults from 20 to 64 years of age, the percentage of male-to-female violence was 19% (with the worldwide rate at 21%), while mutual violence was 15% and female-to-male violence only 3% (Parish et al., 2004, quoted in Jankowiak and Moore, 2015, p. 124). These statistics are consistent with other reports that 30% of China's 270 million families report domestic violence and that more than 90% of recorded incidents are male-to-female violence, but that female-on-male violence also exists in a minority of cases, as is illustrated in a couple described in Chapter 10 (*News China*, 2020). Another study found that victims of domestic violence only seek help after suffering physical abuse an average of 24 times (*People's Daily*, 2011:2, quoted in Jankowiak and Moore, 2015, p. 125).

Domestic abuse still occurs with alarming frequency despite new marriage laws enacted in 2016 intended to combat it. Marital rape is still not illegal, and poor women are especially open to abuse (Feldshuh, 2018). A survey in 2019 found that over half of the women interviewed in China's 'floating-population' of internal migrants to large cities had been subjected to abuse (Huang Shulun et al., 2019). Even in the middle-class population, there is a persistent level of domestic abuse. The National Bureau of Statistics of China reported in 2010 that 24.7% of women aged between 24 and 60 experienced some form of domestic violence (Gongyi. people.com.cn, 2019).

While I have not encountered cases of severe domestic abuse in the couples and families I interviewed, several have reported verbal abuse and minor episodes of physical violence. Many of the couples we interviewed came from families in which verbal and physical violence to wives and/or to children were a feature of their childhood. Parental physical punishment and harsh verbal criticism in the childhoods of our couples were reported to us frequently, and some of the couples we report on have engaged in a great deal of angry behavior with their children. The influence of verbal and physical violence must be taken into account in these cases. Often, such violence stems from a legacy of trauma and poverty in previous generations, as well as from childhoods with especially severe discipline and angry, depressed parents. While the cases I present do not include severe physical abuse, that possibility has to be kept in mind during assessment of couples and families in China, as it does everywhere.

A Marriage in Crisis

I now want to give an extensive example from a couple that I interviewed with my colleague Jane Prelinger some years ago. As with the other couples and families, we interviewed this couple for an hour over each of five consecutive days in front of an audience of about 75 students and faculty, with Gao Jun as interpreter and another colleague, Michael Stadter, as observer. Each of these couples had given permission for us to use the encounter with them for publication, and in each case, we have disguised personal details and omitted material that could be identifying.

These examples tend not to illustrate single issues, so, in giving this example, I will use the starting point of the misjudgment involved in the couple's choice of each other to illustrate other matters, most of which I will discuss in more detail later. All the couples and families we see are inevitably more complex than can be contained in a single concept, so I want to use each example with as much regard to the fullness of its complexity as possible.

In the couple we will meet now, we will see how the circumstances of their initial meeting, and even their first years together, did not reveal the issues that later formed the difficulties they encountered as a crisis when expecting the birth of their child.

All marriages that are formed with through romance and falling in love rely on a pattern of temporary psychic reorganization – a Romeo-and-Juliet kind of idealization of each other and of repressing both what is bad about the self and about the other, often projecting all that is bad into the world around. Theoretically, this means a magnification of 'excited object relating,' in which the other person is seen as all good and doubts are put underground. Colloquially, we say that lovers suffer from a special kind of madness, one which we celebrate as a culture. As time goes on, the repressed parts of personality that would have threatened the bond in the beginning return from repression, that is, they come back and clamor for recognition, because every person wishes fundamentally to be cared for and related to for their whole selves. It is this process of getting to know each other fully that represents the psychological challenge to couples of accepting each other 'for better and for worse' (D. Scharff, 1982; Scharff and Scharff, 1991).

To put it another way, spouses' choice of each other relies on certain conscious and unconscious features that feel almost purely positive to them at the time, but turn out to have liabilities that are only revealed with time, or, if they had known about them, they had not reckoned with them in the beginning. In addition to seeing the problem of the betrayal and disappointment of their early impressions and expectations of each other, this couple's difficulty lets us see problems encountered in a crisis compounded by expecting a child, extramarital affairs, child developmental problems that lead to adult problems, and problems of trust in marriage. Finally, this example shows us at work clinically and how we endeavor to gather information during these interviews, including our use of transference and countertransference as ways to join with the couple emotionally in their problem area, to gain a sense of what they struggle with from the inside the emotional problem ourselves and to work our way out of the impasse that we have joined.

Fei Yang and Fong Jie

The husband, Fei Yang, and the wife, Fong Jie, were both overvalued children, but the overvalued pampering had opposite effects on their personalities. Mrs. Fong seemed to have been so spoiled that she could barely lift a finger on her own behalf, while Mr. Fei, who had been equally idealized and indulged, was imbued with the messages to value family loyalty, but above all, to look out for himself.

As Jane Prelinger and I met the couple, the husband strode in ahead, paying little attention to his wife, who was visibly six or seven months pregnant. Both were attractive, in their mid-30s. They had been together for nine years, married for six, but Mr. Fei had gotten into trouble with his wife recently for 'some tiny mistakes, and not for the first time.' But this time, she could not accept his transgressions. She had lost trust in her husband, not daring to think that his 'emotional relationships' with women might be sexual. It seemed clear that her pregnancy and the prospect of a child had made it impossible for her to ignore a pattern that she previously tolerated.

Mr. Fei explained that they had bought a new, large and expensive house in preparation for the plan to have a baby eventually. But now his wife, pregnant unexpectedly, was due two months from now. The new house had put them under financial burden, which had been exacerbated by the threat of financial setback in his business. They also bought a new house for her parents near their own. All of this involved a great deal of pressure, which he handled alone without help from his wife. The business setback included the threat of loss of major clients, so his general attitude was not good. In fact, he has saved his business, but the strain was so great that, he said, he had even lost some of his hair. (He pointed out that he used to have long hair, but now it is short. We cannot see that he suffers from any significant hair loss.)

Fong Jie nodded in agreement. Jane and I noticed how little she said compared to her husband, who the couple had put out front from the first.

I said, 'And with all this pressure, you sought comfort from other women?' (He nodded.) I continued, 'But it isn't the first time, and that's what brought you here?'

Fong Jie had overheard her husband on the phone with a woman two weeks earlier, and although he protested that it was a colleague, she refused to believe him.

Fei Yang stared at the ceiling, gathered himself and said in an intellectualizing way,

> So we are inseparable. One person's emotions affect the other. Though for me, it doesn't have any impact on our future. But it happened, and we need to face it. I also need to consider the other parts of our life, like my business and housing. In the process, I've neglected her subtle feelings. My premise is always to set a priority to deal with the most urgent things and delay the others.

I noted, 'But the trust is broken between you?'

Fei Yang agreed. 'Sure.'

Mrs. Fong had lost trust in her husband, but it seemed to be a kind of blind trust founded on misperceptions about her husband. She agreed she was uncertain whether there had been actual affairs, but she was quite worried about the prospect of affairs in the future. But we had also found Fei Yang quite confusing, and so we began to join their experience of a confusion that limited our ability to trust the truth of what he said.

While this couple has much to teach us about the breakdown of trust within marriage, here I want also to illustrate how this marital crisis stemmed from the way the couple did not really know each other, not only in the beginning of their relationship, but in important ways, even in the ensuing eight years, that is, until the pregnancy brought hidden factors to the surface of their relationship.

Fei Yang explained to us that they lived essentially separate lives, seldom conversing. She had refused to do more around the house, even when he bought the new house for her parents to be close. His wife, he explained, does essentially nothing at home. Her mother comes to the house every day to cook and clean while she plays on her iPad. She doesn't even manage their money. Her mother had taken on the role of mother and housekeeper. He said, 'I've talked to her about my dissatisfaction, but nothing has changed.'

Fong Jie, smiling, said, 'What he says is true. I'm not interested in those things, but it's a key point, and if I need to, I'm willing to change.'

Fei Yang said,

I plan for everything, including her career. She hasn't played her proper role, her 50%. I think, for marriage, one plus one equals two. For me, I felt that after our marriage, one plus one only equals one. There wasn't any addition to the sum.

It turned out that Mrs. Fong had been cared for in this manner by her mother throughout her young life, being expected to do nothing for herself. She had done well in school, but at home was doted on and completely cared for.

I asked Fong Jie what drew her to her husband.

She replied simply, 'He's a caring person. That was the most attractive part.'

I said, 'Fei Yang, you pride yourself on taking care of someone whom you care for, but you feel she hasn't done enough in the marriage.'

Fei Yang replied, 'Yes, because we didn't live together or have a chance for a mature loving relationship ahead of time. I wasn't very mature, so things happened that were unexpected.'

Jane asked, 'Do you feel cared for by Fong Jie, even though she doesn't care for the house?'

Fei Yang answered, 'I have a sense she is holding me, and gives me time and space to feel safe and secure at home.'

The couple agreed that despite the fact that Fong Jie does little at home, her husband feels held and contained.

We asked about Fong Jie's family. She said she and her family were an ordinary Beijing family, young enough that they had not been so much affected by the Cultural Revolution, only being sent to a rural area near Beijing for its last year. Her father was strict and worked as a driver. Her mother, a physician's assistant, was kind and cared for the house. Fong Jie went to school and university, and did reasonably well in an uninspired way. Her parents fought because her father had an uncontrolled temper. Her mother had to contain his periodic explosions, although that had been better in recent years. Both parents were from large families, but only her mother was close to her own family. She felt her parents had supported her well, but after college, 'I decided to do things on my own.' Throughout, she gave sparse answers so that we felt we learned little from her.

Fei Yang's grandparents had owned a business before the Cultural Revolution, and so the business was confiscated and they were sent to the countryside. His parents, as 'young intellectuals,' were also sent for eight years to rural areas of Inner Mongolia to join the troops for reeducation. That was where they met and married, and afterwards worked in the same factory, his father in electronics, his mother in the office. He said,

> My father would listen to my mother, and my mother would listen to me. My father did small, detail things, while my mother would rely on her ability for complicated things. My father didn't have a lot of friends. He was serious at work and never took leave, even when I was born. My mother never worked hard, but she made the big decisions for the family and for my father. When my father had difficulty in his career, my mother could always solve it. She was closer to me and said that 'I was as precious as her eyeball!' She would sacrifice everything for me. I learned to care for people and for detail from my mother. My character is a mixture of my father and mother. I have a good brain and work hard, but I don't have a good temper. Although my father had a temper, he was very responsible. After he retired, he took a low-paying part-time job. He felt he had to keep contributing to the family. All his friends said, 'Your son now drives a BMW. He would send the car and take you home, but you keep a humble job.' But he thought he was still doing his job as part of the family. My mother had more impact on my intellect. She was the major decision-maker and the family beacon. So, they both influenced me and I appreciate them. But I seldom talk to my parents now, and I don't want to listen to them.

Jane, feeling we were hearing much less from the wife, asked about her views.

Fong Jie said,

> I agree with his story somewhat. There was a huge contrast in our two families. My father was the authority figure. As a child, I didn't have conflict with my parents. In his family, if he had conflict with his father, his

mother would take his side and criticize his father. He doesn't like my family. I feel his mother dotes on him too much. His mother says to him, 'I'm too fond of you.' Perhaps his character problem comes from his mother, too.

In response to our further questions, Fei Yang told us that while he was satisfied with his life, he has a temper, finding it difficult to accept disagreement or criticism. He knows these things already, so it just feels like nagging if his wife says this to him. He said,

I want someone who can guide my life. Perhaps my mother is a model for my ideal woman. I need to be taken care of by others. For men, responsibility matters, so I worked hard and took more responsibility. I worked for several years for a man who taught me how to do business. He was good to me. I still work for him now, but I have my own business, too. Therefore, I have a good life, but now there's a gap between my ideal and the reality. I want somebody who can change me. Somebody has to convince me.

Jane asked, 'So that problem in trust would count for us, too! Do you feel you can trust us?'

Fei Yang said, 'At the beginning I trust people, but I need to see real behavior and I favor outcomes.'

Turning to Jane, I exclaimed, 'We have quite a challenge!' To the couple, I said, 'We're working, but we haven't solved things and won't in one week. If we said we could, you should be suspicious of us.'

Fei Yang said, 'I have some expectations. I want an experience I have never had before.'

Jane said, 'I can see that if we don't perform it will seem as if we're no good.' To Fong Jie, Jane said, 'You have a hard act to follow with his mother.'

At this moment, Jane and I both felt the challenge of being able to get through to the couple, and especially to make a difference. Mr. Fei seemed to be longing for a father who could have set limits, perhaps a longing his mother had also felt when, lacking the feeling she had a strong husband, she paired with her son instead. But this still left him without a sense of a father. It was as though without a father, he was unable to feel he could control himself. And we felt that the difficulty with trust was an issue for both members of the couple. The man he worked for seemed to be a model of the father he wished he had and that he was looking for in consulting with us.

Fong Jie said, 'No. I'm different from my mother-in-law. I can accept his relationship with his mother. But I don't want to be like her.'

I said, 'But he *wants* you to be like his mother.'

Fong Jie said, 'I became more aware of that after this talk. I appreciate my mother-in-law. She has strengths, but I'm different.'

Towards the end of this interview, I said,

> You both have a block to taking in each other's experiences. Fei Yang feels he has to take care of things himself, and, Fong Jie, you think he has to take care of things for the two of you. The result of this is that Fei Yang feels isolated and on his own.

So far, we had seen this couple for two hours. We felt we could begin to put together a picture of a couple who had early expectations of each other that had not been met. Mr. Fei expected an idealizing and caretaking mother figure who would always take his side – and who would tolerate his doing whatever he wanted, including seeking motherly understanding elsewhere. We could see his oscillation between arrogance and vulnerability. Mr. Fei had an internal ideal maternal object that he sought in the other women, while his wife had become the denigrated and rejecting female object. Mrs. Fong expected to be taken care of. What seemed to unconsciously cement the relationship for the couple was Mr. Fei's desire to take care of someone, to be responsible like his father and to be more in charge like his mother, while Mrs. Fong longed to have an endlessly caretaking mother, as she had all her young life. She had become helplessly passive when he either became demanding or failed her.

Their mutual disappointment was embedded in their initial choice of each other and the failure of those unconscious hopes.

I asked Fong Jie, 'Have you met the partner that you want to love and be with?'

Fong Jie answered, 'When I got married, I thought so. But after some difficulties, I wondered if he was the one. It would be difficult to find someone who could meet my expectations.'

We got more clarity a few minutes later when we talked about their expectations for their child. They were both pleased it would be a girl.

Fei Yang said, 'Boys are naughty!'

I asked him to say more about boy's naughtiness.

He said, 'My mother said if she didn't have me, she would have lived another ten years. If a boy is disciplined, he can be obedient. I was pretty naughty, but I was 80% on the main track.'

I said, 'I'm wondering about the part that cost your mother ten years.'

Fei Yang replied,

> She loved that part of me. I have early memories, though. For instance, I have a scar here on my temple from when I fought with a boy in eighth grade. There's a scar on my nose from when I was one or two and tried to climb out of the toddler seat. In second or third grade, I fought with a girl and her finger was hurt. The teacher nagged me, so I got out a small knife, cut myself on the palm and held up my hand to her and said, 'Shut up teacher!' I wanted to control my life

I said, 'I'm really taken by that story.' (Fong Jie is smiling, and looking at the ceiling.)
Fei Yang said,

> My teacher liked me, there wasn't any trouble or criticism. Like in painting class, the teacher would take the picture I drew as a model for others to copy. My music teacher wanted me to lead the chorus. My primary school teacher said, 'If you succeed, don't forget me.' Girls liked me, but I would think that they had no brains, so I had no time for them.

Fong Jie tells us that she has heard these stories often and can imagine them. She volunteers that her husband is still a naughty boy who clowns and cracks jokes with others, but she was an obedient girl who caused no trouble and was a good student.
Jane said,

> We see that the two of you appreciate the differences between you, but they also create problems. Fei Yang, you would like your wife to be more assertive, and Fong Jie, you would like your husband to be gentler and less 'naughty.'

I added, 'But, Fei Yang, you want more, so you turn to other women. And Fong Jie, you then feel betrayed. So, the difficulty between you is about the things between you that leave each of you not fully satisfied.'
Jane asked, 'Is there enough for your marriage to last?'
Fei Yang: 'It's just a little question about what I want. I'm satisfied with 80% of my life, so I shouldn't be so greedy.'
I said, 'If you're 20% dissatisfied, there's still a question about whether you have to be on the phone with other women, and if he keeps doing this (to the Fong Jie), would that break the marriage?'

Fong Jie exclaimed, 'I can't accept that. I told him that's my bottom line. There are some problems between us. We try to solve them. If not, we will have to break up. I don't want third persons involved in our life.'

Jane said, 'I'm feeling this is a complicated moment in your life. You're in your late 30s, and you start to wonder what the rest of your life will look like, what will be an authentic life.'

(At this moment, I felt that Jane was trying to protect the couple from the confrontation that Fong Jie's direct bottom-line answer posed, so I decided to interrupt. In that way, acting on the complex countertransference to the total situation, I was taking over much as the husband so often does.)

I interjected, 'I am thinking about something more specific, Jane. There will soon be a different kind of third 'woman' coming into their lives. I wonder about that. While you, Fong Jie, wanted the baby, are you, Fei Yang, also frightened?'

Fei Yang answered, 'Never! But I have some doubts. There must be new challenges. For my part, I can see taking care of the new challenges. I always believe problems can be solved.'

Fei Yang seemed to react with another retreat to confused self-contradiction. Beginning to say 'Never!' followed by admission of difficulties, followed by evasion of the question that had been posed.

I asked, 'How about you Fong Jie?'

Fong Jie, smiling, said,

I'm anxious, but I don't know where it comes from. Many new mothers give me a lot of information. There's anxiety about what's coming. Life changes, but you don't know what it will feel like, so, I don't know what the challenges will be, but I do feel prepared.

We then returned to discussing Fong Jie's anxiety that her husband would continue to behave in ways she could not tolerate.

Fei Yang said,

I just want my wife to feel safe, to enjoy an easy life. I also wonder how to solve things. For example, when I was young, I quarreled with my parents. Every time, my mother would be angry and cry. Therefore, I thought about it before I went to bed each night, and each time I decided that I would never quarrel with them again. But it would happen again. Every time I decided not to do it, I had the same determination, but it happened anyway. As I got older, this problem seldom happened with my parents, but it's not that I found a way out. I just got more mature and my character improved.

Fong Jie said,

> It was a problem that he never suffered any consequences from his mother because it was so easy for him to be forgiven. He didn't care because he never suffered for anything he did, so maybe that's why things don't change now.

Fei Yang agreed, 'My mother said to me, 'If your father had beaten you, you wouldn't be the person you are.' Maybe that's at the root of my character.'

I said,

> There's a question as to whether Fong Jie's threat that she might have to leave the marriage would be enough to stop you from calling the women, or if you will do it again, just like the way you would keep promising your mother to reform but you never did.

Fei Yang said, 'I don't have a clear answer to you now, but I think if I had talked with a man, then there wouldn't be the same problem.'

It is clear to us immediately that his last statement was double entendre. It meant on the surface that if he were talking to a man on the phone all those times on the balcony, his wife would not have cared. But more importantly, he also conveyed an unconscious meaning that if he were explaining this problem in general to a man (like his mentoring boss, or here in the session like me), either the man wouldn't take it so seriously as we now do as therapists, or most importantly, Mr. Fei would be able to feel that the man would understand and be able to help him in a way that women, and his mother, could not. This was the most direct experience we had so far of his hunger for a father.

Understanding this double meaning, I said, 'And perhaps a man would understand your position better.'

Fong Jie also seemed to understand the double meaning, and said, 'It would be okay if it were a man.'

In this, our third session, we saw more clearly how the husband negated much of what we said while often contradicting himself, creating a deadly repetitiveness in the first half of the interview. In our countertransference experience, we took this in as a confusing stifling repetition. These feelings culminated in the striking anecdote of cutting himself and telling the teacher to shut up. This story seemed to clarify his contribution to the transference in which he presented himself as willing to be dramatically self-destructive in order to defeat any attempt to control him. This revelation was followed by more straightforward comments by Mrs. Fong on the immediate risks to the marriage. The couple then seemed immediately more engaged. We could now clearly see Mr. Fei's underlying longing for a father ('a man would understand!'), and how, especially in addressing me, he would come around to agreeing with things that he originally skirted or dismissed. Nevertheless, Mr. Fei's confusional tone remained, now contrasted more clearly with Mrs. Fong's emerging clarity and strength.

In reviewing this session, we also noted that in cutting across my co-therapist, I had taken over, and thereby formed a pattern of interaction between us as a therapist-couple similar to the marital pattern. We thought this represented an unconscious identification with the couple, as the husband cries for help in a confused and desperate way that both asks for help and denies his need at the same time. In the discussion with the audience after the session, Jane described her sense of being in a timeless, deadened state because so much of what she said had gotten killed off. We identified that experience as similar to the wife's apparent state of mind. After the session, an experienced member of the audience volunteered, 'It's like you're in a spider's web, caught in deadly repetition.' As a group, we then elaborated on his metaphor of the spider spinning a web, catching a fly and anesthetizing it to eat later. It was a perfect image of the kind of web the husband spins for the wife and of the parallel way that we had felt caught by his confused self-contradictions, from which we struggled to escape.

The highlight of the fourth session was the way that the interview came to a point of transference confrontation. We rely on such moments in the immediacy of sessions to catalyze change in both brief and long-term therapy, because they represent times that the central issues come most into focus in the here-and-now of the session, and most importantly, in the person-to-person encounter with the therapists.

Early in the session, I asked Fong Jie, 'Do you have much hope for the relationship?'

She paused and looked at the ceiling. 'It's just that I hope I have hope, but I can't say I have confidence in it.'

The quality of hope is central to all marriages, and especially to marital repair after the inevitability of damage. Without any hope, or at least a 'hope that there can be hope,' nothing is possible. With her forthright statement, we began to see the possibility of repair for this couple whose trust was so damaged.

We soon felt more discouraged again, however, when Fei Yang explained to us that he had been distracted from his marriage, even during this week, with business crises that threatened their financial well-being. However, he had been able to solve them. Today he was due to sign an important contract after our meeting. He felt that his wife should understand that and give him some slack. Fong Jie said that this was his typical excuse. She admitted that the crisis in the marriage was too great to tolerate if they were to have a future together.

Fei Yang then said, 'In fact, I'm not so interested in being here. It never occurred to me that I would be on the spot with so many people looking at me, and being a subject of examination.'

We felt that this transference reference gave us a point of entry, just as our own sense of frustration was mounting. It helped us that Mr. Fei had been so open about his discomfort being on the spot in a public way.

I said, 'I'm glad you were able to say that. It might help you to know that we feel on the spot, too, in trying to offer help in front of this audience, but we don't think of you as a 'subject of examination.' We as therapists are on the spot about whether we can actually help the two of you. That is, we understand you feel under pressure, but so do we. Fong Jie said she can give you a week or a month, or at least some amount of time. But the question is whether you can give attention to your marriage in the same way you do with your business. [Fong Jie nods.] What do you think, Fong Jie?'

Fong Jie then said that, because they had never had any therapy before, either individually or as a couple, neither of them had known what to expect. For instance, she had never understood that he wanted her to be like his mother in taking care of him and tolerating his behavior. This revelation let her say clearly that while she appreciated his mother, that was not a role she was willing to play, that she had to be her own person. However, she also was coming to understand that she needed to change, to be more active at home and to rely less on her own mother. Now she feels willing to do that.

The couple tells us that they do want to take in what we say, but, Mr. Fei says, he needs time to digest what we say, a few days or a week. Mrs. Fong says she understands this about him. She can give him time. She knows putting him on the spot would backfire.

This exchange allowed us to understand that they were saying that even though it was hard, if we could grant them time, they were more likely to be able to absorb what we said and to accommodate. We began to have hope they could benefit from our time with them.

We then turned to Mr. Fei to ask if he felt he was learning anything. He said he wanted advice because when a man gives him advice, he might fight it because, as his mother had said, he was very stubborn, but it was nevertheless important to him if he thought the advice was right.

Jane said, 'Let me play a little game. If I said to you, 'Don't speak to other women!', would you be able to follow that advice?'

I said aloud to Jane, 'You know, that's exactly the advice that I was thinking of!' At this, Fong Jie laughed even before the translator could speak the Chinese, making it once again clear to us that she understood English.

Fei Yang said, 'I knew that before I came. I said if I talked with a man, it would be okay. It just goes very well if a man talks to man. I desire a pal, a man. I want a person I can talk to and find advice.'

In this session, the way the couple recruited us emotionally into their impasse and the fashion in which they then 'supervised us' about what they needed to begin to change gave us the feeling that they did have the potential to form a therapeutic partnership as a precursor to their own growth. We also began to see how their developmentally determined styles had both provided the basis for their getting together, and had come to form the impasse between them, just as those styles had formed a temporary impasse in our treatment relationship with them.

We were encouraged that the wife had realized that the husband wanted a woman to be like his mother and this differed from the way she wanted to be herself. And we could now see that the confusion we had felt in the husband's speech organization represented an ingrained way of distancing himself from his demanding, pampering and intrusive mother. Then he also had to withdraw from his wife, lest she actually be like his mother, seeking that kind of 'understanding' from the distance of a relationship with other women, even while trying to care for himself vicariously by caring for his own wife who was disabled by her ingrained and pampered passivity. And finally, we heard a much clearer message about his hunger for a man who could understand him and from whom he could learn.

In the discussion with the audience after the interview, one of the senior trainee women gave us another wonderful metaphor, suggesting that the couple presented like a tiger (the husband) fattening up a rabbit (the wife) so the rabbit would then be better prey. She said, 'The husband plays with her, like saying, 'I'm here because my wife asked me to be.' Then, when she insists, the tables turn and he feels that she's the tiger and he's the rabbit.'

In this way this trainee summarized the unconscious organization that the couple now shared and feared: that they were in a tiger-and-rabbit (or cat-and-mouse) game. But, this woman said, things were reversible – that is, the couple would take turns with who was the tiger and who the rabbit. The game was repetitive and frightening, and as a couple, they could not find a way out.

On the day of the last session, Fei Yang was 15 minutes late, citing urgent business. But he quickly acknowledged that he had also been reluctant to come. Nevertheless, when Fong Jie said, 'I want to say to him, 'You have to take this seriously!'', he responded that he would try his best. We acknowledged that he would have to take the marital problem just as seriously as he took his business crises, and we finally had a sense at the end that he just might do that.

He said, 'Now I see the pressure she's under is as big as mine. I have to give something now.' Looking to one side in a thoughtful way, he said,

> A wise man doesn't only accept the ideal. He has to accept reality. No one can realize their ideals. I think I've got it now. We had a private discussion about how I could overcome the state of my mind. If I'm in a good state day by day and week by week and month by month, I'll have a good life. I will try. I have lots of thoughts, but I need to try to work on these things to have a better future.

I said, 'You don't have to be perfect every day; you just need to have more good days than bad days.'

Here, in the last moments of the brief intervention, the couple started to look more like an actual couple who would wish to accommodate to each other and to take the kind of help that can be offered. It was only in this session that we got the feeling that the couple, as a couple, had enough feeling for each other to face their shared and individual fears and thereby take advantage of the positive elements that had brought them together in the first place.

This intervention also illustrates what our colleague Michael Stadter (Stadter, 1996; Stadter & Scharff, 2000) has described as the 'dual focus' in brief therapy: A focus, on the one hand, on the symptoms and, on the other hand, on a central dynamic element, brought together in the transference-countertransference interchange. The symptom of Fei Yang seeking other women, the dynamic element of their mutual projective identification around caretaking and the transference-countertransference encounter with us about his fear of being on the spot in public combined all these elements. The enlarged view of the symptom of the couple's marital crisis consisted of the wife's passivity and the husband's turning to other women, brought into focus the dynamic issue they shared of dependency and fear. She longed for caring, and he got a vicarious measure of caring by taking care of her, until an unsustainable imbalance developed because he despised the neediness in himself and therefore had come to attack it in her. This led us to consider issues with their two mothers. Fong Jie's mother pampered her in a way that disabled her ability to care for herself, so that she felt incapable of contributing to the couple now. Fei Yang's mother idealized him in an intrusive way that led to his ambivalence. Now he felt in desperate need of 'holding and containing,' and at the same time he feared a woman's intrusions. We began to see how the initial fit in the couple around need for caring, and his vicarious satisfaction in caring for her while insuring she did not intrude on his prerogatives, had gone badly off track and was now further threatened by the impending birth of their daughter. Both of their longings for mothers, and his longing for a father who could tell him what to do, were echoed in the transference. While we interpreted some aspects of this directly in the 'on the spot' discussion, other aspects of the longing, for instance, the references to the boss who had mentored him, were left uninterpreted in the background of our treatment relationship. Additionally, the couple had the experience of the co-therapists working together as a functioning couple, a model for them as a couple who might also work together.

This couple helped us to see that behind the dynamic they shared of longing for mothers lay an equal longing for fathers and men who could understand. The most poignant emotion in Fei Yang's transference was his longing for me to become a fathering mentor to him in a way that would support his commitment to his wife. It seems to me that longing for fathers is not widely recognized in Chinese clinical situations, and that with the Chinese ideal model of fathers as distant figures, longing for fathers is more prevalent in China than has been commonly recognized. Now, thinking more about it, I believe that this longing for fathers is part of what drives the preference for sons.

As therapists, we did confront the couple, but then, taking direction from them, backed off to give them time to absorb the message before the end of the brief intervention. This also signaled that we respected their needs and boundaries, and that while we would try to help, we would also try not to intrude. This seemed to work, leading to a softening of their defensiveness and the new emergence of a sense of hope. We referred the couple to one of the senior couple psychotherapists in Beijing with the expectation that they would follow through on our recommendation for further couple psychotherapy.

What Does This Couple Show Us about Couples in Contemporary China?

Our work with this couple showed us many things. Their families had been affected, perhaps less severely than others, by the early separations and banishments of the Cultural Revolution. While we could not trace the strands of intergenerational trauma directly, we could infer that traumatic effects had affected these families.

We could hear the effects of the couple's individual developmental stories in the way they had formed a partnership, one that had worked fairly well before the wife's pregnancy. Embedded in this story is the underlying, largely unconscious contract they formed as life partners, she to be taken care of as her mother had cared for her, and he to get both the care through his vicarious care of her and to avoid the intrusiveness of his mother by picking someone who was passive.

However, the excesses of this unconscious partnership formed its vulnerabilities. She had to remain disabled, which he came to resent. He had to conduct an entrepreneurial balancing act for both of them. That is to say, her feeling she could not be active on her own behalf led her to project her own capacity for activity into him. But then his hunger for an active woman led him to form other relationships, whether they were sexual or not. (We were never sure about this, and we thought she was not sure either.)

Both of them longed for stronger fathers, which the husband found through his mentor, and which, in the brief encounter with us, they found in me. However, in this encounter with Jane and me, they also found a functioning and mutually respectful parental couple, something they were also missing, and in missing that, they were having difficulty creating a functioning couple dynamic for themselves, especially while on the threshold of expanding their couple relationship into becoming a family with a child. The anticipation of having that child played a significant role in precipitating the crisis in which the wife could finally face the implications of tolerating her husband's infidelity, and because she did this, he could begin to face the extent of his early deprivation and his enduring sense of neediness.

In these ways, the intimate experience of this couple expresses the dilemma of modern young Chinese adults, the movement from a culture of unquestioned family loyalty even in the face of things like infidelity alongside the urgency to move to an entrepreneurial attitude in order to thrive. The conflict that goes on as a result of the clash of these forces is fought out in the intimacy of many couples' lives.

Chapter 8

The Lingering Legacy of Parental Influence

Parental influence on young marriages has not disappeared altogether. We have seen that parents still carry the legacy of the ancient tradition of the importance of their children's marriages to the continuation of the family and the meaning of their own lives. As we have seen, this tradition is now in conflict with the shift to free-choice marriage that has swept the culture since the rise to power of the Communist Party, changing in nature with the period of opening up and the influence of Western ways of thinking about romance since about 1980.

The couple I describe in this chapter illustrates the confluence of a number of conflicting trends that we have seen repeatedly in Chinese marriages: the lingering influence of the old cultural tradition and family patterns that supported parents' rights to arrange and influence marriages, the rise of free-choice marriage and the painful imprint of childhood trauma and other issues of deprivation or loss. In this case, the husband's mother was not consulted when the couple formed their partnership but reasserted her influence between the time of the formation of that partnership and the actual marriage. She had continued to attack their marriage until the time they saw us. These elements frequently combine either in the history of one of the spouses or come together from both partners when they form their marital partnership.

We have seen that Chinese young people have largely shed direct parental influence on their marriages in moving from marital contracts that are formed in the interest of family, economic and kinship interests, and instead employ free-choice, romantic interests. However, the influence of the parental generation is still often represented often in the form of attacks on these marriages, which, in the eyes of the previous generation, represent a betrayal of the parents' right to the loyalty of their sons and their cultural right to determine and control their marriages. The parents, imbued with the old values of the sanctity of the family line, feel it is their duty to safeguard the family's heritage and chafe at their children's insistence on independence, their flouting of the right of parents to influence or even control the children's future and the young generation's lack of respect for millennia of Chinese regard for the greater good of the family.

The couple we are about to meet exemplifies the situation of the many educated young Chinese who go abroad, often with the intention of permanent emigration, and the issues that ensue if they return to the pressures of Chinese culture and ancient family tradition.

Julia and Max

Julia and Max, in their mid-30s, came to see Jill Scharff and me with Gao Jun as translator and our colleague Damian McCann, who aided us by observing and reflecting on the couple's issues. They were an attractive couple who spoke an educated English, although our interview was, as usual, conducted in Chinese for the benefit of the audience. They met while studying abroad in Germany. In the beginning, they felt they would have an ideal marriage that would flourish with a new life abroad. Max had been a student leader and had offered emotional support to Julia as they lived together in a university town, waiting for her while she finished her studies a year behind his doctorate. But with the financial crash of 2008, Max's prospective job offer in Berlin collapsed, and with that, his chance for immigration to the European Union. They returned home with Julia three months pregnant, ready to marry. Max had not seen his mother for ten years while studying abroad, and his mother was over the moon to welcome him, but was unenthusiastic about Julia as his partner.

From there, things rapidly deteriorated. The couple asked both his mother and her mother for advice about whether to keep the child or have an abortion, hoping for their support to keep the pregnancy. Julia's mother said she would support her decision either way, but Max's mother insisted on abortion.

While Julia's mother was sympathetic and supportive, Max's mother continued to disapprove of her as his wife on the pretext that she came from an inferior family, but it seemed the real motive was that she wished to claim Max for herself.

Julia had been depressed ever since the abortion, even though they had married two years later and now had a five-year-old daughter. She also had a hot temper that Max would try to mollify, often without success, and would then withdraw. But then a psychiatrist told her that she had bipolar disorder and prescribed a low dose of antidepressant medication, which helped some. Nevertheless, their marital conflict continued. Julia said, 'I transferred the way I related to my parents to my marriage. Now I don't know how to stop being so angry.'

Max agreed that they were in crisis. Max said,

I'm a listener. The way Julia talks to her parents and sister, she uses the same pattern with me. In a Chinese family, it's rude for people to quarrel. When people in the family are hurt, it should be covered over. My wife can't connect with her family. Every interaction ends badly, so she's worried that our marriage will end badly, too.

He puts his hand on his heart.

It's easy for her to lose her temper, and I fight back. If we could predict the end of all this … I'm afraid that either we'll divorce or we'll try to endure unhappily until the end of our lives. I don't know which path it will be. There's no model we can follow.

The couple had little sense of hope.

During our interviews, we began to see the origins of their individual and shared distress. Julia reported being warmly treated by her mother until, at the age of five, a younger sister was born who then displaced her as the favorite. From then on, Julia had to care both for her sister and her parents in a kind of Cinderella picture. Her father had a temper, so her parents quarreled while Julia did the speaking for herself and her sister. Although her sister was still difficult emotionally, she had lived with Max and Julia when they were first married. They were close until Julia's daughter was born, when the sister became more difficult and the couple had to ask her to move out. Now the sister is married with her own child, but Julia can barely stand to make short visits to her.

We explored the childhood situations for each of them to try to understand how their individual development might still be influencing their difficulty. Julia said she was forced to be mature early, to parent both her own parents and her sister. She would walk long distances to buy breakfast. When her mother would leave home in the middle of the night after a fight, her father would awaken her to go find her mother. She was their mediator, listening to her mother complain that her father wanted sex every night.

Julia said, 'When I once burst out, 'Then get a divorce!' My mother snapped, 'Then who will take care of you?' She blamed me, saying I was cold-blooded. When my mother left the house, my father would blame me saying, 'It takes so much energy to raise you, how could you allow your mother to do this?' So, to find a way out, I would say to him, 'This is the only way I can keep her from leaving you.' Now I think I have transferred the pattern from my childhood to myself and my husband.

In this way, Julia was both her parents' battleground and their interlocutor. In the process of being responsible for keeping them together, there was deep damage to her personality. She now felt she was visiting these scenes on her husband. She added that she had gone to Germany on her mother's advice, and she now understood she was living out her mother's wish to have amounted to more herself.

Max was brought up by his mother, a single parent. He said, 'I must not have seen my father. In reality, I don't know if I ever did or not.' Max's mother was a party chief with a dominant personality. He was a good student who never felt prejudice about being in a single-parent family. 'My mother did a good job, but she was a dominating person.' It was really his mother who decided he would go first to Shanghai and then to Germany for advanced education. Although he initially said little else about his mother, even these few facts began to tell us of his hunger for a father and a family, and of his loyalty to his mother.

In the second session, the couple focused on the difficulty they had with Max's mother. Max resented what his mother had done. He had not wanted to involve his mother directly in their relationship 'because it would make a mess.' He had hoped they would be reasonably close. But now when he tries to involve his mother in their life, Julia gets upset even if he calls her. Julia told us that his mother had spoken against her ever since they moved back to Beijing.

Max confirmed this. 'My mother would call and say, 'You don't have a good wife,' talking so loud that Julia would hear.'

Now he told us the story of the abortion.

He began, 'Before we married, my wife had an abortion. My wife wanted the baby, but we both weren't so sure, so we asked both mothers. Her mother supported either choice, but my mother was clear: 'Get rid of the baby!' My wife hates my mother for having done that. Since then, they dislike each other and keep their distance. Perhaps I should have resisted more to save the baby.'

While Julia was getting the abortion, Max had gone to Beijing with his mother to find a job. Julia said,

They even stayed in the same hotel room, which pissed me off. I had to do the procedure all by myself. Afterwards, my mother cried, and said, 'You make yourself so miserable.' My mother changed her position from being neutral about keeping the baby to regret. I was weak and vulnerable. So that's how my hatred for Max's mother developed.

Julia said, 'We never said goodbye to that baby.'

Jill asked if they had since imagined what the child would have been like. Julia said she was often reminded of the 'lost child' and the age he or she might have been. 'I've said that we need a ritual to say goodbye to our first child, but Max has not been interested.'

Max said it had also been sad for him, too. 'The way the past generation would try to comfort us was to say, 'We had the same thing,' in order to cover things over.'

Bringing these historical facts into the sessions allowed Julia and Max to begin to mourn in a way they had been unable to previously. It was not just the aborted child, although that was the single most painful loss; it was also the idyllic life and their hopes for a wonderful future that had ended when they had to return to China, punctuated by Julia's disappointment when her new mother-in-law disparaged her and ordered her to have the abortion, even while emotionally claiming her son for herself. The couple's marriage had never recovered from these losses, and the losses themselves were compounded by the way Max acceded to his mother emotionally, especially when he was in retreat from Julia's labile anger. The anger itself was a feature of Julia's inability to handle all the losses and disappointments, which, because Max tried to cover things over, felt even more painful and lonely to her.

Max added,

> Perhaps both of us are castrated. She is responsible for feeling, and although I try to think, it's useless. I have to try to do something. If you think without doing, it's a fantasy. That division has had an impact on our relationship.

Julia said, 'Now, when I'm with my daughter and husband, I become my father. I try to repress my anger in order not to be like him, but then it bursts out and my daughter and husband have to bear it.'

She spontaneously connected this to losing her mother when her sister was born. So, in the next pregnancy, when she had complications in the pregnancy with her daughter that threatened miscarriage at 20 weeks and necessitated an emergency appendectomy, she said,

> Those memories activated my desire to protect her and myself. When she was born, I couldn't tell where danger was coming from, so I abused my husband and he alternated between withdrawing coldly and showing hot aggression. So now, we dare not be together. And whenever we are, it's filled with sadness and suffering.

Julia continued by talking about Max's parents with detail he had not given. When Max's mother was pregnant with him, his father had kicked his mother in her pregnant belly, causing his premature delivery. But his mother had the courage to divorce him and care for Max herself, using the toughness and commanding personality she developed as a party leader. In this way, physical aggression had permeated both families, although with different effects.

A transference event in a session helped us all to see how Max's longing for a father had influenced him and the couple's relationship. Reacting to a confrontation I had posed to him, which he initially rejected as 'dealing him a blow,' but which he then accepted as helpful, he said, 'I don't have a father. I've never seen my father.'

We connected his sadness to two blows: first, the time his father kicked his mother when she was pregnant with Max, and secondly, his mother's ordering his father to leave so he never had a father. In his struggles to avoid that happening to his own family now, he had felt disempowered, using the word 'castrated' to describe his feeling about himself. His inhibition of aggression and assertiveness lest it harm his family also left him feeling impotent. Work with these issues touched the couple deeply.

Julia said tearfully,

> I felt for so many years I could not reconcile with my father because he brought me so much trauma. He would shout, 'You're stealing my money. Where did you hide it?' Only at midnight, when it was pitch black, would he allow me to throw out the trash. He made me guess what he was thinking and when I got it wrong, he cursed me. When you confronted Max, I felt I had two wise and caring parents telling him he could be responsible and that it's not all my fault. Because when I was pregnant, his mother shouted, 'It's your fault!' When I saw the two of you trying to help us work things out, it was wonderful.

Now Julia could begin to feel more sympathetic to her own parents too. Jill asked her to say more about her parents' own hardships, something that Julia had mentioned early on.

Julia said,

> I feel like my parents were two children without protection, alone, having to fight and hunt. There was a lot of hatred, but I understand them more now. They had more trauma than we did, and then they still had to bring up two children. Growing up, my mother was neglected and had to work. There were a lot of deaths – by snakebite, childbirth and so on.

She lived in the shadows, brought up by her father's mother, always hungry or eating decayed food.

My father's parents lost two children from famine before he was born. Later, he buried two younger brothers. All his love went to his mother, and he was always cursing his father. He's an obedient and polite son-in-law, but on my grandmother's deathbed, he couldn't help cursing her. He projected hate from his mother onto her.

Jill said, 'And he projected the hate onto you. He turned into his father and could be cruel to you.'

The appearance of Julia's empathy for her parents marked another turn within the sessions, fitting with her new-found ability to mourn her own losses.

In the last session, we asked if Max could tell us more about his parents.

All he knew about his father was his name, and that he was a soldier who lived locally. The marriage was not his parents' own choice. Max said,

My mother was very beautiful and had many suitors. Finally, she followed her parents' advice. A military man is an honorable man, so she chose him. But during her pregnancy, there was conflict and violence, so she wanted a divorce. She only told me two things about my father. First, when I was still in her belly, he kicked her in the abdomen, resulting in my premature birth. Secondly, when they signed the divorce contract and were dividing assets, my father said, 'So do you want the TV or the child?' I was the only thing she took from the marriage. That's all the memory I have of my father. He settled in another city with a new family and children, but we never had contact.

Max's mother was the eldest of five and his mother's father was high up in the Red Army, but during the Cultural Revolution, his grandmother was in prison, so his mother had to raise her sisters and brother. She emerged from this experience believing only in herself. His mother treated him well. Julia supplied details Max seemed to have forgotten, that he had been farmed out to two women for some of his childhood because of his mother's work, and so he must have missed his mother terribly.

Julia reminded Max of still more details: that his mother's parents had a difficult history, too. His grandfather's early retirement perhaps hinted at scandal. In addition, his grandfather apparently had two wives. Max's grandmother was the daughter of a landlord, and there was a question of embezzlement, perhaps also a reason for her imprisonment and her father's early retirement. While this history was a bit confusing to us, it seemed to document the generational trauma Max's mother had suffered. She had been determined not to pass misfortune onto him. Later, she spent her savings sending him to Germany. Max added that his mother was a mixture of mother and father to him. She was demanding, just as she apparently was in her role at work, rather authoritarian, dominating and insistent about her opinions.

When Max acknowledged that he often couldn't remember these kinds of things, so that Julia had to give elements of his history, Jill said, 'You forget uncomfortable things.' Max agreed, 'These things are useless to me. But sometimes Julia uses such things to attack me, like 'You said this before.' And I don't remember it.'

Max's grandmother is still alive, living with her younger son and daughter. It now emerged that one of his mother's sisters is a model for Max, with a nice family and a husband who is a local judge. Max now remembers that this uncle used to pick him up from kindergarten, and to our question, Max agreed this man was a good father figure.

As we neared the end of Max's story, I said, 'We can see that your wife has the details.' And Jill added, 'And all the feelings.'

Late in our time with the couple, we asked about their sexual relationship. It had initially been vigorous and loving, but was essentially killed off by the abortion. Max had never had an affair, although there was a woman with whom, briefly, he had a strong emotional connection. Julia let us know that the only important emotional affair was with his mother.

Julia said,

There was an important date six years ago. His mother phoned and said, 'You've been married so many years, you should produce a baby.' I was angry, but he said that made him feel safer. But every time we had sex, it wasn't satisfying like before. It was practical. He needed to have permission to have sex or else it was illegal.

In this way, the conception of their daughter had been prescribed and programed.

Discussion

Our encounter with Max and Julia sheds light on many aspects of the ways Chinese culture and China's history impinge on the intimacy of couples. It was only in the latter stages of our interviews that we learned of the direct trauma, in this case a legacy of the Cultural Revolution, that had traumatized Max's family. His mother's poor marriage was the result of the overvaluing of surface qualities in the later days of negotiated marriages, in which loyalty to the family superseded individual preference. Julia's family had been traumatized by the poverty and starvation of the Great Leap Forward at the end of the 1950s, leaving her parents to struggle practically and emotionally.

Then, Max's mother had clung to him in compensation for her loss of a husband and did so in the language of the wounded and draconian mother-in-law, lashing out at her vulnerable daughter-in-law, who was undefended because of Max's impotence and by his traditional but personal regard for his mother over that of his wife. In this way, the couple lived in the old pattern of the often-hateful mother-in-law claiming her son and domineering the hapless wife.

The pain that this couple had inherited from all these elements crippled their initial love and enthusiasm, which each had experienced as a benefit of having initially escaped from China and the legacy of what its ancient culture and the relationship to their parents meant to them. The unmourned losses, of opportunity abroad, of loving and caring parents, of the legacy of family trauma, had all come between them following the catalytic episode of the abortion. Until now, they had been unable to mourn and to recover.

The sessions with us offered an opportunity to begin their healing, as both individually and as a couple, they had grasped eagerly what we offered. They would need more time in therapy to take full advantage of what they began with us, but they seemed to have an innate resilience that would enable them to do so.

Chapter 9

Sex and Sexuality in China

The standard story goes that in the Maoist era, sex was only for procreation and was generally severely repressed. The overall result of this anti-sexual policy was to tie sex to marriage and to disconnect it from pleasure. However, Jeffreys and Yu (2015) have argued persuasively that repression is only part of the story and is even a distortion of official policy. The People's Republic of China's (PRC's) first Marriage Law on May 1, 1950, outlawed the traditional 'feudal marriage system' including bigamy, polygamy and arranged and mercenary marriage, and authorized free-choice, monogamous marriage based on sexual equality. Young people were no longer to be bound to marriages arranged against their interests. The PRC also worked to end prostitution and venereal disease. It preached a new equality for women and the importance of sexual hygiene, promoting a policy that appropriate sex was to be adult, monogamous and practiced in heterosexual marriages. It was not so much that discussing sex was taboo as that such discourse had to be couched in appropriate ways (Jeffreys and Yu 2015, p 4–5).

During the Cultural Revolution, there were claims of an unrelenting repression of sex, but actually, many young people were either sent to the countryside without parental supervision, or were roaming the country in mixed gender gangs, cohabiting and having sex. There were new, unfettered opportunities for love and sex, as documented only after the Cultural Revolution. Sent-down youth circulated handwritten copies of pornographic stories and earlier novels featuring romance and sex (Honig, 2003: p. 161, quoted in Jeffreys and Yu, 2015; Link, 2000: p. 243, quoted in Jeffreys and Yu, 2015). At the same time, many Red Guard factions bullied their peers for being immoral and choosing 'love' over 'revolution' and even destroyed potential careers for having premarital sex, especially if these resulted in pregnancy (Honig, 2003: 151–153 quoted in Jeffreys and Yu, 2015). Jeffreys and Yu's conclusion is that the relationship of sex and sexuality in this period was complex, and as much related to power as it was to the imposition of cultural dictates about sex and relationships.

Since the opening up of the 1980s, several factors changed this picture radically, resulting in a sexual revolution that came far more quickly in China than it had in the West (Zhang, 2011). In the mid-1970s, an anonymous, hand-copied novel had circulated widely by hand. *The Heart of a Young Girl,* said to be drawn from the experiences of an imprisoned girl, described the sexual use of a young girl by two men. Officially disapproved, its purported message was to describe the depravity of sex while actually providing an opposing message. In 2003, *The Left-Behind Love Letters* by journalist Muzi Mei, drawn from a blog describing her sexual life, circulated on the internet, followed by many copycat online authors conveying the message of the pleasures for women of sex unfettered by love or dedicated relationships. This time, there was neither censorship nor official disapproval like that given to *The Heart of a Young Girl* of 30 years earlier (Zhang, 2011, Jeffreys and Yu, 2015). It was clear that times had changed radically and that it was no longer possible to control what people thought. Among events contributing to this dramatic change were the emerging independence of thought of a more individualistic, business-driven modern culture. For instance, the practice of *goudiu* – the offering of advantages to businessmen who met in nightclubs with sex workers in attendance, became an open feature of doing business, in some ways returning to the prerevolutionary practice of men who had concubines or other women in addition to their official marriages.

The policy of the Chinese Communist Party (CCP) towards marriages, which had to be approved by the work units beginning in the 1950s, had the effect of equalizing sexual rights between women and men, and for officially sanctioning sex only for propagation. Shortly after the beginning of Opening Up after the Cultural Revolution and with Mao's death in 1976, the One Child Policy was implemented in 1979–1980, with its impact felt forcefully in the early 1980s. We have discussed the unintended consequences for skewed gender ratios, the aging population with insufficient workers and diminished family structure, all from what must be the largest experiment in social engineering in human history. Another of the unintended consequences of the One Child Policy was the decoupling of sex from procreation. This meant that sex progressively came to be seen as offering pleasure for its own sake, and for women as well as men. Furthermore, sex became separated from romance, much as it has been in the West, so that both men and women came to see sex as something capable of offering pleasure outside intimate relationships. Men were now widely encouraged to seek treatment for impotence through advertising. Since procreation was no longer the goal, women also began to see that they had a right to sexual enjoyment. Premarital and extramarital sex became more prominent. Extramarital sex, which had been a factor before the communist era, now reemerged. Some men now began 'having a second pair of breasts,' a practice offering a more satisfying situation than prostitution or one-night stands. Women were also more likely to seek affairs when their marriage was unsatisfactory.

Although the CCP had declared war on prostitution, there developed an industry of sexual tourism for men from Hong Kong and Taiwan. It later emerged that many of the men seeking women for affairs, as mistresses or through prostitution, were mainland men (Jeffreys, 2010, 2009; Zhang, 2011).

In the twenty-first century, things shifted further towards sexualization of popular culture with sexually suggestive images and songs, the appearance of openly romantic couples in public settings and the increasing acceptance of homosexuality, which formerly was shamefully hidden. Homosexuality had been widely accepted in ancient China but was attacked in the nineteenth and twentieth centuries. While not officially encouraged, it was legalized in 1997, and while still a shock to many parents of young gay and lesbian youth, is increasingly accepted, with even the formation of parent groups openly in support of their homosexual children. Overall, acceptance of LGBTQ persons and issues is still in flux (Jeffreys and Yu, 2015). Recently, however, there have been calls for the legalization of same-sex marriage as China prepares for revisions of its civil code (Lau, 2018).

However, perhaps the most dominant trend since the Cultural Revolution has been the emergence of ideas of love and intimacy as an expectation for both men and women, and as a force that is now, in many ways, more powerful than filial piety. Women and men have come to expect both romance and sexual satisfaction. All these factors, the reemergence of 'love,' the One Child Policy, the rise of an individualism that supports the legitimacy of sexual desire and a rising commercialism that decouples sex from reproduction and promotes the role of sex and love by the media and the culture in general have changed the face of romance and sex in the Chinese character (Zhang, 2011; Jeffreys and Yu, 2015).

As a result of these factors, the age of first intercourse has fallen in China. Most Chinese youths wait until adulthood to lose their virginity even though they are considered adults from the age of 18. China's leading scholar of sex, Pan Suiming, reports that university students lag behind their less-educated peers, being one of the more conservative communities in contemporary China. For instance, although in 1995, only about 10% of both college men and women reported having sex, in 2015, 27.5% of college men and 22.6% of college women reported having sex. However, this compares with 60.7% of non-college educated men and 56.3% of non-college women (Pan, 2018).

In general, Pan reports that Chinese youth are increasingly open about sex. Nevertheless, his surveys show that youth are not all that interested, with 12% of men and 27% of women aged 18–29 saying they had not been interested in sex in the previous year, with these numbers having doubled in the previous 15 years.

All in all, this adds up to an impression of a waning of sexual interest and a proliferation of sexual problems. Unlike Pan's research, mine is not a survey of the entire population, but an in-depth survey exclusively of a few couples and families experiencing distress. However, I find that Pan's survey results fit well with my experience.

Finally, we can see a large difference in the number of single men and women resulting from the gender imbalance caused by a combination of the One Child Policy and the traditional and residual preference for males. When Pan Suiming and his colleagues surveyed large samples of men and women, at age 28 approximately 20% of men and 9% of women were single, but by age 34, 10% of men and virtually none of the women were unmarried (Pan, 2018).

According to Pan Suiming, these statistics reveal

just how widespread this phenomenon is, but also show that men are far more likely than women to remain unwed later in life. After the age of 30, there are far more unmarried men than unmarried women. Again, the reasons for this are numerous and varied. But I would like to make special mention of a phenomenon colloquially called 'A-grade women and D-grade men.

(Pan, 2018)

China's unmarried population is dominated by men from the lower rungs of society and women from its upper reaches, which makes it difficult for the two to pair off.

The proliferation of older unmarried youth is not purely the result of individual choice. More often, it is the result of class differences. This is especially true of men on the fringes of society – particularly rural men with low incomes – who often have difficulty finding a long-term partner. Given their social and financial circumstances, it is natural for them to experience periods of involuntary celibacy or infrequent sexual activity.

Young Chinese people have indeed grown more open when it comes to sex. But the real story lies in their emerging anxieties and the ways in which structural imbalances are leaving many young people unable to get married or find a live-in partner.

(Pan, 2018)

We can see therefore that the situation of the sexualization of Chinese youth culture is complicated, and that no single factor, not the unintended consequences of the One Child Policy on liberating women, nor the media-led sexualization of the youth culture can fully explain these complexities.

Sexual health can still be a problem for unmarried Chinese women. Lin Qiqing, a 26-year-old woman living in Shanghai, reported on the difficulty single women have in obtaining a pelvic exam with medical staff afraid to discuss sex or perform sexually related exams, partly out of fear of being accused of disturbing patients' rights to claim they are virgins, even though close to 70% of single Chinese women have had sex, and partly out of the discomfort of older medical staff. The result is significant difficulty in obtaining through medical care (Lin, 2017).

A recent report described the case of an unmarried woman who sued a Chinese hospital for refusing to freeze her eggs. Chinese law denies fertility services to single women. The case was refused by several courts until the lawyers changed the wording of the dispute to 'infringement of the right of personality,' arguing that the policy violated China's law on protecting women under the principle of gender equality because single men are allowed to freeze their sperm. Although she lost the case, the woman managed to raise many supporting voices (Kui and Xie, 2020).

One of Pan Suiming's findings is of particular relevance to the population of married couples I have seen and report on in these pages. It extends beyond simply not having sex to problems that accompany sexual opportunity: In Pan Suiming's survey, almost half the men and two thirds of the women reported feeling performance anxiety in the past 12 months, and of married or cohabiting people, about 10% of men and 14% of women report having sex less than once a month in the previous year. Sex was responsible for anxiety in 48% of men and 64% of women in the sample (Pan, 2018).

Many of the couples we saw reported a diminishing of sex in their marriages. For some, sex had virtually disappeared, although for most of these couples, sex had been either enthusiastic and frequent, or at least satisfactory, during their courtships or early in their marriages. For some, it had diminished gradually, while for others, it seemed to have diminished at the time of a particular development in the marriage, such as the birth of a child, or, as in the couple reported in the previous chapter, at the time of her abortion. My clinical experience has included several couples in which sex and sexual satisfaction diminished or died, a victim of the couple's overall difficulties.

Children in the Parental Bed: 'That is the Chinese Way!'

Family living arrangements can also impinge on couples' opportunities for intimacy. It is common in Chinese families for most preschoolers and half of school-age children to sleep with one or both parents (Huang et al., 2010). While this may not always disrupt parents' sexual life, I have certainly seen cases of its disruptive effect, and I have had the clinical impression frequently that this kind of co-sleeping has been used in the service of making sure there was no opportunity for sex.

During one of our teaching institutes in Beijing, our colleague Christopher Clulow was lecturing on a case from his practice in England, explaining that because the couple he was treating had their two boys in their bed cuddling with the wife, the couple's sexual life had been disrupted.

There was a kind of stir among the students, all of whom are clinicians, so we polled them to see how they felt about the practice of having children in bed. Two women volunteered that their children are, of course, in bed with them! That is the Chinese way! The first woman said that the child would be in bed with her, while husband might be elsewhere, or actually the child might be in bed with the grandparents as well. This woman has two children: One is in bed with them and one with the grandparents. She said, 'Maybe my father-in-law will go looking for a bed elsewhere.' The second woman said that her four-year-old child is in bed with her, of course, and will be until he is about six. That is Chinese way!

We then asked what happens regarding sex for the couple. There was a kind of titter in the audience. Then the first response was that a couple might take a hotel room for the night so that they could have sex. There was general agreement, hotels being the exception, that couples might have sex when their child was deeply asleep, or that they would send the child away to be with the grandparents so that they could have sex.

The group agreed, however, that sex becomes much less important for couples once their child is born, and that is not really a problem. This also led the discussion to agreement that it is really the grandparents' job to raise the children. These clinicians, who are about 70% women, generally do not expect to raise their own children.

There was less agreement about how often this situation might lead to extramarital affairs and general infidelity once sex waned for a couple after they had a child.

An Example of Couple Sexual Difficulty

The couple I now describe illustrates two crucial points I want to make about sexual dysfunction. Couple sexual difficulties are first, problems not of the single individual but of the couple and their relationship. Second, they are always intertwined with the whole structure of the marriage, sometimes caused by other issues like the accrual of fears or anger, the changes in the partnership with the birth of a child, or parental intrusion. Even if sexual difficulty has a physical origin or was present in one partner before the marriage, the result is inevitably expressed throughout the marital pattern. If therapists fail to understand the intimate relationship between sex and the overall marital relationship, treatment will be futile. This holds true both in the West and in China. I have written about this throughout my career, most thoroughly in *The Sexual Relationship* (1982, 1998) and in *Object Relations Couple*

Therapy (Scharff and Scharff, 1991). (Both these books are available in both English and Chinese.) This case also provides an example of using dreams in therapy to better understand the unconscious situation of the couple. The couple's dreams led to conscious issues that had remained unspoken because of the shame involved in voicing them – often the very issues involved in sexual difficulty.

Yolanda Varela and I interviewed this couple, with Jill Scharff as the observer and Gao Jun as translator, once again with an audience of students and faculty.

Chao and Lan

Chao, the husband, and Lan, the wife, both in their early 30s, came to us with distress because Lan no longer felt Chao cared, while he felt overrun by her demands. In the third session, we learned about the decline in their sex life, only voiced after they told us dreams.

In the first two sessions, we heard about the couple's basic complaints. Lan wanted Chao to do more at home and to show more care for their one-year-old daughter. He would retreat into silence, feeling criticized and misunderstood. He forgets to get her gifts for occasions, and if he does, he fears they will not please her, which they often do not. Lan had been raised by her mother's sister's family, because her father was an international businessman, mostly away from China, and required that Lan's mother accompany him. Her parents were nevertheless demanding. Now she feels that nothing she does is good enough to please her parents.

Chao lived in a stable family, but his parents quarreled. He grew up wanting his family to be different. His parents were not demanding of him, perhaps because he never had difficulty performing at the top of his class. His feeling was that he was free to do his work and nothing else mattered.

The couple met in science class in middle school, where, in the beginning, she was the better student, but by high school, he was winning major awards and now has a PhD, while she has given up work to be with their child, with his approval.

They did not date in school but met again later and dated for a long time before marriage. Then things got worse with the birth of their daughter, when Lan felt urgently that Chao should do more to help. We could see that her fear of being uncared for, a fear that stemmed from her childhood experience, was exacerbated when her daughter was born. She had the fantasy that she would get approval from her parents at last for having a wonderful husband and a new baby, but Lan's father, who was once again overseas, kept her mother from coming to see Lan and the new baby. When they did return, Lan's mother criticized her relentlessly.

Now between Lan and Chao, it is often 'her way or the high-way' in her effort to compensate for the feeling that he is miss-ing from their shared life. Although she knows he is basically a good husband, she cannot back off because she feels so let down that he does not seem to care for her or the baby. Chao feels that he cares deeply, but when she demands more and criti-cizes him, Chao retreats silently. We said that this is a replay through projection of Lan's feeling that she can never meet her parents' expectations, projected into Chao who says he will do things but never does.

Both of them feel that what he does is never good enough, but, unlike Lan's father, he does keep trying. They give the example of preparing for an appointment together. When Lan put Chao's wal-let in her bag to get ready for the next day, he insisted on going out to his car where he usually keeps his wallet to look for it, which infuriated her.

I said,

> Chao, I think you do want to take care of Lan (Chao nods) but you are afraid she will take you over (Chao nods again), so you have to hold things out. You went outside to find the lost items in your car because that is where you wanted them to be, outside the home and outside her grasp. Lan, you want to take these important things of his inside you, to secure the feeling of safety that you want him to offer you. But then he feels he has lost parts of himself because they are inside you. You, Lan, are afraid of losing him, and you, Chao, are afraid she will swallow you up.

Yolanda said,

> Lan, part of you is scared that if you stop trying to control him, some-thing awful will happen and you won't be loved. Chao isn't worried about having to do well in order to be loved. He feels loved anyway. But you worry if you don't do things well, if you don't keep the wallet safe from Chao's forgetting and losing things, you'll lose his love.

Lan now connected her pattern with the repeated disappointment with her parents. She said,

> When I got pregnant, my mother was going to come to China and take care of me, but my father objected. When they finally came, he paid no attention to me and she criticized me for things like my cooking.

In the first two sessions, we had formed a good understanding of the shared fears and of ways both partners defended themselves against these fears. This set the stage for developments in the next two sessions that gave us a new depth of understanding, and gave us specifically a view of how this caused problems in and interacted with their sexual difficulty.

Lan began the third session by saying that what we said the previous day had touched her deeply: 'I realized that I want to know him again because I now see many of his true feelings that he never told me before. I feel the biggest problem we had were not the differences, but the lack of communication.'

Chao said,

I thought it was after our daughter was born that problems started, but now I think it had more to do with the return of Lan's parents to China at the same time. That's when her mood became unstable. When we got married, we talked a lot, but now she can't accept any criticism, so if I say anything like that, she reacts in a volatile way.

Yolanda said,

Chao, you try many ways to get it right with Lan, but you end up feeling you can't, and then you feel like the unwanted part of Lan who struggled to meet her parents' expectations. Lan, there's nothing he can do to please you, but he keeps trying – unlike your father.

A little while later in the interview, we asked if either remembered any dreams.

Chao said, 'Usually I dream of something that had happened in the daytime. For instance, in my undergraduate days, I would dream that tomorrow will be the day of the National College Entrance Examination.' With some prompting, he continued, 'In the dream there were many questions I couldn't answer, but then I would tell myself, but, you're already in college. So what if you forget how to do stuff at high school level?'

Lan then volunteered, 'I've had a repetitive dream for the last year. I dream that I ask Chao to do something and he fails to meet my request.'

I noted that Chao could always do the science in school, so he should have been okay for the test.

Chao corrected me. 'It's not science that I can't do. It's Chinese literature, which I was never good at.'

Yolanda said, 'The dreams go together. Chao, with your dream, you're telling Lan that although you didn't fail, first you doubted yourself.'

I added, 'The task in the dream is like everything on the lists that Lan gives you to do, but then she says you're going to fail.'

Yolanda said, 'I think there's something else you want him to do that you're not able to ask for.'

Lan, laughing, 'Yes. That could be. This is embarrassing to say.'

I said, 'This is your chance. We hear a lot of embarrassing things.'

Lan said, 'It is related to sex.'

I said, 'I was wondering about that.'

Lan, suddenly with more energy, said,

> We have different romantic histories. He never had sex with his girl-friends. I was his first woman. He was a good boy, never looking at porn movies or books, but I had boyfriends before. I could accept that difference in experience, but in my heart, I expected the quality of our sex would improve. Since I had more experience, I felt it my responsibility to talk to him about it, but I couldn't.

I said, 'Chao, she had expectations you didn't know how to meet. Did you know what she wanted?'

Chao said, 'I don't know.'

Lan said, 'Well, I do know. There's a big gap between what I want and what I get. If it wasn't so big, I could communicate better. I once suggested maybe he could see some porn.'

I asked, 'What is it you want that you don't get? Is it that he doesn't know how to make love, be tender or engage in foreplay?'

Lan said,

> He's not good at it. He's not that interested, but that actually makes me feel safe. If I had a man who was more interested, I'd have another set of worries. I don't have high expectations there. All I want is average performance from a husband.

I asked, 'Do you mean, if he was good at it, you'd be afraid he'd have lots of women?'

Lan agreed, 'Yes. I'd worry that in the future, there'd be problems. I'd be getting old, he'd still have desire, and there would be many temptations out there.'

I said, 'So then he'd find another woman?'

Lan said, 'I'd worry about that. So, I chose Chao as a man who's not that interested in sex.'

I said, 'So, you picked Chao because he's safe and that way you avoided that problem. But now you have the other problem: that he doesn't give you enough and doesn't want enough sexually.'

Lan again agreed, 'Right!'

I asked Chao, 'So how do you feel about this?'

Chao said,

It's not that I didn't have interest in sex when we first married. But once our daughter came and the criticisms began, I lost interest. I'd start to be interested, and the criticisms would begin and interrupt my interest. Like, I'd propose sex and then assess her response.

Lan interjected, 'The reason I'd interrupt his interest is that I had no interest because it wasn't good enough.'

I asked, 'He did it all wrong?'

Lan said, 'It just wasn't what I wanted. I wanted something not so boring.'

Chao said, 'I realized I wasn't good enough, so she lost interest. And I thought, 'Well that's that!''

Yolanda said, 'So you stopped trying?'

I said,

So here's the same pattern we've been talking about. Lan, you have high standards that you feel Chao has to meet. When you feel he's not good enough, and Chao, when you feel you don't measure up, you both call the whole thing off.

Lan disagreed. 'For sex, I don't have high standards. But the gap is still there.'

I said, 'It seems to me that you want to learn to enjoy sex together, but the atmosphere of criticism kills it for both of you.'

Lan said, 'I'm not as interested as I was before. For sex, I have even less hope. Yes, I've given up.'

I said, 'The trouble is that without sex, it's hard to make your marriage work. So, I'm glad we still have time to think about this and how it relates to other things that follow the same pattern.'

In this session, asking about dreams led to a succinct summary of the couple's overall difficulty, and that led Lan directly to talking about their sexual problem. Their problem is typical of the complexity of sexual difficulty. Sex represents a couple's overall difficulty, and then the sexual difficulty itself acts to further erode the couple's overall relationship.

In this case, Lan picked Chao at least partly because he was *not* highly sexually expressive or interested in order to save herself from the fear that, if he were, she would be in danger of an abandonment in the sexual arena, which would echo her abandonment by her parents, and especially by her father. The trouble in couples like this is that when the man is not good at satisfying the wife's sexual needs, she comes to feel abandoned anyway. Just what she fears boomerangs back onto her. Lan had hoped she would be able to teach him and thereby help him become more sexually competent, an area in which he felt in need of remediation, much like his dream feeling of incompetence in Chinese literature and unlike his competence in science. So, having made the original pairing of shared intellectual interests but with differences in sexual competence and confidence, their potentials for disappointing her and for him to feel overwhelmed and criticized came to the fore. While they managed pretty well early in their marriage, the birth of their daughter, Lan's identification with the baby as needy and vulnerable, and her mother's returning to criticize her added up to make these unconscious matters problematic. Then the vulnerability of their sexual relationship made that the stage of their shared conflict.

The work in this session set the stage for further work the next day, during our fourth session.

Chao said,

We both had more dreams. I had two short ones. In my first one, I returned to my parents' house and was playing mahjong with my grandparents. Lan didn't come with me. In my second dream, we were sleeping. In the dream, we woke up and found we'd been sleeping in a classroom. I put a quilt around myself and tried to find a place to dress. I looked for a washroom to dress in, and there were two people working on exam papers, doing advanced science. I told them how to solve the homework. Then I went back to the classroom. The course hadn't started yet, but the classroom was crowded. I tried to find Lan, but I couldn't. Now Lan can tell her dream.

I said, 'No, let's see what comes in connection to your mahjong dream first.'

Chao said, 'I was very happy with my parents and grandparents, but it was short, so not much comes to mind about it.'

I asked, 'Did you play mahjong with them?'

Chao said, 'Before I married, my ex-girlfriend and I played mahjong with them. It was very relaxed, but that was several years ago.'

I asked Lan, 'Does anything come to your mind about his dream?'

Lan said, 'I was concerned why he dreamed of going home without me. I felt that he may feel being with me causes too much pressure.'

Chao added, 'We also discussed the second dream that was easy to explain, because yesterday we discussed something very private when we discussed sex here in the session.'

Lan said, 'When he first told me about the dream, he said there were many people looking at us in the dream. So that fits.'

I said, 'In the dream, you went to the washroom to get dressed, as if you had felt undressed and exposed here yesterday. But then you were solving the science problem for two people?'

Lan, laughing, said, 'He connects everything to science.'

Yolanda said, 'How so?'

Lan said, 'He uses science to express his ideas.'

Chao nodded yes.

I said, 'Your life is more complicated than a scientific problem.'

Chao said, 'Yes, it is.'

I now asked Lan about her dream.

Lan said, 'It isn't connected at all, and it's not as clear as his. There were two or three groups playing at a mahjong tournament. I thought I wasn't participating. I was more of an observer than a player. There was one group of four, who were all Japanese. Then it changed to a performance contest and one by one, they all had to show their talents. Then it was our turn. The woman beside me was ordered to play the piano. She played wonderfully, a symphony piece, very grand. I thought suddenly that I could never compete with her. Then the dream ended.

'What came to me is that we are going to Xi'an to compete in a national mahjong contest. About the Japanese, I thought of the China-Japan fight over the Diaoyutai Islands. The face of the pianist was the face of a girl I interviewed a couple of days ago to be a nanny for our child. But I didn't figure out what the dream meant.'

Yolanda asked, 'Did this nanny make any impression on you?'

Lan said, 'We thought she isn't the right one, too young and inexperienced.'

I asked, 'Was she attractive?'

Lan said, 'No. Just average. She had a ponytail and big eyes.'

I said, 'Tell me about the island incident with the Japanese.'

Lan said, 'I'm not very familiar with political affairs. Japan isn't friendly to China. They want to occupy the islands, to take over something that belongs to China.'

I asked, 'Chao, do you have any thoughts about Lan's dream?'

Chao said, 'Well (hesitating). In her dream, there's a competition and someone else is better. She compared herself with others. That's who she is in daily life.'

Yolanda said,

> Both of you had dreams about mahjong. Chao, in your dreams, you play at it and work without pressure. You do what you excel at. You, Lan, want to play, but someone else can do it better. This, coming in a dream, says maybe you realize you do it to yourself, rather than feeling it is outside you. You, Chao, don't put that kind of pressure on yourself, while you, Lan, put the pressure on both of you all the time. Your dreams picked the same image and then they showed that you had very different attitudes about the challenge in playing. What do you think of that?

Lan said,

> That's our normal pattern. Every day at home, he's happy as long as I'm happy and don't force him to do something. But in the past six months, his state makes me unhappy because I have so much to do. After dinner, he's finished but I have more to do.

Yolanda asked, 'Why do you push yourself so hard instead of asking him to push himself hard, too?'

Lan said,

> I put demands on him because my parents put demands on me. Our child is one now and ever since she was born, I've felt so hurt. I understand why Chao has problems, but I can't deal with my anger at my parents and feeling hurt by my husband. I can't get out of it, and every small thing reminds me of the hurt. I've been in therapy for two months, and nothing's changed.

I said,

> You'll need much more time. It can't happen this fast. I'm glad you're in therapy. That's the first step, and there's no shortcut. Like Yolanda, I think these three dreams go together to help us understand how the two of you work together. After the stress and exposure of yesterday's interview, you, Chao, had dreamed of relaxing with your grandparents. Your associations to the dream connected that state to the relationship with your easygoing ex-girlfriend as a way out. Then your second dream showed us that you felt stripped bare and exposed here. Lan,

your dream is a contest where figures are taking over your territory. Four foreigners fighting over disputed territory, which might refer to the four of us, indicating Yolanda, Jill, Gao Jun and myself, and then this other woman who is connected to someone you were considering for taking care of your child. She plays so beautifully that you can't compete with her.

Lan said, 'Her performance was better than the four Japanese.'
I asked, 'So who might that be?'
Lan said, 'I couldn't figure that out.'
I said, 'She's some woman who does things much better than you. Someone you considered as a substitute mother for your child. If she could fulfill a task, she would be better at everything.'
Lan shakes her head, not knowing.
I said, 'It's not who she is in real life, it's who she is inside you.'
Lan said,

Okay, I see. She's more like who I'd like to be. If I could be like her, I'd be wonderful. I learned piano for seven years because my mother wanted me to, but I didn't enjoy it and I was only average. If I tried hard, I could excel even now, but I don't want to because it would be for her.

I said, 'This dream woman is the woman you wish you were, but you can't get there. If you could, you would win the contest. Who is it that you are always in a contest with?'
Lan said, 'With everyone. I'm against everyone. I'm envious all the time.'
Chao said, 'She doesn't think I'm better than her.'
I said, 'I think she does.' I asked Lan, 'Do you?'
Lan said, 'He has a good temper and he's patient.'
I added, 'Science?'
Lan laughed, 'Yes, he's better.'
I said, 'His family?'
Lan said, 'Yes, I'm very envious of his family. I'm envious of the unconditional love they offer him.'
I asked, 'Do you think you're envious of the unconditional love that *he* offers *you*? He loves you even though you make his life difficult. He's steady as a rock. Do you wish you were like that?'
Lan said, 'I'm trying to be like that, but I'm not good at it like he is. I find fault with him. And yet I hope he'll encourage me.'
Later in this session, we turned to discussing reasons for Chao's silent withdrawal.

Lan said, 'I told him I thought he didn't tell me the things he's saying here because if he revealed his true feelings, he'd feel unsafe because I would criticize them.'

Chao said,

I thought, 'Why is it difficult to speak?' I hoped to say it here. This is not the best way to do it, but at least we have this platform to say something hard. My parents quarreled and that had a big impact on me. My mother would shout at my father for being out late at night. I hated their quarreling. When I was young, I thought, 'I will never have this kind of quarreling.' So, my goal is to avoid quarreling. She thinks I should express my thoughts, but if I do, that increases the risk of quarreling, so when I disagree, I keep quiet. I want to change this, but she's very domineering. It's difficult to change.

Lan said, 'The quarreling isn't frightening to me. Communication is more important. We had a nice time at dinner talking. We should try, and I should control myself and let you speak. I wish you could stop the pattern of starting to speak and then withdrawing.'

I said, 'Chao, you're so frightened of quarreling that you don't say things that need to be said. What do you think your parents were quarreling about? Where was your father late at night?'

Chao said,

There were two themes to their quarrels. One, when I was young, we lived with my father's parents and my father's grandfather. My mother had to take care of three elderly people all alone, and she was exhausted. Two, the financial dealings. My mother worried about 'saving for our son.' She hoped my father could earn more than he did in the state-owned enterprise where he had to obey the rules.

Lan said, 'His mother thought his father was too timid and should have made more from the business, like taking gifts and bribes, which he wouldn't do.'

Chao said, 'In China, that's the usual way, but my father has standards.'

Yolanda said, 'You said your mother was wrong, but now you see she was right?'

Lan said,

His parents have an interesting relationship. His mother was not highly educated, and therefore wasn't persuaded by reason. He and his father decide what to tell his mother and what not to tell her. I think his father is his model for whether to speak to me or not. I understand why his father treated his wife that way, but it's not how he should treat me. He shouldn't follow his father's way and treat me like I'm inferior, because I'm not.

Chao said, 'I agree that my thinking and behavior styles are influenced by my parents.'

I asked, 'Do you think your wife doesn't need to know everything?'

Chao said, 'It's not that I think I should hide ideas from her. But my mother would explode at an event. Lan explodes at ideas.'

Lan said, 'It's not fair to treat me like that. It's a death sentence to our marriage.'

I said,

> Now that you've been able to talk about it openly here, you can begin to decide if you want to conduct your marriage this way or not. Lan wants you to say more, and that's fair. And you, Chao, want Lan, not to explode at every thought, and that's fair.

This session again used dreams to spell out the ramifications of issues that we had learned in the session before that were related to the impasse in their sexual relationship. So even though sex was not directly in today's discussion, the issues that got more focus in this session were critical to the sexual problem as well. That point was borne out in the final session.

Chao said,

> We had a conversation last night, and I want to tell you more. I asked myself, 'When did I start to keep silent?' It was about a year before our marriage, when we first got intimate after dating for four years. We had several quarrels because both of us are stubborn about our ideas and opinions. We had a big fight that didn't end well. For a whole week, we were not in touch. I felt so tired, I couldn't do anything. For two or three days I wondered if I should break up with her? Or could I accept her as she was? I decided, 'I love her! So I just have to change my way and avoid fighting.' But this pattern has continued until now. It's definitely affected our sexual life. When I feel wary of her or angry at her, I withdraw. I think that's why I don't feel very intimate or want sex.

Lan said,

> After the last session, I realized his deciding not to share his ideas was in order to avoid conflict. I didn't know that before. He had many opinions, but he pretty much gave them up by staying with me. He thinks he's

been doing a lot to make our relationship work, and I didn't know that. Maybe he thought I knew of his sacrifice for my sake. For me though, I felt he'd done nothing and that's why I was angry. But he thought he was doing all he could and was at his limit. That's what we've gotten from this discussion. So now he's talking. He was surprised I knew nothing of his thoughts. Now he knows I didn't know. That's why I kept complaining. What he is afraid of is just what I fear, too. We are both afraid that if he says his opinion, and if I can't contain my reaction, he'll withdraw and lose motivation to speak up. The pull to withdraw is very strong and probably very difficult to change. Just like my impulse to criticize him.

I said, 'Lan, you're afraid he will withdraw after these sessions are over and you, Chao, are afraid she will go back to shouting.'

Chao said, 'That's not really right. In these sessions, I've said things I never said before. Now I have confidence we can work it out.'

I asked, 'Is there anything you want to say to us about the experience of being here?'

Lan said, 'I'm appreciative, even though I'm mad he kept a secret for five years. I feel crazy from that. If we hadn't had these sessions, he might have kept silent his whole life.'

I said, 'I understand you can be angry that he kept it from you all these years but also feel relieved that he told you now.'

Lan nods. 'I'm not that angry. I'm more surprised and relieved. He finally admitted that I knew nothing of what he thought.'

Chao said, 'I've already said what I wanted to say to you. It helped me individually. Because of these five days, I can think in a new way. I hope I can get more help from therapy.'

Lan laughed, 'He admires you, David, because of the dream analysis. He said it was very scientific.'

In these sessions, we came to see how the decline in the couple's sexual life was inextricably tied to the anger and fear in their overall marriage.

We would have expected that therapy that focused on the troubles in their overall pattern could, therefore, be enough to restore their sexual function as well – if their sexual pattern had been satisfying to them earlier. However, Chao indicated that there was trouble in the relationship that seemed to stem from the first days of their sexual intimacy, and they also agreed that their sexual relationship had never been particularly good. We could see that sex itself had been a dangerous area for the couple because it threatened to bring them emotionally and unconsciously into the zone of becoming like the painful models of their parents. It would take more time to learn about that, and in this brief encounter, we did not have the time to learn more. If they turned out to need some direct focus on sex in the way of behavioral sex therapy, that could be folded into an overall plan for the couple's therapy at a later date.

Conclusion

The point I wish to make through this example is that sexual difficulty in marriage is hardly ever simple. This couple illustrates how their sexual impasse was constructed from developmental factors for each of them as individuals, from the current interactions with their extended families, from heightened expectations and fear of sex, from family developmental factors that included the beginning of sexual encounters, and later the birth of their child, and from a culture in which discussing sex and emotion are not easy. It is attention to the complexity of these factors that allows us to offer the understanding the couple requires and that offers the best opportunity for their growth and repair.

Chapter 10

Extramarital Affairs, Sexual and Emotional

The revelation of an extramarital affair is often the trigger that compels couples to ask for therapy. In the popular view, it is the men who more often seek emotional and sexual relationships outside marriage, but this begs the question of who the women are that the men are finding, and it ignores the fact that women too often feel dissatisfied in their marriages for the same variety of reasons that men do.

I co-authored the report of a case of a woman's affair several years ago, a patient who had sought treatment in the clinic of Dr. Shi Qijia (Shi and D. Scharff, 2011).

Mrs. A and Mr. B

Both members of this couple, who we will call Mrs. A and Mr. B, seen many years ago, were born before the establishment of the One Child Policy. Mrs. A was a 33-year-old nurse who had been experiencing anxiety, lack of attentiveness, insomnia and diminished functioning at work for about a year. After a heart procedure, the details of which were not clear, she began an extramarital affair with her 40-year-old boss. They had worked closely together. Her boss initiated sex while they were on a business trip. Though Mrs. A had no orgasm, she enjoyed the sexual experience. Afterwards, she felt so guilty that she immediately took her whole family on a trip. When her boss paid ever more attention, promising to elope with her and start a new life, she abandoned herself recklessly to the relationship. Mrs. A recalled, 'I even ignored my seven-year-old son. Though I felt guilty, I lost interest in caring for him.' Soon, however, the boss began to criticize her. When she complained to her company and to his family, the boss became hateful. In therapy, Mrs. A wanted to understand why he broke his promises and treated her badly. She said, 'Despite all these problems, if he were good to me again, I would give up everything for him. I was like a slave to him and I'm still willing to do anything he asks.'

Mrs. A grew up with her poor parents who favored her younger sister. Her father was violent, often blaming and beating her. Mrs. A remembered that once when she got a poor grade at school, she went home and cooked a meal. Nevertheless, her father gave her sister rice and she was only given watery congee. During her childhood, she got up early to carry out most of the household duties. Now, besides her nursing job, she also worked as a super-market cashier and as a waitress. Deciding to impress her family by earning money, she bought them a house and found her sister a job, supported her parents and let them live with her. She was so competent at work that soon she became a head nurse, earning more than her husband. She claimed she was the boss at home, proud that she could take care of her parents and sister.

When Mrs. A had met her husband, she did not think he was the one. However, after three years, he was still waiting for her. So, they got mar-ried, even though she knew he was not the right man because he had a low-level job and no sense of competence. But he had neither bad habits nor any obvious shortcomings. They married and their son was born a year later. Following the birth of their son, the couple only made love about once a year. Sometimes Mrs. A wondered whether her sexual desire was too strong. Once, learning that a co-worker had an abortion, she felt jealous because her co-worker must have had more sex. She also had heart surgery for an undefined ailment some years ago, a turn-ing point in her desire to get more out of life.

Mrs. A's disappointment towards her husband increased over time because she found that he had no motivation and no pros-pects in his menial, deteriorating job situation. More importantly, he showed little interest in sex and had difficulty with erections, making her wonder if her own sexual desire was excessive. At the beginning of her extramarital affair, she felt guilty and made many attempts to improve marital sex life. Failing in that, she recklessly threw herself into the affair, where sex made her feel real and no longer the lonely, independent woman who had to control every-thing. She felt that her son was now afraid she would abandon him, so he, too, placated her and acted humbly.

When the therapist saw the couple together, he was able to con-firm that the husband was passive and lacked ambition, and the wife was controlling and critical. The picture confirmed Mrs. A's description in which, although she had been a high-performer, she had not thought she would find a partner and so had settled for a man she did not respect. The marriage had never been vibrant or satisfying to either of them. She felt rejected by his passivity and he felt controlled by her demands for more from him, resulting in frequent quarrels.

Mrs. A had adapted to her childhood unhappiness by becoming competent and taking care of her entire family, an adaptation that was agreeable to her less-achieving husband. But she then tired of having to do everything for him and her family, and sought emotional and sexual support, which she found with her boss. The husband, used to being pampered by his mother, wanted only for his wife to take care of him. His sexual and emotional potency faded under the pressure of her personality and her demands of him. The therapist suggested to them that the husband should become more assertive, taking appropriate masculine control of his relationship to his wife, but the couple agreed that he was unlikely to do so, and that if he tried, his wife would defeat his efforts in any event.

The history of this marriage, from Mrs. A's point of view, shows how her early-life disappointments, and the way she compensated by developing her hard-charging personality, were folded into the collapse of marital satisfaction, with the result that she turned to an affair for the satisfaction she felt was badly missing in the marriage.

Mrs. A began, 'When we were dating, I told my father that our relationship was very plain. He said, 'Which is better for you, water or coffee every day? Water is better for health."

The therapist responded, 'It seems your father supported this relationship ...'

Mrs. A continued, 'My parents think he is a dull but good man with no bad habits, such as smoking, drinking and gambling. My parents persuaded me to take him because his temper was always good – at least better than my brother-in-law's. My matchmaker advised that I needed to wait to know him better. I wanted to separate from him, but my husband said gold would shine ultimately and he hoped that I would give him a chance. Now I think I actually was clear then. When I got married, I already had my own savings. He had almost nothing in his bank account and was already over 30. People say that one should be established at the age of 30, yet he had nothing. He is the youngest son and lived with his mother who patted his butt or touched his head! Maybe she still hugs him when I'm not there. I'm the eldest child and am seldom intimate with my parents. My family thinks I should bear the family burden. I want to express my love, but if I expressed it directly, my father would worry that I had changed.

'Since childhood, my father has blamed me, not my sister. My sister is not healthy. I am the eldest, and I have to take care of her. My relationship with my mother is better than that between my sister and her. My father cried at my sister's marriage, but not mine. I am independent. My parents don't worry about me.

'My father was a worker and is arrogant. Our relationship is bad. I told my mother that I hated him because he was mean to me. I can't forget when he gave my sister rice and gave me congee as a punishment. At that moment, I swore that I must be more useful than my sister and let my parents depend on me and not on her. I have hatred in my heart that I don't express. Others see me as a filial daughter. When I started to earn a little money at work, I bought my family expensive items and luxuries. My grandma suggested I save money for myself. I replied that my only thought was to improve my parents' living. I enjoy this responsibility and that my father makes requests. When he said he wanted a leather belt or pair of trousers, I told him to follow me to the shopping mall. I can afford whatever he chooses. I feel satisfied when he gets what he wants. When I got married, I wrote in my diary that I wanted to marry someone who was like a younger brother so I could control him and continue to arrange my life. When we married, I thought at least I was in command and could make him listen to me. Now, when I feel contemptuous, I treat him even better so as to make him feel guilty towards me. I will not hurt him or withdraw my support.'

Mrs. A makes it clear that she chose her husband in the mold of the relationship with her family, a man she could care for and who therefore would have no right to challenge her authority. She has contempt for her family and for her husband, but she has grown up devoted to taking her own satisfaction through satisfying their every whim. With her husband, however, the pattern has worn thin.

The therapist said,

Your relationship with your father is a foundation for your relationship with men. When you were young, your father was rigid and critical of you. Now you try your best in everything in order to earn their respect, and, actually, you succeed.

Mrs. A differed, 'I looked down on my father all the time, and after I know a man well, I start to look down on him in my heart, too.'

The therapist asked about the extent of her contempt for men. 'Do you look down on all men after you get to know them?'

Mrs. A said, 'Once a relationship is established, they need to listen to me. I'm stronger than they are in the end.'

The therapist suggested, 'So with your husband, you wanted to find a younger brother you could control?'

Mrs. A said, 'I had many suitors, but no time to think about love affairs, as I had five or six jobs at a time. Men pursued me, but when I looked up, he was the only one still there.'

The therapist asked again, 'You devalue him, like you do with your father. Do you do the same to every man?'

Mrs. A admitted, 'I have adored some men before.'

The therapist inquired, 'Are there men whose control you accept?'

Mrs. A explained further,

I really want to be controlled. After I had heart surgery, I felt tired and thought that if I died now, this man still would never have known how to look after me. I want someone who can take care of me, someone to rely on. After that incident, I preferred someone to do things for me. Someone told me that women do not need to think at all and should let men do the worrying. 'Just wait to be served.' I thought that was right.

In extramarital affairs that are realized sexually, the psychosomatic sexual bond becomes a vehicle for the expression and satisfaction of emotional issues that have not been satisfied in the marriage. In this view, the affair is a symptom of marital dissatisfaction and expresses hope for something more fundamentally nurturing, not simply for sexual freedom.

From the clinical segment above, we can see that Mrs. A has an internal psychic organization of a domineering self and a subservient other. In her marriage, the subservient other is her husband. However, such internal psychic organizations are reversible, which is to say that, as she tells us, she longs to be in a situation with a dominant man who loves her and to whom she can be subservient. This was the situation with her boss, even when he became contemptuous and cruel, just as she ordinarily is to her husband. Underneath her dominant and castrating relationship to her husband is a meek, solicitous little girl longing to be loved and dominated at any cost.

Mrs. A said,

The house my family lived in was small, only one bedroom and a living room. Sometimes when I went to the toilet in the night, I saw my parents making love and felt embarrassed. I only realized what they were doing when I was older.

The therapist asked, 'Did you talk to your mother about your sex life?'

Mrs. A replied,

My mother also felt sad about my marriage. She saw that we seldom talked to each other and had no romance. When I told her about our sex life, she was shocked. She was surprised it had been five years. She understands that because he looks like a good man, it is difficult for me to give him up. I am worried that even if I met a new man and we loved each other, could I tolerate it if I couldn't control him? I have never met a man who can control me, even though I long for a man who is stronger than me and could control me.

The therapist asked, 'If you both were able to cooperate to improve your sex life, would you feel better?'

Mrs. A said,

I think so. I felt all right that we had sex only a few times a year. A few times are better than none. But now my desires have become stronger. I have talked to him many times! I told him to watch pornographic movies or take some medicine. I tried everything to let him get into my body, but in the middle, he says he's tired! I wait patiently for him to penetrate. Then he gives up. He believes he is impotent. When he can't satisfy me, I want sex desperately. In my dreams, I beg others for sex. I dreamt that I kneeled and begged my boss to do it with me.

The therapist drew the connection between his patient's inheritance of a hateful, contemptuous attitude towards men and her need to be in control, which was a conscious reaction formation that covered over her resentment towards her father and her family. Satisfying others sets up a projective identification of her inner desire to be satisfied, the other side of her unsatisfied rejecting object. She found a husband who is like a younger brother, but eventually the unsatisfied repressed object relationship returned as a vicarious way of gaining control. When this unconscious defense failed, it left her once again feeling unloved, bitter and sexually rejected. The extramarital affair brought a union with a man with elevated social standing, money and authority who cared for her. As an exciting and idealizable object of her longing, he satisfied her needs and compensated for the rejection from her father and husband. He provided sexual satisfaction, even without orgasm. This Oedipal triumph was an opportunity to take revenge on her internal rejecting father.

In the couple therapy with Mr. B, Mrs. A claimed the therapist for herself, reenacting the pull towards an ideal man who could offer a kind of relationship her husband could not. Sharing the secret of the affair with the therapist and not the husband was a way to draw the therapist into an Oedipal quest to enlist his help to find a man to love her. Thus, the therapist became a new exciting and idealized object who she felt could understand her disappointments.

The Couple Unconscious and the Social Unconscious

Although we know more about Mrs. A than about her husband, the therapist learned enough to see that there was an initial unconscious fit between them in which, through the action of mutual projective and introjective identification – that is, mutual unconscious communication – each partner could, in the beginning, find missing and longed-for parts of themselves. Mrs. A found the pampering and care she longed for in the inner world of her husband, while Mr. B found the aggression and the dominance he dared not show actively through the assertiveness of his wife. Each supported these aspects of the other because they identified with them unconsciously. Through projective identification, Mr. B's aggression supported the rejecting object organization of his wife, while Mrs. A vicariously found an exciting object in the perpetual care she gave to her parents and husband. Ultimately these unconscious mechanisms failed to satisfy, becoming frustrating and returning each partner to the feeling of deprivation and suffering they had sought to escape. On behalf of herself and the couple, Mrs. A sought to regain an exciting and satisfying relationship through her sexual affair, supported by Mr. B's obliviousness because unconsciously, he hoped another man could supply what he dared not. Ultimately, this also failed.

We can also see wider cultural issues expressed in this couple's dynamic. The couple's story and their relationship to their Chinese therapist illustrate how social unconscious issues are internalized as a force in their conflict. China's changed opportunity for women presents Mrs. A with a chance to make up for her family's and her own deprivation. Her outward traditionally compliant demeanor is a reaction formation masking her wish to exert control and dominance, a revenge for the deprivation imposed by old cultural values. Mr. B, the pampered favorite of his mother, had developed a character structure of passivity and demand for care. Together, the couple relationship is a tragedy of intersecting cultural values. All this was delivered into the transference relationship with the therapist who, in his countertransference, identified with the cultural imperative for male authority. In an enactment, he tried to reassert male authority on behalf of the repressed life of the couple and of the culture, suggesting that the husband should take more assertive control, but the forces of change in the couple and in the culture defeated this enactment, as the spouses agreed that such a reassertion of the old values would be personally futile.

Affairs in China, as in the United States, are one of the most frequent reasons that couples seek therapy. While affairs used to be understood as largely conducted by men, clearly women were always involved, and now it seems likely that as things move to more equality generally, women will continue to have affairs more often than in previous years. Nevertheless, women's discovery of their husband's infidelity remains a frequent cause for legal action and divorce. Jeffreys has reported on the rise of private Chinese detective agencies for catching the errant lovers, establishing a small but well-publicized industry that has found a niche for investigating marital misbehavior in an area where the police cannot be bothered (Jeffreys, 2010).

Affairs occur with infinite variety, so we could never offer enough examples to cover all possible reasons they occur, nor to illustrate the variety of possibilities for repair. (For a more through discussion of the root causes of affairs, see D. Scharff, 1982; Scharff and Scharff, 1991.) The couples who do seek help run the gamut of those in whom there is remorse, regret and a shared wish for repair, to those couples for whom the end of the marriage seems inevitable.

An Affair, a Pregnancy and Couple Violence

In a couple who consulted with Jill Scharff and me, the husband said, 'We have long-term difficulty of quarreling over small things. Because of that, I did something that should never happen in a marriage.' The husband, a university professor, had a sexual affair with his young assistant, who became pregnant and had an abortion. In the initial session, he raged at his wife for 'ruining the young woman's reputation.' His wife had confronted him and the young woman for having an affair after finding evidence on his Twitter account, where he professed his love for her. He at first ignored and then refuted his wife's accusations, despite the fact that the girl later became pregnant. In the first session, he then acted as though it all did not matter, because his wife was at fault in any event. He behaved in a way that seemed completely outrageous to us. The wife contended that there had been many affairs. The young woman he had the affair with had later attempted suicide and still had considerable power over the husband, since if she reported him to his department, he might well lose his job.

As we got to know the couple better, it turned out that the wife's temper was frequently outrageously explosive, driving her husband away at just the moments that she was frustrated at his coldness and lack of concern. The couple had an eight-year-old child, and their quarreling had increased when the wife's parents came to live with them to care for the child.

In the interviews that followed, we came to see how the couple's angry relationship was rooted in the family situations in which they had grown up. The husband had a poor relationship with his father, who was absent in his childhood, and both his parents had always been cold to him and his wife. He said of his mother,

> She was a typical old Chinese woman of the countryside. She's traditional and lives with no thought of emotion or love. Survival came first. My mother may not be sensitive as to expressing or receiving love, but that doesn't mean there is no love and caring between us. These were poor economic times. My parents had to work to make money. My mother had to stay in the countryside. There were many families like that. Poverty was everywhere.

With his father absent, the man in his life was his maternal grandfather, who had a fierce temper. In our sessions, he compared his wife's temper to his grandfather's.

The wife's biological father died in the Cultural Revolution, and her paternal grandfather, with whom she lived, died soon after the Cultural Revolution when she was seven or eight. That grandfather had angered easily. She said,

> He wasn't violent, but he was aggressive and would smash dishes. I spent a long time with my grandfather. I never saw him attack a woman. Only one time did I see him throw hot rice on my mother, burning her neck.... My mother's younger brother had a great temper. It's true he hit his wife.

When Jill suggested that while she was well treated, she had seen these men express anger physically, she said,

> Yes, but I never saw it. I only heard it. My grandfather had a bad temper. He was abusive with words when he was angry, like with the rice. Mostly it was about food. He would be angry if the food was salty because he thought his wife or daughter made the same mistake over and over.

We could sense confusion in her story about what was violence and what were just angry words.

The problem in their marriage, and now in the room with us, was the continual replay of her own anger. Each time she felt frustrated at the impasse in their marriage, she would erupt. The confusion we heard in the wife's history about whether there was violence or not in her childhood came to life in the sessions about whether she was violent or not. There was arguing between them, but the physical violence came from her.

We had been discussing her grandfather's verbal abuse, and I said to her, 'Your husband said you verbally abused him.' The husband replied, 'No, I said she was violent and hit me.'

The wife said, 'I did hit him. Once I used the blunt side of a knife to cut his side. Do you think that using the blunt side of the knife is violent?'

When we said that was indeed violence, her husband said,

> Whether the knife is violent is not important. When she is furious, there's a painful impact on me and on the family. She'll be explosive, really violent. Afterwards, she regrets it and doesn't know what she did.

The wife's temper was so bad that her parents, who kowtowed to the husband, had warned her that divorce might follow, and even suggested to him that he should divorce her. The only times he was tender was in attempting to soothe her when she was out of control. The pattern of her fury followed by his solicitous calming had become so engrained in their relationship that it looked as though one factor driving her rage was the tenderness she received only then.

Slowly, we helped the couple to see how the interaction of his cold condescension, which came from his family experience, and her temper, which came from hers, had now led to the growing disaffection in their marriage that preceded and essentially caused the affair. At the end of our time with them, we had begun to make inroads into understanding the complexities of her anger, which had been replayed in the sessions. Slowly, she got the message that when her anger erupted as furiously as it did, it became the story, overtaking the difficulties of his cold withdrawal that caused her to erupt in the first place. When that happened, she could no longer get anything she wanted from her husband, even when he tried to reach out to soothe her. We said that her anger exploded on behalf of the two of them, and while she would need to work to calm her anger, he would need to understand his own buried resentment that had led to his provocations of her, his withdrawal and his search for love outside the marriage. They left the consultation with an agreement to accept referral for couple therapy and a shared wish to reconstruct their marriage.

A Couple Formed on the Principle of Always Needing an Affair

The next example describes a couple in which the husband brought into the marriage an inability to maintain a steady relationship, while the wife brought with her an inability to claim him but also an inability to leave. We were able to establish that each of them had difficult early relationships, characterized by anxious and unstable early attachments leading to considerable disorganization of their personalities. Throughout our interviews with this couple, we had trouble seeing them as being married in an emotional sense. However, they were also unable to face the possibility of divorce. This dual inability – either to be emotionally married or to be emotionally divorced – was a legacy of the shaky and anxious life-starts they had each experienced and had never overcome.

I interviewed Michael and Mei, both in their mid-30s and only children, with Janine Wanlass, while our colleague Yolanda Varela observed and offered commentary. At the time we saw them, they had been separated for eight months and were living apart. Michael had had three affairs. In a denigrating way, he blamed Mei for his need to have affairs. They had a four-year-old child born after they had married while Mei was pregnant. Now Michael neither has steady work, nor does he help in childcare, paying little attention to Mei or to their child.

Michael was living with another woman in distant city when he met Mei online. When Mei became pregnant, because he desperately wanted the child, he agreed to leave the other woman on the condition that they marry. All four parents were against the marriage, and Mei considered abortion, but Michael persuaded her to keep the child and marry him. However, he was still with the other woman not only after the birth, but still while Mei and the child were ill.

Mei said, 'Why does he tell the other woman he loves her? He told her he was single. I don't know if he loves me. He doesn't show it if he does.'

When I asked if Michael had been unfaithful from the beginning, she said,

> We first met before I knew of the girl. When I found out about her, I said you need to decide. He said he would end the relationship. But soon, although I knew he had not, I was pregnant, and so we married. I thought, 'Everyone makes mistakes.' I decided he could change.

Michael was unclear if he had loved Mei or not. In response to our questions about why he married her, he obfuscated about the nature of love and diverted the discussion to all that he had given up to be with her. In the beginning, he seemed to have been wanting to take care of somebody who was in need and alone, and then he quickly became disgusted by her emotionality.

Throughout our time with him, his disorganization and dissembling persisted. The couple agreed that he lied and hid things from Mei. In the interviews, we were never sure of the truth of what he said, and beyond that, his evasiveness and confusion frequently left us in doubt about what he meant. What did come through was his concern that marriage would impinge on his desperation to be his own person.

Michael said,

> The critical point is not the marriage, but the two persons in the relationship that matter individually. It's the relationship between the two individuals that is most important, regardless of what form it takes. We both love our child. If our marriage doesn't work, can we be friends? I don't want to be enemies!

In these few sentences, his focus oscillated between wanting to get along, and his determination to be himself. Many of his statements were, like this one, full of internal contradiction.

Michael and Mei's marriage was unconsciously founded on there always being a third person, and on Michael's aversion to being accountable to any one person and equally on Mei's desperation to hang on to an elusive object. They got married – something he wanted very much – but he was still working on being an individual who needed a third person to keep him from being subsumed into an intimate emotional relationship. For Michael, the sexual affair represents a way of getting cared for and loved without being swallowed alive.

The enduring puzzle in this couple's encounter with us was why Mei needed to marry a man who needed constant affairs. Indeed, she had been the 'other woman' with whom he had an affair when they meet online. Early on, her description about why she wanted to stay in the marriage seemed confused. She said that she had gotten married for life, but she also alluded to her insecurity without being able to say why she felt so insecure.

As we spent more time with the couple, it became clearer how Michael repeatedly introduced confusional elements into the relationship and into our interviews. On the surface, Michael seemed to have had a more traumatic upbringing. Early in Michael's life, his father was successful and rich, and apparently had multiple affairs. When Michael was a teenager, his father suffered severe economic reversal and became poor. Michael's mother threw him out, breaking Michael's relationship with his father. He had not reestablished a relationship with his father until a few years ago. The danger of a ruptured relationship with his wife and his child now existed in his marriage. The potential rupture in the relationship with his daughter seemed to be his principal motivation to keep trying at the marriage.

Initially, Mei described her parents as loving of each other, supportive of her and in general undisturbed, but she added that when they quarreled, they might not speak for days. We began to feel that she disconnected herself from any image of them or of a childhood that was less than ideal. She told us that her family had been loving and accepting about the pregnancy. Her father offered to supply whatever she needed for herself and the child. But her early family portrait seemed unreal, particularly because Mei also seemed to have an insecure attachment style, which she then projected into Michael. A narrative like Mei's that is too general, lacking affective immediacy and the feel of more detailed validity often masks aspects of early trauma. We speculated that part of the draw to Michael may have been that Mei could project a bad, anxious relationship into him, hoping to cure that part of herself vicariously by taking care of it in him, or by separating from him and therefore from it. Early on, Mei told us that when she was upset, her mother would say, 'Don't cry! I won't love you if you cry.' Mei's generalized memory of a bland 'good family' seemed to be the kind of characterization that masks an insecure or disorganized attachment that is idealized in retrospect in order to suppress unhappiness. This seemed to stand for the way Mei had to suppress upset and stay the course with Michael, but we could not understand more than this hypothesized generalization.

Later, Mei said,

> Ninety-five percent of the atmosphere in my family was good, but I was
> uncomfortable if they were silent. When I was young, I had no energy to
> fight back if my mother was mad. She didn't allow me to cry. Just as my
> mother said, 'Don't cry or I won't love you,' my husband says the same
> thing: 'Don't cry.' I couldn't be angry when I was young. Now if someone
> says 'Don't be angry,' I can't stand it.

Insecurity in Mei's narrative about her relationship to her parents, her job and her own personality began to come through as
being strongly implanted before she met Michael. Eventually, as
she was able to say more, we learned that Mei's mother's father
was away in the 'American War' in Korea in her young life, and
then when he returned, her mother died. So, Mei's mother had
lost her own mother at age three, and thereafter had been raised
by her father as a single parent. There was, therefore, intergenerational loading for loss, loneliness and anxiety. In addition,
Mei's own father had been away from the home in the army for
much of her early life. At first, she had been cared for by her
grandfather, but after he died, she and her mother were on their
own.
Mei said,

> After I was about three years old, my mother took care of me by herself,
> but she had to work. At daybreak, she cooked me some food and left,
> so when I woke, there no one was there. I was scared and shouted and
> tried to find my mother. I looked through the windows. I finally left off
> looking out the window and took up my comic books and read and ate
> melons. I was left alone so often that I got used to it. I still remember
> it. I was in the bedroom and no matter how loud I shouted, there was
> never a response. Recently, I dreamt that I beat my husband in anger in a
> dream. So, when he and I are together, if it's difficult, I dream that he will
> leave me. I don't know if that's connected.

When we noted how desperate and lonely Mei had been while
seeking someone to take care of her back then, just as now, she
added,

> I felt upset. I couldn't accept that there was no one there because she
> didn't tell me. I asked, 'Why didn't you tell me?' My mother said it was
> because if she did, I wouldn't let her go. And I accepted her explanation.

With this added story, we came to understand this early relationship and her dream as models for her relationship with Michael. Now we felt we understood more about why his turning his back on her in silence and his leaving her for other women both played into her ambivalent and anxious clinging, her original formation of a relationship with him as an elusive object and her inability to separate now.

Among the patterns in couples who come to us because of affairs, we frequently see one partner who unconsciously needs their spouse to maintain a connection to an outside person as a way to fulfill unconscious needs for both partners. For Mei, Michael's affairs provided a series of elusive objects, while she could identify with Michael and project herself into his search for distant objects to satisfy his need. Michael could search for an object that had disappeared as his father had and could maintain a desperate autonomy, safe from being swallowed by his partner. The real threat actually came from his own his needy self – a self so needy that he also wished to be taken inside the caring person. He had felt threatened by his mother's need for him when her husband was unavailable, and now he was threatened by Mei's and his daughter's need for him. The most pressing threat, however, came from the enormity of his own needs.

Why Not Divorce?

We will turn to the vicissitudes of divorce in the next chapter, but the question of divorce is often presented at the same time as that of affairs, so the problems cannot be disentangled. We saw this in the book's opening example of the older academic man and the younger country-born wife, for whom the question of divorce haunted their tenuous marriage. So it was with Michael and Mei. Both of them gave confused and inconsistent statements about the possibility of divorce, although their unconscious reasons were different. Mei said that she had gotten married for life, but she also frequently said that if Michael could not change, she would be better off alone. She remained ambivalent about marriage and divorce throughout the five days of our interviews, even temporizing when, through his confusion, Michael was more or less clearly saying he could not guarantee future fidelity. He would ask, for instance, 'What is marriage anyway? Do I need to be faithful, or does it only matter that we have a child?' Over time, we came to understand her ambivalence. In one state of mind, she was clear that her marriage was beyond repair, that she was facing divorce. However, being unable to stand that fate, she would then retreat to another state of mind that could retain a futile sense of hope.

We developed a conviction that Michael constantly lied to Mei, asking provocative questions like, 'If I'm having an affair, does that mean things aren't working?' It was hard to trust anything he said. It was not only that he wanted things both ways but that he seemed to oscillate between scattered parts of his own mind without a firm place to stand emotionally. Until the end of our encounter, he vacillated, saying that what really mattered was the individuals and not the marriage. He said, 'Love and marriage are not a religion. Maybe we can be better friends if we divorce.'

Chapter 11

Beginning Treatment of a Couple Who Presented with an Extramarital Affair

In the previous chapter, we saw two couples who demonstrated quite different aspects of how extramarital affairs expressed marital dysfunction, and in which the chances for substantial repair seemed remote. In the case I describe in this chapter, as in all others, the cause of the affair cannot be understood as limited to a single factor, because a presenting symptom of marital distress always condenses other elements of the couple's difficulty into the affair-as-symptom. However, we also see a resilience in this couple that the previous two did not have.

This couple also illustrates several dimensions of the difficulty of becoming a couple in China. While each couple is unique, in this couple we can see the influence of society-wide pressures that play on many families – of the pressure to succeed, of the change from old family values to those of the emerging modern world, and we can see the way a formerly loving couple lost their way and were fortunate enough to seek – and find – help.

> The couple, Thomas and Lila, in their early thirties, were eager to be seen. Thomas appeared wearing a hat emblazoned with 'University of Technology.' His shirt, sporting a Pacific Coast insignia, shouts, 'Get the Wave.' Lila wore bright purple sunglasses and a shirt that proclaimed, 'The Best Time to Be Crazy.' Janine Wanlass and I introduced ourselves, with our translator, Gao Jun, between us, and Elizabeth Palacios behind us as discussant.
>
> Thomas explained that they had come because of loss of trust since Lila had a baby three years ago. She has not recovered from an ensuing depression, and sex is not good. Finally, he continued, 'I made some mistakes, for which I confessed and tried to correct them, but my wife is disappointed.' She broke down after a recent 'big mistake.' It was initially unclear what the 'big mistake' was. He had lost 30,000–40,000 RMB (between $5,000–7,000) with a partner, but gradually we learned that he then tried to soothe his

friend by arranging 'some special services for him' – that is, a prostitute. Lila found this out by seeing internet chats and thought the prostitute was for Thomas. As Thomas tells us this story in a confusing way, Lila sits stiffly without obvious emotion. He then adds another confusing story about business dealings, starting companies with complications, bad news in the market, investors who have let him down and time on his hands because of little to do.

Finally, he said, 'There is a second problem: We don't have a good relationship because I made a mistake. I had a bodily affair.'

We turned to Lila, who said,

> The first time he had a problem, it was a huge blow. I thought I knew him, and it never occurred to me that he would do something like this. He explained, and I believed him, but I still had some suspicion; I didn't know if he was telling the truth and whether I could trust him.

Thomas had explained that the arrangement was for his friend, whom he wanted to help. They quarreled, she cried and remained suspicious.

Janine asked whether he had first told Lila about the prostitute for the friend, or about the affair?

Lila said that she had been doubtful, but finally found a text in which Thomas asked the prostitute if she had time.

Their difficulties had begun three years ago, Lila told us, with her delivery and her serious depression that followed. She cried all the time and had pains. A couple of therapy sessions, Traditional Chinese Medicine and jogging had helped; she returned to work where she once more got along well.

But the seeds of their problems went further back. Lila said,

> I didn't want to be pregnant when I was, but because his family put pressure on us, we went ahead. I still have little interest in sex because of my body and my mind. He put pressure on me, and every time I rejected him, there was more pressure. I tried to communicate and hoped he would try to learn how to help, but he didn't. There were painful fights and conversations. Also, he hoped that I would have a child that would make his family happy, so I gave in. It took me three days to deliver my daughter, and finally I had a cesarean section. But because it was a girl, his family was unhappy. They didn't accept that I had a daughter. From then on, no matter how I suffered, I couldn't get anything back from them. There was no pity from them and no care. After that, I didn't want to do anything to please them.

Janine said, 'So you didn't want a baby yourself. You did it for him and his family. Then, because it was a girl, they were disappointed and down on you?'

Lila said, 'Yes, and for a long time they wore black faces and didn't even want to see my daughter.'

Thomas nods in agreement and said,

I agree. First, because of me, she gave birth to a girl. We planned to have it later, so it was an accident to have it now. Second, my parents — perhaps because it's a traditional thing in rural China. When she delivered the baby, I was very busy. I wasn't mature enough to take care of her. Third, when she delivered the daughter, my parents and her mother took care of her.

We noticed that his sentences did not really follow on each other, despite the way he introduced order by numbering his points.

Problems followed. Lila had returned to her hometown for her mother to care for the baby and to find medical help for her deteriorating health. Thomas came on weekends but was always on his cellphone. She fought with her father, and eventually returned to Beijing, and her daughter, now three months old, was sent to her in-laws. When Lila joined the baby there, they tried to stuff her with eggs. Now retreating to her own parents, she had some psychotherapy, which enabled her stand up more for herself. By the time the baby was eight months old, things were better and Lila returned to work, but with lingering resentment for Thomas and his parents for 'what they did to me.' Now her in-laws are basically raising her daughter, doting on her while she lives with them in the countryside near Beijing, sleeping in their bed. Thomas and Lila visit only on weekends.

Thomas said, 'I think it was a most difficult situation in her mind, so since then, the old experience has led to the current situation.'

I said, 'It's a painful story!'

Lila said, 'Before I was about to deliver, his family came to Beijing and said that it was equal whether it was a boy or girl, so no pressure on me. But they changed once she was born. I felt cheated and betrayed.'

We asked Thomas how he felt about having a daughter. He said it was fine, and that he had tried talking with his parents but had neglected his wife's feelings.

Thomas said,

I forgot to explain to her that it didn't matter, and so for my wife it had a big impact. I didn't believe it would change the course of things. Because after delivery, my parents had the wrong attitude. But now they love their granddaughter. When I took the baby to stay with Lila's parents, my parents had a lot of difficulty separating from her.

Janine asked Lila to tell us more about conflict with her father.

Lila said, 'It seems trivial. Probably it was because I was in a bad mood. My father is immature. It's difficult for him to understand others. We haven't talked much over the years.'

Thomas added, 'She lacks a father's love. Her mother did everything for her.'

I said, 'Lila, since you feel unloved by your father, when Thomas didn't have time for you, did that feel the same way as not being loved by your father?'

Lila thought her father was not that important.

I didn't have a strong feeling towards my father, so I don't compare them. Before I had a boyfriend, I depended on my mother and I always talked to her. But after I married, I hoped my husband would care for me, and then it was difficult to talk to my mother. When there was difficulty, if he wouldn't take care of me, I had to bear up myself.

As we explored further, Lila told us that she has an identical twin sister and, because her countryside family had girls, they were exempt from the One Child Policy and were allowed to have another child, producing her younger brother. The twins had been inseparable until Lila's marriage, together taking care of the younger brother.

Thomas is the elder of two with a seven-year-younger sister. His family claimed an exemption through political connections.

Thomas said, 'It's the Chinese style. You try to find relationships, and my father found relationships at the government level that gave my parents an exception. And because it was in the countryside, the policy wasn't so strictly enforced.'

As we closed the first session with the couple, we briefly explored their family situations. Thomas came from a relatively well-off family from a small town. While his parents treated both him and his sister well, it was understood that as the son, he would eventually inherit the family apartment. Lila's mother was a clerk, while her farmer father became jobless when they moved to the city, then opening a grocery store. They had frequently struggled financially, often relying on relatives for assistance.

On this first day, we saw evidence of the traumatic effect of the traditional Chinese preference for boys and the One Child Policy, seen in the grandparents' disappointment. Although both members of the couple had siblings, at the time they had their own child, the One Child Policy was still in effect. In earlier years, their families had, in different ways, skirted the One Child Policy: Lila's because in her farming family, the first children were girls, and Thomas' family through the corruption of that policy for relatively well-connected and wealthy families. We guessed that pampering by his mother represented the storied pattern in China of treating boys as 'little princes' and 'women as nothing,' but that surmise was not yet be confirmed.

This likeable couple seemed to us, however, more like sibling children trying to pass as adults, hardly a couple, dependent on both sets of parents to whom they had ceded their daughter. Lila's marriage and pregnancy brought an emotional impact that revived the feeling of the loss of her mother and twin more than the gaining of a partner. We wondered how much their emotional situation related to recent Chinese social history and how much to older Confucian patterns.

To the second session, Lila again wore her purple sunglasses. Today her shirt read 'BLOW!' in capital English letters.

She said,

I was disappointed with Thomas. I'd heard everything he said before yesterday, so I was considering whether we would still choose to be together or how could I rebuild my confidence. I don't trust him because I'm afraid I'll be hurt again. I hope these sessions will produce something so I can change my mind and contribute to our family's future. But if there isn't a good outcome, I'll consider separating. Whichever outcome, I wouldn't want a life of unhappily clinging to each other.

I said, 'It seemed you were doing okay until your daughter's birth and his family's rejection. Perhaps that recalled, Lila, how you felt rejected earlier by being a girl in a family that preferred boys.'

Lila nodded. 'My parents preferred my brother. My mother took care of us twins, although she wasn't really aware of us. She helped us go to university and get master's degrees, but she preferred him.'

I said, 'That must have hurt.'

Lila continued,

Yes, but I want to make another point about my grandfather. My father was the only son with a sister. His father didn't really like the three of us and preferred his daughter's daughter. So, my mother would tell us to work hard to win his respect so he wouldn't despise us.

The strategy had not worked. Her grandmother had died young, and her grandfather always preferred her cousin, even though Lila and her sister were more highly achieved.

Thomas confirmed Lila's story. 'It was hard to change her grandfather's or her mother's minds, even though she tried hard. Her mother, like my parents, prefers boys. Both girls felt their mother didn't love them. It depressed them.'

I said, 'So you, Lila, looked to Thomas' family to love you more than your mother did. Then you were hurt again when you had your daughter and they turned against you.'

Lila agreed,

> Before I married, his parents valued me a lot. They cooked food I liked. They treated me well and I tried to satisfy them. I brought them presents and visited them instead of my parents. I treated my in-laws as though they were my parents.

Janine said, 'So when they turned against you, that was awful.'

Lila said,

> I felt lost. I knew that they wished for a boy, but they never said they wouldn't accept a girl. For a while, I felt Thomas would divorce me because I'd had a daughter. He didn't have any reaction, but he didn't comfort me. It had never occurred to me that he wouldn't accept her. He had no intention of taking care of me.

Janine asked Thomas for his view of the situation. He brushed off his neglect, blaming the press of his work. He said he had tried to persuade his parents to accept his daughter but couldn't change their minds. He continued,

> The fourth problem between us was that I didn't react. She believed I was negative. She thought I didn't value her or our daughter, but we had been together nine years and I never thought of divorce. I want to keep the marriage.

Janine asked if he had been aware that Lila felt he was so distant and unavailable. He had not, but he had 'tried to negotiate with his parents about their 'black face' reaction to the baby.' He thought their unhappiness had somehow influenced him, resulting in his neglecting Lila.

I asked Thomas if his parents' reaction had hurt him as well.

He said,

> Yes, and the first thing was, I was disappointed because my parents had signaled that a boy or girl was equal. Then there was a big turn, and they said I had disappointed them. Secondly, I had to work long hours. I was so tired I didn't know what to do. She was so depressed; I didn't know if my work was valuable. I decided to change jobs.

I felt deflected from the emotional path we had been pursuing, but we followed Thomas' lead and asked about his job. Lila picked up the lead, saying she had a well-paying, stable job at the time, while he was not earning much, so she had suggested he move into a different part of the financial sector. He did and his income increased dramatically. We also asked about Lila's job and initially felt quite confused, eventually learning that she is also in finance. Here we felt there was another element of vagueness and confusion that seemed to be protecting secrets.

Moving back, we asked Thomas again about the family situation.

He said, 'That's the miracle of blood ties. Like magic, they soon came to care for her. They've taken care of her from when our daughter was three months old. Since then, she has never left them.'

Lila interjected, 'But his parents never changed their preference for boys. Now they're pressuring us to have a second child.'

I asked Lila how she felt about that.

Lila said,

> When the One Child Policy changed last year, I broke down. I knew that his parents would try to persuade me to have another child. I didn't want to. Thomas tried to negotiate with his parents not to bother us for perhaps a year, but still, it was only for a time. We gave the excuse about our financial pressure, but we know they'll pressure us again.

I asked, 'How do you feel about that?'

Lila said,

> I don't want a second child. Mothering is hard. I'm not mature enough for a second child. I would never be able to take care of myself. I'm not crazy about having a child. Thomas isn't either. I don't want to sacrifice my life again.

Janine asked, 'Thomas, do you want a second child?'

Thomas said,

> It depends. Maybe when our daughter is six or seven, if our income and our family environment is better, or if Lila were willing then. Many

of our friends have second children. Perhaps an only child is too lonely. Now with the aging as a problem of the population, I'm also concerned about that.

Even though I am interested in the social factors they were discussing – the effects of the One Child Policy, the parents' pressuring the young couple to have more children and to accede to their preferences for boys, the pressure from an aging Chinese population, I felt that in the session, we had experienced Thomas deflecting us once again from an important emotional path. So, I suggested we get back to his parents' disappointment.

I asked if Thomas had felt feel jealous of his sister while growing up. When he denied that, saying he had taken care of her, we asked about other disappointments. This led to a new avenue.

Thomas said,

My parents had a strict attitude about educational performance. They wanted me to go to college so I would not be a disappointment. My older cousin went to a good university, but I only scored average on the national entrance exam, just above the cut for an ordinary university. They scolded me. I blamed myself, but I was hurt. Day after day they criticized me. Finally, I just let them talk and tried not to take their criticism seriously.

Lila added, 'His mother is harsh. When his sister failed to get into a master's program, his mother said 'Leave home and don't come back!' I couldn't bear it. His mother was so critical.'

Thomas continued,

This had a huge impact on my personality. The second point is for my father. He was in a high position and so was very strict. So, if you failed, he was harsh. *That influenced how I talked to my mother.*

(This was a slip in translation: Thomas had said 'how I talked to my wife,' but Gao Jun had translated 'mother' instead of 'wife.')

When we heard the slip in Gao Jun's mistranslation of 'mother' for 'wife,' we were immediately interested in the unconscious meaning of her slip. I should explain that Gao Jun's English is excellent, and we have invariably found that when she makes a mistake in translation, it is for helpful emotional reasons, exactly the same way that our own or a patient's slips in treatment present important clues to unconscious meaning. In this case, her emotionally determined slip in translation was an important clue, helping us connect Thomas' mother's harsh treatment with his own treatment of Lila.

Thomas continued, 'I also had a harsh tone. She felt that I was criticizing her. Actually, I had that happen in my family, which was a problem that she didn't understand.'

Now we felt we had help from Thomas' insight.

Janine said, 'So you got criticized by your parents, and then you behaved like that with Lila?'

Thomas nodded. 'Yes. Recently I became aware of it, so I tried to change it. But I need her help to break my habit.'

I said, 'Now things begin to connect. That harsh criticism and disregard that each of you experienced has led to blowups between the two of you.' (Lila nodded.) 'This has contributed to Lila's depression and to you, Thomas, turning to other women for comfort.'

Thomas seemed at first to nod in agreement, but then took it back.

I don't think so. First, I don't recall how I felt treated by my parents. I just wanted to calm her, but I let her down. I just said, 'I'm sorry.' I knew she wasn't physically okay, but I didn't try to find women for this reason.

I insisted, 'But there's a similar pattern to the way you fend off your parents. You listen to Lila without reacting, like you listen to your parents' criticism without reacting.'

Thomas said, 'Yes, when her mood was intense, it would happen. Recently I want to open myself up, to tell her my thoughts so she doesn't have to guess.'

I said,

Okay, but I believe you turn to women for sex in order to get your needs met when you cannot get them met with Lila. Lila couldn't feel sexual even if her body didn't hurt because she's so angry and feels so rejected.

Lila nodded. 'Yes. In the beginning, sex didn't feel like that. Recently, it isn't good. He was pressuring me. I say, 'Okay, if you just take time to shake hands.' But then he wants to hug me immediately.'

I asked, 'What was it like in the beginning?'

Lila said, 'In the beginning, sex was okay, but now I just feel he is using me. Otherwise he ignores me. He only kisses or hugs me for sex. Otherwise there's nothing.'

I said, 'So, Lila, you were angry and depressed, and Thomas, you got more and more desperate, leading to a cycle of desperation and mutual rejection. That is the story of the breakdown of your marriage.'

Lila said, 'Yes! Yes!'

Janine added,

Thomas, the more you distanced yourself, the more emotional Lila became in order to get to you, and then the more you would try to create distance in order to calm yourself. It's another way of wanting something from each other, but missing each other in the process.

We continued to feel that this couple was more like brother and sister than husband and wife, both needing parental confirmation that eluded them in childhood. She was not the preferred boy, and he did not live up to his parents' hopes, and only the birth of a boy would have restored them to their parents' good graces.

But we also began to see positive things. They had come for help and were beginning to talk, but they were still unable to use love and tenderness for repair. Lila still suffered from the BLOW (as on her shirt) from the loss of an idealized fantasy, experiencing instead repetition of traumatic rejection. She didn't want to be dragged back by another baby, while Thomas temporized, saying, 'Perhaps in seven years we can have another child.'

During discussion, one of our students likened Thomas to a porcupine. Trying to get close to Lila, he sticks her, leading her to fearful withdrawal, an image that describes their sexual and emotional relationships. His distancing attachment style is magnified in reaction to her anxious and demanding clinging.

On the third day, Lila began by describing how Thomas ignored what she wanted in favor of imposing things on her, including sex. His family, similarly, pressed things on her without regard for her limits or preferences.

I took her lead, and asked more about sex early on.

She said, 'It was okay early on because I could feel he cared about me and could understand me. Later, I gave him a lot, but he was like a little child and stopped taking care of me.'

Janine asked how this compared before and after the pregnancy. Lila said,

There were similar episodes before the pregnancy. If we disagreed about something small, he would say, 'Let's separate,' or he'd leave home. But that was just something he threatened. But there were only the two of us without our parents, so I tried to deal with things alone. Sex was normal. We didn't reject each other.

Janine turned to Thomas, who said,

One, I was not mature. Secondly, we had just graduated from the University and started living together without conflict. Secondly (*again*), I would insist on my opinion. For example, I wanted to take care of her. She has low blood pressure, so I would try to persuade her to eat. She felt I was insisting. Third, my parents and I had different life customs. I like to repeat things. That's my problem.

(Janine and I looked at each other. We felt the confusional element creeping in again as we had trouble following his pseudological and badly numbered connections.)

Lila followed his segue into talking about his parents, describing more about how they imposed their ways of thinking on her and ignored what she said, for instance, about what and how much she ate. Eventually, she became unable to eat in their presence, although able to eat at work or with friends.

We turned to what their relationship had been like in the beginning. They had met as university classmates. Lila was moved by Thomas' consideration, which however later fell away, leaving her feeling she had to take care of him.

Thomas once again gave a circular series of explanations, so that as the session progressed, Janine and I began to feel that as soon as we saw something, it disappeared.

Feeling swept in a swirl, I dragged us back to a point we had fled from the beginning, about Thomas searching online for sex. Thomas said it was the deterioration of sex, but he also felt it followed his boss, who was his mentor, leaving the company he was working for. Lila once again said she wanted to help him, but not by tolerating the prostitutes. She is now exhausted and feels he has to handle things himself.

Lila said, 'I was very upset. The more I gave, the more he became distant. I don't know: Maybe he'll be there for a few months, and then give up again.'

Janine conjectured, 'You're so hurt now that even if he tried, you wonder if it would be enough.'

Lila said, 'I feel numb like a wooden figure. I don't feel I'll get better.'

We discussed how each of them would have to find ways of reversing their withdrawal if they were going to reconstruct their marriage, something we thought they would need couple therapy and individual therapy to accomplish. We did not recommend they start with sexual reconciliation, but with a shared commitment to finding emotional paths towards each other – if they both still wanted that.

Our comments elicited the other side of Lila's vision of a future that would lead to divorce:

> I was thinking mostly about what would happen after we separated, about how I would deal my life, leaving the city, changing my job, learning to take care of myself. I always thought if I lost him, my world would collapse, but after this incident, I wondered if we would separate and if I would live alone.

(She was crying, reaching for tissues.) 'I thought what it would be like to be with the child, alone in my family.'

Janine now highlighted the way Lila's depression added to her bleak view, and continued that she thought Thomas, too, was depressed. He nodded, and we asked him to think about that idea out loud.

Thomas considered this possibility briefly, then ran from it in favor of a vague action plan.

> My own depression never occurred to me. About my parents, first they have a style that's hard to change. I don't think they can change to meet her standards. I suggest that I take her parents as mine, and she take my parents as hers. Then she wouldn't be so upset. Also, we could live separately from my parents. We could have our own space, and they could be close by, so we can go there to visit the child and eat with them and then go home at night.

Trying to follow, I said, 'You've given your daughter to Thomas' parents?'

Lila said, 'Most of the time, they take care of her. She's in kindergarten, and we accompany her or take her out to play, and then she sleeps with her grandparents, so we're less involved.'

Thomas said, 'We will go to kindergarten and take care of her in the evening. The most important thing is to give my wife space to recover.'

I said,

> I'm slowly coming to understand that we have to suggest one step at a time. The first thing would be to help reestablish the two of you as a couple. Apparently, you were loving couple in the past, so it would be important to draw on that to repair the decline. It's important, Lila, to see Thomas' turning to prostitutes as symptomatic of last year's problems in your marriage and his own way of dealing with his hurt, just as you withdrew from your hurt.

Lila nodded. 'I could accept and forgive his behavior. But I worry whether something like that will happen again in the future.'

In our ensuing discussion, we noted Lila's 'no entry defense' developed against repeated rejection and hurt throughout her life. By 'no entry,' we mean that she cannot allow anything in, lest it poison her from the inside. This has showed up with food: Lila accepts only the exact food she wants, and she requires a perfect double, to re-find a twin to feel at one with, something that cannot happen in a couple relationship. Before the baby, there may been a oneness that was no longer possible once they had the baby. Now anything that gets close to her hurts because of all that it is not.

On the fourth day, Lila's jacket covered her shirt, but Thomas' shirt proclaimed, 'Jaws Beach.'

We were particularly struck by his shirt, given our formulation the day before of her fear of being devoured by her in-laws' wish to subsume her.

Lila began by referencing what we had said the day before that we thought Lila was depressed. She had agreed and thought she had been blocking all Thomas' efforts to get through. Last night, as her mood improved, she thought, 'I should give our relationship a chance.'

She continued, 'I wanted to approach our sex life as if I were meeting a new man. So, we would have to get to know each other all over again in order for me to accept him sexually.'

Janine said, 'You're trying to find a new beginning.'

Lila said, 'Yes! If we started over like friends, you'd start by shaking hands, like a new beginning.'

Now Lila suddenly unzips her jacket, revealing the words 'New Balance: Boston, Massachusetts.'

I was quite struck by the new message on her shirt that meant to me finding a 'new balance' with an American location, meaning that it was in relation to Janine and myself as Americans. I thought it might signify a resilience that had been covered up until now, but that she might feel hope in the message her clothing conveyed in its reference to the transference to us.

The couple now agreed that they could try new ways of dealing with each other. For instance, Thomas thought that instead of simply confronting her when she was in a bad mood, he could invite her to do things together instead of withdrawing. At the same time, Lila began to understand that this was his way of managing painful things.

Lila said,

> So, I can understand him more and try to calm myself, to be less angry. Although I'm still concerned that if I express my will or reject something, he'll keep repeating requests that I don't know how to deal with. Should I change the way I speak?

I said, 'Yes, and therapy can help with that. But Lila, have you noticed what's written on your shirt?'

Lila looked down and read, 'New Balance' in English. She laughed, and repeated 'New Balance.'

I said, 'That's what you want!'

Moved, Lila said, 'Thank you. But can you offer suggestions to help us change our minds and deepen our understanding so that we would know each other better?'

Janine repeated what Thomas said he has been learning here, and asked what interferes with being able to hear Lila.

This time, Thomas worked with us in a new way.

He said,

> It relates to my work. I was born in a rural area. I had no background or family connections. I had to fight for my position. I got promoted, so I could do big orders quickly. Lila expected I could do the same in our life together, but I didn't know how to do it at home.

Lila said, 'In his work, he did well because he listened to his boss. Why can he hear others but not me?'

Thomas said, 'At work, there's only one chance for people like me. Several subordinates failed my boss. I succeeded and got promoted. At work, I had to guess what the boss thought and produce the right outcome. At home, I didn't want to guess at what Lila liked, so I overlooked her.'

Janine said, 'Thomas, you said you're a single-focus person. In the beginning, Lila was your focus. Then you dropped her to focus on work.'

Thomas said, 'I devoted too much to work. I wonder how I can find that new balance and take care of both home and work.'

Janine said, 'So Lila is wearing the shirt for both of you.' (They laugh.)

With a different tone of gratitude, Thomas tells us how Lila supported him when she made three times his salary, telling him she was willing to continue to do so. Then he found his way and began to earn much more.

Janine said gently, 'Lila, you're beginning to cry.'

Lila said tearfully, 'I supported him and I was pregnant. I did so much, and everybody around me hurt me so much. I was pregnant, alone and his family and mine both dropped me. I couldn't even eat in my early pregnancy.'

As she cries, Thomas leans over to offer a tissue. There is a new feeling of intimacy in the room.

She continues, 'It was so hard. Despite all my effort, I got nothing in return.'

Janine asked, 'You want Thomas to understand that?'

Lila nodded. 'I think he knew. I wondered if he could understand how I suffered. I don't know if he understands the pain he inflicted.'

I asked, 'Thomas?'

Thomas said,

In the last month, I've been reflecting. I remember how I overlooked her support. I knew how she was suffering when she was crying. I didn't know what to do. Perhaps how I comfort people is wrong. She said I should encourage her, not blame her. If I encouraged her, perhaps her mood would recover.

I asked Lila, 'What would you like from Thomas when you're upset like this?'

Lila said, 'Just to be there, and hug and comfort me. He doesn't necessarily have to say something. He just has to not leave me alone to do his own stuff.'

Thomas said, 'She's making a good point. I will do it. I should be with her sincerely.'

I asked, 'Thomas, do you sometimes feel like Lila is like your mother telling you that you weren't any good?'

Thomas looked thoughtful now.

I need to think about that. My mother had high expectations. She would blame and criticize me. Once she said that I owed her one million RMB. But even if I pay her 100 RMB per day, I calculated that I couldn't repay her in my lifetime.

I said, 'Now Lila has become like your mother saying, 'You're never good enough.''

Lila nodded.

Yes. I just wanted to make the point that he owes me and has to work for it every day. You need to try every day. I didn't want to give the impression that if he paid me back, then he could give up. I was trying to motivate him.

Janine said, 'You want him to keep working at it, but what Thomas heard was 'You can never do enough."

I added, 'Lila, you're afraid that if you don't keep his feet to the fire, he will lie back and let you support him?'

Lila said, 'He often lies back or his attention drifts. He doesn't take care of me anymore. I want him to make an effort all the time. Maybe I hurt him, but I don't know how to hook him otherwise.'

I said, 'That strategy backfired.'

Lila said, 'I realize that. It was probably the wrong action, but I don't know a better way for him to see me."

I said, 'You have to find a way out of a lifetime of slave labor and discover a relationship in which you can see each other.'

Lila said, 'I don't want to oppress him or squeeze things out of him. I want to help deal with his upset, but when I'm not in good shape, I don't know how to get him to help me.'

I asked, 'Was there something growing up, Lila, that you feel that unless you work all the time, nobody will care about you?'

Lila said, 'In my childhood, I always worked to find solutions and get rid of adversity. I don't know how that fits.'

Janine asked, 'Did you feel you were always responsible for the others?'

Lila, thoughtfully, said,

> No. I took care of my younger brother for my mother a lot. It was so hard for her. (Now she begins to cry again.) She had so much hardship, she devoted so much to her family. My father never understood what a difficult life she had.

Janine asked, 'So you watched your mother work so hard, which your father didn't appreciate?'

Lila nodded tearfully. 'He never appreciated her.'

Janine said, 'Now you have that feeling with Thomas. You work, and he doesn't see you.'

Lila, wiping her eyes, 'That's right. I feel I lead a difficult life.'

Janine said, 'So when you met, you thought he understood and things would be different. But then you felt your marriage became like your parents' marriage.'

Lila said, 'In the beginning, we understood and supported each other. Later, no matter how much I tried, it didn't feel like that.'

Thomas said,

> I treated her like a queen in the beginning. But after we got married, with more monetary pressure, I thought I only had to provide more and more money. I thought it had to be one million RMB (about $150,000),

then five million, then a house. Then I got anxious because of my job and the high rate of inflation in China, more than 12%. The price of an apartment would go up because of inflation, and later it would cost 100 RMB (about $15) to buy an apple. You have to have a safety plan, and buy and sell apartments, and other ways of safeguarding our money.

I said,

I can see you have a strategic plan and that you are actually very worried about succeeding. But there's a real danger that you could become wealthy financially and poor in your family. And as Lila has showed us, you need a 'new balance' between work and home.

Thomas said, 'I agree. I want to understand things about our family difficulty. I took a wrong turn and I'm trying to find that balance.'
Janine said,

You were trying to take care of your family through money, but you went missing. Lila is telling you what she wants you to do just as much as she wants the money. In fact, Lila wants you more than she wants money.'

Thomas nodded. 'She's been telling me that all the time, but I couldn't grasp it. If we continued as we were, perhaps we'd have a good financial life and a ruined emotional life.'
Lila said,

I always tell his parents, 'People count more than... even if we're poor, if we supported each other it would be enough.' They value money more than affection. I don't think he can change in two or three sessions. How long will he be able to sustain this new attitude?'

Janine said, 'That's the worry you had earlier, about whether it will last.'
I said, 'This can only be a good start. We recommend that you continue the momentum from our sessions here with a therapist in Beijing because this is a pattern that the two of you have built together, not separately.'
They nodded.
I continued. 'Lila, I want to go back to an issue we haven't followed up on. Is your sister an identical twin?' (She nods yes.) 'What was it like between you?'
Lila said,

We did everything together growing up. If I was upset, I would talk to her. But before Thomas' incident, she had arranged to move overseas to work in America, to settle there permanently. After the prostitute episode, she stayed behind for a few days to help me, but then she left.

I said, 'She left and you felt alone.'

Lila sobbed harder than any time before.

I said, 'She understood you better than anyone.'

Janine said, 'This is very painful. Did Thomas understand the loss of your sister?'

Lila said, 'I don't think so.'

I said, 'He didn't understand that you are in mourning for your sister since she left?'

Lila said, 'She could take care of me. I was lost. I depended on her. I lost him and I couldn't depend on him, then I lost her. I couldn't recover.'

I said, 'Thomas, of course it's not your fault that her twin left, but it's important that you understand what it meant to her.' Thomas nodded solemnly.

Today, we felt the hope of a new beginning, heralded by Lila's 'New Balance' shirt and continued by their work on reversing their destructive cycle. For the first time, Thomas could listen to Lila telling him how hard life has been, echoing with her mother's hard life that her father failed to appreciate. And we could hear how Thomas felt criticized. For both of them, the harsh judgment of the other echoed with their own internal judgment that they were failing in the eyes of internal parents.

We noted that Lila had cried three times. First in despair, because she couldn't get Thomas to understand her suffering while she was trying to help him with his issues. But today, at such a moment, Thomas was able to give her a tissue in a sign of listening and understanding her. The second time she cried because her relationship with Thomas echoes the way her mother took the family burden without her father's appreciation. That let us link her past situation with the situation now in the marriage. Third, and most movingly, when I brought in the loss of the twin, she cried at losing her sister just when she felt the marriage was failing.

These episodes, and other moving moments in the session, marked significant turning points. The couple could see that five sessions would not be enough, but they began to see what interferes with their being a couple. They still did not know what love and tenderness were, or how they could forge a different marital link. So far, their logic has been, 'I've invested, so I have to get something back through money or single-minded attention, not daring to hope for love and tenderness.' So, Lila says, in effect, 'I need to hook him.' She doesn't say, 'I need to find a way to bring more love into our life.' We now felt hope that fondness or even love would follow.

On the last day, Lila began. She had left yesterday's interview feeling sad, thinking about her sister. But this time, Thomas had listened, and said, 'You're far apart, but you're also together.' That comforted her and helped her recover.

Thomas said, 'We talked last night about our lack of trust. So, we're taking steps. There's a Chinese saying, 'A small step can become a big smile.' You said these five classes wouldn't be enough, but I hope it's a good start. I'll be there for her for her treatment. Thirdly, you said we had a wonderful experience in school. We've been married six years. We had happiness and sorrow. It's a good basis. Finally, about new goals: I told her I would try to earn money and she wasn't satisfied. I still want to share my success, but we need to negotiate our goals, hers and mine and the family's. If we disagree, we can work on our differences. I think we can talk now.'

Lila followed. She still wants to talk and share, but she wants to decrease her need to cling, to be fused so she would not pin excess expectations on him and then fear her world would collapse. We agreed that her idea of 'taking care of herself' could add to a healthier give-and-take.

Lila said, 'Thank you. I think I've learned a lot from these classes. I've made huge progress. I'm really grateful. We want to stay in therapy. For these days, especially since the third day, I've been less exhausted. Then I thought about my daughter. When I'm in a bad mood, she wants to stay with me, to find me. (Now Lila is tearful again.) I wondered if she wanted to comfort me.'

I said, 'I'm so glad you mentioned your daughter, because we are concerned for her, too. Tell us more about her?'

Lila wiped her eyes.

After she was born, his parents took care of her. We weren't so fully involved in her life. When I disagreed with them, it was hard to correct them. We only visited her two days a week. I'm concerned that she doesn't communicate so well with others. I wonder if my mood affects her. If I'm in a bad mood, I don't want her to see that I'm so sad. I hope to give a better psychological environment so she can have a better life

Janine asked, 'What's she like?'

Lila said,

At home, she would sing and dance and play. For instance, she'll make a house for horses. She talks for a long time to herself even though we're there. She enjoys playing alone. Recently, I found out she doesn't want to play with the other kids so much and is kind of afraid of them. She doesn't have playmates because she is constantly moved, and his parents aren't very sociable.

Janine asked if she was having trouble with kids at school.

Lila said, 'She says the others don't want to play with her. The teacher said she is shy, that it's not that others exclude her. I worry about our impact on her.'

We said that we were glad to hear about their daughter, who is with grandparents who are isolated themselves, and we wondered if she was learning to isolate herself rather than burden her mother, who she misses terribly.

Tearfully, Lila said, 'When I'm in a bad mood, I don't let her see it.'

We were now able to discuss how the couple, in their preoccupation and depression, may not have given their daughter enough of themselves, perhaps leaving her feeling insecure. We wonder if Lila was worried that she would burden her daughter as she felt burdened by her mother's depression.

Lila said,

> I learned from my mother. For example, I gave birth to my baby, and then his parents took care of her. My mother said, 'You have to be grateful,' and they demanded gratitude. My mother thought they were taking care of me, but she couldn't understand my suffering, so I suffered more. I can't talk with her or my father at all. Before college, I was dependent on my mother. After I got married, I tried to use her ways to treat others, but I just got traumatized. Now I don't agree with her ways, so I distance myself from them.

I asked, 'Has your mother has suffered in silence?'

Lila said, 'She kept saying, 'You should not think too much.' Her way was to ignore both her suffering and mine.'

I said,

> Today we've been focused on you, Lila, but Thomas, you've been hearing about how Lila's mind works. Now it's starting to work in a new way. So, she wants to tell you, Thomas, that when there's difficulty, please don't turn away from her.

Thomas nods.

Janine said, 'You also said you were learning about yourself, Thomas. That it was important to share with Lila.'

Thomas said,

> During these five classes, I've been thinking a lot. For example, on the way here today, Lila's parents called to get her involved in her father's broken foot and their difficulty getting along. I told Lila to ignore them until later.

I asked Lila how that advice sounded. She said it soothed her. Thomas had offered to visit and help her parents later, so she felt supported.

We discussed the improvement in the couple, cautioning them that in the days ahead, there would inevitably be mistakes and reversion to the old ways. They responded that they were beginning to feel hope and the beginnings of trust.

Lila was again in tears, but this time of gratitude. 'When I think about our love, I was so happy during our courtship. I hope we will have that again.'

Near the end of the hour, we came back to their daughter, whom Janine and I had concern for.

Lila said,

I haven't experienced pleasure in being a parent. Her birth was a lot for me, so I didn't dare to give her too much. I should take more responsibility as a mother, but when I do, it feels like a demand, not a way of pleasing myself. It's not her problem but mine. I need some help with this.

We discussed the infringements on Lila's enjoyment in mothering, probably transmitted in part from her own mother. We said that one focus of therapy should be on helping Lila, and both of them, to enjoy being parents of a daughter who loved them but wanted more from them. 'As you find pleasure together as a couple, your daughter will enjoy that, too.' Lila smiled and Thomas nodded.

As we finished, Lila said, 'It was so lucky for me to have this help. I learned and felt understood, so that let me feel more relaxed. It's been good.'

Thomas agreed.

We're very lucky. I feel grateful for this chance. In terms of feedback, at first I felt five sessions would be too long, but now it feels like not enough. It's hard to get things out of me like this. But we'll continue with this work.

Discussion

These sessions closed with expressions of gratitude, with acknowledgement of what the couple had learned from their experience with us and with new seeds of hope. In this way, they confirmed the hope we had felt the day before, when we sensed a turning point in the encounter.

A word about their direct expression of gratitude that replaced the desperate expressions of hopelessness in the first couple of days: This seemed to us to be more important than a mere 'thank you,' an indication of their recovering a capacity to feel gratitude, not just to us, but to each other. This contrasts with Lila's relationship with her father. She was able to experience the therapists as a different kind of couple from whom she could get something good. The positive transference represented the hope extended from the therapist couple to this pair to become a working and loving couple. That we cared to listen without shutting them down gave Lila and Thomas new hope.

One sign of their fledgling hope was a new ability to discuss their daughter. Because they were symbolically cared for like children in the brief intervention, they could then begin feel that it is possible for them to take care of their child. To be a mother, you have to feel cared for as a child.

Now, after the good experience with us, Lila is able to give a good description of her daughter, to describe how the daughter tries to take care of her, to soothe her when Lila doesn't feel well, as Lila did with her mother before. Lila wants to protect her daughter from her own depression rather than repeat what her mother did to her in projecting depression and fear onto her daughter. We could then say to Lila that we did not want Lila to have to be a mother only out of obligation, but out of a capacity to love.

Thomas and Lila learned through the experience of our intervention. This modeled what they could expect from a longer therapy, as well as the way a child learns and grows from the experience of her parents, giving a first-hand experience of how growth occurs from feeling cared for and understood.

The Process of Assessment and Treatment

This example began with the symptom that brought the couple to ask for consultation – the affair. It shows how that symptom condenses the full range of problems such couples face: the growth of misunderstanding, difficulties facing pressures from their parents, the legacy of problems carried from their developmental years and the pressures brought to bear on them from their parents and from the wider culture. It illustrates what we hope to offer couples clinically and what we hope to teach Chinese clinicians. In this case, as with most of the couples and families that we see, it demonstrates that change is possible when we can help a couple re-find their resilience. Thomas had it in his business, but the couple had lost their capacity to grow and had now re-found it once again in the brief therapeutic encounter. We, and they, knew that they needed more therapeutic nurturing in order to sustain their innate resilience.

Chapter 12

Divorce

We have already seen examples that demonstrate how, when couples struggle over time, divorce often threatens as an alternative to the pain of a crippled marriage. In this chapter, I begin by discussing several aspects of divorce in China, from the problems and inconsistencies in divorce law within the social and legal setting, to problems that ensue in the wake of divorce, and reasons for commitment beyond love that often bind couples together, even when emotional connections are severely damaged.

In the last generation, divorce has increased dramatically in China, rising in waves since the 1950s. As many returning Communist soldiers left their farms and rural wives to move to cities, there was a need to free couples from marriages of obligation that had previously been forced on them. As result of both the empowerment of women and of the introduction in 1950 of a new marriage law, there was a sudden rise in the availability of divorce, unlike anything China had seen previously. Women initiated most of these divorces, resulting in this new marriage law being popularly referred to as 'the women's law.' These were not necessarily unopposed. Local cadres, dominated by men and reflecting the traditional patriarchal bias, were often unwilling to grant divorces. Their efforts were countered, however, by party leaders' insistence on every person's right to choose their spouse and to leave marriages into which they had been forced. As a result, the divorce rate soared, but by 1953, once the many women trapped in unbearable marriages had managed to divorce, the rate returned to the traditionally low levels. After the Cultural Revolution, there was another dramatic increase in divorce, and a third wave of divorces ensued in 2003 after legal procedures were streamlined and the requirement dropped for permission from employers or neighborhood committees (Jeffreys and Yu, 2015; Jankowiak and Moore, 2017).

Divorce rates have steadily climbed since then. The website *Facts and Details*, quoting the Chinese Ministry of Civil Affairs and *China Daily* in 2015, stated 'The number of divorces in the country is rising.

The number of couples who filed for divorce in 2013 climbed 12.8% to 3.5 million according to the Ministry of Civil Affairs. That compares to around 458,000 in 1985.' Divorce rates were highest in the big cities, with the divorce rate approaching 25% in some urban areas. For China as a whole, the rate is currently approximately a quarter of that of the Unites States, where the rate is above 50% (Hays, 2015). One major reason for divorce, about 15% of requested divorces, is domestic violence (*News China*, 2020).

In the first part of 2020, during the COVID-19 pandemic, rates of domestic violence and requests for divorce increased dramatically, first in Wuhan and then nationally, as couples who had regulated their not-so-good marital relationships by maintaining distance or having affairs could no longer do so. As of this writing, we cannot know whether the level of these trends will return to normal, now that the need for quarantine has receded in China. I should also note, however, that the spike in divorces is balanced by reports that many other couples reported improvement in their relationships, as the closeness renewed their love for each other (*Global Times*, 2020; Feng, 2020; Deese, 2020).

Divorce Law

Although Family Law is in place in China, its execution is subject to social and family pressure at every level. I have said that women were given the right to divorce shortly after the Communist victory in 1949, but over the years, in practical effect, and since state approval was required, divorce was rare and once granted, people were often demoted or banished to rural areas. New marriage laws in the 1980s made divorce relatively easy, although husbands could not apply during a wife's pregnancy or within the child's first year. The wife, however, could apply for divorce, even while pregnant. Nevertheless, permission from the couple's Working Unit was usually required, and this pressure often resulted in couples' reluctance to seek divorce. And during a month-long imposed waiting period, divorce officials would try to talk couples out of divorce on pain of having their process denied.

Divorce law became a matter of legal contention in the mid-1990s. The old ways were criticized as offering an imbalance of state paternalism over individual freedom and choice (Alford and Shen, 2003). After divorce laws were reformed between 2001 and 2003, divorce rates soared once again as many unhappy couples took advantage of the new ease of divorce. There were also new laws allowing wives to divorce unfaithful or abusive husbands, and requiring men with mistresses to pay compensation to their spouses, including 'one law that allows a spouse to claim all family assets if her partner is considered to be 'at fault'' (Hays, 2015).

The new access to courts is, however, not without political complexity. In an article entitled "No malicious incidents': The concern for stability in China's divorce practice,' the legal scholar He Xin (2017) describes the pressure on judges in highly contested and potentially explosive cases not to allow things to get out of hand and cause instability. The judges are encouraged to employ mediation over judicial imposition because they are responsible for keeping the parties in check. This has led judges to employ more skills as counselors in the mental health sense. However, in cases where there are direct or indirect threats, the legal criterion of 'the breakdown of mutual affection' is eclipsed by the political principle of 'no malicious incidents.' The emphasis on maintaining social stability paradoxically can produce the very instability it seeks to avoid, because it produces incentives for domestic violence and gender inequality. The judges are more likely to believe threats of suicide or violent retaliation against the judge or the spouse from men than from women, thus making them more likely to be swayed by threats from men. The overall effect is often to place the political evaluation of judges' performance in maintaining peace and stability above the best interests of couples (He Xin, 2009, 2017).

A 2019 case reported illustrates the vagaries of how divorce law is imposed in China. The headline in *SupChina* read, 'Court denies divorce to woman after she was paralyzed from a jump to escape domestic violence.' The woman from Henan Province had been abused for years. She was seen on closed-circuit TV being beaten by her husband. She then jumped out a window to escape another of her husband's beatings. A year later, the court had still refused to grant her a divorce, ruling that her divorce request would not be approved because her husband wanted to continue the relationship. She was also told that in order to obtain sufficient evidence to prove her domestic violence accusations in her divorce case, she would need to file a criminal complaint against her husband. However, even with the medical records, the local police decided that her paralysis was a result of her 'attempted suicide,' without direct relation to the husband's abuse. She persisted and was still denied divorce, with the court ordering her to try to resolve the issues in her marriage (Feng, 2020).

The New York Times later reported,

In a bid to pressure the court, Ms. Liu uploaded the video of her beating to WeChat, China's dominant social media platform. Thousands of Chinese internet users rallied to her defense, and a hashtag about her case was viewed more than a billion times on the microblogging site Weibo. News media interviews soon followed. Before long, a judge called Ms. Liu to say there was no need for mediation and the court would issue a verdict soon. On July 28, three weeks after she released the video, she was granted the divorce.

(Wee, 2020)

Many also pointed out that Liu's case was an alarming example of how China's policies that promote marriage and couples sticking together make it more difficult for victims of domestic violence to leave their abusive partners. In 2019, in a bid to reduce the country's soaring divorce rate, China introduced a new clause in the family and marriage section of its revised civil code, stipulating that divorce-seeking couples must wait 30 days before their request is approved. Since then, the so-called '30-day cool-off period' has been met with a fierce backlash from critics who argued that the legislation does nothing but add unnecessary obstacles to people who are in dire need of a divorce, especially those facing violent domestic abuse. When this year's Two Sessions meetings took place in May [2020], there was a widespread online campaign calling for China's policymakers to remove the proposed clause. . . Despite the strong opposition, the controversial clause was still included in the final version of the new civil code, which was approved and is slated to take effect on January 1, 2021' (Wee, 2020).

Despite increasingly fair laws, after divorce, the ex-husband is still likely to get child custody and the ex-wife to experience social ostracization and/or employment difficulty. For these reasons, as I have seen in several marriages I have interviewed, women are apt to endure. This is different than in the old days when the men would take a concubine while ignoring their wives (Hays, 2015).

The climate of spying and of devious behavior around divorce is often vicious. Rules governing such behavior are lax compared to the West. There are also many regrets voiced by the older generation, who viewed divorce as shameful and as a betrayal of family loyalty. This attitude is prevalent enough that often neither party is apt to seek divorce but rather opts to endure a marriage. For instance, I interviewed a Chinese woman who divorced her husband. At first, she did not tell her parents, but when she finally did, her parents did not tell the rest of the family and asked her to keep the divorce secret. Then they lobbied her to remarry her ex-husband in order to have children.

The situation of child custody is also difficult. Joint custody is rare, with the majority of awards favoring fathers. In addition, there are many cases of aggressive action to bar the spouse, most often the wife, from seeing the child, or effectively to kidnap the child prior to court hearings, since judges are highly likely to rule to maintain the status quo as being in the best interests of the child (Thomas, 2016; Zhang, 2019; *Reuters World News*, 2016).

New Wrinkles about Divorce

There is a new phenomenon called 'parent-driven divorce.' In these situations, parents who disapprove of their child's spouse drag the couple into court where they speak for their child, demanding divorce, often while the young adult child sits passively. I had been unaware of this development and have never seen a case clinically. So, I asked some of my Chinese students if they were aware of this pattern. 'Oh yes,' they said. 'This is common and we hear about it frequently.' In this way, the legacy of parent-negotiated marriages is resurgent. While the parents may have less to say about the formation of modern marriages, in parent-driven divorce, the old role of parents in determining marriages comes in through the back door of divorce. Then their right to interfere is often upheld in a practical way. Yan Yunxiang argues that parent-driven divorce is, in a paradoxical way, one expression of the new mode of individualism in China in which there are challenges from a lack of social space for youth to organize themselves independently from family, even while the culture is dominated by a consumer materialism, forcing the young people to seek financial support from parents. The conflict over individualism that lies behind the surface of struggles to become independent from parents, even while being beholden to them, can show up in divorce court in this way (Yan, 2013).

Alternatively, parents may pressure the couple by continuing to voice their negative opinion during the early phases of the marriage, often with a gathering force that either disrupts the marriage or operates as a wedge between the spouses, taking advantage of marital difficulties that might otherwise have come to therapy. We have already seen an example of this in Chapter 8, in which the husband's mother attacked the marriage from the beginning. This trend contradicts the idea that Chinese young people have thoroughly moved into the modern age in which their parents have no influence over their family life. We can certainly say that this could be true in some Western marriages, and indeed we hear stories clinically of parents who are opposed to their child's choice of a spouse and remain antagonistic to the spouse throughout the life of the marriage, but this pattern seems more formidable in China with its ingrained legacy of a parents' right to influence their adult children's marriages.

In the light of all the difficulties in the divorce process, and of inherent disadvantages to wives in divorce, many wives take it as a given that they will stay in bad marriages, suffering disappointment, affairs, abuse or contempt out of fear, or even virtual certainty, that divorce will be worse or that they may lose access to their child.

Finally, there are many legal and economic loopholes that have made it advantageous for some couples to have pro forma divorces while continuing to live together. For instance, there have been real estate laws that advantage single people and transient laws that have compensated divorcing partners, thereby promoting sham divorces.

On the positive side of the divorce picture, there are now websites offering solace to grieving divorcees, a sign of a small but growing awareness of the needs of divorced spouses (usually women) for advice and social support.

Seeing Couples Who Are Considering Divorce

We need to know the facts about divorce and divorce law in China, in the same way that knowledge of the legal and social context in our home countries constitutes a background that informs our clinical work with all marriages in which divorce is in consideration. Working with a couple clinically, however, offers dimensions that cannot be dealt with through law or understood only through cultural constructs, even though these play a role.

We have already seen several cases, beginning with the case that opened this book of the older academic man and the younger country-raised wife, in which one or both spouses were considering the possibility of divorce if things did not improve, and who weighed this possibility against the cultural and personal downsides to divorce with its economic and social disadvantages. Several of the wives have said that divorce would be a disaster for them. Recall, for instance, Nicole's family in Chapter 6, in which her father was out most nights drinking with colleagues, had lost a great deal of money and her mother would send him to beg for understanding from 14-year-old Nicole because she had no tolerance for him when he was drunk. Nicole's mother could not bring herself to consider divorce, feeling that there was no place to go, despite the 'reassurance' from Nicole that she could easily take care of herself and her mother.

Many of the couples we have seen have discussed the possibility of divorce with us from the beginning of their consultation. This is true in the United States as well, and as there, most of the couples who seek marital therapy, as opposed to divorce therapy, are predisposed to repair their marriage rather than to divorce. Nevertheless, couple therapists need to bear in mind that there are more than a few marriages for which separation and divorce are a better outcome for the individuals involved than the maintenance of an unhappy marriage.

This chapter is informed by the couples we have seen, several described earlier in the book, who considered divorce, but most of whom then moved to renewed hope and the possibility for repair of their marriage, a shared expression of couple resilience. Another of these cases is described in the next chapter. However, to give a more rounded picture of divorce, I will give two examples here.

A Case of Inevitable Divorce

Early in our China teaching, Jill and I saw a case of a demanding husband, Dr. T, and a disappointed wife, Mrs. B. They had married in their 30s for practical reasons, because time was getting on and so he thought he should, and because she thought he was well-educated and virtuous. In the sessions, he was peremptory and demanding. He announced that his wife was 'poor material' and only 5% satisfactory, which surprised him because he had thought she would be intelligent and good when they got married. He told us that he had cut off his family, not speaking to them for eight years because they cut him off from his first love, demanding that he give her up, which he had done. His father had been a model to him, an electrician in a mine who had been denied university education because of the Cultural Revolution. He said that he was like his father who sat alone and could not communicate, and always wanted things his own way. Now the couple did not sleep together because she did things that bothered him. She would have liked to have a child, but he was opposed to the interference a child would mean in his life. He wanted to handle these difficult things on his own, and only then pull his wife in so he could join her ideas with his own self-reflection, because, he said, she could understand even though she is not that smart.

When we asked about their dreams, in an attempt to reach below the obvious, Dr. T said that he dreamt about doing experiments and writing articles, and also dreamt of quarreling with his wife. Mrs. B dreamt about her grandmother who raised her during her first five years. Her grandmother, who had been her kind principal caretaker, and her father had died in the same year, when her grandmother was 88. Her father had beaten her mother, but not the children. As a child, she had tried to keep quiet when her parents were fighting, because she did not want to call attention to herself as the child of quarreling parents.

Dr. T had beaten Mrs. B only once, only with a slipper on her bottom, and then he shoved her against the refrigerator. On that occasion, she said if he did it again, she would divorce him. After that, he began to treat her better. He had unexpected but frequent outbursts, which she felt threatened by. For instance, he had smashed a laptop in anger.

They had been sleeping separately, but after our second session, Dr T did come back to bed with her, but when she tried to comfort him by offering a pillow and positioning his laptop for him, he resented her interference and yelled at her, calling her vulgar names. In the session, she cried about his mistreatment, but she said she believed that he would like to change. He said that he was afraid she would not be able to wait for him to change. She knew his thinking was idiosyncratic, self-involved and not susceptible to dialogue. He agreed that, because he is a scientist, he only believes in logical thinking and she is incapable of that. Mrs. B then said she would like to live alone. We could see that Mrs. B had been trying to accommodate him, but it appeared that over time, he had become psychotically self-referential and increasingly unavailable to outside influence, including anything his wife or we had to say.

In the fourth session, we asked if they were considering divorce. Dr. T turned on us for not giving him enough advice and telling them specifically what to do, while she said that what we had to say had been helpful to her. She said she did not want to divorce, because she did not want to give up on him. He replied more angrily: 'It is actually a question of whether I will give up on you for being so slow and unintelligent.' He was suddenly even angrier at us, finally announcing that he was leaving. He strode out of the room. His wife left with him but came back a few minutes later to tell us that this is what he was like these days. He was probably going away to think and be able to control himself, and that he was likely to be back the next day for the concluding session.

However, he did not return the next day. We saw her alone to discuss the question of what she wanted to do and whether or not she wanted to separate, which now seemed to us inevitable, given not only his sudden departure the day before, but what seems to have been a steady drift into an isolated and idiosyncratic state of mind. We acknowledged her dilemma: She had been reluctant to give up on her husband all along, but she could now see that he was becoming increasingly impossible. Her resolution to the marital impasse remained unclear when our time was up.

This case was unique in our interviewing experience in China, although not in our longer clinical careers. Its uniqueness reminds us that there are marriages that are characterized by the kind of self-referential intransigence that Dr. T displayed, and that suffer from serious mental illness, which likely afflicted him. Even here we saw the wife's extreme reluctance to face separation and divorce because she was still considering both the cultural and family consequences for each of them, even though he was blocking her and her family's wish for a child.

A Family after Divorce

The next case is a divorced family in which the arrangements were, as is typical in China, disadvantageous to the mother and therefore to their daughter. I interviewed this case with Jill Scharff, with Kate Scharff, as the observer. We had requested that, if possible, our host and collaborator, Fang Xin, find a case involving divorce because Kate's clinical and research specialty is the study of new ways of facilitating better outcomes for divorce in the United States, having two books published on the mitigation of divorce processes and their effects on children (K. Scharff and Herrick, 2010, 2016).

Rachel, Alexa and Tom: A Family Consultation with A Family of Divorce

Rachel is a 13-year-old girl whose parents divorced when she was four. She lives with her father, Tom, and her stepmother, who is referred to as 'Auntie.' They are strict disciplinarians with high expectations, while her mother, calling herself Alexa, is indulgent. To us, Rachel seems immature, more like a young child. Both parents said that their own parents were strict, but while Tom has continued in his parents' mold, Alexa has reacted against her parents' methods. Rachel was clearly fashion-conscious, dressed in matching bright pink pants and a jacket. She sat between her parents in their muted colors. Her face reflected the features of both parents, but her overweight body was unlike either of them. Her voice was incredibly high and halting, like that of a four-year-old. From the beginning, we noticed that Rachel had a facial tic of irregular blinking that was more prominent at stressful moments in the sessions.

In the first session, we learned that Rachel's school performance vacillates, but the bigger problem is that she is not well-liked and is frequently teased. It was easy to imagine her being teased and even shunned at school for not fitting in because she does not like pop culture and is interested in classical music, philosophy and ancient history, which her classmates are not.

Emotionally, Rachel lives in-between her parents, bringing them together every day. While she resides with father, her mother lives nearby and comes to his house every day to care for Rachel. Tom thinks Rachel should be like him, while Alexa thinks that Rachel should be coddled and allowed to live life as she wants. Rachel described herself as being like two people: a six-year old who likes pink and cartoon movies, and a 40-year-old who likes classical music and philosophy. She is jealous of her half-brother, aged four, who is indulged by his own mother, Rachel's step-mother, even though she is strict with Rachel. Furthermore, Rachel thinks it is not fair that people tell her she should take care of him. Tom has told Alexa that she must not get remarried because a stepfather would be bad for Rachel. Alexa feels bound by her ex-husband's opinion.

In the first session, it remained obscure why they had divorced, and Alexa does not want us to ask that question. Since the father seems quite strict and demanding, demonstrating an off-putting demeanor with us, we thought that perhaps she just wanted away from him. We entertained other fantasies, especially of affairs.

Alexa said, struggling, 'It's because of me.'

Tom said,

> We got divorced because we are from different family backgrounds and cultures. Conflict developed over many things. I discussed it with her as my dissatisfaction grew. She felt dissatisfied too. She no longer loved me. I looked down on her and she looked down on me. We weren't right for each other.

Jill asked, 'Alexa, why do think that the divorce was because of you?'

Alexa said, 'Conflict had been accumulating. Then I got somebody else.'

Rachel rejects the idea we propose to her that she has the power to bring the parents together as if they were still married. She complains of her father's threatening strictness.

She says,

> For example, we visited an amusement park. I was timid and didn't want to play on the equipment. My father threatened me: 'If you don't play, I will go away and leave you here alone.' I was seven or eight, so I had to obey because I didn't want to be left alone. My mother felt that threating me was completely not okay.

In this session, we already felt that Rachel wielded a great deal of power with her parents, but she denied that.

For the second session, we saw the parents alone in order to hear more about the divorce. Tom and Alexa grew apart after Rachel was born, developing mutual contempt. Tom had looked down on Alexa as not being his cultural equal, but she was contemptuous of him, too. It all developed gradually until, in the wake of the changed emotional climate, Alexa had an affair.

Tom said,

I felt angry, of course. I wanted to say that when we married, she was very young. We almost never quarreled. The problem in the relationship was that we ignored each other. Rachel didn't see us fight. We just didn't relate.

I said, 'So there was an empty space that led to the affair, which then led to Tom's anger and the divorce. (Alexa nodded.) What was that empty space like for you, Alexa, and for how long did it go on?'

Alexa said, 'It came on gradually. Before Rachel was born, we had a good relationship for seven years, but after she was born, we had different ideas. We seldom fought. It's hard to explain how we were gradually driven apart.'

Jill asked, 'Did having Rachel drive a wedge between you?'

Alexa said, 'Yes. Because of her being a small child, there was so much to do. My time was totally occupied by her. I complained to Tom. He said everybody lives like this. How can you complain?'

Although Alexa's parents had taken care of Rachel for the first year, Tom then asserted his opinion that the family should move to an apartment complex with *his* parents, who promptly took over. From this point on, Tom's attitude determined pretty much everything. That has since included insisting that Alexa should break up with the man with whom she had the affair because of Tom's strongly voiced opinion that stepfathers were bad for a child, even though he was equally sure that his new wife was a not bad influence on Rachel. In fact, the stepmother has been critical of Rachel with a tone similar to Tom's. But living with Tom's edict had meant that not only did Alexa lose some of her access to Rachel, but it also meant that in a personally tragic way she lost her partner. So, she was made a second-class citizen, doing the caretaking, essentially acting like a nanny, a role she has accepted.

We also learned another important new fact. At the time of the divorce, Rachel had been enrolled in a kind of boarding situation, sleeping at the kindergarten where the other young girls were not nice to her. It sounded as though she was neglected and tormented in the boarding preschool. This became the reason for taking her back home at night after about a year. So, Rachel had the additional trauma of early separation from both parents. It was at this time, age four or five, that Rachel had a personality change and became difficult, complaining that she did not like to stay overnight when the other children did not have to. In addition, Tom told us that he thought the teachers were inexperienced, young, unmarried girls who were harsh, treating Rachel's distress as a nuisance to be punished.

We could see that now Rachel was identified with her depressed and powerless mother, and had a negative attitude towards her father, whom she felt was too strict and bossed her around in a way that was similar to the way he bossed her mother around.

We suggested that the next day we see Rachel along with father, stepmother and four-year-old brother, but Tom absolutely blocked this idea, saying it was 'not convenient and would not be good for a four-year-old boy.' In this exchange, we again had first-hand experience of his authoritarian way. We let them know that although there are other ways of seeing our suggestion, we accepted his decision. In this episode, we experienced Tom as an authoritarian boss, one to be obeyed and feared, much as Rachel and Alexa must experience him. As he deprived us of one kind of opportunity to learn and be helpful to them, we developed a countertransference feeling of the kind of tyrannical domination and deprivation that Alexa and Rachel must be feeling at his hands. This connected to our sense of Rachel as wanting to be a baby in order to go back to the time when her parents were together and she was well-treated, and before she was in the depriving situations of the kindergarten-boarding school, of the divorce or of having to put up with her new half-brother. We felt this helped to explain our sense of her as regressed and infantile, having to defend herself against growing up with the deprivations and losses that had entailed.

In the third session, attended once again by the three of them, we noticed an exacerbation of Rachel's tic, especially when her mother discussed issues about visitation. We began by asking Tom about his time growing up and the history of his family. We were able to establish a connection between his family, which was treated badly in both his grandparents' generation and during the Cultural Revolution. All his grandparents had early separations. Then, during the Cultural Revolution, Tom's parents were accused of having the 'wrong roots,' meaning they were rich, and his father of being a 'rightest anti-revolutionary,' bringing serious attack onto the family. Tom's mother's personality had always been full of hatred and disdain, which Rachel had experienced with her.

Tom said,

> My mother was asocial with her peers. When Rachel was in elementary school and complained about having no friends, my mother would say to her that she understood because it had been like that for her, and that it didn't matter, because if you're good at school, you can ignore them all.

We thought that the disdain Rachel experienced with her maternal grandmother was part of the model for the teasing and put-downs she had repeatedly experienced in the classroom. Tom did not want to talk about all this, and never really did tell us what happened to his family in the Cultural Revolution, except that it was bad. We noticed Rachel's blinking increase as he talked about his family. He questioned whether Rachel would have any knowledge or ability to understand the family's history, but Rachel insisted that she could. We said she needed to know these things, because she was living out the legacy of that history without knowing where these elements came from. We focused heavily on Tom's history in this session, saying to Alexa that it was our intention to do that with her the next day.

We also got a feeling for how Tom's own treatment as a child influenced his treatment of Rachel. His father had hit him repeatedly to motivate him into doing his homework, so, he said, it was natural he would hit Rachel: It was just ordinary. But then he had noticed it hurt her, so he stopped.

This session confirmed our impression of the severe effects of the Cultural Revolution on Tom's family, including how he was frequently hit as a child. But we also know that strict punishment of children is sanctioned in Chinese culture, even absent this kind of trauma, so in all probability, the two forces of culture and family trauma added together. In an unknowing way, Tom therefore hit Rachel, only stopping because she was a girl who complained that his blows hurt, but he had continued his harsh words and critical imposition of standards on her as a consequence of the way he was treated by his parents, all along considering it to be normal. Since neither his mother nor he had had friends in school, he had thought that Rachel's friendless experience was simply the way things always were.

In the fourth session, we explored the relationship between the parents and their parenting of Rachel. Rachel moves between them in a way that promoted splits between them and in her, while reinforcing their mutual disapproval. In addition, there was the continuing silent expression of their hostility on the basis of their failed relationship. We learned that Alexa was also beaten at home as a child, but more for her behavior than for her grades. She thought her bad temper was a result, and she finds herself yelling at Rachel in ways she wished she did not. Rachel's blinking again becomes more prominent as her mother says this. Tom and Alexa discussed Rachel's appalling manners, which had meant they were embarrassed about her in public. We proposed that her 'greedy' manners might represent her hunger to compensate for the void that she has felt both in the past and now. Rachel thinks she is bad and is the cause of her parents' discord and of her father's disapproval. She also believes that both parents think she is bad, which they denied in the session, but she has been criticized both for her academic performance and for her behavior at family dinners.

Rachel said,

> I get to eat last, when the food I want is gone.... I think I'm bad and my parents think so, too. My father thinks the biggest problem is my school-work and his relationship with me, and also the relationship between me and my brother. But mainly, it's the academic problem. If I were a good student, everything would be solved. My father blames me, but my mother blames my peers. She speaks on the internet platform with the other parents and tells them to discipline their own children. My father blames me while she supports me.

The parents' disagreement over disapproval seemed again to relate to the way that both parents had been treated harshly by their own parents. Tom took his own way of being disciplined and treated that as a model, while Alexa was determined to undo her treatment as a child through her relationship to Rachel. In this way, Rachel became the battleground about which way of dealing with harsh parenting was better. Not surprisingly, she preferred her mother even though she knew her father cared for her, too. Throughout the session, Rachel's facial tic was obvious, only subsiding when we got to talking about what she wanted from her parents in place of the way that her father treated her now. Rachel's obvious distress affected our translator, Gao Jun, Jill and me in a countertransference that the three of us shared because her demeanor conveyed a great deal of her distress.

In our discussion after the session, Gao Jun articulated her countertransference, which spoke for Jill's and mine as well. She said,

> During the session, I was upset. I felt Rachel cut her mother out of discussions and used her mother as part of herself, leaving no room for the mother's self. There were so many things stuffed into me emotionally that I could hardly translate. I felt her tic in myself, as though I couldn't open my eyes because there was too much to digest.

In the last session, we honed in on a paradox: Although Tom seemed harsh, in fact, Tom and his wife were often passive in the face of Rachel's behavior, and let Rachel boss them around, while Alexa could then become strict and demanding. Rachel's anger at her father was magnified by deflecting onto him the anger she actually had at her mother for abandoning her, even though her mother was now with her every day.

We pointed out to the family that Rachel was powerfully in charge of the family in a way that was painful both for her and for them, forming a destructive cycle. In part, she provoked battles with her father to prove she should live with her mother. When we said this, Rachel began to tear up, and her blinking stopped as her anger gave way to sadness. We now saw that the blinking-tic was a bodily representation of trying to hold back her tears. Later, trying to recover, Rachel focused her anger on Jill, although she actually seemed angry at all of us for daring to accuse her of being powerful.

As we ended, we said to the family that Rachel should have more time in each family and not have the boundaries be so blurred between the two families. This would mean having more time in her mother's home. To our surprise, Tom seemed to have changed his attitude, accepting what we said, while now Alexa had become more resistant, looking, in these moments, much more in line with Rachel's staunch and stubborn resistance.

After the session, Jill said to the group of students, 'I felt an enormous relief when I saw Rachel's tears. Her eye blinking and her tics stopped because she no longer had to use her body to defend against deep feelings. At that moment, she became angry with both of us for confronting her, and only then could we see the deep unhappiness. This is the kind of moment that we welcome therapeutically, as the transference gathers and focuses on the therapists, and especially today on me as representing the mother with whom Rachel cannot afford to be angry. What I learned is that the anger at the father is also the anger that is unconsciously deflected from her mother, but that she can't afford to express directly to her mother. I could only see this when it was delivered to me in the session when she became furious at me, although now I can see that it was there at the end of the previous session when Rachel refused to shake my hand.'

Rachel's individual therapist, who had been observing from the audience, told us after the family left that he had long felt helpless in the face of Rachel's stubborn resistance. We recommended continuing individual therapy for Rachel, as well as family therapy. We understood that having Rachel alone in individual therapy would continue to be difficult because any real motivation for growth resided in her parents, who did want to help her. They themselves would need help about how to be better parents, both individually and together.

Concluding Thoughts About Divorce

Considerations of divorce in China could fill another book, so in this single chapter, we can only consider divorce in a partial way. Couples who face the possibility of divorce are scattered throughout this volume, because so many of the couples we have seen came for help while facing crises that threatened to destroy their marriages. Most of those couples were able to pull back from the edge, which is also my experience in the United States where I have the opportunity to follow through with treatment, unlike the situation in China where we either have to return them to the therapist who has sought consultation with us, or, if they have not been in therapy, refer them to a Chinese colleague in their home area.

Nevertheless, in these two examples, we have seen many of the elements that stress couples to the point of divorce, involving issues from the culture in which they live, as well as issues specific to each couple, such as family pressures, the trauma of previous generations, limitations of personal development and mental illness. In this second example, we could see how these vulnerabilities get passed through to children of divorce. Throughout this book, we also see the resilient attempts of couples and families to move past the shortcomings of their pasts, to achieve new adaptations and to improve in their own generation on the vulnerabilities inherited from the past.

Throughout this section on marriage and divorce, we have been examining the intersection of the inner sanction of couples' lives and the social forces that impinge on and partially construct those lives. While our focus has addressed the clinical questions I posed at the beginning of the book, there are always also the questions about how Chinese history and culture affect the couples, how current large-scale social forces impinge on them and how couples' current challenges relate to evolving Chinese culture. Social forces and the intimacy of the family are always intertwined. In the next section on families, we will examine how this is so for families who wrestle with how to best facilitate their children's growth.

Part 3

The Changing Face of Families

Chapter 13

The Young and Changing Family

As we have already seen, the Chinese family has changed and is changing still. In three generations, it has undergone several transitions from the model of a traditional family centered on a kinship-based economic organization with a preference for large families based on filial piety, reverence for elders and obedience to the father with considerable emotional power held by the mother and grandmother, to families that were in many ways subservient to the state and in which marriage was to serve the state more than the family itself, to the One Child families that were characteristic of urban and much of rural China from the mid-1980s, and finally now, to families allowed to have more children.

In relaxing the One Child Policy, and now in urging young couples to have more children, the government has hoped to compensate for the demographically and economically handicapped and dependent elderly population supported by a diminished young workforce with no solution in sight for the next generation. The government's estimates for increased birth rates have so far proven to be overly optimistic as governmental urgings to young people to produce more children have resulted in relatively small increases and a good deal of pushback by the childbearing age group that now wants the government to leave them to their own devices. The preference of modern young adults includes delaying marriage and a general desire for one child, or at most two children. There is also an increasing percentage of young adults who wish never to marry or to have children. This follows trends around the world for developed countries with two members of the family in the workforce and increasing costs of raising and educating children (Haas, 2017; *News China*, January 2017; Eberstadt, 2019).

The particular Chinese pressures on families include the way in which the 'only children' carry the hopes of their families solely on their shoulders, receiving some combination of pampered idealization and anxious harassment from a young age. But as they mature, it becomes clear that these adult 'only children' will face a future of shouldering burdens alone, burdens not only for fulfilling the family's hopes and dreams, but also for literally supporting the family economically. In a study of comparative transfers of wealth at varying ages, Wang Feng and his colleagues (2019) found that in Western countries, a combination of governmental and family provisions means that the aged members of families receive a good deal of economic support from the state. In the United States, they receive Social Security payments that represent both monies paid into the government during a person's working life and transfers from taxes that younger workers currently make. China has only about 65% coverage for any level of social security support, and even that is meager – unlike the days before 1980 of the 'Iron Rice Bowl,' in which all were guaranteed a basic living. The burden of supporting the aged now falls largely to families' own adult children. The government has put into law the right of the elderly to be supported by their children. This means that a child-rearing couple is likely to have up to four aging parents, and perhaps also surviving grandparents, who need financial support, including support for health needs. I have already described that it is generally now acknowledged that young adults are increasingly unenthusiastic about this role, feeling it is too great a burden. They are afraid that they will not be able to uphold this kind of obligation. These strains have shown up already in changing patterns of relationships to the grandparent generation.

Rural Families and Families of Poverty

As I have previously noted, rural families were less subject to the strict One Child Policy, although forced abortions and severe social and economic penalties were still often enforced. But there have been other forces operating, as much of the adult population left the small towns for the cities where employment was available. One result was a large population of 'Left-Behind Children' raised by grandparents or other relatives, or even by unrelated villagers. I referred earlier to the way the documentary 'Last Train Home' (Lixin Fan, 2009), which tells the tragic story of such a family and the loss of linkage between the parents working in the city and their left-behind children.

As the government now pursues a policy of moving rural families into cities, it is building a large number of mid-sized cities where there is no traditional social infrastructure, a paucity of meaningful employment and little or no family support for those being moved off the land. More than one million families, many of them rural, whose only child has died by accident, disease or natural tragedy, have no hope of extending their family name and no one to support them in old age (Yuan Ye, 2012).

My encounters with Chinese families have been limited to urban middle-class families, although many of the families I have seen began their lives in the countryside. It is to the children of these families that the leadership will fall in business and intellectual fields, as well as in senior governmental affairs.

In the chapters that follow on Chinese families, I will examine how the pressures on families and their children are displayed in symptomatic vulnerabilities, and how many of these families that we have seen respond with innate resilience that is a feature of Chinese character.

Planning for Children

As we have seen, the question of whether and when to have children has changed radically in China. While Chinese couples are waiting longer to marry and to have children, their parents, who have only one child capable of producing grandchildren, grow increasingly desperate, fearing that their child will fail to have a child at all.

This has led to the phenomenon of couples who agree to have a child essentially for their own parents. One couple I saw said this directly. They had the child that their parents demanded, and then deposited the child with the wife's parents in another city, visiting the child from time to time but otherwise continuing to live as if childless.

Once a couple has a child, the age-old tradition of grandparental care of the child is apt to take hold. While there is no longer the extended family of the old days, now that both parents are likely to be working in the city, childcare from one or more grandparents is welcome. This carries the complications of living with or nearby to one or both sets of parents, with the attendant jealousies between sets of grandparent in-laws. There are also problems when the grandparents want control of family life when most young adults want more independence.

Childhood in China

Childhood in China has changed dramatically in the last 100 years during China's various stages of modernization that are ever more affected by global considerations. Middle-class childhood has changed the most. We could say that middle-class Chinese children now look more like Western children – more autonomous, wealthier, better educated and given more of a voice in the family. But tension with the old ways of filial loyalty to family and group remains. There are also large differences between urban and rural children, and between those legal middle-class urban children and the children of urban migrants from rural areas without *hukous*, and therefore without rights to education and medical care. There are also differences in equality of city girls and rural girls. For middle-class city girls, there is something like gender equality, as the parents of only-child girls cherish and nurture their only-child girl.

In the countryside, however, the fact that families of first-born girls have often been able to have a second child has eroded the worth of girls, leaning towards the traditional preference for boys and thereby diminished the gains compared to city only-child girls. There are many other tensions in national policy about children that reflect the government's interest in what child-rearing and education should strive for in the continuing transition to a market economy, and there are tensions between parents' wishes to give their children a kind of life and an autonomy they could not have, and their simultaneous adherence to traditional values of family fealty and group identity (Naftali, 2016).

A Contemporary Chinese Family

The family I will introduce now is one with two young children, something we will see again in later chapters on late adolescence. We commonly conduct family therapy with children of all ages. This family shows some of the issues that families with preschool- and elementary school-aged children have and how we work with them. It also illustrates many of the important contemporary issues for many Chinese families: the wish for a second child before the ending of the One Child Policy made this easy, the role of the ambition of the parents, educational and behavioral pressures on the child and difficulties living with grandparents.

In this family, the play of the children and the inventiveness of the family helped them to begin to overcome the distress that brought them as a couple to consult us. Then we found that the couple's issues were also producing symptoms in their children.

The family came for evaluation as a couple with the presenting problem of dealing with their ten-year-old son. Fortunately, they agreed to bring in the son and the daughter so that we could have a family meeting, offering us a chance to see how the unresolved issues and resulting dynamics of a struggling couple affected their children. This example of family also gives us further opportunity to reflect on how social issues impinge on families and on the children's development.

When we see young children, either alone or in a family, we rely on their play even more than their words. Two of the sessions I describe below demonstrate how we incorporate the play into our understanding of the families of play-age children, using the play as a language for speaking to the children and to the whole family. This family was especially good at using the play as a psychological vehicle. It is a tenet of our clinical work that play *is* children's way of communicating, because their play is more articulate and shows more of their inner world than their words (Winnicott, 1971a; Scharff and Scharff, 1987). This example is given in more detail than some others so that we can recreate the visual interaction.

The Family of Becky and Dr. Liu

Jill Scharff and I greeted a nice-looking couple who entered the room. The usual audience of 75 Chinese students and faculty was gathered in front of us, our colleague and translator, Gao Jun, was sitting between us, and our teaching colleague, Mary Morgan, was behind us. The couple spoke fluent English, but we conducted the interview, as usual, through the translator in Chinese.

With the husband's nod, the mother introduced them. She asked us to call her Becky, and her husband said he was Dr. Liu (again, not their real names). They are older parents – she 50 and he 47, and have been married a little over 12 years, with a ten-year-old son, Michael, and a four-and-a-half-year-old daughter, Anna. Michael's symptoms, which first appeared about three months ago, alarmed them and brought them for this evaluation, for which they immediately expressed gratitude. Michael has been withholding his saliva, washing his hands repeatedly, taking as much as two hours to decide what to wear each day and is frequently paralyzed with indecision over small things. Doctors have diagnosed obsessive compulsive disorder and suggested medication, but the parents, thinking it was a psychological condition, sought further consultation. Becky is a businesswoman and Dr. Liu a medical researcher. They both work hard, employing nannies for the children and, in the past, living in a complex of apartments with his parents and with her widowed mother, all of whom helped with the children.

> Becky said, My mood has not been good for several years now. It should go up and down in an ordinary way like the temperature, but it has just been low. I cannot understand why. And our couple relationship has big problems. We don't talk except about the children. We are both busy, so we have no time for the relationship.

Dr. Liu agreed with his wife's description, adding that his hospital was far from home, and with his travel to conferences, he had little time for his wife and children. He added that his son is extremely sensitive to criticism, and there is a heavy family atmosphere and the stress of school. He said, 'I wonder how to improve what's wrong with us, and how to help the children, especially Michael.'

Jill said, 'As I listen, I get the feeling of tremendous pressure. You're asking what you can do while suggesting you don't have enough time for the children or yourselves. How do you change that?'

We noticed that the couple had already shifted focus from Michael onto the difficulty in their relationship that they thought affected Michael. Becky enlarged complaints about her husband's unavailability, from preoccupation with his work to being glued to his cell phone at home. Dr. Liu added that she was frequently angry at him for forgetting family arrangements, like whether the children were to have tennis lessons.

Dr. Liu said, 'I ask her and she doesn't answer. She thinks I should know. I feel she despises me, so I retreat. Perhaps because I know she's like that, I shouldn't take it personally, but I do.'

Becky responded,

> When I ask those questions, I don't know why you don't have the answer, if you don't remember or you don't care. I conclude you don't care and aren't paying attention to me or your family. Then I have to remember everything.

I asked, 'Are you mad at your husband often?'

Becky said, 'Mmmm, maybe 80% of the time.'

I asked, 'Almost all the time?'

Becky said, 'There's still 20% left over.'

Dr. Liu said, 'But in that 20%, she doesn't see me. Well, that's just a joke.'

Jill said to Becky, 'Your husband has said that you despise him and that you're angry. But, Dr. Liu, you also said her judgment was good. So why did she marry you if you're so unsatisfactory?'

Dr. Liu said, 'Because I was good and decent.'

We now discussed how their early affection had declined both because of their careers and because of Michael's sensitive temperament. At Becky's insistence, Michael had displaced Dr. Liu in the bedroom. The couple had been living in the United States because Dr. Liu had an exchange academic appointment when Becky became pregnant a second time. Although Dr. Liu had not wanted a second child, he acceded to her wishes. Because their daughter was born during that year, she is a US citizen. Therefore, they were not subject to the financial and social penalties of having a second child when they returned to China. (We would learn later from other families that often that was not the whole story on that issue.) Jill asked about the deterioration of their affection for each other. Occasionally breaking into English, the couple explained a gradual shift. Dr. Liu has become less patient and more absent; Becky has become angrier. We discussed how Michael ended up in their bed. Becky said she was getting angry now because her husband forgot the important detail that Michael had to stay in the hospital after birth, and once he came home, he was often sick in those early years. She had to take care of him so that he would not disturb his father's sleep. She described the incompetence of the nannies who were supposed to care for Michael.

I asked, 'There was conflict over where the boy would sleep?'

Becky said, 'We never discussed it.'

I said, 'But now there's a battle going on through your boy.'

Becky said, 'It never occurred to me to use the word battle, but maybe it is.'

Dr. Liu said, 'There are many unpleasant conflicts over parenting. Maybe this sleeping thing is important, but we also disagree about a lot, like his snacks.'

We now learned that they disagreed over many parenting decisions. For instance, Becky, when shopping, will tell Michael that candy is destructive for his teeth, but he can decide whether to have it anyway. Dr. Liu says his candy should be limited. He has 'rules without exceptions,' while she wants her children to be free. But then, when they ask Michael to decide, he's unable to.

I said that Michael was paralyzed trying to please both parents. Jill followed by asking if their differences might stem from differing family experiences.

Becky said,

I don't see how my parenting reflects my family experience. I was born during the Cultural Revolution. My parents were absent early on because my father was sent to the countryside for reeducation, and my mother had to work long hours in a factory. I was raised by my mother's parents, and then later I lived with my parents and my father's parents for three years before my father moved away again for work. Things changed often. I don't see how this affected me, but I vowed to be more flexible than my parents were. I did well in school, and then moved to Beijing for university.

When Jill said, 'I can see that you became flexible because you had to move and get on with things,' Becky nodded assent.

Dr. Liu's mother was a rural farmer, his father a teacher in the regional school. His mother was carefree, loving to sing and dance, while his father was more serious. Because his father had to live in another town during the week, Dr. Liu would often stay with him. His father, although strict, was kind to him. His grandparents, labeled 'rich farmers' during the Cultural Revolution, had their property confiscated, but his parents were apparently not directly affected. His father was not deprived of an education, perhaps because like many rural families, they kept a low profile and were spared. Because Dr. Liu and Becky had been able to buy three apartments in the same building, they had lived with both sets of parents in a complex, but with considerable friction. The families fought over decisions about the best care of the children and were unfailingly critical of the nannies, resulting in the couple changing nannies frequently. Eventually, they sent his parents back to live with his sister in their hometown, and later left their apartment to Becky's widowed mother because she was constantly critical of everyone. They bought themselves a new apartment across town from Becky's mother.

I summed up our first impressions: 'Today we have more questions than answers. There's a lot of conflict that you haven't discussed. Your son probably tries to solve your conflict for you. We think it would be helpful to meet with your children.' This resulted in a kind of crisis, with the couple expressing reluctance about exposing Michael and offering to bring just their four-year-old daughter instead. Feeling uncomfortable with a sense of pressure on the couple to do what we wanted, Jill said it would be best to leave the decision to the couple, which we agreed on, therefore not knowing if we would meet the children.

We noted that Becky was incredibly angry at her husband and that both parents were using Michael as a displacement from the parents' conflict. It seemed as if they existed only as parents, not as a romantic couple. Jill particularly noted the informative value of her own discomfort at the end of the session over whether the couple would bring the children. She thought that her feeling might be much like the boy's emotional situation, caught in the headlights of parental disagreement. We all agreed that the wife's anger and the husband's flight represented the frustration and distance between them, and that the boy must be expressing this in his paralyzed preoccupation with decisions.

The next day, we were pleasantly surprised to see that the family brought both children. We scrambled to find paper and markers, as at home in our own offices we would have known to supply appropriate toys. We placed paper and pens on the floor between our seats and theirs, and welcomed the family, who introduced us to Michael, a good-looking boy of 10, and Anna, a cute, petite four and a half. Anna had toy in each hand, which we eventually discovered to be a tiny doll and a spoon attached to a ball that could be tossed and caught in the spoon. Michael holds a small action figure. Soon after arriving, Anna shows her mother that her doll has lost a leg. They all search for it without success.

Anna sits shyly. Michael wordlessly urges Anna to show us her toy. His parents try to put him at ease. Becky gently prods him to tell us about his problem about holding his saliva. Both children are stuck, unable to speak, which does not surprise us. Michael hesitates, thinking; Anna checks with him, waiting for a cue from him, following his lead. Begin here

Seeing their difficulty, Jill gets down on the floor, inviting the children to join her. When that is not enough, she asks me to join her in the 'Squiggle Game' (Winnicott, 1971b). She draws a wavy line, asking me to make it into a picture. I humorously say that my effort will show everyone what a poor artist I am. I draw (Figure13.1) and hand my drawing to Jill, who describes the sun and clouds on a mountain with a river or path.

I then hand a squiggle to Jill, as we continue to model playing in order to invite the children to engage. Jill draws (Figure 13.2).

We ask Michael if he can guess what her picture is. Again, he hesitates painfully. *(We remember that his hesitating is the main symptom his parents worry about.)* I indicate I cannot really tell either, so Jill asks the family, 'Do they have snails here?' Becky

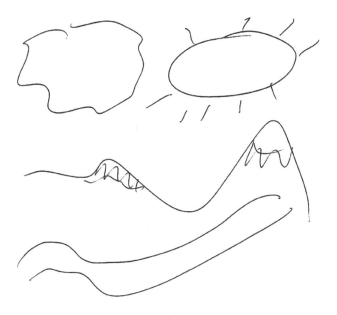

Figure 13.1 David's Sun, Clouds and Mountain

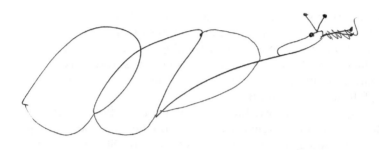

Figure 13.2 Jill's Snail

nods. Jill continues, 'I started to draw a snake but got scared and changed it into a snail. Then I thought it was interesting because a snail leaves a trace like saliva.'

In this way, Jill has associated to Michael's holding his saliva, with the addition of her own feeling a kind of fear in her counter-transference, a sign that Michael's fears may lead to this retention of his saliva.

Now we ask Michael to help Anna draw, but the children remain stuck. Suddenly Michael bursts out, 'I can draw.' He draws a squiggle and enthusiastically shoots it over to Jill, but then changes his mind and says that his mother, Becky, should draw. She draws an apple tree with many apples and a worm in the middle of one apple tree (Figure 13.3).

'A worm!' Jill exclaims. 'Maybe a rotten apple.'

Becky explains, 'No, the worm means that the tree is organic, so it's healthy. In China, it is commonly said that a worm in an apple indicates that there is no contamination from pesticides.' (*Later, our translator, Gao Jun, confirms the accepted truth of this Chinese wisdom.*) As Becky adds flowers to the tree, Anna has frozen again while Michael is playing with his action figure.

Suddenly, Michael pulls on his mother's arm. He points to Anna's doll's missing leg wedged between the wall and the riser we sit on. There is a family-wide effort to retrieve the missing leg, to no avail. Feeling this event is important, I stand and ask the family to move so that I can shift the riser. Dr. Liu joins me, and we quickly move

Figure 13.3 Becky's Apple Trees, One with a Worm in an Apple

the riser so that Anna and Michael are now successful. Together we replace the riser and the chairs.

Jill and I now comment on the family's cooperation, and then return to asking Becky to say more about her drawing. She explains that the rain makes a creek that waters the tree and the flowers.

Jill, on the floor again, says that she is remembering about Dr. Liu's mother. If she was a farmer, she would know about healthy cultivation. What about Becky's family? As both children relax into playing with their toys, Becky says that her mother worked in a factory, while her father first worked for a company making food products, and later opened a store selling groceries, liquor and candy.

We now ask Michael to give his father a squiggle in order to be fair in not challenging only his mother. He eagerly gives one to his father, a line running up and down the page vertically. Mr. Liu scratches his head, rotates the paper, and draws a sports car on a road (Figure 13.4).

Meanwhile, Becky asks Michael if he's hot and wants to take off his coat. Michael shakes his head, 'No.' Then he whispers energetically to his father, who tells us that Michael says that he should've drawn a national flag because Michael meant the line to be up and down (like an upright flagpole), not sideways.

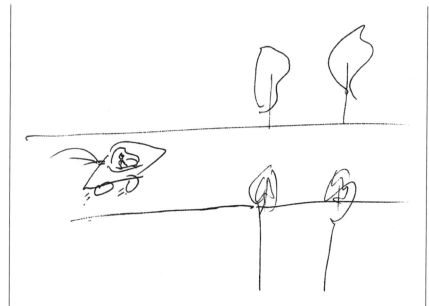

Figure 13.4 Dr. Liu's Sports Car on a Road

I ask Michael what he wanted. Michael replies in clear English, 'I think … . I drew a vertical line for a flag.' His father says he didn't think of that. I say, 'That's the trouble. You can't really tell what each other is thinking unless it's discussed.'

Michael asks his father to now draw a 'national flag.' But Anna jumps in first, saying, 'I can draw one.' She gets on the floor and draws a tiny yellow flag.

As Anna is drawing, Dr. Liu asks Michael if he's hot. Michael nods and promptly doffs his coat. Jill asks why he does so now when his dad asks him to, but not when his mom asked him the same question. Michael says, 'I didn't notice when my mother asked me, but now I feel hot.' Jill and I exchange a glance about his saying 'No!' to his mother and 'Yes!' to his father.

Resuming drawing, Michael shows his mother a 'National Flag' (Figures 13.5 and 13.6). Anna says there should be a ball on top. Michael adds one, and Anna says, 'That's right.'

I now venture that everyone had cooperated except Mother. Jill corrects me: 'I think you're wrong, David. You thought Dr. Liu did it because his car gave Michael the idea of the flag, but Becky had encouraged Anna to make a flag.'

Apologizing to Jill, I said, 'Thank you, Jill. I was wrong. Sometimes you and I disagree and we have to talk about that.' Turning to Michael, I ask, 'Does that happen in your house with your parents?'

Figure 13.5 Anna's Tiny Flag

Michael hesitates once again. He then says to his mother, 'You should answer.' Becky encourages him, 'Say whatever you want.' Michael says, 'They only disagree a few times.' Immediately Anna chimes in, 'Most of the time!' in English. Michael corrects her, '*Not* most of the time.' There's laughter. The disagreement between the children, while lighthearted, seems important, and although it seemed clear to us that Anna said, 'Most of the time,' the family

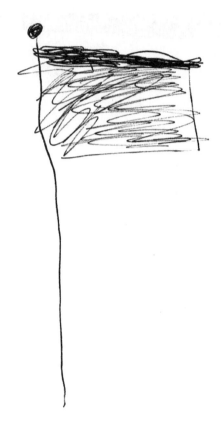

Figure 13.6 Michael's National Flag

now debates this and in the end changes Anna's mind to 'Not most of the time.' But Becky says clearly now, 'Mostly we disagree.' Michael now says, 'Anna said, 'a lot of the time." Becky says that Anna had said it *wasn't* most of the time, and Michael follows, again in English, that Anna had said it wasn't most of the time. Becky also follows in English, trying to explain Michael. Gao Jun tells us that Michael is now asking Anna what she meant, and Becky says, still in English, that they all got confused trying to interpret what Anna meant. Finally, Anna, tossing her ball into the cup quite competently, says in Chinese, 'That's right. It <u>wasn't</u> most of the time.' Dr. Liu translates this to us in English, and Becky, in English, notes how confused everyone now feels.

The mood of the session has now changed, as Michael sits forward and asks his mother in English, 'Can I say?' Becky nods.

Michael says his parents argued about buying the tickets for a train trip. Becky had bought the tickets to visit Dr. Liu's family for Spring Festival. This required Anna's passport information because Anna is legally an American citizen, but the clerk could not process her serial numbers. Dr. Liu had said not to try to argue with the clerk, just to buy another ticket and return the original. Their voices had been somewhat raised.

As they explain this 'disagreement,' I notice that Anna is staring at her toy, blowing bubbles with her saliva, indicating that she is feeling the growing tension in the family. Jill meanwhile says that the passport story makes her remember the different citizenship between the two children. Becky says China does not allow dual nationality, so Anna is American. The family doesn't discuss this difference often, because it's not a problem. Jill says nevertheless, it reminds her that the children both wanted to draw a 'national flag,' which would be a different one for each of them. This could be a story about Michael and Anna, who are brother and sister, but Anna has an American passport while Michael is Chinese.

Dr. Liu gives other examples of small disagreements. I say to Michael that all parents disagree sometimes. He nods. Becky says, 'And we have a lot of disagreements. For example, Michael, you want a lot of chocolate and your father says 'No!' and I say 'Yes!"

Michael nods, 'Yes, more or less.'

We now explore this situation. Becky says, 'I tell the children it's bad for their teeth but they can decide for themselves.'

I say, 'So, Michael, your dad says, 'No! Or just a little candy,' and your Mom says, 'Whatever you want, but it's not good for you.' Then it can be really hard for a guy to decide.'

Michael (checking with Becky) asks, 'Can I say? If I ask my mother, then, I do what her idea is. If I ask my Dad, I do his rule. Is that okay?'

Becky says, 'That's okay. But sometimes he asks me first and then asks his father. Then it's hard for him to decide.'

In summarizing something we learned today, I say,

It's impossible for you, Michael. You're trying to be so helpful to Anna and to both your parents. We see it's really hard because one parent is often upset, or at least you worry that they're going to be upset, so you spend a lot of time trying to fix things between them.

Michael smiles, 'Yes!' in English.

We indicate that we would like to see the children again the next day. Dr. Liu counters, 'Since it will be Monday, they'll have to go to school.' Michael echoes, 'We have to go to school.' Anna nods.

So, we say we'll leave it up to them to decide, but that if they do decide to bring the children, to please bring toys they would enjoy.

As they leave, Anna hops off her chair. Indicates her father's backpack, and asks, 'Can I have an apple candy?' Dr. Liu hesitates, then says, 'Yes. OK.'

In this second session, we worked to establish comfortable holding for the family and especially for the young children who were entering our public setting. We noted how Jill's removing her jacket to sit on the floor had led the way eventually for Michael to remove his, and eventually for the children to be able to play.

The example of the apple tree and the candy brought out the most anxiety in the family, emblematic of the many major disagreements over 'small things' about the children. It was then that Anna looked right at us and blew bubbles. We wondered whether Anna's playing with her saliva was symptomatic of that anxiety, just as Michael's holding his saliva might be.

The drawing of a flag that was 'just a national flag' of undefined nationality also pointed to anxious territory that was clarified in the discussion of the passports. The theme of the family's conflict over disagreement was echoed at the session's end, when Anna asked her father for 'apple candy,' echoing her mother's picture and the grandfather's store. Dr. Liu then hesitated before agreeing. That is to say, we thought his momentary hesitation was a source of Michael's symptomatic paralyzing hesitation about how not to displease either parent. This paralleled Michael's hesitation about whether to swallow candy or spit it out, or his not taking his mother's suggestion to remove his coat – and even changing the story to say he had not heard her when he had actually told her 'No!,' but agreed to his father's suggestion soon thereafter. These confusions, like the one around whether Anna said there were many disagreements or not many, expressed a confusional anxiety in the family and the children's difficulty pleasing their parents by saying the right thing.

Jill added that she had sat on the floor to enter the family play space, but it was lonely because there is no play space in the family. That echoed the couple saying the day before that they never have fun anymore.

Finally, we noted that the first event in the interview was Anna's saying her doll had lost a leg. That the family, with Michael's leadership, retrieved what was missing, was hopeful for this trial of family therapy.

On the third day, all four family members showed up, with toys and a small canister of markers. The family explained that the children had come because of Michael.

With his father's encouragement, Michael says, 'Yesterday, when we discussed how people had different opinions, I said if I followed my mother, I didn't think she would be upset because she would ask me to use my own judgment. So, if my Dad asked me to eat only a little bit ...'

Becky interjects, 'What if you follow my rules?'

Dr. Liu corrects her, 'He hadn't finished.'

Michael, looking at Becky, 'I don't know what to do now.'

Dr. Liu says, 'My differing opinions from my wife lead to difficulty for Michael. If he follows my rules, maybe it would upset her, so he prefers her rules.'

Jill says, 'Michael, I see you often check with Mom before you decide what's okay to say. You don't want to say the wrong thing.'

Michael looks puzzled. He makes mouth gestures indicating he doesn't know what to do or say. Finally, he manages, 'I want to add something like my Dad said ... Well ... Maybe when my parents have different opinions, it's hard for me to make my decision.'

Jill asks, 'Dr. Liu, you said last night you asked the children if they wanted to come back. Was Michael realizing that point about his decisions the reason they returned?'

Dr. Liu answers, 'Yes, because it helped him. Also, he liked the two of you.'

Jill asks, 'What does that mean, Michael?'

Michael replies, 'You can help me understand myself.'

Anna is now holding her eyes shut. Jill says, 'Anna, you're looking sleepy.'

Becky asks, 'Why did you want to come back, Anna?' (Michael holds the microphone up to Anna's mouth, trying to help her speak through her shyness.)

I ask Michael to speak for Anna. Michael says, 'She thought we were coming so she would come, too.'

Anna now wants to draw, so I get on the floor. She hands her pink and white toy to her mother. I ask what it is.

Anna says, 'It's a flying super hero.'

Michael demonstrates her Transformer that looks like a super hero helicopter with skis. (See Figure 13.7 for pictures of the toys.)

Then Michael explains that his toy is a Lego 'good guy' who can win because he has a gun. His parents bought it, and he made it himself. Michael clambers onto the floor and begins manipulating the Lego, saying, 'It's a little bit broken.' Anna shows me that one antenna is broken. Michael shows me another figure, the 'bad guy,' and then extracts from his father's backpack a huge Lego Transformer robot with impressive weaponry.

Figure 13.7 Michael and Anna's Toys: Left to Right: Michael's Small Lego Transformer and Action Figure; Anna's Pink Super Hero Helicopter and Lego Figure; Michael's Large Lego Transformer

Michael says, 'This one is a bad guy, but the one with the gun, the good guy, will win because the bad guy can only use his hands.' Anna chimes in to agree, then asks Becky to help with her Transformer, which Becky does. Michael takes the little good-guy figure and shows me proudly that his little guy fits neatly into a sort of 'control center-cockpit' in the chest of the giant robot.

I say, 'So this guy sits there and drives the big machine, like a Star Wars machine. What I really like is that it's like a kid is inside a grown-up deciding what the grown-up should do.'

Dr. Liu, leaning on Michael's shoulder, holding the microphone for Michael so he can be heard, says, 'There's a child inside the adult.'

Becky agrees, 'Yes, there's the little boy is inside the man.'

I say,

I think that every grown-up has a little kid inside, and also kids want to be grown-ups. Michael, you think you have to fix the grown-ups in order to be stronger yourself. And Anna, you'd like your superhero to fly in and rescue everybody. Michael, do you think you should be better at fixing your parents? ... . Hey Anna, where is your helicopter-hero flying to?

Anna says, 'I don't know.'

Becky says, 'He wants to run around the planet to rescue people.'

A bit later in the session, while the children are now playing on the floor, Jill says, 'I see a family group of three figures plus the tub of markers ...' But before she can finish her sentence, the kids introduce another figure to the family making it four figures (plus the tub of markers), but then promptly taking one of them away.

I, recalling how the family had gotten rid of the grandparents, asks, 'Is somebody missing?'

Michael pauses, anxious, not knowing how to answer.

I say, 'That toy family changed from four to five, and back again, reminding me that your parents told us that you had a grandmother who used to live with you.'

Anna says, 'My grandmother used to live with us. It's better now though.'

Michael says, 'Now we have to take a bus to see her.'

Becky volunteers, 'I agree with Anna. I don't want to see my mother much. We upset each other.'

Michael says (in English), 'I hear them fighting.' Then in Chinese, 'There's fighting at my grandma's apartment.'

Anna says, 'I knew it, too. It was noisy and I can't even sleep.'

Jill says, 'What was the fighting about?'

Michael says, 'I almost forgot.'

I say, 'Saying you 'almost forgot' means you do remember some.'

Jill says, 'Did Grandma and Mom fight more than Mom and Dad?'

Michael says, 'Yes. Mom tries not to fight. She tries not to be with her.'

Anna says, 'If they meet, they fight. Grandma says something to Mom and, if they disagree, they fight.'

Still on the floor, I arrange the toys. 'Here's Grandma and Mom fighting. Grandma's pretty strong, so everybody is worried about Mom.'

Michael says, 'I worry about their fights.'

Anna says, 'I worry about their fights, too. I worry about them both.'

Michael says, 'I worry the fights will get bigger and bigger.'

Jill says, 'Grandma's very bossy?'

Michael says, 'No. There just is a big difference. It's not my business. I don't want to be concerned.'

Jill asks Michael, 'How does Grandma treat you?'

Michael answers, 'Good, but I don't like it that she's so noisy and annoying. In the winter, she would make me put on more and more clothes. That was my business.'

(I think about how he kept his coat on when his mother asked if he was hot yesterday.)

Anna says, 'It's my business, too.'

I say, 'You don't want Grandma to boss you. You have enough bosses with Mom and Dad. Dad, what you think of all this?'

Dr. Liu answers, 'My wife and her mother had different ideas about the children. I tried to mediate the fights, but Grandma was very stubborn and wanted things her way.'

Anna is now squirming and needs to go to the bathroom, so we indicate Becky should feel free to take her. But we also realize this is probably an indication of Anna's anxiety about the fights. When Anna and Becky return, I ask if things are better between the couple without Grandma.

Dr. Liu says, 'It's not better between us, but at least I don't have to mediate between the two of them.'

Now Michael, then Anna, climb onto the floor with me to draw pictures. Anna draws another flag in bright yellow, like yesterday's but bigger (Figure 13.8). I compliment her flag and ask Michael to tell us what his picture is.

Michael points to powerful figure drawing that recreates the big Transformer. He continues to draw while Anna returns to her seat. (Figure 13.9)

I say, 'I see in Michael's picture that Grandma is surrounded. And I see, Michael, that you began by drawing a tiny figure on a big piece of paper, although the other figures are even smaller.'

Figure 13.8 Anna's Second Flag

Figure 13.9 Michael's Picture of his Transformers

Anna interjects, 'And the big space is the sky.'
I say,

That's a nice way to see it. In your family, there's a lot of fighting, which Michael and Anna find painful, and so do you, Mom and Dad. It's better without your mother nearby, but how you two get along is still a problem.

Michael continues to draw. Anna says his picture is good.
I ask, 'Michael, do you think the main problem is how Mom and Dad get along?'
There's a pause. Michael hesitates while he considers the question.
Becky chimes in, 'Maybe!'
I repeat, 'Maybe?'
Becky shakes her head, 'It's for sure!'
I ask, 'Do your parents fight much, Michael?'
Michael answers, 'Not so much.'
Anna disagrees, 'They fight much.'
Becky says, 'We don't fight so much.'
Following Becky, Anna corrects herself, 'That's what I meant – 'not so much." (She gives in to agree with her mother's correction.)
We notice this repetition of yesterday's confusion, with Anna being emotionally forced to take back her initial response that they do fight a lot.
Michael now draws a larger toy behind the other toys in his picture of his toys. He says it's imaginary, not an actual Lego.
Jill says, 'The question is about the parents fighting, how that shouldn't be the children's business.'
As time is now up, I borrow a phone from the audience to take pictures of the toys. Michael lines up the toys for the picture. Becky

offers to take the picture because she has a better angle. We leave it to the family to decide whether the children or just the couple will return, acknowledging the family agreement that the central problem is how the parents get along. We tell the children that we are grateful they have come. We will be glad to see them again, or glad to meet with their parents alone.

In the discussion today, we noted how the parents so often disagree, while Michael and Anna always try to agree, Anna looking to Michael for cues. Once again, Anna felt she had to change what she had to say about the fights, indicating the enormous anxiety about the parents' disagreements and the threat to the children that they might say the wrong thing.

The play with the rapid changes in the toy-family configuration suggested to me that Michael might be worried about being sent away as Grandma was, but I felt that theory was not confirmed. The children had led the way in talking about their parents' fighting as the central family anxiety, but the couple had facilitated the kids expressing themselves and related to the play as expressing family concerns despite the parents' own anxiety about the children seeing their fights. We note how cooperative and open the parents were in both facilitating the children's play and in joining in the drawing – a good sign for their potential to be more engaged with the children.

On the fourth day, the couple came alone, although the children had been eager to return. Becky said they decided to come as a couple because they felt that Michael's problems stemmed from them. 'We have a lot of battles between us that we project onto the children, but rarely discuss ourselves.'

Jill agreed, but added, 'It's also clear how much you do right. Your delightful children are very capable.'

We turned first to the differences in their interests. Dr. Liu described himself as 'sporty,' enjoying biking, badminton, swimming and climbing mountains. Now these have all been replaced by accompanying the children to tennis and swimming.

Becky says she never objected to his sports,

But, for example, we have two apartments. I ask him about washing the plates. He wastes water and gets them very clean. I don't feel I have to get them so clean, so I complain about his using so much water, while he thinks I don't clean the plates enough. So, we decided that in his apartment, washing will be thorough, and in my apartment, we'll only do ordinary washing. There are a lot of differences around the children, too; for example, about eating candy or about homework. We never discuss how to reconcile our differences.

Dr. Liu disagrees: 'We discuss things, but there's no consensus. I say, 'For all the children's matters, we will follow your rules.' But my wife felt that maybe I just gave up. It's evidence to her that I don't want to participate.'

Jill says, 'That you surrendered!'

Becky interjects in English: 'Unwillingly!'

Jill asks, 'Becky, do you want him to surrender willingly?'

Becky demurs, 'I prefer that we discuss things. Perhaps we could debate.'

(Dr. Liu tries to come in here, but gives up as she continues. Then she sees him and gestures that he should speak.)

Dr. Liu says,

> There are character differences. I'm from science; she's from liberal arts. But she's logical and uses data. I do photography and artistic things. I don't really follow data. I just make a decision. For instance, about chocolate, she asked me what medical sources tell me that they shouldn't have chocolate. I don't have the data, so I surrender.'

I comment, 'So, if you give an opinion, Becky challenges it, and you, Dr. Liu, just go away.'

Becky, again in English, responds, 'And then I get angry. But I don't say so.'

I say, 'But he knows.' (Dr. Liu nods even before the translation.)

Jill says, 'It's silent anger, but the look on your face must signal your fury. I can see traces of it here.'

Becky says, 'I try to be happy and settle things without emotion. As a result, I don't know what he thinks.'

Dr. Liu agrees, 'This is all true.'

Jill comments, 'It's difficult for you to come together as a couple. I'm thinking about the two apartments with two separate standards.'

The couple explains that each of them lived with their parents before marriage, so they came together with different lifestyles. We ask what they each want now. Becky said she wants to be able to have frank discussions without the inhibition of foolish worries.

Jill says, 'I'm surprised you're worried about being foolish, because you're very confident or maybe even a little bossy.' (Becky smiles.) 'I see you as a powerful person, and I don't mean to be rude.'

Dr. Liu says,

> I tell her sometimes that she shouldn't be so pushy. When I'm very calm, I don't take her style personally. But if we're arguing, then I'm charged with emotion and can't remind myself that being a bit bossy is just her way.

I say, 'This is a central underlying issue that you fight about.'

Jill turns to our translator, Gao Jun, to ask if she feels Becky has a peremptory manner of speaking. Gao Jun confirms that she does, more so than comes across in translation.

The couple gives another example. Dr. Liu had an idea for planning a trip, but Becky did the research. Then they give a second example about Becky's mother. Because Becky and her mother fight constantly, and because Dr. Liu is in the profession, he usually accompanies her mother to medical visits. But often afterwards, Becky will challenge him about whether he had asked all the relevant questions. He feels, 'If her doctor thought those were important, he would have said so, and so I didn't need to ask.'

Jill suggests we explore Becky's relationship with her mother a bit more. 'I don't know if she is very difficult. Or does being with you make your mother upset?'

Becky says her mother is difficult, but Dr. Liu says his view is that she is not so much difficult as stubborn. 'You can't ever change her mind!'

Becky says, 'She tries to impose her values. She's tried to change me all my life.' She went on to list the critiques her mother had about her hairstyle, her school performance, her friends.

> She wasn't even there until after I was six. Once I was helping her fetch water from the village well. The bucket was too heavy for her to carry alone, so I had to help. She told me to go faster than I could go. The barrel fell and she cursed at me saying, 'How could you be so slow? Time is urgent.' Now, when she criticizes how I raise the children, I say, 'You never raised me, so how do you know what they should do? You don't have the right!'

I now feel ready to give an individual interpretation:

> Your mother wasn't there, and then when she was there, she criticized you. I think there are two pieces of your mother that you speak from. On the one hand, you try to be *not like her*, and so you say to your children, 'You can have all the candy you want,' because that's being *not like* your mother. But then you say, 'But it's going to poison you!', and that's being *like* your mother.

Becky nodded tentatively.

Jill says,

> I was trying to have sympathy for your mother. Those six years, not knowing where her husband was, she had to work in a factory, and

maybe during this time she didn't like the way that her parents were raising you. I wonder if they were too indulgent for her taste.

I add, 'Maybe she was trying to 'bully you into being a good girl.' But what you felt was that she simply was a bully.'

Jill says, 'She still is a bully. But Dr. Liu is not a bully. He's easygoing except about cleaning the house.' (He smiles).

I want now to build our thinking back to the couple's dynamics, so I add, 'But the bully comes back because Dr. Liu feels that you, Becky, bully him. And Becky, it seems to me that you feel he makes you behave like a bully. And you hate that.'

Becky, in English, 'Indeed I do!'

They now give two examples that underline the problem. The first involved Dr. Liu giving their nanny permission to have an egg for breakfast. Becky felt managing the nannies had been delegated to her, so he was undermining her by indulging the nanny. A more telling example was when he forgot to tell her that the children would be flower attendants in a wedding for a member of his family in his home village. So, they arrived in his village without her being able to bring the appropriate clothes. They had scrambled to borrow them, and things turned out passably, but she was angry at his omission.

I now begin to give what amounts to a little lecture about the importance of repair in marriage, but Jill interrupts me to say that she thinks I'm becoming preachy. I accept this idea because I think she is right. Jill asks instead whether Becky had 'lost face.' Becky says no, she was angry because they could easily have prepared properly.

Dr. Liu said, in English, 'This was unforgivable.'

Jill asks, 'Is it unforgivable, or should it should be forgivable, but your wife never lets it go?'

Becky says, 'It's not unforgivable. I solved it, but the important thing is that we never discussed it.'

After the session, we discussed the way that the more Becky controls, the more Dr. Liu absents himself. Then Becky feels alone, as if 'everything is up to her,' and she becomes more controlling. The cycle repeats and she is left feeling painfully on her own again. The couple shares a belief that differences cannot be reconciled, much less be combined creatively. Jill and I thought it was a useful model that we could have a difference between ourselves at the end without being frightened or frightening.

We also noted that we had not heard much yet about Dr. Liu, who cooperates in putting his wife out in front and hiding behind her.

On the other hand, his pride in her capability is clear. Nevertheless, we hoped to hear more about him on the last day.

On the fifth day, again with the couple, Jill begins:

We thought we'd start this last meeting by summarizing things we have learned. We understand that Michael's problems with the saliva, washing his hands and his indecision are in reaction to your couple problems. Then, things build up in Michael and recently have gotten worse. The differences in your personalities are hard for him. Partly that's because of his sensitive nature. Perhaps another thread relates to Becky's father's death coming when Michael was one. And, partly also, Michael's inclination to catch colds made you worry for his health, fueling disagreements with the grandparents. That all concentrates on the question of his surviving.

But now Michael is healthy, and his difficulty is more emotional. The handwashing also reminds us that Dr. Liu likes things to be very clean, while the story about how Michael decides on how much candy is okay reminds us that Becky's father had a store with candy. So, we think Michael's symptoms are also attached to Becky's father who died, as well as to Becky's mother who was absent early in her life and is still problematic. Becky, we see you still carry your anger at your mother for leaving you for your first six years and then returning to boss you around. In fights with her, you try to be different, to be your own person, but in doing so, you've developed traits that are unfortunately like your mother. So, just as she criticized you, you feel critical of your husband. You try to suppress your anger, but it emerges as an angry atmosphere. So, the anger, originally directed at your mother, affects your whole family, your husband and Michael.

Dr. Liu, we know much less about you, but we do know you put your wife out front. So far, we know you had a fun-loving mother and a strict father, whom you often stayed with. Then you fell in love and married a woman who had some of your father's strictness while you've embodied your fun-loving, sporty, agreeable mother. As a couple, you're missing the fun-loving part that you, Dr. Liu, could bring. But now, as you retreat from Becky's critical anger, your fun-loving and sporty self is contaminated. You've become forgetful and a nuisance instead of a joy.

Dr. Liu says, 'What Jill said about having fun: It's an important part of my life. It's become limited. We should learn how to have fun together again.'

The couple responded positively to our summary. Becky added that at birth, Michael had to be taken away to be put under special lights because of a dangerously high bilirubin level that, left untreated, could cause liver disease and brain damage. Putting him under bright lights had fixed the problem, but her point was that a medical concern and a separation from the baby had been there early on. While Anna had the same condition at birth, the parents were allowed to be with her, and they were less anxious, having been through this before. Through this association, Becky seemed to confirm that alarm about Michael's health and survival had been involved in the couple's anxiety from the beginning, and that Michael had suffered being alone, without parents, symbolically echoing her own early abandonment. We explained that if Becky's father's death had affected the relationship with Michael, it would have been mediated through Becky's reaction, but she could not confirm this idea. She could not understand the influence of her father's death, since she did not feel particularly fond of him. While she felt a bit sad at the funeral, it didn't amount to much.

Jill says, 'It's sad when you have a son and realize your own father wasn't that important.'

Becky says,

> When Jill described where my anger comes from, I just felt 50% of the anger evaporate. I realized that I do have a lot of my mother's way in me. As my husband said, she's not so difficult, just stubborn. So, as to what we can do to make things better, we can spend more time as a couple, like going for walks or to movies. Perhaps we – I – can try to make these plans.

Dr. Liu added, 'When Becky mentioned how 50% of the anger was gone, I realized that I agree that we haven't found an appropriate way to live with anger without it having a negative impact.'

We suggest that this accumulation of anger that has such a negative impact should be focus of future couple therapy, while Dr. Liu could work on not retreating and being annoying.

Becky says that nothing is unforgivable because these things were human, except that she cannot let go of the disagreements when they affect the children.

Jill adds, 'And about being a married couple: Is sex also invaded by anger?'

They both nodded. Dr. Liu says quickly, clearly and in English, 'Absolutely!'

I now move off to the disagreement about children, feeling that to address their sex life directly at this late stage would be too exposing in this public setting, but Jill draws us back, saying, 'David, I think you were trying to protect the couple from public exposure, but we want to be clear that the impingement on their sex life must be a significant issue.'

Dr. Liu thinks silently for a moment. We give him the space, feeling that as he looks down and pauses, he's taking a kind of time he needs.

(I later realize that this is exactly what Michael does when he pauses, but then Michael gets paralyzed. Looking back, I can see Michael as identifying with the way his father pauses.)

Dr. Liu says, 'I don't know where to start.' He pauses again.

Maybe it's from my character. For instance, when I disagree with Becky, I'm so concerned about her opinion and her attitude ... No ... I thought she ... I don't have a way to say ... my capacity that equals a negation of my style.

(We notice that there is a kind of confusion in his sudden difficulty responding. Gao Jun later says that his use of the word for 'negation' has the connotation of a character flaw.)

He explains that her attitude affects his self-esteem:

Deep in my heart, I have a sense of inferiority that comes from a lack of confidence. Like that hospital example. She asked me, 'Why didn't you ask the doctor about this or that?' If I was confident, I could say, 'There was no need. The doctor can solve the problem.' Deep in my heart, her attitude affects my self-esteem. I don't know if it relates to my childhood. When I was young, I talked less. I remember when my mother would try to get me to speak, I would pause and my mother would say, 'He's shy and doesn't want to talk.' Living with my father, I had to walk home from primary school. When an aggressive boy blocked my way, I wouldn't fight. I'd find a detour. All that influenced my self-esteem. When I grew up, I purposely tried to be an extrovert, but deep in my heart, I don't feel confident.

He paused.

The repetition of the phrase 'deep in my heart' conveyed the pain of his vulnerability to her criticism and bossiness. For the first time, I could really feel the pain that caused him to repeat.

Jill says,

Becky comes right out with things, while you need space to find the words. Becky's brain is verbal and linear, and your brain, Dr. Liu, is more intuitive and technical. You like putting things together like a scientist, with energy and physicality.

Dr. Liu agrees, 'I'm good at problem-solving, like in my medical research.'

Jill says, 'Your two brains function very differently.'

Becky adds, 'And that's a good combination. I speak with little consideration, while he raises good points. That's good. At work, everyone thinks he's a 'sunshine boy.' He's sociable, treats everybody well, and there he can chat with everyone easily.'

I say, 'He has a nice way, but you're afraid that he won't be strong enough.'

Becky says, 'So he makes me be strong.'

I say, 'Which you resent. Do you feel that you're a nice person?'

Becky says, 'Yes. I'm a nice person.'

I ask, 'So how about when you're angry?'

Becky answers, 'I don't like it. I want to relax and have a good time.'

I say, 'We hope that couple therapy will help you rebalance so you each feel you can be both nice and appropriately forceful.'

Dr. Liu says,

I feel, mostly, I can be 85 out of 100% of a person for a lot of things. And I feel for Becky, she can be 95 out of 100%. And I feel whether your 85 or 95 doesn't matter, but she hopes that I'll be 95 out of 100%.

Becky agrees.

Jill says,

I'm asking you, David: The couple told us that they have lost their sexual life, and I felt that you went back to Dr. Liu's childhood. I felt sad about the lost opportunity. Maybe it's a lost opportunity, but maybe they were hurt. Maybe you diverted to protect them. (Dr. Liu smiles.) I wondered: 'If a man were vulnerable, how could he approach his wife in their angry situation?

I feel this is another moment in which Jill is helping us stay on a useful track, leading to my next question.

I say, 'Thanks for bringing us back to this, Jill. What do you think, Dr. Liu?'

Dr. Liu answers, now with more confidence,

I think our sexual life is not the cause of the problem, but it's a result. I agree with you that David was protecting us, but I understand that he was also trying to help us. I agree with his protecting us but helping us. Perhaps if we get the relationship to be lighter, then the sex would flourish.

We agree that it will be important to address their sexual issues in time, perhaps after work on the overall relationship. We then review Michael's situation, which may also alleviate as their relationship improves, but we agree with Becky when she asks whether he should also have his own therapy now. She came with a long list of questions and said we had answered all of them. But she has one more question: 'Is Anna okay, or does she need help too?' We say that right now, she looks sturdy, although she cues on Michael and shows some vulnerability to carrying the family burden, too. They could afford to wait to see how she does with the other interventions. We promise to arrange for referral for couple therapy to one of the faculty members in the room with us, with whom they were already acquainted, and indicate that therapist can give them a referral for Michael, and if necessary later, for Anna. We thank them for coming and sharing so generously, and wish them the best of luck.

In our discussion following this last session, we note that Becky has a double dose of being the worried researcher, while Dr. Liu has a double dose of sunshine, so they have become polarized and conflicted over time. The result is a type of 'projective gridlock' described by Mary Morgan (2019) in which their unconscious projections into each other add up to a stalemate in their capacity for intimacy.

We can see that they were attracted to each other with the idea that through their partnership, Dr. Liu could borrow from her authority, and Becky could get from him the idea of having more fun. We agreed that Becky's being immediately relieved of 50% of her anger is a good start, but still only a start. They will need couple therapy so that the mutual resentment does not wash back in. Furthermore, Becky had said that she still could not tolerate disagreements about the children. We feel that position marks a family vulnerability where remaining problems are likely to lodge.

The Intersection of National and Personal Issues

Becky was born just before the Cultural Revolution began. Her early maternal deprivation, probably because of the Cultural Revolution, was compounded by separation at age six from the grandparents who had been raising her, and by her mother's critical personality, which is common in many Chinese families, but which may well have been hardened by her mother's traumatic experiences during those years. Dr. Liu apparently escaped the ravages of those years. He offers an opportunity within the couple's relationship to leaven Becky's trauma, but only if they can develop a new pattern that offers more containment for her anger and in which he can become more understanding and less prone to the emotional flight that is triggered by his own wariness of anger.

In this family, the children have become vehicles for the expression of their parents' individual and shared unmetabolized anxieties. Although his early physical vulnerabilities played a role in setting the stage for Michael to become a vehicle for the parents' impasse, all children are shaped by their parents' strengths and weaknesses, both those of each parent individually and those of the parents as a couple. We can see how Michael – and potentially Anna – was vulnerable as each parent individually off-loaded unresolved issues through projective identification, and how the couple, through their relationship itself, conveyed further unconscious problems to him in the daily link of their interactions. Thus, Michael's and Anna's preoccupation with pleasing each parent had become an impossible problem because, as a couple, the parents could not be satisfied when it came to the problem of their unresolved resentments and the fears expressed in the question of whether to be strict or indulgent. Both parents feel they are in danger of harming their children if they get the discipline wrong, but they disagree about what constitutes the right way to set limits.

Finally, the narrative of the sessions demonstrates our ways of working with couples and with families with play-age children, regardless of which culture we are in. Despite the unusual setting of having an audience, the differences between their Chinese and our Western cultures and the use of translation, we felt we had achieved a level of understanding of and dialogue with the family that was comparable to that we would hope to reach with a Western, English-speaking family. More would be possible with experienced Chinese family therapists – but few of these exist as of yet. The project we are engaged in with our Chinese colleagues aims to train a group of Chinese therapists so that, in the future, they can constitute a strong, indigenous resource within China.

Early Childhood Separation

This family illustrates many issues that show up repeatedly in our interviews.

The first issue is the all-too-frequent pattern in China of early childhood separation from parents, with grandparents often filling in. The social patterns of the last 65 years made this problem epidemic, especially so during the Cultural Revolution, when parents and children were often forcibly separated. There was already a tradition of grandparent care for children, with fathers often working at remote sites, but in the period of the Cultural Revolution, these separations became more common, more thorough and more troubling. These days, when both parents are more often working, grandparent care of the one child has assumed a new pattern, even though having grandparents in the caretaking role is also based on the old tradition.

This, however, has also introduced many other elements of vulnerability. First, there is the persistent 'mother-in-law problem,' although for slightly different reasons. Now the wife is no longer automatically consigned to the husband's family to be relentlessly under her mother-in-law's thumb, but when a young mother needs support from her own mother or from the parents of her husband, she is still subjected to the possibility of criticism and control, especially when the grandparents are under their own pressure from cultural tradition and their personal need to have grandchildren.

Mother and Father Hunger

Second, there is the common unconscious condition of hunger for both mothers and fathers. We tend to think that hunger for mothers and their kind of 'maternal understanding' is more fundamental than for what fathers offer. This supports the idea that a mother is really the parent who provides the most crucial care in the first period of life. Therefore, most Western developmental literature speaks simply about mothers, motherly care and love, and the baby's need for that. What we are really conceptualizing in this way is the need for early *parental care*, not that it must only come from a mother. Nevertheless, when either parent is missing, children carry a concept of the missing parent in their minds, and this includes both missing mothers and missing fathers. Becky did not necessarily have deficient care during her early years. Neither she nor we can tell for sure at this point. But she does carry a longing for something that continues to feel that it was lacking from the beginning. She carries it as a longing for a good, caring and uncritical mother, while at the same time feeling she can only keep trying to get care in a relationship that is suffused with criticism. In her exchanges with her husband, she keeps trying to get care by doubling down on being critical, much in the mold of her own mother, even though she knows consciously this is self-defeating. She just does not know how to look for love in another way because the internal object organization of her mind keeps putting this way of interacting first, even while she hopes to get a different result out of her angry plea for understanding and love.

My point here is that this is a longing for both a loving mother and for a father who could compensate for the unquestioning kind of love that she has been missing. So, when she lost her father some years ago, she was losing the person who had provided more of the kind of parental love she had longed for all her life. She lost her father near the time of Michael's birth, presumably increasing her concern for whether Michael would survive when he had medical issues.

Many of the Chinese patients, couples and families I have encountered long for both mothers and fathers, but often not so much for the parents they had as for the ones they wish they had, an unconscious fantasy of an endlessly giving, understanding and loving parent who would not express their parental concern by being critical, demanding and punishing, but through care, concern and even indulgence. We see this longing in Becky, but it is there for Dr. Liu as well. He got care from his father that he felt he could not get from his mother. His father was strict but also kind. His relationship to his parents was more positive on balance, but there is still a longing for more unconditional love. He also indicated that there had been a role of the Cultural Revolution in his family's background. That national trauma apparently had a more direct effect on his grandparents, but we do not know how much of the anxiety that affected nearly everyone in that period might have therefore affected his parents, too, and so would have been passed on to Dr. Liu in an indirect form. In any case, we could see that he, too, is longing for a kind of love that has disappeared from the marriage as mutual resentment and wariness has grown.

Grandparents, Fathers and Mothers

Another issue for Chinese parents becomes clearer if we reverse our lens and think not only of the family that was in front of us, Becky and Dr. Liu and the children, but of the family members we did not see – their parents, now identified as grandparents. Thinking of them as equally warranting our interest, which they surely do, we need to remember that parents around the world have always expected in part to live through their children. Chinese culture has developed a particular tradition of expectations and obligations in this regard, often leading to diminished parental flexibility and adaptability to the current rapid evolution in family patterns. It should not surprise us that aging parents still harbor hopes to live through their children and grandchildren, and therefore suffer bitter disappointment when unexpected obstacles appear through the cultural and personal shifts that characterize the current generation.

Children express our hope for the future. We expect and hope that they will live after we are gone, and will be vital when we are no longer productive or able to take care of ourselves. Psychologically, they carry more than our genes or family names. They carry in their minds and psychological make-up all we have instilled in them of our hopes and fears through the way we have provided for their education, socialization and, least understood, through what we as parents have communicated to them both unconsciously and through daily interaction. So, the fate of these children, as well as the quality of their relationships with their parents when they are children and when they reach parenting age themselves, is of fundamental importance to all aging parents.

Our interviews have not focused on the older generation, and so we have not considered their needs directly. Nevertheless, we should consider them just as surely as those of children and parents. Grandparents, and all of China's elderly, have been displaced as new family patterns have taken over. Many seem to welcome the role of taking care of their grandchild, or, nowadays, increasingly often more than one grandchild.

But as we have seen in this case, as the children of this aging population change in their own expectations, there is frequent conflict, and at least some proportion of these adult children will limit the roles of the grandparents or even turn their backs on their parents.

This involves the cultural shifts that have occurred so far and are still evolving. I have mentioned the many young adults who delay marriage or do not wish to have children. Others emigrate to the West, partly motivated by ambitions seeded in them through their parents' provision of educational opportunities abroad. Or they migrate internally in China in ways that cut them off emotionally from their parents and rural roots.

But the most unseen migration is one of values and expectations, spurred by the changes in the culture in which these young adults live. That emotional migration begins in the ambivalent attitude of parents who waver between wanting their child to be loyal to the family in the old ways, and who nevertheless gave the message of the need for the young person to be entrepreneurial and more individuated (Fong, 2007). This oscillating attitude that the parents give began in the 1980s and is now bearing fruit. We have seen the benefits for some of the couples and families we have seen in the economic success of this generation. In other cases, including the one in this chapter, that legacy must have also borne bitter fruit, turning the interests of the now young and middle-aged adults against the interests, if not the emotional fealty, of their parents. For these aging parents and grandparents, particularly if they are or were based in the countryside, this leaves them emotionally barren, no longer supported by the large extended family of years ago and often economically impoverished as well (Eberstadt, 2019).

The mental health implications of these shifts are clear. In the West, we see epidemic depression in the older age groups, especially among widows and widowers. Surely the same is and will be true for China, especially in the rural areas that are increasingly depleted of young family members.

I remember a time in 2007 when Jill and I first came to China. As part of being tourists in Beijing, we visited a Beijing *hutong* where we met an old woman living in a traditional *siheyuan*, a courtyard house that was typical for more than 2,000 years. Now most of these have been destroyed to make way for urban development, except for the few kept as tourist destinations. The hospitable elderly woman we met invited us in for tea. She had lived in this complex all her life and had no interest in leaving. She told us cheerfully, however, that her three children thought she was crazy to cling to her old house. They lived in high-rise apartments in Beijing with their spouses and children. They were highly educated and worked successfully in the modern economy. This woman seemed to do well with her tourist role in her advanced age. She had children and grandchildren who were nearby and cared for her, and she was possessed of a sunny disposition. Many others are not so lucky.

Chapter 14

Families of Young Adolescents

China's adolescents have been born into a changing world in which the value of family loyalty has been eroded by the exploding market economy, the improvement of the status of women, the One Child Policy and the cultural encounter with the global community. Chinese youth, as everywhere, now spend their lives online and on their phones, chatting, picking up the latest culture and struggling to achieve independence from their own childhoods and from their parents. The increased importance of the peer group looks more like the picture in the West. These changes cause chagrin to most parents of adolescents who face a variety of problems their own parents did not. In some ways, this would feel familiar to Western parents, but in China, the most important clash is with old ways that are more radically different today than in the West.

Whenever we see early adolescents, we also bear in mind the revolutionary personal changes that are happening from inside the adolescent's mind and body. Research tells us about the large-scale changes in the adolescent brain, including the explosion of capacity for abstract thinking but with incomplete frontal lobes that will later help in modulating behavior. At the same time, in hormonal, anatomical and emotional ways, adolescents become sexual beings in ways they previously were not. In these years, their bodies change in the growth of pubic hair, breast and genital size and function, and their bodies change in overall shape, size and strength that results by mid-adolescence in the development of an adult body with a child's mind. The young adolescent feels somewhere in between, still a child, yet restless to be accorded full adult rights. A newly rich fantasy life, usually saturated with sexual fantasies, results in new ways of feeling with the conviction that the adolescents' parents simply cannot understand how their world works. In this way, adolescents are cut off from their parents at precisely a time of entering a new world of sensation and interests. Because of the rapid evolution of Chinese culture – under the influence of global culture in a way that was unheard of a generation ago – the ubiquity of phones and the internet, and the influence of a newly invigorated influence from adolescent peer culture, the vulnerability of parent-child relations has been magnified enormously in recent years.

Also, as we have been seeing throughout, Chinese parents have their own ambivalence about the degree to which their child (or beginning now, their children) should owe fealty to the family, which the parents still harbor as a culturally inherited value. This clashes not only with parents' wish for the child to be able to make good in the competitive and increasingly materialistic and opportunistic culture, but also with the parents' anxieties about whether they will have grandchildren and about whether their child will be willing to support them in their old age. These last two forces are mostly latent and silent when the children are in their early adolescence, and mainly come to the fore later when the children are of marriageable and child-rearing age.

So, the forces that are in play in young adolescents and their families most often focus on academic and extracurricular success, and the chances of getting into university, or into the best university. Early in my time in China, beginning in 2007, the parents of young adolescents came mainly from the generation that had missed out on education and opportunity because they were caught up by the Cultural Revolution, in which their parents or they themselves as children were sent to the country-side. The couple I described in Chapter 2 represents this problem, as did the girl Scarlet, who I described briefly in Chapter 1, whose parents had missed out on education because of the Cultural Revolution.

The families we have seen more recently, half a generation later, are less likely to have been directly affected by the traumas of the twentieth century, although their grandparents and parents often were. They are more likely, however, to have migrated from rural and farm villages to the city, presenting other issues of cultural acclimation. So, we continue to see families dealing with the threads of intergenerational trauma, poverty and cultural dislocation.

In these families of adolescents, and in many cases I have heard about from students and supervisees, I hear of two related epidemics: adolescent suicidality and school refusal.

Adolescent suicide is epidemic in China, the leading cause of adolescent death (Caskie, 2016; Chelala, 2014). It is not just the number of successful suicides, but the climate in which adolescents become suicidal, talk of suicide and read about suicide. This represents the most fearful consequence of depression. While some of these children and adolescents are not depressed but are more impulsive, in most cases, adolescent anxiety and depression are the main problems, with suicidality as their most extreme expression. Related to this is the high number of adolescents who are on the verge of, or who actually do, drop out of school, something we also see in epidemic numbers. As a child psychiatrist, I understand school refusal as an emergency that requires urgent, active intervention, with efforts to reinstate a child in school and to understand and deal with the root causes as promptly as possible. Child psychiatrists think of this as an emergency precisely because the longer the situation goes on, the harder it is to reverse, and because it stands for and exacerbates a halt in the growth and maturation of the adolescent's capacity to move out into the world as a productive adult.

However, with a few exceptions, the principal causes of school refusal lie in the family. I can cite a case of an American high school student I treated who was an A+ student but poorly socialized in her school, and who suddenly became unable to sit in class or stay in school. The cause was her extreme anxiety, expressed in an obsessional illness, traceable to the unconscious family pressure to perform to perfection, family distress between the grandparent and parent generations and the girl's fantasy magnification of emotional differences between her parents.

The same approach has been upheld in research on Chinese families of school-refusing children and adolescents. Hu Jingmin and Li Xiaobai (2012) found that paternal severity of punishment, paternal rejection, maternal overprotection and maternal rejection were associated with school refusal. Yang Xiao et al. (2017) found that boys were more likely to drop out of school than girls, younger children were more likely to drop out of school than older children and the proportion of drop-outs was higher in families with breakdown or in single-parent families. Wang Linghua et al. (2012) found a high degree of emotional disturbance in these children. While these sources do not specifically mention family-wide difficulty, they certainly point towards it.

The major treatments that have been attempted with the adolescents I have seen or heard about in supervision have been psychiatric and biological rather than psychodynamic. Clinicians have thought that a child is depressed, perhaps psychotic or bipolar, and so have prescribed an antidepressant or antipsychotic medication, often combined with hospitalization. It is possible that this approach has worked in cases we have not seen, but in the ones that have come to us or to the therapists I have supervised, the biological approach has not worked. Invariably, we have been able to discover family dynamics that accompany the adolescent's distress, which is then expressed in school refusal, depression and, often, suicidality.

The factors that seem to have led to these symptomatic expressions cluster around three factors: First, and most frequent, the pressures the parents and the child feel that their child should perform well to make it to university (or, with more pressure, to a prestigious university); second, the child's struggle between family loyalty and peer allegiance; and third, couple and family stress and/or breakdown. Adolescent peer allegiance is not mentioned in the literature I have seen on traditional Chinese culture, so it is my impression that it was much less a factor in development in the old times that privileged family loyalty. That is no longer true. Teen culture is as rampant in China as it is elsewhere in the developed world, which is evident in Scarlet's telling me that she learned her fluent and 'with it' English from watching the American TV show *Desperate Housewives*. We see it also in the way that their sports outfits announce they *are* teens, even as they attend nonstop to their phones,

WeChat, Snapchat, TikTok and whatever new platforms will dominate even a few months after this writing.

The Fearful Tyranny of the Only Child and the Decline of Parental Authority

We have earlier seen a picture of an adolescent who dropped out of school in the example of Nicole in Chapter 6, whose so-called psychotic illness formed an articulate narrative of her parents' difficulties and her father's alcoholism, and who, in her own way, took control of the family narrative.

In another case presented in a group of Chinese therapists I supervised, a 15-year-old boy dropped out of school and stayed in his room playing video games on his computer, blithely unconcerned about returning to school. This boy had absorbed strain from his parents' conflict, which had recently been exacerbated when the father was hospitalized with a serious medical illness from which he had now recovered.

The parents succeeded in persuading the boy to attend family therapy, but once there, he refused to talk, saying, 'There's nothing I want to discuss. If you push me, I'll leave.' The parents fell into anxious silence, and when the therapist gently but firmly persisted, he became abusive to his parents and walked out. The therapist explained to the parents the power the boy was wielding in the family and worked with them on the need to set limits with him.

This case demonstrated, as one member of the supervision group put it, 'the fearful tyranny of the only child and the decline of parental authority.' The group agreed that many parents surrender authority and unconsciously empower their child in destructive ways because they are terrified both for and of their only child, fearing a loss of his affection just as much as they fear for his future if he cannot perform in school.

Formerly, when families had several children, they could afford to exercise authority over each of them because even if one were defiant, the affection of the others was there to buffer the difficulty. But the Only Child is so precious that, in many families, he or she usurps control of the family because the parents fear losing that child's affection. In many families, this extends to a fear that something untoward might befall that child, who might die if the parents mishandle things. This often takes the form of an unspoken fantasy that the parents' mistakes will drive their child to suicide, which is the parents' side of a shared unconscious fantasy that is often spoken openly only by the child who toys with the idea of suicide, partly as an aggressive attack on the parents and partly out of the shame of letting them down. The supervision group agreed that if a family has three or four children, losing one is tragic, but manageable. With only one child, even the very idea of that child's death threatens catastrophe. This unconscious constellation silently augments that child's ability to wield power, seen most clearly at the extreme in suicide threats that bludgeon parents into acceding to a child's demands. But it is not that the child is the villain of these pieces: the parents' frightened abdication of authority plays an equal role that induces the overly confrontational stance in their child. This kind of pattern is jointly constructed by the parents and children.

We will now see another variation of parental abdication of authority in the face of adolescent distress in the following example. It also illustrates the kind of work with a family that can enable adolescents and their parents to find a constructive voice and move beyond the depression, suicidality and reluctance to attend school that brings such families to seek help.

A Young Adolescent and Her Family

A 14-year-old Chinese middle-school girl whom we will call Clover had been cutting herself, putting Chinese stones into her mouth, was afraid of strangers and had become preoccupied with love and suicide. We were told that she had been sexually provocative, falling in and out of love with male and female teachers. When she joined suicide chat rooms and erotic porn sites, and formed a suicide club at her elite school, her teachers became concerned and informed her mother who taught at the same school. Clover's mother Cindy, an authoritative, accomplished and well-respected teacher, liked to be on top of things. We heard that she felt deep shame that her daughter had been open about her suicidality with others and not with her. Her father, Hong, an engineer, was more laid back, but both parents perceived the need for help. Clover began weekly individual therapy while her parents went into parent–couple counseling, but up to the time we saw Clover and her family, there had been little improvement. The parents' couple co-therapists suggested the possibility of a family consultation with myself and Jill Scharff, and Clover's therapist agreed.

We were somewhat apprehensive about these particular parents' participation in such an open setting, given their concerns about others knowing too much about their child. It seemed that they overcame any discomfort in order to accept the teaching setting and get the clinical help they wanted. Their shame, or more particularly *loss of face,* would emerge later, delivered into the transference where it could be worked on. But at the point of meeting them, we could not know this. We could only imagine the parents' tremendous worry about their only child, whose life was so precious and who was so determinedly interested in death.

This case illustrated elements of the difficulties that Chinese adolescents and their families face, including the enormous pressure on the only child to perform academically so as to become successful and make the parents proud. The child who does well in school will be most able to support parents and grandparents in their old age, carry the burden of hopes and difficulties of older generations and survive the influence of the peer group in adolescence. Finally, the case shows that anxiety about school performance gathers currents of family and cultural concern resulting in pressure at home and at school, self-harm, suicidality, and conflict with parents.

Session I

For the first session, we were seated opposite the family with Gao Jun, again our translator, sitting slightly behind and between us, and two colleagues, Michael Stadter and Jane Prelinger, observing while seated slightly behind us.

As they sat down before us, 14-year-old Clover smiled at us, while her mother, Cindy, seemed close to tears and her father, Hong, anxiously checked that his family had enough water and tissues. Clover sat between them, looking from one to the other parent as if holding them together and keeping them apart at the same time.

Cindy began, explaining that Clover is more sensitive than are other children to criticism from teachers in her highly competitive middle school. Cindy worried that she and Hong had been too demanding about Clover's falling grades. She told us that this concern would be like that of any other parents of children at that school. Clover had then felt pressure both at home and school, and so the parents had tried to lessen the pressure by dropping their expectations. Cindy said, 'I used to set standards for her, give her a work plan, but I have stopped because life comes before success. It's okay to be average. I've given up expecting more.' Hong agreed that they had backed off confronting their hypersensitive, secretive daughter, but they missed the child who used to talk to them freely. He said, 'We can't accept her actions, her extreme thoughts, her wish to hurt herself. We can't understand her inner world.' With no apparent empathy for her parents' distress, Clover said amusedly as if to end the worry, 'I don't want to live. It's just my style. It's no big deal.' They were at an impasse. We tried to encourage conversation, but they did not know what else to say.

We felt that Clover's suicidality was about much more than falling grades, something to do with the usual worries of adolescents about family, friends, social life and sexual questions, wishes and fears. As the family did not volunteer information, I, feeling some anxiety about making the meeting a good clinical experience for the family and good material for the students in the audience to learn from, began asking questions to reach these areas, but I kept not getting answers until Jill and I felt that we, too, had hit a wall.

In this way, early in the first session, already the family had delivered the problem into the therapeutic space. Facing a family in distress before an audience of our peers and trainees, we felt that our performance as therapists was slipping. In having that feeling of not performing well, we were like Clover. At the same time, we felt we were being demanding (like her parents who wanted more) and getting nowhere in our attempts to communicate and understand (like the whole family). Our usual way of working is to reflect inwardly or between ourselves on our countertransference that was represented in these feelings during the session, and then to speak from having emotionally shared the family's experience. We thought we were now feeling what the parents felt, so Jill said, 'I feel we are becoming part of the pressure. It is hard for us, sitting here, knowing you want help and not knowing how to offer it to your daughter, in front of these all these observers.'

Hong admitted,

> With so many people out front of us, I feel nervous. It is hard for us Chinese to reveal what is buried deep in our hearts. I feel that there must be something lacking in our way of being as a family.

I asked, 'There is such a block to telling us about how you feel; it makes me wonder if Clover is being unhappy for all of you?'

Cindy said, 'No, my marriage is stable.' (Clover started to cough, as though sending us a signal that this was a vulnerable moment. Hong offered her water.)

> But every family has conflicts, and I'm not sure if our occasional quarrels stress her out or not. Mostly I complain about trivialities, like he didn't sweep the floor well enough, or he should have closed the kitchen door. He's in charge of science homework, but she doesn't want to learn from him.

Hong intervened,

> My wife just likes to complain. I support her, I do things over, I smile and I laugh things off. I know I don't do a good job, but I don't think it matters. I'm easygoing. It is difficult to change.

Clover said simply, 'I can't meet their standard. I'm lazy and I let things go. I'm like my Dad who has a lazy part, too. But I don't feel bad for being lazy. I don't cry at night about that.'

Jill said, 'Clover, you don't cry about it: You jump right into cutting and thinking about killing yourself.'

Clover nodded.

Jill continued, 'And Mom cries all the time. In your family when you were growing up, Cindy, who was perfect and who was lazy?'
Cindy replied,

> My father was very relaxed, and my mother was industrious. My older sister is high-achieving, good at math and science, a successful accountant. My mom preferred my sister because she was more obedient and better than me. My dad preferred me. When I was in middle school, I liked to play. I was relaxed and busy with social life. I didn't like to work too hard, but I was not lazy. It was in high school that I started to work because of a particularly good teacher.

Jill said, 'You liked to play, and Clover likes to play with her friends on the internet, but for her, play takes the form of playing with her body in scary ways, like cutting and playing about suicide.'
I said,

> Clover, I sense that you think it is better to die than be unhappy yourself, but then somehow the unhappiness falls upon your mom and dad, who want you to live. Then there is a family argument about living and dying.

Discussion of Session I

By the end of the first session, we felt we knew little. We had few clues as to why this attractive, lively, young girl would want to die. What might she be escaping from and to? The audience was most concerned with Clover's suicidality as a response to academic pressure, which they all understood. We felt that in telling her friends and teachers all about it, she also seemed desperate to be known and understood. Yet in keeping her thoughts from her devastated parents, and to a large extent from us, she wanted to remain private and undisturbed. Her secrecy seemed partly a typically adolescent stance, and partly a dissociative response to deep and disturbing conflict. We noticed that the focus was on death, not sexuality, suggesting that sexuality was even more upsetting to Clover than thoughts of death or the academic expectations of teachers and parents. We were able to confirm the way that the parents seemed traumatized by the knowledge of their daughter's preoccupations, and the mother additionally by the humiliation of not having learned of the depth of her concerns directly from her while her colleagues at school knew all about them. There seemed to be an unconscious shared family assumption that death is preferable to unhappiness, and that excellence is the best defense and perhaps the only defense against criticism and shame. But the perfection blocks chaos and conflict also leads to the death of hope and belief in growth and progress. Clover's preference of death to unhappiness formed an early clue that shame might be at the

heart of the family's problem, because shame is a frequent cause of suicidality, even in the absence of clinical depression.

Session II

The second session began with Cindy speaking about how she had
learned of Clover's suicidal nature from her teacher colleagues, and
had been dismayed – shamed, really – that they knew about it
when she had not. The discussion moved on to Clover's tendency
to feel numb or to forget what has been said. Then, in response to
our asking about her adolescent physical development, the family
joined in talking about her first menstruation as a joyful event that
speaks of her life in the future as a woman and possibly a mother.
We noted that nevertheless, now they live in fear of death. We
asked about anger at the parents, thinking that angry moments
might connect to underlying 'bad thoughts.'

Clover told a story: In fourth grade, she had been furious at her
mother for saying she could not play with her grandmother's lamb
because she had not done her homework. Clover said she had
strong feelings from that event, but she could not remember them.
The more Clover reversed herself, or simply said 'No!' in response
to our attempts to explore the parents' experiences, the more stupid we felt at not getting through to her or her family. As before,
we spoke to our countertransference of feeling stupid as a way to
communicate our understanding of their experience.

Jill said,

> We are having an experience of feeling controlled, and then helpless,
> and desperate, as your parents must feel, and stupefied by your situa-
> tion. Clover, that makes me wonder if you want us to know that feeling
> puzzled is how you feel, too.

Cindy said, 'That's exactly how I feel—helpless and stupid. I
don't know what to say or do, and there's no feedback.'

I said to Clover, 'I think you feel helpless inside about thoughts
you can't share.'

Nodding, Clover said, 'Yes, I do.'

I continued, 'And these thoughts are driving you, like you drive
your parents.'

Clover again said, 'Yes.'

I continued,

> Clover, you're in the grip of forces that you are too frightened to talk
> about. Your parents and teachers value your life, and we do, too. I think

there is a part of you that values your life, too, because I see that part of you sitting here, full of life and laughter and teasing. We're searching in the dark, but the dark is really in you, Clover. You're more frightened of talking with your parents and us than you are of being in the dark by yourself.

Clover said, 'Inside me there are many thoughts and there are many selves flying around.'

Jill asked, 'Can you tell us about how the selves different? What do they do?'

Clover gradually explained, 'One is talking normally; one is judging me; one is having wild thoughts; one is killing herself; and there is also an observer.'

We closed by saying we would look forward to a chance to hear more about Clover's four selves the next day, and Clover nodded.

Discussion of Session II

We tried to open the space for the couple and for Clover to think, feel and talk together more openly than before so that they could become curious about one another's experience. We noticed that Hong, in his desperation to care for his family, left no space for Clover (or indeed, Cindy) to experience need, and so Clover appears to have found a perverse way of achieving separation. Commenting on the countertransference of feeling stupefied and frightened ourselves allowed Clover to acknowledge the helplessness inside her. We talked to each other aloud during the interview about how each of us was feeling stupid, and how to proceed in the light of that feeling. That open conversation was different from the parents' way of working and withdrawing. In discussion after the afternoon's interview, an audience member said that my telling Clover that I could see that she was also full of life was 'a golden moment.'

This session began to open our understanding as we registered how we had taken in the feeling of hopeless stupefaction, a countertransference that we could then use to interpret the family's unconscious experience, and get confirmation from Cindy and Clover of their own dilemmas.

Session III

We were surprised when the family did not arrive on time. After ten minutes, Hong hurried into the room, desperately out of breath. He said that his wife and daughter had had a terrible fight in the car on the way here and he could not deal with it. His wife had erupted at Clover, saying that she was so upset that all her colleagues knew about Clover's bad thoughts when Cindy did not. She could not stand them looking at her with pity and sympathy. She had said to Clover, 'If you are going to kill yourself, why don't you go ahead and do it, and I will follow you.'

Hong was horrified. Not knowing what to do, he tried to get them to come in and talk, but they refused. So, he had left them in the car and had run straight to the interview room.

I went out to the car with Gao Jun while Jill remained in the therapy space. I found Clover and Cindy huddled together in the back seat as if in a state of fusion, Cindy in tears and Clover glued to her. Sobbing, Cindy described the humiliation she had experienced in front of her colleagues, while Gao Jun translated. When I used the word 'humiliation,' it did not seem to mean anything to Cindy, but when I then said that I could understand her 'loss of face,' Cindy agreed readily. After talking more about her situation, Cindy agreed to return to the interview room with Hong, but Clover, while seeming calmer, preferred to stay outside the room with her parents' therapist to keep her company.

Once back in the room in front of the audience, Cindy repeated that she now feels so ridiculous, so much loss of face, that she is not able to face going to school at all. She hoped that I would give her a doctor's excuse so she could miss school. Jill responded by empathizing with her 'humiliation and shame,' but Cindy disagreed. Knowing that Cindy had previously accepted my comment about 'loss of face' and that loss of face is a more culturally accurate phrase for what in Western culture we would call shame, I modified Jill's comment by saying again to Cindy that it was her 'loss of face' that had been intolerable. Cindy readily agreed to this way of putting the emotional situation.

It later occurred to Jill that it may also have been the female sympathy that Cindy could not accept, rather than a semantic difference between 'humiliation' and 'loss of face' creating a block in understanding.

The session continued to focus on Cindy's feeling of upset about not knowing about Clover's trouble at school. After a few moments, Jill spoke of feeling lost and deeply split off from me, since I had not briefed her on where Clover was nor about my experience at the car. She felt in the dark and disempowered.

In this way, the session repeated the situation that Cindy herself had been in for those terrible months.

When Cindy was close to tears again, Hong instantly offered her water, then tissues, both of which she refused. We asked what that refusal was like for him. He responded in terms of what it must be like for her. We guessed that it must feel as if there were too many sympathetic people too close in, including teachers, counselors, Cindy and Hong, all trying to help Clover.

Cindy apologized that her outburst in the car had spoiled the opportunity to talk about Clover's four selves, because her upset and Clover's reaction to it kept that from happening. She had ruined their chances of understanding, and she thought that Clover would have trouble accepting her solicitousness when they returned to their apartment in the evening.

Jill said, 'Therapists' kids are like teachers' kids. They feel their parents know too much, and therefore there is no private space, which Cindy and Clover both want.' Hong smiled at Jill's saying that therapists' kids feel this. He told us that Clover had sent a message to her classmates that said, 'It's hard to be the child of a teacher!' He and Cindy took this to mean that there is no room to think because the teachers know everything about their topics, rather than that Cindy knew too much about Clover and her life at school. We now learned that both Cindy and Hong's parents were also teachers who helped Clover each night with her lessons. I asked about their treatment during the Cultural Revolution, wondering if they had been sent to the countryside, seeking to know if there might be intergenerational trauma to account for the anxiety around Clover. Cindy and Hong agreed that neither of the two families had been affected because their parents trained after those years of persecution for academics, Cindy being 41 now and Hong 44. The couple gets along well with both families and gave no sign of any cultural trauma or unease with current or past societal changes. So, in this case, our concern about the possible influence of that national trauma was not borne out.

Hong said that talking about old things was too hard, and maybe it would be better to 'let painful things alone.' But Cindy shook her head in firm disagreement, insisting, 'No. I know now that we have to talk!'

Hong said,

In that case, I think you should tell Clover your experience here of talking, and then feeling better. And I think you should apologize for your outburst. It is better if Clover comes here, because it is best for the family.

Cindy agreed.

They left looking somewhat cheerful and determined.

Discussion of Session III

As Clover was about to reveal things about her inner world that had been withheld from her parents, her mother 'cracked' and said things that she had previously been too frightened to say. Cindy's show of anger, which was usually hidden and was clearly also a factor in Clover's suppressed anger at her parents, had felt too dangerous to express. Instead, both parents had become depressed and helpless while quietly seething at Clover's covert attack on their love and support. This paralleled Clover's anger at the way their lifelong solicitousness and demands had invaded her and her sense of well-being. We felt we also heard of the family-wide pressure on Clover, with not only her teacher-mother but her teacher-grandparents as well helping her every night with homework, something that had come to constitute not so much 'help' as pressure and a demand for academic performance.

When I went outside by the car and heard Cindy's 'loss of face' and her anger displayed openly for the first time, I felt a sense of relief that the family's encapsulated rage had burst to the surface. I felt cautiously hopeful that the family might begin to build on this event, since it had brought into the open the venomous feelings that had been buried because they felt too dangerous to be aired. For much of the session, Jill felt left in the dark in a way that echoed Cindy being locked out of Clover's inner world, until Jill and I could straighten out this omission after the family left the interview.

This is the kind of dramatic, and sometimes cornerstone, session that can make or break a crisis intervention.

Session IV

Cindy began, 'I feel so good about all this. I am thinking that if I get better, Clover will feel better. And if Clover is better, the whole family will feel better.'

Clover, who had come to the session willingly, said, 'I don't need your help,' and continued to refuse to have a conversation.

I began to speak about academic pressure, the need for space, social anxieties and so on, as if giving a lecture to fill the space. In the tone of my delivery, there was a kind of desperation to help.

I later thought that in giving a kind of speech like this, I had enacted the parents' giving Clover help when she wanted to be free to think things through for herself.

There was no response, and I said, 'What do you think, Jill?'

Jill replied (in a somewhat teasing way),

I think you should stop talking! We need to allow space so Clover doesn't feel smothered here, too. By her reticence and her one-word answers, she does evoke our wish to give her help. If we keep asking questions, all we will get are answers, but no conversation.

We would learn during the discussion that the audience was surprised and later reported that they felt Jill had been rude to me. But I explained that I did not 'lose face' over this because I understood the larger intent of Jill's teasing remark, and because I appreciated the wisdom in it. I also knew it modeled a couple being able to talk through their disagreements, which the family needed to see.

Hong said, puzzled, 'You mean we should chat freely? I can't think what to chat about. Can you give us a hint?'

The parents spoke about their young life: meeting, falling love, studying together and having fun. They also told us that Clover had frequently been up late at night on her cell phone, texting her classmates and on internet chats. They had tried to take the phone away at night, but Clover had begged them not to, saying she needed it because she could not sleep, so they had given in. We noted that Clover had managed to be in charge of what happened, and that the parents had been unable to set limits because they were so worried.

Later in the interview, Jill said to Clover, 'I feel you don't want anyone to know of your longings and your various selves. Is there any place where you do talk about them?'

Clover said,

There are girls at school who say they love me. It can appear to be a homosexual thing, but it's not. It's part of a whole family. For instance, I'm in a family at school. But I'm the father because this girl asked me to have a family with her. So, I got her as a wife. We have one child. In that family, I have a father, who is a girl. All the boys are called sisters.

Cindy understood. 'I've seen this in my class. I know her 'wife.' She's the class monitor.'

Jill said, 'Now that you're an adolescent, there is a next step that is missing. Where is the dating before thinking of a family?'

Clover said, 'We don't date because we would mature too early, so we make a family out of our schoolmates and that's safer.'

I said, 'What do the four parts of yourself think about your family?'

Clover said, 'They don't feel anything about it, and they don't think about it. They just tell me what to do.'

Hong said, 'I'm very confused. What is happening here? You have a good time with your family at school. Parts of you are a wife, a father, a girl and yet not a girl?'

Cindy explained, 'If there is someone Clover likes, that person takes a role in her family. She will say, 'I treat him well because he is my sister.' I think that is to cover her true feelings.'

Discussion of Session IV

They had all returned, but it was difficult at first to get the discussion going again. The family members were unfamiliar with the culture of family therapy, saying whatever comes to mind and associating freely to what one another would say. We had a sense of pressure and awareness of the limitation of time remaining. When Jill and I spoke together about the wish for more space and about the pressure they were feeling in the interview, Clover became more connected to the process. We learned about her complex social world, about inventing a play reality with her peers and creating virtual experiences of life, death and family relationships so as to bridge the adolescent gap between latency and adulthood. We appreciated that Clover's explanation of her family game at school had taught us how she and her peer group pretend-played at family life in a way that felt safer than acting on their adolescent sexuality and noted that her capacity to play was reassuring (Winnicott, 1971a), but we also noted that she did not explore the various selves that had piqued our interest before Cindy's collapse had diverted attention from it, nor did she want to explore the sexual or gender issues that were suggested by her family game. We regretted that loss, but recognized that there are limits to what is possible in such brief interventions and that the family had diverted our attention. We speculated that Cindy's blowup on the previous day must have been partly triggered precisely because she was frightened at the possibility of hearing about Clover's secret inner world, or perhaps out of some personal resonance with it.

Session V

Jill began: 'Clover, I've been thinking about your families with your friends at school. There is a life family in the classroom and a death family on the internet.'
We could see quickly however that Clover could not connect with this idea of a split between life and death.
Cindy said,

Yesterday she told me she has stopped having those thoughts about suicide! I am 50% glad and 50% still concerned. My husband really supported me when my child witnessed my despair. I met with my principal, and he supported me too. I feel much stronger today and I feel I can manage now. If a colleague expresses compassion, I can tell her the story without losing face.

Hong said, 'After these days of counseling, we can sit together with a new way of communicating. I'm happy about that.'

Cindy said,

I'm much better, but not totally happy, because the problem isn't gone. Yes, I got a message from her class teacher that Clover no longer has the thoughts about suicide, but I don't know if they could return. Clover says she doesn't know either. Can you suggest how to keep her stable? Do you have any advice for us?

I said, 'It's true that Clover might feel down again and then the thoughts might return, but the difference is that now you can talk about it and talking is what helps.'

Jill said,

Our advice is that both parents should agree. Talking is one part of it, and another is that you need to have the confidence to set limits. One limit we suggest is that there should be no cell phone after bedtime.

Cindy said, 'I get it. After Clover had those bad thoughts, she got to be in charge.'

I said, 'Yes, because you were so frightened. Then, when you can't set limits, she can't stop, feels more guilt and feels out of control when no one can help her. When she can't stop, it keeps getting worse.'

Cindy said, 'Hong thought I was too strict, but mostly he followed what I thought.'

Hong said,

Sometimes my wife will overdo it, but mostly she is right. About the cell phone, I thought, after the quarrel, Clover was very upset and couldn't get our support, and so the cell phone became her friend. Her therapist told us that she might feel worse without it.

During this exchange, Hong kept trying to pass water to Cindy even though she didn't want it. This reminded us of the earlier session when Hong opened a bottle of water for Clover even though she had not wanted it.

Jill said, 'I think Hong is afraid that Clover won't be his friend. Indeed, if you take away her cell phone, she will be mad at you. But that would be okay.'

Hong said, 'Her mother will have to take it away. I'm not that assertive.'

Cindy said,

I'm the bad one. He is the good one. When I didn't allow her to play video games, he snuck them into the house for her, and he would watch them with her. I was very angry about it, but they did it again, and so I was angry again.

I said, 'The worst thing for you, Clover, is to come between your parents. You'll feel best if they support each other.'

Shaking her head, Clover said, 'I don't know about that.'

Jill said, 'I would rather Clover be mad at both parents than so mad at herself and so guilty that she has to hurt herself and think of suicide.'

Clover said, 'It is none of my business.'

I repeated, 'You're right. It's the parents' job to say 'No' when 'No' needs to be said, and then to take the anger together. It's hard to do, and it's why grown-ups have to be in charge.'

Cindy said, 'Hong and I do agree mainly. I can take the anger, but I can't bear the silence and the upset.'

I said, 'But that is how Clover expresses her anger. She gives you the silent treatment. You have to be able to understand that's what it is, and you have to be able to take it.'

Hong said, 'There are different kinds of anger in different people. When she is silent, it's suffocating. It's harder than a fight.'

Clover said again, 'This is none of my business.'

I said to the parents,

So our advice is you have to talk together, make a decision and stake out your position. We know it's hard to do, and that's why we advise you to continue therapy in this family format, if you think it's a useful way to work, and if your current therapists agree.

Jill summarized what had been achieved and what had not been addressed. She said,

You came together as a family to work on things. The stress of doing this brought about a crisis of despair in Cindy, which you survived and which brought important things to the surface so that we could discuss them here. Hong stepped up as the father to keep the appointment when you, Cindy, could not, and then brought you in to face your despair here. That helped you recover and enjoy some good family time. You've improved your communication. We have understood the pressures of parenting, the intense academic pressure on Clover and the appeal of the internet over the ordinary work of middle school. We have heard about a time when Cindy herself used to play and yet recovered her ambition by the time she was at high school. We've learned about Clover's creation of a life and death family as a way of exploring life and death anxieties, but we have not dealt with the social and sexual anxieties of adolescence. We began to hear from Clover about her inner selves, but we didn't learn more from each of them. It's important that Clover tell her therapist about these inner selves, and that her therapist talk with each of those parts of her.

Hong stepped forward to take his leave of us and of the audience. He explained that they were grateful for the help, and he handed us a gift of stones on which our names had been etched. On the end of each stone, he showed that a traditional 'chop' had been carved for stamping letters or drawings. Hong explained proudly that Clover herself had made this gift yesterday for the family to bring to us. We were moved by the gratitude and the choice of the gift, and encouraged by its being a creative product of play, work and carving on stone, a much better activity than carving her skin. Clover explained that the chops she had chosen to make for us said 'Calm' and 'Harmony.'

Discussion of Session V

Advice to parents of the sort we gave in this last session also functions as a psychodynamic interpretation to the whole family. We knew that Clover could not use direct interpretations about guilt and anxiety to help her regulate her behavior, but the family therapy setting allows for us to speak to her through speaking to the parents. We had not forgotten that Clover saw herself as having multiple selves, one or more of which is an observing, more mature part that can identify with her parents. So, in giving advice, we were simultaneously saying to the family group that it needed to be governed by an integrated parental ego, which would operate best through the thoughtful, mature collaboration of the parental couple. And we were speaking to the group of selves inside Clover. As parents, the couple had been invaded by the fear of losing love and losing face, and this had disabled them so that they could not set ordinary limits to help Clover with her mounting adolescent anxiety – limits they themselves would have preferred. Clover had been pairing with her father in a sneaky pleasure that was forbidden by her mother, who had not been able to keep them from pairing in this way. In this way, Clover's developmentally appropriate sexual interest and curiosity were either constrained by the gratification of Oedipal triumph or transformed into guilty excess with peers. Unable to tolerate her guilt and shame, Clover short-circuited her anxiety by turning it into a self-punishing suicidal idea that went viral by contagion in the adolescent peer group. Clover's anxiety about confronting her parents directly with her anger, guilt and sexual longing had turned into malignant self-punishment and self-harm.

Clover's individual therapist and one of the parents' couple co-therapists were in the audience watching and learning from our way of working and from the contributions of their peers to the large-group discussion. It was not our task to consult to them or to change their way of working. Their approach had been to work in parallel, with therapy for the adolescent and couple therapy separate for her parents, a common approach in the child guidance model in Europe and the United States, and one that has a history of being effective. We have found family therapy more conducive to developing shared understanding of family difficulties, a shared approach to solving problems and more effective group strategy for moving on through the life cycle (Scharff and Scharff, 1987). Our task was to augment the didactic teaching on theory and technique of analytic family therapy by demonstrating our way of working, from which Chinese therapists could take whatever aspects they might find applicable in their work within their own culture.

Concluding Remarks

We have been seeing how treatment of any family occurs within the context of the culture in which the family lives. The highly competitive Chinese educational system that is so important to educated families tends to exert pressure on children and parents far greater than we generally see in the United States. We are familiar with the pressures of school on adolescents and their parents, but we have had to explore and adjust our approach to the circumstances of the Chinese family. This includes work to give family members permission to speak freely, encouraging their free association and adopting language that fits with their way of understanding, for instance, using the term 'loss of face' when the word 'shame' is not adequate for conveying our understanding that 'loss of face' can feel worse than death (Stadter and Gao Jun, 2020). In the United States, parents are free to choose the size of their family. In China, the degree of investment in their one child's future has often felt unbearable for all concerned. Added to that is the effect of the culture in the specific select-entry middle school in which mother and child were together. As it is among the most prestigious of the local schools, Clover's school would be likely to open the door to a first-rate university.

Clover's play 'family' was her particular expression of adolescent culture in response to concerns about sexual maturation and gender roles. The play family puzzled Clover's father, but it made sense to her teacher-mother, who knew the school culture, but we had never heard of that in the North American, Central American or British adolescents and families we have interviewed and treated. We understood it as an adaptation specific to Clover's family and school environment, and an expression that was at the interface of individual development and Chinese culture. It also occurred to us that her family game at school was like the way many adolescents live through trying out different personas as 'avatars' in internet games. Clover sought a space of her own with her young adolescent peers in the world of burgeoning sexuality and romantic preoccupation with death, a space apart from her loving parents, whose investment and interest in her felt intrusive. That constellation is similar to what we work with at home. Allowing freedom and setting limits, and offering discretion but not secrecy, are conflicts that American families wrestle with, too. This has been our experience: In China, things are different and yet the same. With attention to culture and also to the particularities of conflict and loss unique to each case, we have learned to adapt our work to the specific needs of Chinese families and couples.

When family therapy offers an opportunity to dissolve the capsules of shared trauma in a family, turning pain and self-inflicted harm into a positive experience for the family, therapists feel hopeful. This family showed us their resilient potential for shared self-exploration, mutual support and concern, and trust in a therapeutic experience, despite the unusual barriers of being translated and observed. We left the situation feeling that the family would do well in ongoing family therapy with their Chinese therapists.

Chapter 15

Older Adolescents, Youth and Two-Child Families

Older adolescents are close to leaving school, moving into higher education in university or may have already moved into the wider world, either instead of higher education or afterwards. In the West, this period of young adulthood, also termed 'youth,' has come to be understood as constituting a phase in which personality and identity are still fluid and when many of the traits traditionally attributed to adolescence remain prominent. This newly recognized developmental period now seems to apply to China as well. There is often family-wide worry about these late adolescents that includes desperation on the part of the teenager himself or herself during the pressure of the transition into full adult life. This might be life in university, as these young people are often away from home for the first time, or concern with their entry into work and living alone.

Older adolescents often struggle with the new prominence of sex in their lives. They now have fully sexual bodies, the hormones of adults and minds that are usually full of sexual thoughts. For these late adolescents and young adults, there is a challenge about whether, when and how to become sexual. Formerly, sexual development would have taken place in the shadows in China because it was officially forbidden during the Cultural Revolution. On the other hand, being in the Red Guards or being sent down to the countryside allowed young couples a freedom for sexual experimentation as they roamed the country unchaperoned. Now, the scene has changed radically, so that in China, as elsewhere in the world, sex is everywhere as the media feature young bodies in sexually suggestive scenarios (Jeffreys and Yu, 2015).

For many of the older adolescents we have seen directly or heard about in cases presented to us and in supervision, school has been difficult. Almost always, family relations are at the heart of these struggles, as in the following two cases that capture many of the currents of middle and late adolescence. Often, difficulty giving up childhood overlaps with struggles with parents. Adolescents who drop out of school may not have significant academic problems, or if they do, their struggle with schoolwork is often caused by family difficulty. These adolescents are often also suicidal, turning anger at their parents onto themselves in identifying with their parents' harsh treatment of them or at the shame of their situation.

One family that was presented to Jill Scharff in supervision involved a mid-adolescent boy who had stopped going to school two weeks earlier after a fight with his father in which his father, who was frequently critical of him, had hit him. The situation was complicated by the fact that the father's senior job required him to live away from the family. The boy had already been depressed after changing schools, and in so doing lost contact with friends, including a girl who had a crush on him. The girl's interest in the boy had alarmed both families and was part of the reason for school changes. When the boy came to family therapy, he was despondent, suicidal and unable to express his anger at his father. He was, however, able to talk in the family session and willing to continue therapy.

The next case also illustrates how school problems intersect with suicidality, and both of the next two cases demonstrate the adolescent struggle for autonomy in the light of preoccupation about relationships to parents.

The next two families both had two children. As China became used to one child families, jealousy between siblings was virtually extinguished. The relaxing of the One Child Policy, beginning in 2013, and its virtual ending more recently, has reintroduced both a resurgent preference for boys and the whole area of sibling jealousy (K. Huang, 2019). In the first of our cases, the older daughter insisted that her brother was not a problem for her, and the brother felt that he got on well with his sister. Although we felt the daughter's jealousy for her brother was there, it was a buried theme we could not explore in the sessions. His birth was one of the events associated with the beginning of a change in her personality. The anger at her parents could be seen to derive at least in part from her feeling unfairly targeted compared to her brother. The second case, in which two sisters get along well, features the problem of the 'excellent older sister' and the dependent younger one.

'Daughter' and Her Family

Janine Wanlass and I interviewed this family, with Michael Stadter as observer and discussant, and Gao Jun as translator. They were referred because of the depression, acting out, self-cutting and anger of their 16-year-old daughter, who refused to tell us her name. We initially thought of her as 'No Name,' but in the second session, she agreed that we could call her 'Daughter,' a designation she clearly enjoyed. It was immediately clear that she was the family spokesperson. The family also had a ten-year-old boy, Lowell, who said that he feared in an unspecified way that the family would break up, while Daughter said that things were better since she decided she had no relationship with her parents. She thought that her relationship with her brother was good, however. Her mother was concerned that Daughter had spent time looking at gory movies and images on her phone. During these interviews, Daughter looked at her phone as a way to gain space and time in order to get away from emotional moments, a kind of dissociation from the pressure of the interviews.

Daughter made it clear from the first moments that she trusted no one, not her parents, not men and not us. However, after an initial show of balky reticence, she quickly became the most outspoken member of the family. Throughout our sessions, she discussed fears that seemed to her to be more important than her loneliness – fears of impingement, fears men would do violence to her and fear that I especially would not be on her side. She objected to her mother's pressuring of her and taking her phone away to force her to do homework, and she relentlessly criticized her parents' relationship. The father acknowledged he had previously been focused on earning money for the family, but now when he tries to approach his daughter, she rebuffs him, while the mother explained that she was constantly worried about her daughter to no avail.

Daughter and Lowell both insisted that their relationship was good, but we noticed that Lowell always managed to stay below the radar of the family fights. The other three members of the family also all collaborated in keeping him out of the fray, so there seemed to be complete unconscious family agreement that he was to be spared and never dragged into family disagreements. Nevertheless, he was clear that he remained frightened about the breakup of the family. In this way, his anxiety was not spared, even though his direct involvement was.

Eventually, we heard more about the parents' fights that had been severe some years ago, although not now. Mother had threatened to leave the family if Father brought his own debilitated mother to live with them. There was an unexplained but severe rift over Father's gifting an Amway package to a female colleague, which left Mother with a suspicion that he was having an affair. We learned, too, that Daughter had trouble thinking in school when she was preoccupied with her parents' fights, that she had trouble getting along with peers, that she had been cutting herself in order to feel something when generally she felt numb and that she had been hospitalized a few months before. In the hospital, she got in trouble because of interfering in the treatment of a younger psychotic girl.

Daughter explained,

> It was because she had severe auditory and visual hallucinations. She would kill small animals without being aware of it. I felt she was foggy, like they're not even there. It wasn't so dangerous, but it felt... I don't know.... Both of us had very bad parents. Perhaps hers were worse than mine. I talked to her parents once. I never met anybody so disgusting. I felt that I met the aggression of darkness. It was like all the evil things put into the body of a monkey. I told the father to take the girl out of treatment because it was hurting her, but he said that she needed that treatment. He didn't understand that the hospital was making it worse. He was like my parents that way.

Trusting our comments now more than she had done initially, Daughter agreed that she was identified with this younger girl, and through her way of seeing the girl, could express her anger and disgust at her own parents.

We began to feel the sadness in the numbness and deadness of Daughter in her reactions to the parents' angry relationship that still threatened the death of the family. While Daughter attempted to contain the family distress in her symptoms, her younger brother Lowell distanced himself from the distress, which was easier for him to do because he was less of a target of parental concern.

The first two days of interviews were on the weekend. On the third day, a Monday, the parents refused to bring Lowell because, 'While we are willing to be guinea pigs ourselves, we don't think it is healthy for Lowell.' Once again, we could see that Lowell was spared, although we thought that would mean that he would be bearing his anxiety about the family alone.

Daughter said that she felt markedly differently about therapy than her parents: 'If it weren't for therapy, I would be dead!' The degree of parental disaffection was slowly clarified, as was how much of Daughter's difficulty came from trying to distance herself from her parents while being painfully unable to stop caring how they felt about her. She cried when I pointed out that she really still cared, and that her self-cutting and cutting her parents off emotionally were related.

In the fourth session, we moved from Daughter's anger at her parents to examining Mother's anger at her husband. Both Daughter and Mother would try to get close to him, only to have him pull away. Our attention then shifted to Daughter, who now painfully admitted to getting more and more symptomatic, cutting herself and acting crazier, as strategies aimed at getting her parents' attention.

Janine said, 'In some ways, you're like your mother. Like you both try to get something from your father, and you're frustrated when he pulls away.'

Daughter said,

Yes, I do. But my point is that my parents don't tell me anything of what they think because they're afraid it will make me worse. So, I think I just can go ahead and be worse to get what I want.

I said, 'I think you just gave away your secret of why you misbehave.'

Daughter reacted to Janine and my insight. There followed a kind of repartee between us.

Daughter said, 'It doesn't matter. I'll just try new things.'

I said, 'Like what?'

Daughter said, 'Like killing myself!'

I said, 'Yes, logically that would be the worst thing.'

Daughter said, 'There are worse things.'

I said, 'No! There aren't. And really, it would be deeply disappointing to everyone. But I think you need a new strategy.'

Daughter, unconvinced, said, 'Perhaps?'

Janine said, 'And if you kill yourself, you would have given up all hope. So, you need another way.'

Daughter said, 'Yes. Maybe you're right.' (Now she's pondering this problem.)

I said, 'I want to say something about suicide.'

Daughter said, 'You're not going to change me!'

I said, 'No, I agree that you're more stubborn than I am.'

Daughter said, 'You think I'm stubborn?'

I said, 'Definitely! But I understand that being stubborn comes out of being in a corner that you can't get out of.'

Daughter said, 'I think I can get out of my corner though. I have other ways to get out of the difficulty.'

I said, 'Good! So, I want to talk about suicide. A lot of people think that if you kill yourself, you can still be alive. (Daughter nods yes.) But actually, that would be the end of everything.'

Daughter said, 'I know it, but at the same time, a lot of people think they can control the degree of the suicide so that they don't really kill themselves. But I won't take such a risk.'

I said, 'I'm glad to hear that.'

Daughter said, 'Thank you!'

I said, 'We actually agree on a lot of things. So, have you thought about killing yourself?'

Daughter said, 'No, I won't take the risk. In the past I would have, but not now. So, things change.'

I said, 'So things do change?'

Daughter said, 'Yes, but it's a gradual process.'

Mother broke in to say that she is afraid all the time, at home and especially here, that she will say something that will damage her children.

Daughter had expressed many things she was afraid of, but we could see that this had been useful. When I said that Daughter had said valuable things, she was extraordinarily pleased. This led to a discussion of which things she could say, and in what settings saying things helps, and at what times actions and words become self-destructive. The further into this we went, the more Mother opened up about her own fears and dissatisfactions, and although more slowly, the more Father told us, too. He said he was reluctant to be here because of his own distrust of others, and so we could now see how his innate suspiciousness parallels Daughter's and is probably one source of her mistrust.

Daughter described two parts to her mind, so I invited her to bring the two parts in. One part was always trying to fight with herself, and then there is a crazy part that she cannot get rid of. She would watch TV shows about the eleventh century that were full of bloody scenes. She remembered how a teacher earlier, in junior school, had prevented her from putting two cups of milk tea together to look like a human eyeball from which she would drink.

This material enabled us to see that Daughter's adolescent development had been skewed. We are used to seeing adolescence as a time of flux. During that time of identity diffusion, and with the pressure of family strife, vulnerable adolescents can look very crazy, often resulting in diagnoses of Bipolar Disorder or Borderline Personality Disorder. These two diagnostic categories describe people with labile emotions, extreme reactivity and difficulty with relationships, often including high anxiety, promiscuity, poor academic performance and suicidality. However, we have also come to understand that, with strong emotional and often therapeutic support, such adolescents can reintegrate and recover a path to growth and maturation. We thought that this potential for growth was there for Daughter, and we wanted to see if we could find signs of this kind of resilience in her and in her family during the remainder of our encounter.

We discussed with Daughter how another way of seeing the two parts of her mind was to say that one part of her longs for love from her parents, while a second part has to try to get away and forget. That second part can act crazy as a strategy to escape. She acknowledged not wanting to hear this because it was so painful, even though she acknowledged that it was true.

We found Mother to be frequently rejecting of her daughter. When Daughter said, 'I can grow on my own,' I asked the parents if they liked it that she wanted to live on her own. Father said 'No,' while Mother said, 'Yes, it's okay for me if she would have a psychological separation.'

Now we were able to describe how it is not just Daughter but the whole family that was trying to forget painful things. There was a transference-countertransference reenactment of the forgetting: I was trying metaphorically to liken the pattern of family forgetting to 'holes in the ground that swallow everything,' but in the moment, I could not remember the right word, so I asked Janine for help finding it. Janine supplied the word, 'sinkhole,' which sufficed, but it was only later that I recalled the word, 'quicksand.' My counter-transference event of forgetting a common word became a meta-phor for the process of how having to forget painful things takes everything else with it. In this way, the family's problem had gotten into me and into Janine, too, and this event facilitated our work on the use of forgetting as a defense that removes painful memories for the moment, but is self-defeating because this kind of forceful forgetting takes everything valuable with it into the quicksand.

In this session, we managed to discuss the important question of suicide and how the risk of suicide was tied centrally to Daughter's relationship and frustrations with her parents. She used fantasies of suicide to exert power over her parents, which she said was the only way to get through to them. The discussion of this led both to her being able to acknowledge the severe risk of acting on this fantasy, and to the sadness about whether anyone would really care if she died.

At the end of the fourth day, we asked Daughter's therapist, our Chinese colleague Zhou Jie, to tell us more about the family's his-tory with her. We had not wanted to hear this until we had our encounter with them, but now, because we knew we did not know all the relevant facts and because we would be returning them to her care, we wanted to know the essentials of what we did not know.

Zhou Jie told us that the patient had come to see her a year ear-lier, after seeing another therapist for year before that, beginning when Daughter was 14. At that earlier time, she had been diag-nosed with 'depression with schizophrenic qualities' and had been prescribed antipsychotic medication. Mother refused to give her daughter the medication. Daughter was living in a boarding middle school before coming to see Zhou Jie. She had begun cutting herself at about nine years old while in third grade. Mother confirmed that her daughter had been timid and clinging from that time on.

An important part of the history the family had not told us was that Mother had a first surgery for breast cancer when Daughter was five and Lowell was 10 months old. Then Mother had a second surgery, a mastectomy, for recurrence when Daughter was nine. Six months before we saw the family, Daughter found lumps in her own left breast, which fortunately turned out to be benign.

This related to Zhou Jie's report that the daughter had many sexualized thoughts, but when she had suggested that Daughter's fears came from having normal sexual desires, Daughter replied, 'That's disgusting, and it's disgusting to see my own naked body.' Her mother's breast cancer and surgery, and then her own recent breast cancer scare, had joined up with the ambivalence many adolescents feel about the anatomical sexualization of their bodies to create a kind of terror about sexual development.

Zhou Jie also briefed us about the parents' childhoods. Mother grew up in a rural village, having to care for a younger brother and feeling that her own mother had no understanding of children or of Mother. Mother was a good student who got no praise because her parents only complemented Mother's little brother, who was a poor performer.

Father had grown up in the same village, but was from a minority group, so the village people were prejudiced against his father, who struggled to support his four children. Father and one of his sisters went to college, but not the other two sisters.

On the last day, we felt there was significant movement for all three members of the family. Daughter became, despite herself, more trusting and cooperative. She said she had 'failed herself' because she blurted out, 'Thank you!' to us, despite having been resolute not to. She said that she has started working on not being vengeful. She had said that remembering was painful, but she now agreed it would be necessary.

Daughter, her head to the side, began, 'I was thinking about things I forgot, and how I feel bad when I try to remember them. So now I say to myself that I should never forget them.'

Mother recalled, 'When she was young, she bit herself if she was angry.'

Daughter said, 'I'm trying to analyze it. It's the remembering, going back to that scene is painful.'

I asked, 'Which scene?'

Daughter said, 'I don't remember which scene. Well, I remember my mother yelling at me, like, 'How could you perform so badly?' And she would hit me.'

I asked, 'Mother, do you remember that?'

Mother answered, 'I did hit her, but not because she didn't perform.'

Daughter corrected her, 'I did something to not perform.'

Mother insisted, 'Not because of school, but I don't remember exactly. I told you not to do something and you didn't obey.'

Daughter, insisting, 'No, my memory is not failing me. It is the way I remember it.'

Mother said, 'Yes, I criticized you. But I didn't hit you for the school things, but for other things. There was pressure on me. I couldn't accept that she wouldn't perform in school. I felt helpless to educate her.' Mother now agreed that she sees herself in Daughter. We said that Mother had been vicariously hitting and reprimanding herself when she had been so self-critical, in addition to criticizing and hitting her daughter. The disagreement about whether Mother was critical about Daughter's school work or other unspecified things led Daughter to insist it was about school. We said to Mother that even if her memory is different from her daughter's, and that her criticism was about behavior rather than school, it is important to acknowledge how Daughter remembers it.

Janine now asked Father what he thought.

Father replied,

> I think whether my daughter performed well in school or not, we shouldn't hit her. I wanted her to be a better student, but my wife couldn't control her temper. I couldn't get involved, because then we'd have a fight.

I said, 'So you were helpless in case you and your wife would have a fight? And your wife had a temper she couldn't control?'

Father replied, 'When my wife is stressed, she has a temper.'

Janine asked Mother why she was so worried about Daughter.

Mother answered, 'I hoped she could go to university and get a job to support herself.'

I inquired, 'Was it out of concern for her well-being that led to your anger and the hitting?'

Seeing that Daughter was smirking, I asked, 'What's that look, Daughter?'

Daughter said, 'I didn't realize I had a look. I thought that even if it was out of concern that you hit me, you were still bad to me.'

I commented, 'You really didn't like it!'

Daughter said, 'Especially for that reason. It's not normal.'
Janine said,

> You're surprised that your mother said she was concerned for you, and
> therefore there was pressure on her, and that's why she hit you. It was
> still terrible for you. Are you surprised that she was concerned, or that
> her concern led to her hitting?

Daughter said, 'Maybe both. I thought, 'How come you treated
me like that out of simple concern?''
Mother said, 'I don't remember. But I've always been concerned
for you.'
Janine requested, 'Can you say more about your concern for your
daughter?'
Mother reflected,

> Let me think... She performed quite well. Why I was so worried?... I'm
> not that concerned right now. I can't remember why I was then. Maybe
> I was afraid if I didn't put pressure on her, and if it went wrong, then she
> would blame me in the future.

I said, 'Daughter, it sounds like that doesn't make sense to you.'
Daughter said, 'Of course not.'
Janine commented,

> It's not what I wish your mom had done, but I believe that she felt
> doing it was to help you, just like your dad felt it would be better not
> to intervene, so things between you and your mom wouldn't turn into a
> conflict between your father and mother. (Wife and husband nod). But
> they both were afraid that you, Daughter, would experience difficulty or
> cause damage. And then, of course, that's what happened. The difficulty
> is that you, as parents, tried to help, and the way you did it hurt her. And
> that resulted in just what all of you were trying to avoid.

Mother responded,

> Well, about character and personality. I'm sensitive that my daughter's
> like me. So, when I experience her bad voice or tone, I would hit her
> so she wouldn't be like me. But I've also discovered that it was hard for
> others to get along with me. I'm not easy, and maybe that's why I don't
> have many friends. So I hit her for being like me, so she'd do better.

Now we were able to see that Mother has had hope for her daughter, but she feels herself hit by the daughter's symptoms and especially by her school problems in getting along. The problems in

relationships have hit Mother harder than academic matters because of how Mother feels about herself. When Mother says she herself is bad with people, so there are no good relationships with her daughter or with others, this offered a way towards mutual understanding and empathy.

All three of them were more forthcoming in this last session.

Father said, 'I do want to get closer to my daughter and to my wife, but I can't find any peaceful way. I tried, and then they dislike me or hate me.'

This let us show Mother and Daughter that he was hurting, too, and feeling that there was no way for him to get into the family emotionally.

Towards the end, I said to Daughter, 'You're caught between two things: teaching them what love is, and trying to teach them a lesson by taking revenge. You're not sure which to do.'

Daughter said, 'I have thought about that while we have been here. From yesterday, I've been trying to give up my revenge.'

Discussion

This family let us see how family events were woven into Daughter's symptomatic picture of school refusal, suicidal depression and psychotic-like behavior. We are used to seeing this kind of vulnerable picture clinically in the United States, where family conflict, trauma and deprivation are deposited into the mind of a child or adolescent in developmental flux. Now we see something identical in China. In both countries, such developmental struggles are often misdiagnosed as psychosis and treated only with medication and emergency procedures such as hospitalization. The case of Nicole, presented earlier in Chapter 6, is another example, and I have heard others in supervision.

Bei Bei's Family

I now turn to a second family that also had two children in order to illustrate something of the variety of presentations that appear. The adolescent in this family was less disturbed but was nevertheless struggling. The picture presented by the siblings is also quite different. We expect that because every family will present a unique situation and differing attempts at solution, no two examples will look the same, and no number of examples will cover the infinite range of possible family situations.

This case also presents another family in which the adolescent was struggling to stay in school. It provides a study of another family in which family-wide tensions led to difficulty with school attendance.

The Zhou family was also a two child family with an identified patient, who we will call Xiaoling, whose nickname we will disguise as Bei Bei, 18, and her sister, Xiaoqing, 31, whose nickname we will give as Tian Tian, who is married with a baby. These nicknames convey something of the sense of the actual names as infantile. Bei Bei had been out of school most of the previous two years, hospitalized for depression and desperate emotional turmoil, but without the psychotic or suicidal features of the previous case. The sibling relationship featured prominently in this family, although not with open jealousy.

I saw Bei Bei and her family also with Janine Wanlass, this time with our colleague Christopher Clulow as observer and Gao Jun as translator. We expected to see a family of three, but when they arrived, the family had expanded. We met with Mr. Zhou and Mrs. Chen, in their 50s, Bei Bei and Tian Tian, Tian Tian's husband, Mr. Huang, also in his 30s, and the young couple's 14-month-old baby boy.

Bei Bei had missed most of the last two years of school and was still struggling. The parents put her in a boarding school to try to support her. She has always been urged to be like her older sister Tian Tian, whose school performance was always excellent.

During the interview, Bei Bei was frequently in tears, and her sister stroked her chest. I could see that she had little breast development, giving the feeling that this stroking was like the care of a baby sister, much like the toddler sitting in Tian Tian's lap, playing and holding everyone's attention. The toddler, at the age of 14 months was beginning to move away from babyhood, seeming to provide a metaphor for difficulties Bei Bei faced in separating from her parents. Both Bei Bei's mother, Mrs. Chen, and her sister, Tian Tian, had spent time at the boarding school helping Bei Bei with homework and care of herself.

In the first interview, Bei Bei said that she feels that her mother, sister and the baby care for her greatly, but her father does not. Mr. Zhou identified himself as a person who gets on with things. He admitted that he is frequently critical of Bei Bei. He and his wife are teachers. It is important to them that Bei Bei perform in an excellent way. They are deeply distressed about her depression that started in junior high school two or three years ago and was treated with medication and psychotherapy.

In the first interview, they hint at family problems. Mrs. Chen tells us in passing that some years ago, her younger brother was in a terrible car accident that was a major blow to the family.

Bei Bei says she has always been under pressure in school, although she was an excellent student until recent years. She was compared to children of father's colleagues as well as to her excellent older sister. Her difficulty began early in high school, and it became important that her sister help with homework, help that Bei Bei readily accepted.

Tian Tian said that she was always happy to help her little sister. She describes doing the kind of mothering and hovering that she and Mrs. Chen both did for Bei Bei at the boarding school.

As we talked, we saw Bei Bei coming alive in playing with the baby. The baby takes things from her, throws them away and Bei Bei fetches them, playing a game of separation and return that is a metaphor for Bei Bei's adolescent separation struggles with her family.

Bei Bei told of an occasion when her parents did not visit her when she was sick at boarding school. She said she began to hate her father for not caring. This episode was reported by Mr. Huang, the brother-in-law, who says he understood that Bei Bei did not really hate her parents, but was stressed as she tried to recover from depression. Bei Bei added the teachers wondered why her parents did not visit, and when they finally did, her father had said to her, 'A big girl like you shouldn't cry like that.' When her father said, 'You shouldn't cry,' she felt completely misunderstood.

Mr. Huang continued by saying that two years ago, when Bei Bei first became sick, his wife, Tian Tian, was pregnant and could not take care of Bei Bei as usual. Now his infant son is the family mediator, making everybody feel good when there is strain. He said that Bei Bei, being a second child, experienced a big gap between her and her sister. He thinks that first children do better because their parents are more attentive, while second children have older parents with more financial resources but less emotional ones. He grew up in a similar situation, taking care of his much younger brother. 'My wife treats her sister more like a kid, not an equal. That satisfies her inner needs.'

When I asked Mr. Zhou about being able to have two children during the time of the One Child Policy, he said, 'In some provinces, we could make things happen by different means, but it is better not to talk about that.' Mrs. Chen added that they were both government employees and that some people in that situation could have a second child. She said, 'We were jealous of others who could have a second child and wondered about that, but we were very busy then. Eventually, years later, it became possible.' She added,

> I was very busy with my first daughter when I was 25. With my second daughter, who I had at 38, I was less busy and could give her more

attention. We traveled and had picnics. Some would say I doted too much on her. I was very young when I had Tian Tian, but with Bei Bei, I was always with mothers who were much younger.

The baby was now throwing things and giggling, throwing a small figure and expecting its return from his mother or Bei Bei. Soon everyone is playing the game. Bei Bei says that the baby really gives her hope. When she was at school and being stressed, she would look at videos of the baby to be happy. She said, 'I cared for him even when he was in my sister's uterus. I would talk to the fetus.'

I said, 'Your sister has been caressing you like you are a baby.'

Bei Bei said, 'Yes, because Tian Tian really takes care of me. She helps my parents take care of me. I feel love from my sister and my mother.' (But she pointedly omits saying that she feels loved by her father.)

Discussing this first interview afterwards, we wondered about the parents being middle-aged and their possible loss of sexuality just as Bei Bei is 18 and would be becoming sexual, but we also noticed how there was a push from the whole the family, including her sister, to treat Bei Bei like a baby. So, it might be that the idea of Bei Bei becoming sexual not only threatens her, when her infantile needs are so strong, but also threatens the whole family.

Bei Bei showed up for the second day in a T-shirt emblazoned with:

MODERN PROMETHEUS
A BEAUTIFUL NAME

The family talked more openly today. Mr. Zhou said that although he had been skeptical, he now realized this was a wonderful opportunity for all of them. He apologized to Bei Bei in front of everyone, saying, 'I'm very sorry, dear.' He realized that his telling her to be strong was based on the model of the advice he had lived by himself. He thinks that much of his own irritability and impatience comes from his lifelong sleep disorder that began when he was in university. As parents, they wanted Bei Bei to have a happy time in university after high school. 'It's not for a good job alone that we want this, just for the opportunity for her to enjoy university.'

We note silently that Mr. Zhou must have become anxious at the same point in his life that Bei Bei now faces.

Today, Bei Bei was able to talk about how she never felt as strong as her older sister. We said how, in many ways, especially in the way she's used her illness, she is actually stronger than Tian Tian. Mr. Huang agreed. He sees Bei Bei as stronger than his wife, who has unacknowledged problems. His wife agreed, and the whole family then agreed that the uncle's car accident had been a huge blow, and finally, that the birth of the baby had produced a rival to the attention previously paid to Bei Bei.

In this way, the strength that Bei Bei exercises has now been put on record, a theme we would follow throughout the rest of our time with them.

The family began to discuss conflict between Mr. Zhou and Mrs. Chen. Mostly, it had centered around the difficulty of Mrs. Chen being so indulgent of Bei Bei. Mr. Zhou said that he thinks his daughter should buck up. He was raised in the 1960s, when it was completely crucial to be able to take care of yourself. We could see there was more to learn about his growing up, but all we heard so far was that his early days were ones of 'hardship and individual striving.'

We began to understand that the family has been indulgent and overly supportive of Bei Bei out of fear she would not be able to make it on her own. Paradoxically, this indulgence contributed to her feeling that she cannot make it on her own, even though she was previously an excellent student. It remains unclear exactly when and why she took a dive. Bei Bei speaks about the way that her parents' friends thought she would never survive in university, but now she is determined to do it and show everybody.

The heart of this session came in the discussion of the parents' fights that have formed the basis for Bei Bei's fear of family breakdown. Speaking for the first time in this session, older sister Tian Tian said she experienced her parents fighting but never thought they would divorce. She sees that Bei Bei is more frightened of that. We agreed that Bei Bei uses her illness both to hide and to express anger at her father for his angry outbursts at her mother, and also to draw attention to herself and therefore away from the couple in order to avoid the couple splitting apart.

Tian Tian's husband now talked about the way his own father's younger brother was less successful than his father, and this led to a discussion of how it is that many younger siblings feel unhappy when compared to their older siblings.

I said I thought Bei Bei was furious at her parents for comparing her to Tian Tian. Bei Bei agreed.

I said,

Now that you've caught your father in the crime of causing the trouble, you keep on prosecuting him by staying sick. Because if you stop being sick, it would prove that he was right that you could be tough. Actually, I think you're very strong.

Bei Bei said that other people don't think she's strong, but Mr. Huang said that he agrees: Bei Bei is the strongest person in the family.

Bei Bei said, 'I don't know who I am or what kind of person I should be. With each competition, I need to get others' approval.' This returns the discussion to the way her mother and sister treat her like a baby. She craves this baby-love but then feels that she can't live without it. Bei Bei continued, 'Nobody's confident in my ability, so they can't let me go. So only I can prove to myself that I can do high school.' Referring to when she began high school, she said, 'They didn't believe I could manage on my own until I finished, and then they were all surprised.'

Mrs. Chen said,

> They thought you lived in your sister's shadow. I felt I gave Bei Bei so much care. If there was a rock in front of her, I would pick it up so she wouldn't fall. My husband and I aren't so successful, but we have a certain amount of recognition in our small town. People would say 'Oh, you're Mr. Zhou and Mrs. Chen's daughter.' She was eager for recognition, but the pressure led to conflict between father and daughter.

I said, 'Bei Bei, your mother and sister have had their arms around you like a baby, because a baby needs to be held, but that kind of love doesn't really support you.'

Janine added, 'It's like they're holding you up, and when they do that, you don't know if you can stand on your own.'

Bei Bei cannot deal with Janine and me talking about her infantile needs. She continues to talk about her parents, not herself: 'My father loses his temper and accuses my mother who doesn't fight back. My father says, 'Don't blame me all the time."

Mr. Zhou agreed. Growing up, he had to rely only on himself, but his wife is indulgent. 'No matter what my daughter says, my wife agrees with her. Therefore, we have conflict.'

Bei Bei said, 'I think sometimes my father doesn't have the right point of view and my mother does. If they disagree, he thinks my mother just sides with me.'

But constantly working to win her mother over to her side has left Bei Bei with an increased fear that her parents would divorce.

After this session, we noted that Bei Bei is a female version of a 'Modern Prometheus.' Having stolen fire from the Greek gods, Prometheus' punishment was to be eaten alive forever – a heavy price for Bei Bei's efforts to become her own person through resisting her parents. In a way, this is a metaphor for modern Chinese youth as they struggle against the old ways. When Bei Bei, the precious second child, came along after so many years, everyone agreed to protect her in a way that apparently had not applied to her older sister. Mr. Zhou's attitude puts him on the outs with the three women in the family and reinforces his idea that he has to take care of himself. But his anger is there, some of it residual from his difficult childhood. It is frightening to everybody, but most of all to Bei Bei. Mrs. Chen and Tian Tian constantly protect Bei Bei from his anger, while at the same time, Bei Bei is trying to protect her parents as a couple from her own efforts to split them, partly driven by her Oedipal attraction to her father, about which she cannot allow herself to know.

On Day Three, we learned that Bei Bei had actually been staying with her sister and brother-in-law, where she feels more comfortable. Bei Bei feels ready to go back to school, already feeling relief from anxiety as the family has begun to talk.

Mr. Zhou began by apologizing, again in a heartfelt way. He sees now that he misunderstood Bei Bei, thinking that she just had to buck up and take care of herself. He assumed he was being good to her by being critical. This comes from his own experience. Although his parents were government workers, they really were from a hardscrabble traditional farm family. His success was through hard work and determination, but always with anxiety.

Mr. Zhou was raised by his grandparents while his parents lived apart from each other and from him in other cities. He was always closest to his maternal grandmother. His mother did not live with him until he was 10. His grandmother, who was still alive when the couple married, took care of Tian Tian. Mr. Zhou developed extreme anxiety during school, which he solved by jogging many miles a day. He still does not sleep at night and still handles his anxiety by running. Mr. Zhou's story brought the themes of early separation and anxiety into the room. Bei Bei listened with interest.

The greatest impact today came from hearing about Mrs. Chen's brother's death, which had earlier been mentioned only in passing. Tian Tian described how the mother's brother, her uncle, was hit by a bus crossing the street, and the anxious days in which he was in the hospital before dying. Tian Tian had been taking care of Bei Bei and the uncle's young son, and had to act as though nothing was wrong, meanwhile feeling awful herself. Mother's brother was beloved by the whole family, so everyone felt the tragedy.

Bei Bei said, 'After that, whenever my parents went out, I was afraid something bad would happen. If I didn't warn them to drive carefully, I'd be more afraid of a car accident.'

Janine pointed out that while Bei Bei was afraid they might die in an accident, she was also worried about their relationship.

I added, 'Janine, I was thinking to say, 'Were you also worried they would kill each other?"

Bei Bei said that having an accident like her uncle's was always a 'low-probability event.' From then on, even though something was low-probability, like her uncle's accident, she would worry. She needs to have her parents visit her to reassure her they are alive, especially that Mr. Zhou is alive. We said that one thing that endangers Mr. Zhou's life is the anger at him in Bei Bei's mind, so then she needs him to visit to be sure that he is not harmed by her rage. So, when Bei Bei rebukes him for not visiting, it is both because he is not paying attention to her, and, more importantly, because without seeing him, she gets no reassurance he is okay. Bei Bei responded that since a 200-kilometer trip is dangerous in itself, even its low probability of catastrophe does not reassure her or stop her from fearing he will be killed during the trip. But, since she demanded the trip, she also feels responsible for putting him in danger, so her anxiety knows no relief.

Today, we also heard more about the father's explosive temper and Bei Bei's worry whenever he blew up. Mrs. Chen and Tian Tian are used to his temper and do not take it personally, but for Bei Bei, it induces fear and a feeling that she has to protect her mother, and therefore side with her mother against her father. Then her anger at her father, which she unconsciously fears endangers his life, increases her anxiety. The whole feeling today was one of a relief of family-wide tension as they talked for the first time.

For the fourth day, only the parents and Bei Bei came because the baby, sick with a cold, begged both his parents to stay with him. Bei Bei sits between her parents, buckling and unbuckling the shoulder strap on her overalls, which partly looks like baby play and partly like an adolescent striptease. Her teasing anger at her father, we can see, reinforces her bond with her mother against him.

We dug into the origins of Mr. Zhou's anxieties and temper. He says more about being raised in a rural farm village. His parents were engineers, but during the Cultural Revolution, it was precarious to be somebody with skills, even if the skills were valuable to the community. Because of not raising their own food, his family was a 'social minority' that had to pay for food and were therefore vulnerable to criticism and in danger of losing face. Consequently, when he now is in a difficult situation, he still feels in danger of losing face.

In the early years of his marriage, his low-level government job did not provide enough money to improve the family's situation.

Mr. Zhou said,

> Because I graduated in the country, I didn't have particular difficulty. After we married, we moved out of the small family house. I began to teach, but I wanted to be promoted and tried to get into the leadership. I was in the CCP at a municipal level. I also sold vegetables and plastics, did farming and had a small business. I was the first to buy stock, I borrowed money from the bank. I even bought stock in the USA. I was thin but very strong.

His activities led to the improvement in the family's resources. Eventually, they did well.

Mr. Zhou said,

> There is a common expression, 'just like a farmer,' meaning someone who is easily angered. Among my 10 colleagues, I'm least likely to be angry, but I'm often angry at home. It's because I think no one should ever make a second mistake.

Mrs. Chen agrees that he is generous and mild-tempered with colleagues, but at home, he has to have things right and is intolerant. We said this relates to his feeling that he is always anxious to get things right in order to improve his station in life and to ward off potential loss of face.

Mrs. Chen's growing up was easier, with a brother and two sisters, all of whom have been successful. While she feels she has more temper than she would like, a temper that is modeled on her mother's, as a teacher, she transforms her anger into her devotion to educating her students how to be less angry.

Bei Bei said,

> My father doesn't do anything around the house. It's not fair. He thinks it's enough that he earns a good living for the family. Therefore, he doesn't have to wash dishes. He should do things like everybody else, even though my mother is okay with this.

Bei Bei then admitted she is as intemperate as her father, turning her intolerance for his mistakes against him.

In this way, Bei Bei and her father form an intense bond through battle, an angry, sexualized way of fighting that covers over and superficially denies an Oedipal bond, substituting intense anger for intense longing. Paradoxically, her anger also comes from a struggle inside herself, wishing for independence despite longing to be a dependent baby.

Nevertheless, there had been significant thawing this week between Bei Bei and her father. On their way home, she put her feet on his shoulders in the car and asked teasingly if they were smelly. Mr. Zhou welcomed her gesture, playfully asking for a back massage. This loving playfulness had eluded them until now. They both welcomed the closeness.

The three of them came again on the last day and asked to have their picture taken with us, Bei Bei all smiles. There was a new sense of working together.

We learned on that day that Bei Bei returned to school just before the consultation with us and thought she could continue going, although she missed most of the last two years. Mr. Zhou and Bei Bei worked on their relationship, rehashing disagreements and wishes for each other to change, and demonstrating a beginning capacity to work on difference.

When Mr. Zhou described being angry at Bei Bei for being on her phone all the time, she replied that he was the same in his perpetual preoccupation with the stock market.

I said, 'Okay, Bei Bei. Here's the thing. Your mother says it's okay because he takes care of the family, but you say he has to do what you think!'

Bei Bei said, 'No! All family members should do their share. But he feels if he makes the money, he can do what he wants.'

I said,

> You're just like your father, actually. You pick up on his inconsistencies, but you behave exactly like him. You're turning his personality against him. You say it's to protect your mother, but she doesn't care. I think you're doing it for yourself.

Bei Bei said, 'Yes. I use his own rules against him.'

I said,

> Here's what I think. Bei Bei uses her 'illness' in a fight to the death with her father. She targets her father's loss of face growing up and in the family. The conflict is often set in the family's kitchen. So then, my question is, 'Why is Father so angry in the kitchen and so concerned about his disorderly family?' I think he feels ganged up on by his wife and daughter, displaced in his own home, a lonely man in a sea of women.

I linked that to his upbringing and described the current family in which all three are 'the odd man out.' Mr. Zhou's family was threatened with loss of face in the farming community. Thus, his family's humiliation is replicated in the kitchen when he feels he loses face in the family.

We made the further interpretation that Bei Bei's friendly fighting with her father was a way of keeping their relationship close when otherwise things were difficult for them, but that idea seemed too much for her to accept.

Near the end, we suggested that Mr. Zhou could afford to stop trying to control Bei Bei, who really wants to go to school and do well, just as he wants her to. Letting go of control would give her the control to do that for herself. We described how Bei Bei exhibits strength in order to fight with her father, and then the fights with her take over family life. We wanted her to employ her strength to fight for herself instead of fighting with Mr. Zhou. This led Bei Bei to remember times when she was young when she and Mr. Zhou had a tender relationship. Now, Bei Bei feels he is against her when in fact, his criticism is driven by intense concern for her. Bei Bei nods. She says her father's visits always led inexplicitly to her suddenly feeling better.

Mrs. Chen says, 'They used to be friendly. My husband loves his child so deeply, but he's afraid that she won't have a happy life.'

Discussion

These two families, both with two children, give contrasting pictures of sibling relationships. Even if many Chinese families choose to have one child in the future, others will opt for two or more, so sibling issues will soon become common. However, I believe it is safe to say that sibling relationships in the twenty-first century will be qualitatively different than those of the traditionally large Chinese families before the 1949 advent of the Communist Party and before the One Child Policy. While the new possibility of two child families, and the probability that there will occasionally be families of three or more children, that increase in birth rates will still not be enough of a boost to the demographic problem of a shrunken workforce. It will nevertheless present another change to China's nuclear family structure and to the overall structure of family kinships. Cousins will once again become more commonplace. There is still a residue of the traditional preference for sons, but I doubt the gains for women will be substantially reversed in a world of increasing consciousness of the rights of women to be treated as equals. Whatever happens, and however much a preference for sons might remain for some as a background, the new ways will not replicate the old pattern of large, male-dominated families. The psychological issues will be new, buffeted by China's changing culture, economic pressures, and the continuing climate of intense competition. Because of all these unknowns, the shape of the interior of Chinese families of the future, and the shape of the strains they will face, also remains unknowable.

Chapter 16

A Couple Therapy[1]

This final clinical chapter shows what is possible with long-term psychotherapy that extends well beyond the kind of five-day encounters that my trips to China have allowed me and my colleagues to conduct personally. It also offers another perspective from the point of view of one of our Chinese colleagues. I have been working with a group of senior Chinese therapists in twice-monthly group consultation for many years. The group is constituted by those who served as leaders of the small affective discussion groups that meet twice each day during our in-person teachings in China. The Western teachers then consult to these group leaders about the process and themes of their groups (J. Scharff and D. Scharff, 2000, 2017). In this design, we have been able to train a number of Chinese group leaders in the methods of leading these Small Affective Groups, and, as in the United States, the twice-daily small groups have come to be a highly valued part of our trainings. In addition, I consult to a dozen of these group leaders twice a month online on the conduct of their own family and couple cases. This provides them with additional training, and at the same time augments my own learning about Chinese couples and families, expanding my experience beyond the more than 20 families I have personally interviewed.

In terms of this book, the case that Li Yanling presented in that group and generously offered to let me share here, lets me close with the ongoing therapy work of a senior Chinese colleague and allows me to discuss the process of the group consultation that represents working together to learn more about therapy for Chinese couples and families. In this way, this chapter speaks to the last of the questions I posed at the beginning: Can we respond to our Chinese psychotherapist colleagues' request to help them increase the effectiveness of their therapy? Li Yanling, a senior psychiatrist and psychotherapist, presented this couple several times during my regular consultations to that group. She incorporated understanding that I and her colleagues offered into her ongoing work before the sessions that she brought to the group and that I present below. She and the family both gave me permission to report here on the treatment in order to show how change is possible during two years of psychotherapy, and also to demonstrate how I work with colleagues like her in their advanced training.

Li Yanling wrote the initial treatment report, the names of family members already changed to protect confidentiality. I have edited her English and added commentary of the kind I regularly share with her and the group on the family, her engagement with them and the progress of treatment. These comments are therefore like the ones I make during these consultations. I wish also to acknowledge gratefully Li Yanling's colleagues in the consultation group, whose comments always add to the collective understanding we strive for together. In this kind of exercise, discussions among colleagues of the consultation group increase everyone's understanding of a family and how to help them.

Initial Presentation

Wang Fan, a woman in her early 30s, made the initial contact with Li Yanling when, after taking some counseling courses, Wang Fan realized that she and her mother were both emotionally compromised. Because Wang Fan's mother was taking care of Wang Fan's three-year-old son, Wang Fan suggested that her mother get psychotherapy for fear that she would negatively influence her grandson. The grandmother saw Li Yanling for two sessions at Wang Fan's insistence, but then refused further treatment. At that point, Wang Fan accepted therapy for herself. After six months of Wang Fan's individual work, Li Yanling suggested that Wang Fan invite her husband to join her in couple therapy. Over the next period, there were a few couple and family sessions that included the son at intervals, but once he began preschool, the treatment became exclusively couple therapy.

Wang Fan had a college degree in commerce and worked in a community center. Her husband, whom we will call Zhou Wei, held a degree in science and technology, and worked as an engineer. Their son, Xiao Ping, was five at the time Li Yanling consulted me in the session we will review after describing Wang Fan's initial work.

Wang Fan's Individual Therapy

During individual sessions, Wang Fan mostly talked about her own and her parents' histories, her conflicts with her parents and in-laws, and differences she had with her husband in terms of chores and child education. She complained that her husband was unwilling to cooperate with her and failed to be a good container for her emotional needs.

Wang Fan reported that in her childhood, her parents were emotionally unstable and often denigrated her. They demanded that she perform well academically and dished out corporal punishment when her grades were unsatisfactory. She was also punished for being headstrong. Her family struggled financially, and Wang Fan's sense of worth was also shattered by the family's financial situation, about which she often felt ashamed. Her grades began to slip after middle school. She was rebellious and resisted studying, underperforming at the National College Entrance Exam. Therefore she was only able to enroll in a mediocre college that led to a low-paying job after graduation.

Wang Fan was uninterested in her current job. She frequently complained about her lazy husband, who she would like to be more ambitious financially. However, her wish was not supported by her mother-in-law – who 'did not have the heart to see her son "suffer",' so Wang Fan had turned to her for money instead.

Giving up on her husband, Wang Fan invested instead in her son, Xiao Ping. She wanted to give him the best of everything in order to grow him into a decent young man. Yet whenever Xiao Ping failed to meet her expectations, Wang Fan admitted that she would become verbally or physically violent. Later suffering regret, she would worry she had harmed him. However she repeatedly said that the problem lay with everyone else – her husband, her in-laws and her parents. If they would change, that would heal her, too.

Wang Fan described her father as a retired worker who was a paranoid whiner, a smart person with terrible emotional intelligence and interpersonal skills. She said he was rarely happy and was needlessly frugal, always purchasing whatever is cheapest.

Wang Fan described her mother, also a retired worker, as an irritating grumbler. She often felt humiliated by her mother's annoying ways. Her mother had rocked her to sleep on a good day and poured scorn on her on a bad day. When the right age came for her to date, her mother asked her to have blind dates with boys with below-average qualities, as if her daughter were 'a pile of garbage' whom no one would marry.

As an adult, Wang Fan refused physical contact with her mother, whose volatility had hurt her – one moment an angel, the next a devil. Her husband, Zhou Wei, shares similar feelings towards

Wang Fan's parents, which is one of the few things about him that Wang Fang finds gratifying.

As an only child herself, Wang Fan has a strong sense of possessiveness of her own child and wants more and more for him. She would like to take as much money from her in-laws as possible in order to offer her son the best of everything. She does few chores, usually leaving housework to her parents or in-laws. When they are absent, Wang Fan commands that her husband take over.

Li Yanling reported that in sessions, Wang Fan was extremely anxious. She seemed exceptionally fastidious in life choices, such as her son's kindergarten, furniture for their new home and itinerary details for family trips. Family trips had apparently become excruciating ordeals, which the husband and son could not refuse to join, however reluctant they might be. Wang Fan said that she never got to travel when she was little, so going on trips now compensates for past disappointments. If her son gets to live like this, that will gratify her greatly.

Consultation

Li Yanling presented this background about Wang Fan at the beginning of her several consultations and augmented it as she accumulated more understanding. In this process, the group and I learned about Wang Fan's narcissistic orientation, her envy and greed, and her accumulated resentment towards both her parents and her in-laws. Despite the continuing help from the parental generation, her resentment of them and of her husband continually generated painful countertransference for Li Yanling in that she could feel that the people in Wang Fan's life might feel mistreated by her.

In the consultations, we were able to understand the projection from Wang Fan's self-hatred onto family members and the projection of an ideal self into her son. Naming this process enabled Li Yanling to develop more compassion towards Wang Fan and the suffering that she continually tried to relieve through splitting and by projecting everything bad onto the parental generation and her husband, and everything good onto her son, rationalizing her self-justified greed because of her desperation to be compensated for the feelings of neglect and persecution while growing up. This facilitated Li Yanling's efforts to understand and develop an underlying identification with Wang Fan's deprived internal representations, rather than simply feeling sorry for the people in her life who, in outward ways, she took for granted and of whom she appeared to take advantage.

Couple Therapy

After six months of seeing Wang Fan for individual therapy, seeing that Wang Fan inevitably placed blame for her complaints on others, but especially on Zhou Wei, Li Yanling suggested that they change to couple therapy. This recommendation followed from ideas developed in the consultation group, where we considered that without having the husband actually present in the therapy, all that Li Yanling had access to was Wang Fan's own inevitably one-sided version of her husband. Furthermore, the husband had no opportunity to benefit from being in the therapy himself.

Zhou Wei agreed and they began therapy together, during which the then three-year-old boy, Xiao Ping, participated in about 10 family sessions. However, when he started kindergarten later on, he no longer wanted to come to therapy. The couple agreed to revert to couple therapy, as the presence of the son sometimes made their conversation uncomfortable. The couple turned out to be highly motivated, never missing sessions except for holidays or planned travels.

Once she began seeing the couple, Li Yanling heard how the couple's marriage was characterized by bickering. Wang Fan bossed her husband around relentlessly while doing little herself. Zhou Wei resented her entitlement and bossiness, and her wanting everyone else to nurture her. He said he felt exhausted around Wang Fan. They agreed, however, that the grandparents, who take care of both the couple and their child, are intrusive.

Zhou Wei also complained that Wang Fan is inordinately demanding on behalf of their son. Everything for her son must come with the best brand names. She has demanded that Zhou Wei sleep in a separate room for fear that the son would not have sufficient oxygen to breathe if the three of them slept in the same room. So, the privileged child was in bed with Wang Fan.

Zhou Wei's History

Now with Zhou Wei in the room, Li Yanling could learn about him individually, too. He was an only child of lenient parents, loving video games since middle school. Despite putting little effort into his studies, he got good grades because of innate intelligence (which Wang Fan confirmed) and enrolled in a decent university. However, he works a mediocre job with average pay. He is obsessed with online gaming, often playing until the middle of the night. He has diabetes but exercises no dietary control. Like his wife, he feels no guilt asking his parents for money.

Zhou Wei's father retired from a corporate mid-level management position when the company shut down. For a while, the father was immersed in self-pity, but then became immensely vain after making a fortune speculating in stocks. Zhou Wei's mother is a retired worker who wears her heart on her sleeve in that she is easily emotional in reaction to others' troubles.

Consultation

I was not surprised that the picture of Zhou Wei that Li Yanling got once he was actually in the room was quite different than the one that had been presented by Wang Fan. We find this regularly whenever we move from seeing only one member of a couple to seeing the couple together. The group was prepared for this difference because we have been working together over several years, but each time we see it in action, there are surprises. In this case, the equal and opposite complaints by the husband confirmed Li Yanling's countertransference experience of Wang Fan. However, with the husband's complaints and characterizations, Li Yanling had more opportunity both to support the couple and at the same time to confront Wang Fan with his observations. This is never easy, and as a group, we could discuss the tact necessary while confronting Wang Fan's sense of entitlement and the way her persistent attempts to compensate for her sense of life-long deprivation usually backfired. We could also see that some of her characterizations of Zhou Wei were valid. That offered an opportunity to work with him on fears that hobbled his ambitions and that also crippled his ability to form a marital partnership.

The Couple

When the couple began to come together, Li Yanling sought a history of them as a couple. When a friend introduced them, Wang Fan noted that Zhou Wei had a decent background and a good degree. Marrying him would be a fast pass from hell to heaven. They married after three months and now live in the same community as Zhou Wei's parents. After their son was born, Wang Fan's increased contact with Zhou Wei's parents led to friction and intense quarreling, although, the couple agreed, they are dependent on them to prepare daily meals for the family and to pay for most of their expenses, like their travel and car payments, while Wang Fan and Zhou Wei save most of their own income for their future.

Prior to treatment, the couple argued frequently and then took their frustration out on their child. They were sleeping in separate rooms and rarely had sex.

Consultation

Having the couple together in the room offered a new understanding of their relationship from a perspective outside the one-sided version each presented individually. The points of agreement and disagreement offered new opportunities for exploration that Li Yanling exploited over the first sessions in the couple work. As a result, through her enhanced view of them we began to see that the couple was characterized by a shared fear of deprivation and personal inability to take care of themselves. Then through mutual projective identification – that is, by unconsciously projecting the sense each of them had of being unable to take care of themselves – they attempted to locate blame for their shared inability into each other in order to avoid feeling disabled themselves. The problem was that once they located the trouble in each other, they lost the ability to examine and work on their own sense of disability, and could only insist that Li Yanling try to fix the other person, thereby increasing the feeling of helplessness they each carried.

The Course of Couple Therapy

Li Yanling found that although Wang Fan initially had a hard time listening to her in the beginning of couple therapy, she slowly grew to take in more from her husband. Li Yanling would often ask, 'Have you discussed at home what you have just said here with me?'

Some months after the treatment began, the couple resumed sleeping in the same room. Sex eventually increased from once in three months to once a month as they both acknowledged each other's positive changes. Still, Zhou Wei was always the initiator, with Wang Fan often declining his invitation or demanding additional conditions, for instance, that Zhou Wei massage her. Wang Fan attributed her frequent refusal of intimacy to her anger towards her husband.

After six months of couple treatment, the couple moved to be more independent from Zhou Wei's parents and decided to divide chores: Wang Fan was now in charge of cleaning and Zhou Wei of cooking. Zhou Wei stepped up substantially, although his parents still helped with housework on weekends.

Consultation

During her therapy, Li Yanling presented the couple several times. This gave me and the group the opportunity to examine the slow process of change in a way that could never be available in the five-day interventions my colleagues and I conducted in-person. Therapy is always a slow process in helping couples and families alter lifelong, ingrained patterns that have been the best they could manage. Consequently, over time, we could learn from and consult to Li Yanling's work in a detailed way. Any of us stands to benefit from such a close examination of our therapy, and so we all felt privileged by Li Yanling's generous sharing of her work and appreciated this opportunity that she gave us for shared learning.

The Process of Therapy

Li Yanling reports below three vignettes from different phases of the therapy. In order to illustrate the process of change, I follow these vignettes with consultative comments.

First Vignette: Family Therapy

In an early family session, the couple discussed how Wang Fan controlled Zhou Wei at home. Meanwhile, the child, Xiao Ping, played with his father, feeding a school of small fish to a huge shark.

I said to Li Yanling that the theme of Xiao Ping's play, the small fish getting eaten alive by the shark, was the boy's commentary on the way his father often feels eaten alive by his mother, showing that Xiao Ping was taking in the emotional meaning of his parents' arguments. This illustrated what I teach about the role of children's play in family sessions: When parents fight, their fighting relationship colonizes the child's mind. This play confirmed that worry by showing it happening right within the session.

Wang Fan goaded Zhou Wei, 'Go ahead, tell on me.'

Zhou Wei queried, 'What's to tell?'

Wang Fan answered, 'That I made you come home.'

Zhou Wei explained, 'She demanded that I leave work early today. My boss caught me leaving. I was quite upset. She won't stop calling me on days when she gets home early, 'When are you coming back? I'm home with the kid. Come home soon! We miss you.' She demands, 'Come home early!' But, really, I'm coming back to no-big-deal except to cut her some slack.

'The kid stayed home today feeling under the weather. Wang Fan got home, asked my mom to leave. Soon her patience wore out, so she called me. Really, it was for me to save her. When I got home, she just supervised my taking care of the kid. That doesn't feel good.'

Li Yanling said, 'We've talked about similar situations before. What was the distress this time?'

Zhou Wei said, 'If I don't comply, she's cross. 'What are you bustling about at work then? You can't even come home to be with me?' It's phone-call assault. Very unpleasant. If I give in, we fall into her supervising me with the kid. That doesn't feel good.

'One more thing really upsets me – the dishwasher. She claimed she couldn't understand the instruction manual and asked me to read it and teach her. In the end, she simply admitted that the process was clear but she couldn't learn it. Dishwashing is now my sweet burden. She's manipulative even with her own family. She aspires to become someone with disabilities who commands, 'Zhou Wei, get over here! Pour me a glass of water!' (Wang Fan always refered to Zhou Wei by his full name.) Water was right in front of her, but no, she has to recruit me. She says it all the time 'I want to be waited on! I want others to plan great trips for me.... I want, I want, I want!"

Li Yanling asked, 'How does a person with disability go on a trip?'

Zhou Wei said, 'I mean, I feel that's the state she wishes for. 'Disabled' means incapable of functioning, of moving. Things should simply appear for her like magic.'

Wang Fan, smiled, 'Generally, he beats around the bush too much. But at home, he's like a landlord, ordering people around, enjoying life.'

Li Yanling now confronted her, 'Wang Fan, you are more direct about it. You're also a landlord who bosses people around.'

Zhou Wei asked, 'Who torments people!'

Li Yanling asked, 'Wang Fan, do you have something to say?'

Wang Fan said, 'This relationship is a collusion. There is the 'landlord' part of me, which is like my father who was doted on by Grandma. Grandma and my mom dote on me, and my aunt dotes on her daughter, who acts like a boss, too. On the other hand, I throw comments at Zhou Wei when I feel unfairly treated. I'm a straightforward person, I don't play mind games. Like about the dishwasher: I just don't like to read manuals, too much trouble and I wouldn't understand anyway. So I asked to him to read it and teach me. Simple as that. If he insists on pinning this 'it-never-occurred-to-me con-spiracy theory' on me about the dishwasher, then I might as well act as he imagines. Zhou Wei, you repeatedly refer to me that way. Fine! I don't want to fail your expectation that I'm entitled. He aggravates me. He said, 'If we purchase appliances in the future, you have to figure them out yourself. I'm not using them anyway. Don't you go buying stuff like this dishwasher and make me study it. If you don't need to worry about even using these appliances, what are you doing, really?' He said he wouldn't need a new TV, then he watches it more than any of us. Do you see the mismatch he presents? I didn't have a clue which TV to buy or how to handle the installation. I asked him to help out and listen to installer's instructions, but he just stood up and walked away. I was extremely upset. I wonder how he defines his role in our home. It seems that responsibility and account-ability are the ants in his pants, so he shirks them. This is partly why I give him commands.'

Thinking back to the beginning of Wang Fan's speech, Li Yanling asked, 'What do you mean by the word 'collusion?''

Wang Fan said, 'Just that his being irresponsible motivates me to boss him around. And to scorn him. We're in it together!'

Li Yanling commented, 'I observe a pattern between the two of you. Wang Fan wants to get hold of Zhou Wei and keep him close, whereas Zhou Wei wants to run away. Zhou Wei's running away triggers Wang Fan's anger and intensifies her instinct to hold him tight. It also makes Zhou Wei feel that something else is hidden in her behavior, which drives him further away.'

As consultant, I was thrilled to have this report of Li Yanling's interpretation, which seemed to me to make all the important points about the couple's interaction and show them how it hurt them. I said this to the group, who agreed.

Wang Fan agreed, 'Indeed, that's it! You've got the pattern.'

Zhou Wei complained, 'She takes me as an extension of her arms and legs. I'm supposed to do anything she doesn't want to do.'

Li Yanling said, 'You feel disgusted, but mainly you're terrified by being treated as her extension. Is that why you run away?'

Zhou Wei said, 'It's repulsive. Take traveling as an example. She would say 'You said you're not a fan of traveling. How come you enjoy it so much?' I mean, you forced me to go there, so if I have to go, I'd rather be happy than just pout. Same thing with the TV, you brought the TV into our home, so of course I'll watch it. I don't support her squandering money, but once the appliance is here, sure, I'll use it. I think, 'Why did you want to buy a TV in the first place if you don't know how to use it?' She sent me to handle the installation because she was afraid her ignorance would be mocked.

She couldn't growl at the installer, but she sure growls at me, especially when she can't understand. If it were someone else, she would have had to swallow her pride.'

Discussion

When Li Yanling presented this vignette, the group could see that even though the couple was expressing mutual anger, they were talking directly to each other, something they never did before couple therapy. And although Wang Fan is defending her entitlement, now it is contested by her husband. In the consultation, I noted that previously, in individual therapy, Li Yanling would have been in the awkward position in that confronting Wang Fan's entitlement might well have hurt Wang Fan's fragile self-esteem. Now, Li Yanling is in a position to have the couple negotiate these matters themselves in a way that enhances mutual understanding.

In the session, instead of silent, angry withdrawal, Zhou Wei now confronts his wife with the consequences of her behavior and expresses his anger directly. Such confrontations can now occur in the presence of their therapist, who can point out to each of them how they interact in a pattern that actively denies each of them what they most want – understanding and care. The impossibility of their pattern has to register with Li Yanling before she can help the couple understand it. In the group consultation, we could see their pattern of interaction as a couple and help Li Yanling in her work to understand the hurt each of them felt individually and to fashion interventions they could accept as a couple.

We also saw how the couple's fights registered with their child. Before couple therapy, Xiao Ping was the principal witness to their quarrelsome relationship, taking it into his mind in a way that attacked his development. Once the family was in therapy, he no longer needed to shoulder this burden alone. Although in this vignette, he did not speak directly to the couple's issues, his play continued to demonstrate his emotional understanding of it. I pointed out how this enabled Li Yanling to show the couple that their son was registering their fights. In the group consultation, she came to recognize how she could describe his play to the couple and thereby show them for the first time how the fights burdened him.

I would have liked to hear more details of his play, but Li Yanling had not reported its evolution moment-by-moment (in the way I have done in Chapter 13). This did give me a chance to say to the group that more details on a child's play would give us more information about the family.

Second Vignette: Couple Therapy a Few Weeks Later

Wang Fan was complaining about Zhou Wei's obsession with video games.

Zhou Wei defended himself. 'Playing games is an outlet for me. Slashing and battling help me forget things and emotions I'd rather not feel.'

Li Yanling asked, 'What do you want relief from these days?'

Zhou Wei answered, 'That I have to serve her all the time. When we first moved to our new home, she actually did housework. Now she's stopped. She just watches TV, shops online, spends time on social networks and has the robot vacuum clean the house. She identifies with her father, who orders his wife about. Her mom bustles in and out of the house all day. Whatever I'm doing, she interrupts me.'

As Li Yanling recounted the dialogue, I noticed the repetition of the old theme and felt my own countertransference of impatience in identification with Li Yanling. Would the couple ever get beyond this? Suddenly the recital of the old topic shifted to previously hidden concerns, desire buried under anger.

Zhou Wei continued: 'Oh, and about sex! Sex comes with mountains of conditions. I have to massage her for at least half an hour. And when we finally start, she immediately tells me, 'Hurry up, hurry up.' Sometimes I lose interest when I hear her demand a half-hour massage.'

Li Yanling asked, 'So how often are you having sex now?'

Zhou Wei replied, 'About once a month.'

Li Yanling followed up, 'How do you satisfy your own needs then?'

Zhou Wei replied, 'Masturbation.'

Li Yanling tells the group that the couple had sex almost every day during courtship, but when Wang Fan was pregnant, she refused sex. After their child was born, Wang Fan was angry at Zhou Wei's father, reproaching Zhou Wei about him every day, and she continued to refuse sex. Li Yanling continues.

Wang Fan said, 'I refuse him eight times out of ten. Sometimes I'm tired. Sometimes I'm sulking. I know he would spend less time on video games if sex improved, but I can't initiate sex. He's angry. I'm angry. And the thought of his father still upsets me.'

Li Yanling intervened, 'When you're unfulfilled with Wang Fan, you, Zhou Wei, turn to masturbation and video games. It seems there's a 'third wheel' between you two: First, the baby in Wang Fan's body; then, the anger at Zhou Wei's father; later, the games and online shopping. These 'third wheels' don't appear on their own. Together, you invite them between you to sabotage your relationship. These third wheels run on their own, and the baby or your father are just the excuses to take a ride on them.'

Discussion

In the group consultation session, we discussed Li Yanling's skill-ful connecting of the dots between their mutual frustration, their anger and the decline in their sexual life. Li Yanling was able to show them how they repeatedly construct a pattern, a 'third wheel,' that takes the place of positive intimacy and ensures that intimate interaction does not occur. This 'third wheel' destroys their capacity for sexual pleasure, putting in its place an intimate angry relating instead. Although we do not yet see evidence of changed understanding, we do see improvement in their commu-nication and movement in their couple defensive system. As ther-apists, we are used to looking for small signs of change, continuing to work on an issue many times over, all the while knowing how long fundamental change takes. The group discussed Li Yanling's intervention, and the resulting enhanced potential for change in the couple, giving us a chance to study the slow but definite pro-cess of change itself.

Evidence that therapy is indeed working comes later in the ses-sion when, in passing, the couple acknowledges that therapy gives them hope.

Li Yanling said, 'I'd like to ask you again about your goals and motivation to continue therapy?'

Zhou Wei responded, 'I hope that her anxiety will decrease, and she will stop pointing fingers at others so we can live a life differ-ent from her parents. I see hope in our two years of therapy.'

Wang Fan said, 'I'd like to live like everyone else: educate my child so his intelligence doesn't go to waste, live independently and be financially stronger.'

Li Yanling asked, 'To live like everyone else. What's that like?'

Wang Fan replied, 'To earn more, to stop relying on my mother-in-law for house work.'

Consultation

In our group discussion, we noted the importance of therapists being able to see glimmers of light that shine through, almost in passing. Early signs of change are often like that. Zhou Wei is asking for the same thing he has always wanted: peace and quiet. But now this comes after Li Yanling has made an important interpretation about the obstacles to their growth that the couple constructs together. Zhou Wei's expression of hope follows, replacing his earlier hopelessness. At first, Wang Fan gives the impression that she is still wanting more for herself and her son. But now we hear Wang Fan say she wishes she could stop relying on others, implying that she would like to be more active on her own behalf. The group discussed that while Wang Fan and Zhou Wei are not there yet in planning life as a couple, they are on a path towards more collaboration and self-reliance.

Third Vignette: Later in Couple Therapy

In this session, Li Yanling reported that instead of blaming his wife, Zhou Wei recognized and complimented Wang Fan on becoming more stable emotionally.

Then Zhou Wei said, 'Fan pinched me and teasingly said, 'I love you.' She pinched me <u>while</u> telling me she loved me. But I won't let her pinch me.'

Li Yanling asked why Wang Fan approaches her husband like this.

Wang Fan explained, 'I have this liking for his plump parts. My parents play around like that. Mom will yell, 'Hey it hurts!' Dad keeps on, saying, 'No, it doesn't.''

Li Yanling asked, 'What do you make of this behavior and each other's reactions?'

Wang Fan answered, 'I pinch him both to fulfill this physical sensation and to establish more intimacy in our relationship.'

Li Yanling inquired, 'What can you do, Zhou Wei, to better your relationship while getting her not to pinch you?'

Zhou Wei responded, 'If I massage her, she'll just order me about more. This could go on the whole day if no one sets a time limit.'

Consultation

The group examined how love is coming back into the relationship. I commented that it is doing so in a self-defeating way because while teasing, it is also sadomasochistic. In response to Li Yanling's tactful inquiry, Wang Fan tells the therapist and her husband that the pinching is modeled on her parents' physical relationship, which must have also had a teasing sadism. I pointed out that her behavior is nevertheless a hidden sign that she now finds something loving to identify with in parents she had previously only disparaged. Her expression of love is teasing and mildly sadistic, but it is a sign of love and physical intimacy nevertheless. I say that they are both still afraid of expressions of love, she because of the fear of being rejected, and he because he is afraid of being devoured. So, the physical exchange of pinching expresses the central paradox in the couple: love and aggression at the same time that express hope and fear. The group agrees that while there is a great deal of work still to be done, change has begun.

Reflections about the Relationship of Wang Fan and Zhou Wei

Through our consultative work together, we heard a good deal from Li Yanling about her growing understanding of the couple. She told the group how Wang Fan was traumatized growing up. Then, when she had a child of her own, she worried that he, too, would be harmed, but ascribed harm as coming from everyone except herself. Now, Li Yanling can see that Wang Fan is unconsciously most worried about her own potential for harming her son. Wang Fan projects onto her son a kind of pure and noble object, a residue of the Chinese traditional worship of sons, but also a projection of an idealized self that she can only sustain by housing it in her son. At the same time, she carries a degraded image of her husband and her mother, who seem to her to be degraded and menial, therefore also positing potential contamination that would damage her son.

Over time, I could help the group see that these degraded images are also projections of 'bad' and therefore rejected unconscious images of herself. In this split, Wang Fan projects the lovable parts of herself entirely onto her son but is then psychologically emptied out of everything good and is therefore even more at the mercy of her 'bad' internal objects. Wang Fan was extremely disappointed with her own parents, and therefore idealized Zhou Wei and his parents when they first married. During their early relationship, Wang Fan idealized Zhou Wei with the hope that he could become a container that could endure and digest her emotions, and cure the 'bad self' she carried inside. With time and disappointment, this idealization turned into contempt and denigration for him as an embodiment of her bad inner self.

Zhou Wei has unconsciously identified with Wang Fan's powerlessness in the process of their interactions, joining in her deep distress. Although well-endowed intellectually and well-educated, his inhibition about becoming a more active man keeps him from fulfilling his potential. His parents coddled him, thereby supporting his passivity and contributing to a fear of his own assertiveness. When his wife challenges his passivity, albeit for her own reasons, he is more than just annoyed. He is frightened of being devoured and so he has retreated emotionally and sexually. But now he is speaking up for himself, and she sees in him a reflection of herself that is less denigrating. In this exchange, the couple finds some hope for growth.

Li Yanling reported:

Now, after two years of treatment, there are signs of love returning and a beginning understanding of their shared desires for a more mutually supportive relationship and a more active sexual life. There is still continued strong dependency within this immature couple. Each of them fights to be the child in the relationship, often leaving their son on the side. On the surface, Wang Fan appears to be the greedier one, when in reality, they both long to compensate for what is missing inside: Wang Fan thirsts for money, Zhou Wei lusts for food and care.

I have enjoyed working with the couple during more than two years. There are ups and downs, times of turbulence and struggles, but they are robustly motivated. With their reliable rapport in the therapeutic relationship, I feel we will be able to tackle their difficulties. It will definitely take time!

Conclusion

Li Yanling's vivid description of this couple and their treatment gave the consultation group a sense of how therapy always proceeds through hard work that leads gradually to understanding. I could help the group see how change in therapy depends on the intimacy of the therapeutic relationship. We could see how, as the couple argued over the dangers of depending on each other, they came gradually to depend on their therapist because, over and over again, she proved herself to be dependable, devoted and clear-headed about finding meaning hidden underneath their arguments. We could see the evidence of how the couple's alliance with her, their ever-growing trust in her and her good wishes for them despite their shortcomings got slowly installed in each of them individually and in them as a couple. Ever so slowly, their relationship changed and grew, not in a straight line, but, as Li Yanling said, with ups and downs.

That is the way therapy works, and it is why there is hope for this family and for other families who seek help from an increasingly sophisticated group of our Chinese colleagues. As the group continues to meet, I hear about other treatments, other kinds of challenges. We work together towards growing understanding. This is my reward in coming to China over the years: the growth of our Chinese colleagues who continue to learn, not only from us as Western teachers, but from each other as they become more skilled and more able to teach their own psychotherapy students how to help couples and families.

Notes

1 Case presented by Li Yanling with consultation by David Scharff in *(Therapy report and group consultation translated by Chen Yting).*

Chapter 17

China in Light of COVID-19

I finished this book in the time of the COVID-19 pandemic. Quarantined in my home just outside of Washington, DC, in Chevy Chase, Maryland, I have been in frequent contact with Chinese colleagues as together and separately we work to help our patients and our colleagues in America and China. I have been involved in educating American therapists on how to move their practices online when that way of working was still alien to many of them, and working together with others, have been engaged in trying to understand how to think about this unique situation in which colleagues worldwide share in being threatened by the pandemic even while trying to help our patients with that worry, which has magnified the difficulties that brought them to treatment in the first place.

I continue to teach and consult in China – remotely for the time being, because travel to and from China is not possible. We have given lectures for both Chinese and American colleagues on going online and on dealing with COVID-19, both to large-group webinars and to the smaller groups that we teach regularly, and I continue to consult with groups of therapists that I had been working with before.

These Chinese colleagues report that the stresses in China are much the same as the ones I hear daily from friends, colleagues and patients in the United States: fear for the safety of their families and themselves, fears for frontline workers, uncertainty about when things will open up and the dangers that opening up itself is presenting. They report strain on the families and individuals they counsel.

The *Wall Street Journal* reported on the mental health strains worldwide, across Europe, the United States and Asia. It reported (in part):

> The battle to stop the coronavirus pandemic, fought with social distancing and enforced isolation, is taking a psychological toll that some officials warn could prompt another crisis: a mental-health one. Billions of people from the U.S. to Italy have been ordered to stay at home. Germany, Australia and the U.K. have determined that two people are a crowd and millions are cut off from family members, lovers and friends.

Beyond acute stress and anxiety, psychologists say the confinement is beginning to trigger deeper troubles, including depression and compulsive disorders.

A recent review in the *Lancet* medical journal of studies on the psychological impact during outbreaks of SARS and Ebola showed that quarantine can trigger issues such as emotional disturbance, depression, irritability, insomnia, post-traumatic stress symptoms, confusion and anger. Some of the studies suggested long-lasting effects.

(Bender and Pannett, 2020)

While giving responses to COVID and the mental health stresses around the world, one *Wall Street Journal* paragraph described the fallout in China:

A survey of 52,730 people from across China, Hong Kong, Macau and Taiwan, conducted by psychiatrists from the Shanghai Mental Health Center between Jan. 31 and Feb. 10 (2020) on how the population coped during the Covid-19 outbreak found that almost 35% of respondents experienced psychological distress, women significantly more than men.

(Bender and Pannett, 2020)

This is consistent with what Chinese colleagues have been reporting informally. We agree that there is not only a pandemic of the biological virus, but a mental health pandemic, too. So many families quarantined together experience stress. If a marriage or family has significant vulnerabilities, these are strained. Thus, our colleagues in Wuhan have reported increased marital stress in those marriages that were already vulnerable, and this has also made the news, where it was reported early on that requests for divorce had spiked.

The *SupChina* news service (Feng, 2020) reported:

As the coronavirus wanes in China, large numbers of couples across the country are filing for divorce after spending weeks at home together during self-isolation. Per the *Global Times*, the city of Xi'an has seen a record-high number of divorce requests since the local marriage registries reopened on March 1 (2020). In some districts, the numbers were so high that local offices say it will take until the end of March to process the backlog.

According to a Chinese official surnamed Wang, who works at the registration office in the Beilin district of Xi'an, the rise in divorces was partly caused by the coronavirus outbreak, which forced couples to spend a lot of time in close quarters under quarantine, creating an inflammatory environment for marital conflicts. 'As a result of the epidemic, many couples have been bound with each other at home for over a month, which evoked the underlying conflicts,' Wang told the *Global Times*.

People on the Chinese internet (in Chinese) found the news makes perfect sense, saying that marriages were prone to fall apart when couples had to deal with a string of hardships caused by the coronavirus, including significant interruptions to their routines, economic stresses, and increased risk of anxiety and depression. 'When couples spend day and night together, it's hard to gloss over or hide marriage problems. This news didn't strike me as a surprise,' a Weibo user wrote.

(Feng, 2020)

It is much too soon to know what the ultimate fallout for marriages and families will be in the long run in China or anywhere else. Major events such as this pandemic – which harkens back to historic times of plague and world war – have unexpected consequences. But some things already seem certain: that mental health practice will never be quite the same, in that virtually all psychotherapists will now have had experience using tele-psychotherapy; that while some families and couples will have been resilient and emerge with stronger bonds than before the crisis, others will have been strained to the breaking point and, as a family or as a couple, may not recover; and that there will be a pressing demand for psychotherapists and psychoanalysts to help families, couples and children cope with the inevitable disruptions to their old ways of life. In this way, there will be alterations in the contours of family and couple life that will emerge as the decade unfolds. It seems to me that it is safe to say that the need for therapeutic help for couples and families will be greater.

It is up to all of us to help the mental health profession understand and adapt to the changing and growing needs in China, a country that, as we have seen, has a capacity for great resilience in the face of social stress. That large-scale social resilience is based first and foremost on the resilience of its families.

Chapter 18

A Return to Our Questions

Any treatise about China is bound to leave out a great deal. I have tried to cover a large territory in showing the context in which middle-class families live in contemporary China and describing enough of the history and culture to locate the modern Chinese family within the larger picture. And then, I have tried to describe the intimacy of family and couple struggles as they navigate the complexities of modern life.

The life of contemporary Chinese families takes place in a climate of continuing rapid change. Most of the elements of these changes are well-known: the emergence of the family from traditional patterns, and then from the strictures of early governmental domination of the family; the period of Opening Up and entrepreneurial dominance; the strictures of the One Child Policy for 35 years, and then its ending in the last few years; and the opening up of China to world culture, and, at the same time, the resurgence of elements of traditional culture. Less well-known are the factors already in place from the demographic facts of China: a rapidly aging population poorly supported by too few people of working age, a hidden legacy of historical trauma, enduring problems of poverty, the relative absence of a system of social security and the migration of large numbers of people from rural areas to cities, often still with inadequate citizenship rights.

While there are other challenges to Chinese domestic life, such as the environmental dangers of pollution, local and national dissent to some policies, diplomatic challenges and the problems of needing to move towards a consumer economy and away from reliance on the state-supported industries that require cheap labor, these are not the problems that have impinged directly on the families I have seen. Rather, it is those issues that show up in the struggles of the family as problems of conflicted reliance on the older generation, children's school performance, school refusal, suicidality, the ubiquity of the shame culture with its particular consequences, and sexual and marital problems as young people forge new paths to adulthood and productive lives.

Throughout this book, I have tried to show how important widespread social issues in China show up as personal challenges that are lived out in the intimacy of the family, and how these personal challenges appear in the therapeutic setting that constitutes my area of observation and research. Looking at a continuum that stretches from large-scale factors that characterize modern China to their appearance on the small canvas of the interior of family life allows us to see how history and social pressure collide in families that strive for growth and that continue to demonstrate enduring resilience, even as they encounter obstacles that are at one and the same both broadly social and deeply personal.

This brings me back to the four questions I posed at the beginning.

First, we have seen many ways that the ancient history of Chinese culture forms a largely unseen but still influential substructure, a kind of basement on top of which the Chinese house is built. Because of this, there are many, fragmentary, ways that the ancient culture continues to influence Chinese families and individuals.

Second, we have seen many instances of the ways that large-scale social factors get inside families and are expressed in intimate and day-to-day ways. And, in a reciprocal way, taken on a larger scale, what happens in these families influences contemporary Chinese culture, which itself is in rapid evolution.

Third, the current challenges to families are both impacted by and will have an impact on the future of China and its emergent culture.

Fourth and lastly, we have seen ways in which my colleagues and I have worked to demonstrate to Chinese colleagues the tradition of psychoanalytic psychotherapy developed over that past century in the West, which they have asked us to introduce to them. At the same time, I hope to have demonstrated the many things about China and its culture that we learn from our Chinese colleagues, which influence how we work there and how we join with them to teach them and learn from them at the same time.

Some of the most important questions remain, begging for answers that only the future will reveal. What is the future of the Chinese family? What new stresses will fall on families to be worked out in the intimacy of these families in the future? We cannot know now what new, still unformulated national policies, such as the current emphasis that implores families to have more children, will do to families. We cannot know the trends over the next 20 years, during the struggles that are surely coming, to support the aging population. How will families resolve the financial and emotional conflicts that stem from these problems that are both national problems and ones for each family to resolve independently?

In a more focused way, we can see that lending our clinical experience to those Chinese colleagues who wish to learn from and with us can enhance their skill and capabilities, but only if we do it in an open-minded way that eschews any intention to impose our thinking on our Chinese mental health colleagues and instead offers a collaborative hand in a jointly valued task.

The privilege these families and couples, and our Chinese colleagues have accorded in allowing us to learn from them has been, and continues to be, a singular honor for me and my colleagues. We continue to work with and to study the issues they bring to us, and count it a privilege that they have allowed us to share in the task of improving life for China's families.

References

Alford, W. and Shen, Y. (2003) Have you eaten? Have you divorced? Marriage, divorce and the assessment of freedom in China. In W. Kirby (ed.) *Ideas of Freedom in the Chinese World*. Stanford, CA: Stanford University Press.

American Psychological Association. (2014) *The Road to Resilience*.

Becker, J. (1996) *Hungry Ghosts: Mao's Secret Famine*. New York: Holt.

Benard, B. (2004) *Resiliency: What We Have Learned*. San Francisco: WestEd.

Bender, R. and Pannett, R. (2020) Coronavirus pandemic takes toll on mental health. *Wall Street Journal*, April 9.

Bion, W. R. (1962) *Learning from Experience*. London: Heinemann [reprinted London: Karnac, 1984].

Bion, W. R. (1967) *Second Thoughts*. London: Heinemann [reprinted London: Karnac, 1984].

Bion, W. R. (1970) *Attention and Interpretation*. London: Tavistock Publications Ltd. [reprinted London: Karnac, 1984].

Bollas, C. (2013) *China on the Mind*. Abingdon: Routledge.

Bowlby, J. (1958) The nature of the child's tie to his mother. *International Journal of Psycho-Analysis* 39:1–24.

Bowlby, J. (1969) *Attachment and Loss, Volume 1: Attachment*. London: Hogarth Press. New York: Basic Books.

Brenner, I. (2019) *The Handbook of Psychoanalytic Holocaust Studies: International Perspectives*. London and New York: Routledge.

Caskie, S. (2016) The rise of youth suicide in China. *The Week* (online). Accessed December 11, 2016.

Chang, J. (1992) *Wild Swans: Three Daughters of China*. London: Harper Perennial.

Chang, J. (2013) *Empress Dowager Cixi: The Concubine Who Launched Modern China*. New York: Anchor Books.

Chang, J. and Halliday, J. (2005) *Mao: The Unknown Story*. New York: Anchor Books.

Chelala, C. (2014) Will China be able to curb adolescent suicide? *The Globalist* (online), July 20. Accessed December 11, 2016.

Chen, F. and Li, T. (2007) Marital *enqing*: An examination of its relationship to spousal contributions, sacrifices, and family stress in Chinese marriages. *Journal of Social Psychology* 147:393–412.

Chicchetti, D. and Rogosch, F. A. (1997) The role of self-organization in the promotion of resilience in maltreated children. *Development and Psychopathology* 9(4):797–815.

China News (2020) *Domestic violence*, March 1, p. 4.

Davies, J. and Frawley, M. G. (1994) *Treating the Adult Survivor of Childhood Sexual Abuse*. New York: Basic Books.

Davis, D. S. (2014) Privatization of marriage in post-socialist China. *Modern China* 40(6):551–577.

Dicks, H. V. (1967) *Marital Tensions: Clinical Studies Towards a Psychoanalytic Theory of Interaction*. London: Routledge and Kegan Paul.

Eberstadt, N. ed. (2019) *China's Changing Family Structure: Dimensions and Implications*. Washington, DC: American Enterprise Institute.

The Economist (2012) Fulfilling promises: China is beginning to face up to its pension problems, August 11.

Faimberg, H. (2005) *The Telescoping of Generations: Listening to the Narcissistic Links between Generations*. Abingdon: Routledge.

Fairbairn, W. R. D. (1943) The repression and return of bad objects (with special reference to the 'war neuroses'). In *Psychoanalytic Studies of the Personality*. London: Routledge. With a new introduction by D. E. Scharff and E. F. Birtles, 1994. pp. 59–81.

Fairbairn (1952) *An Object Relations Theory of the Personality*. London: Routledge.

Feldshuh, H. (2018) China's Domestic Violence Law of 2016 was celebrated as a victory for women's rights. But two years later, its shortcomings are evident. *SupChina*, October 10.

Feng, J. (2020) Divorce applications spike after coronavirus quarantines. *SupChina*, March 21.

Fong, M. (2016) *One Child: The Story of China's Most Radical Experiment*. London: One World.

Fong, V. L. (2002) China's one-child policy and the empowerment of urban women. *American Anthropologist (New Series)* 104(4):1098–1110.

Fong, V. L. (2007) Parent-child communication problems and the perceived inadequacies of Chinese only children. *Ethos* 35(1):85–127.

Foulkes, S. (1964) *Therapeutic Group Analysis*. London: Allen and Unwin.

Freud, S. (1920) *Beyond the Pleasure Principle*. SE 18: 3–64.

Freud, S. and Breuer, J. (1893–1895) *Studies on Hysteria*. SE 2.

Gallese, V. (2003) The roots of empathy: The shared manifold hypothesis and the neural basis of intersubjectivity. *Psychopathology* 36(4):171–180.

Gallese, V. (2012) Mirror neurons, embodied simulation, and the neural basis of social identification. *Psychoanalytic Dialogues* 19(5):519–536.

Gannon, K. (2019) 629 Pakistani girls sold as brides to China. *APnewsonline. com*, December 7.

Gao Jun (2015) A commentary on 'Brief intervention with a Chinese family' by Jill and David Scharff. In J. Scharff and D. Scharff (eds) *Psychoanalysis and Psychotherapy in China*. London: Karnac. pp. 50–54.

Gilmartin, C. (1990) Violence against women in contemporary China. In J. Lipman and S. Harrell (eds) *Violence in China: Essays in Culture and Counterculture*. New York: State University of New York Press. p. 209.

Goldkorn, J. (2018) Hey, People's Daily – Leave my womb alone! *SupChina* (online), August 7.

Gongyi.people.com.cn. (2019) People's Republic of China Anti-Domestic Violence Law. *Implementation Monitoring Report Released–People's Daily Online–People's Network.*

Greenfield, P. M., Keller, H., Fuligni, H. and Maynard, H. (2003) Cultural pathways through universal development. *Annual Review of Psychology* 54:461–490.

Gullestad, E. S. (2014) Dynamic psychotherapy: Teaching and supervision in China. In D. E. Scharff and S. Varvin eds (2014) *Psychoanalysis in China.* London: Karnac. pp. 231–241.

Haag, A. (2014) Psychoanalytically oriented psychotherapy and the Chinese Self. In D. E. Scharff and S. Varvin eds (2014) *Psychoanalysis in China.* London: Karnac. pp. 21–32.

Haas, B. (2017) China allowed all families to have two children in 2015, a decision described by demographers as 'too little, too late'. *The Guardian Monday*, January 23.

Hansen, M. H. and Svarverud, R. (2010) *iChina: The Rise of the Individual in Modern Chinese Society.* Copenhagen: Nordic Institute of Asian Studies.

Hays, J. (2015) Divorce in China. *Facts and Details* (online).

He, X. (2009) Routinization of divorce law practice in China: Institutional constraints' influence on judicial behaviour. *International Journal of Law, Policy and the Family* 23(1):83–109.

He, X. (2017) 'No Malicious Incidents': The concern for stability in China's divorce law. *Practice, Social & Legal Studies* 26(4):467–489.

Honig, E. (2003) Socialist sex: The cultural revolution revisited. *Modern China* 29(2):143–175, p. 161. Quoted in Jeffreys, E. (2015) *Sex in China.* London: Polity.

Hopper, E. (2003) *The Social Unconscious.* London: Jessica Kingsley.

Hu, J. and Li, X. (2012) Study on the relationship between school refusal and parental rearing pattern in children and adolescent. *China Journal of Health Psychology* 11:1710–1711.

Huang, K. (2019) Unexpected trouble for China's newly two-child families: Sibling Jealousy. *Inkstone Online News*, March 28.

Huang, Xiao-na, Wang Hui-shan, Zhang Li-jin and Liu Xi-cheng (2010) Co-sleeping and children's sleep in China. *Biological Rhythm Research* 4(3); *Current Research on Aspects of Child Health in China*, 169–181.

Huang Shulun, Liu Zishuang and Ren Qiuyu (2019) Half of migrant women in Chinese megacities suffering domestic violence, survey finds. *Caixin*, July 12.

Jankowiak, W. R. and Li, X. (2017) Emergent conjugal love, mutual affection, female marital power. In G. Santos and S. Harrell (eds) *Transforming Patriarchy: Chinese Families in the 21st Century.* Seattle, WA: University of Washington Press. pp. 185–2005.

Jankowiak, W. R. and Moore, R. L. (2017) *Family Life in China.* Cambridge and Malden, MA: Polity.

Jeffreys, E. ed. (2009) *Sex and Sexuality in China.* Abingdon: Routledge.

Jeffreys, E. (2010) Regulating private affairs in contemporary China: Private investigators and the policing of spousal infidelity. *China Information* 24(2):149–167.

Jeffreys, E. with Yu, Haiqing. (2015) *Sex in China.* Cambridge: Polity.

Kelly, J. B. and Emery, R. E. (2003) Children's adjustment following divorce: Risk and resilience perspectives. *Family Relations* 52(4):352–362.

Kernberg, O. F. (1995) *Love Relations: Normality and Pathology*. New Haven, CT and London: Yale University Press.

Kim, K.-H. (2015) China: When an only child dies. *Reuters* (online), December 2.

Klein, M. (1946) Notes on some schizoid mechanisms. *International Journal of Psycho-Analysis* 27:99–110.

Klein, M. (1975a) *Love, Guilt and Reparation & Other Works: 1921–1945*. London: The Hogarth Press and the Institute of Psycho-Analysis.

Klein, M. (1975b) *Envy and Gratitude & Other Works: 1946–1963*. London: The Hogarth Press and the Institute of Psycho-Analysis.

Kleinman, A. and Kleinman, J. (1994) How bodies remember: Social memory and bodily experience of criticism, resistance and delegitimation following China's Cultural Revolution. *New Literary History* 25(3):707–723. 25th Anniversary Issue (Part 1).

Kleinman, A., Yan, Y., Jun, J., Lee, S., Zhang, E., Pan, T., Wu, F. and Guo, J. (2011) *Deep China: The Moral Life of the Person*. Berkeley, CA: University of California Press.

Kui, Y. and Xie, Y. (2020) Frozen out of motherhood. *China News*, March 1, pp. 36–37.

Lau, D. (2018) As China prepares to revise its civil code, calls are renewed for legal recognition of same-sex marriage. *SupChina*, October 30.

Li Yuan (2019) China begins to pull plug on abusive pickup artists. *New York Times*, Business Section December 30, pp. B1 and 4.

Li Zhisui (1994) *The Private Life of Chairman Mao*. New York: Chatto & Windus.

Li, T. S. and Chen, F.-M. (2002) Affection in marriage: A study of marital *enqing* and intimacy in Taiwan. *Journal of Psychology in Chinese Societies* 3:37–59.

Lin Qiqing (2017) Sexual health and single women. *Sixth Tone* (online), December 26, 2017.

Lin Tao (2014) The encounter of psychoanalysis and Chinese culture. In D. E. Scharff and S. Varvin eds (2014) *Psychoanalysis in China*. London: Karnac. pp. 54–61.

Lin Tao (2020) Language in learning psychoanalysis: An obstacle or a bridge? (Unpublished manuscript).

Link, E. P. (2000) *The Uses of Literature: Life in the Socialist Chinese Literary System*. Princeton, NJ: Princeton University Press, p. 243. Quoted in Jeffreys, E. (2015) *Sex in China*. London: Polity.

Liu, C. and Chen, S. (2016) Lost lives: the battle of China's invisible children to recover missed years. *Reuters World News*, December 14.

Liu, M. and Chan, C. (1999) Enduring violence and staying in marriage: Stories of battered women in rural China. *Violence Against Women* 5(12):1469–1492.

Lixin Fan (2009) *Last Train Home (film documentary)*. Produced by Daniel Cross and Mila Aung-Thwin of Eye Steel Film. Distributed by Zeitgeist Films.

Losso, R., Setton, L. and Scharff, D. eds (2017) *The Linked Self in Psychoanalysis: The Pioneering Work of Enrique Pichon Rivière*. London and New York: Karnac.

Ma, J. (2012) *The Dark Road*. Taipei: Asian Culture Press. Quoted in Wang, H. (2020) Femininity and masculinity in Chinese culture. *Psychoanalysis and Psychotherapy in China*, 3:1.

Mann, S. L. (1991) Grooming a daughter for marriage: Brides and wives in the Mid-Ch'ing period. In R. S. Watson and P. B. Ebrey (eds) *Marriage and Inequality in Chinese Society*. Berkeley, CA and Oxford: University of California Press. pp. 204–230. Quoted in Wang, H. (2020) Femininity and masculinity in Chinese culture. *Psychoanalysis and Psychotherapy in China*, 3:1.

Mann, S. L. (2011) *Gender and Sexuality in Modern Chinese History*. New York: Cambridge University Press. Quoted in Wang, H. (2020) Femininity and masculinity in Chinese culture. *Psychoanalysis and Psychotherapy in China*, 3:1.

Ming, L. (2014) Yin Yang philosophy and Chinese mental health. In D. E. Scharff and S. Varvin eds (2014) *Psychoanalysis in China*. London: Karnac. pp. 62–72.

Morgan, M. (2019) *A Couple State of Mind*. Abingdon: Routledge.

Naftali, O. (2016) *Children in China*. Cambridge: Polity Press.

News China (2017) China sees 'fourth wave of singledom'. *Editorial*, January, p. 7.

News China (2019) China's *hukou* reform needs long-term vision. *Editorial*, June, p. 1.

News China (2020) Domestic violence, March 1, p. 4.

Ng, K. M., Peluso, P. and Smith, S. D. (2010) Marital satisfaction, intimacy, *enqing*, and relationship stressors among Asians. In J. Carlson and L. Sperry (eds) *Recovering Intimacy in Love Relationships*. New York and Hove: Routledge. pp. 331–352.

Owenby, D. (2002) Approximations of Chinese bandits: Perverse rebels, romantic heroes, or frustrated bachelors? In S. Brownell and J. N. Wasserstrom (eds) *Chinese Femininities/Chinese Masculinities: A Reader*. Berkeley, CA and Oxford: University of California Press. Quoted in Wang, H. (2020) Femininity and masculinity in Chinese culture. *Psychoanalysis and Psychotherapy in China*, volume 3:1.

Pan Suiming (2018) Sex in China. *Sixth Tone* (online), April 17.

Parish, W., Tianfu, W., Laumann, E., Pan, S. and Luo, Y. (2004) Intimate partner violence in China: National prevalence, risk factors, and associated health problems. *International Family Planning Perspectives* 30(4):174–181. Quoted in Jankowiak, W. R. and Moore, R. L. (2017) *Family Life in China*. Cambridge and Malden, MA: Polity. p. 125.

People's Daily (2011) Home-hidden crime scenes. *People's Daily*, November 4, pp. 1–2. Quoted in Jankowiak, W. R. and Moore, R. L. (2017) *Family Life in China*. Cambridge and Malden, MA: Polity. p. 124.

Ping Wang, Dian Zhi Liu and Xin Zhao (2014) The social ecology of resilience: A comparison of Chinese and Western Researches. *Procedia – Social and Behavioral Sciences* 116(21):3259–3265.

Plaenkers, T. (2010) *Landscapes of the Chinese Soul: The Enduring Presence of the Cultural Revolution*. London: Karnac.

Plaenkers, T. (2011) Psychic impact and outcome of the Chinese cultural revolution (1966–1976). A psychoanalytic research project at the Sigmund-Freud-Institut (Frankfurt, Germany). *Special Issue: Psychoanalysis in China. International Journal of Applied Psychoanalytic Studies* 8(3):227–238.

Plaenkers, T. (2014a) China – A traumatized country? The aftermath of the Chinese Cultural Revolution (1966–1976) for the individual and for society. In D. E. Scharff and S. Varvin eds (2014) *Psychoanalysis in China*. London: Karnac, pp. 33–44.

Plaenkers, T. (2014b) When Freud headed for the East: Aspects of a Chinese translation of his works. *The International Journal of Psychoanalysis* 94(5):993–1017.

Reuters World News (2016) *In China, calls for end to aggressive child custody tactics* (online), December 28.

Rutter, M. (2008) Developing concepts in developmental psychopathology. In J. J. Hudziak (ed.) *Developmental Psychopathology and Wellness: Genetic and Environmental Influences*. Washington, DC: American Psychiatric Publishing. pp. 3–22.

Scharff, D. E. (1982). *The Sexual Relationship*. Northvale, NJ: Jason Aronson (also in Chinese).

Scharff, D. E. (1998). *The Sexual Relationship*, 2nd edn. Northvale, NJ: Jason Aronson (also in Chinese).

Scharff, D. E. (2011) Issue editor and introduction: Psychoanalysis in China. *International Journal of Applied Psychoanalytic Studies* 8:191–195.

Scharff, D. E. (2014) Five things Western therapists should know for working with Chinese therapists and patients. In D. E. Scharff and S. Varvin eds (2014) *Psychoanalysis in China*. London: Karnac. pp. 111–120.

Scharff, D. E. (2016) The contribution of Enrique Pichon-Rivière: Comparisons with his European contemporaries and with modern theory. *Couple and Family Psychoanalysis* 6(2):153–158.

Scharff, D. E., Losso, R. and Setton, L. (2017) Pichon-Rivière's psychoanalytic contributions: Some comparisons with object relations and modern developments in psychoanalysis. *International Journal of Psychoanalysis* 98(1):129–143.

Scharff, D. E. and Scharff, J. S. (1987) *Object Relations Family Therapy*. Northvale, NJ: Jason Aronson (also in Chinese).

Scharff, D.E. and Scharff, J. S. (1991) *Object Relations Couple Therapy*, 2nd edn. Northvale, NJ: Jason Aronson (also in Chinese).

Scharff, D. E. and Scharff, J. S. (2011a) *The Interpersonal Unconscious*. Lanham, MD: Jason Aronson.

Scharff, D. E. and Varvin, S. eds (2014) *Psychoanalysis in China*. London: Karnac Books.

Scharff, J. S. (1992) *Projective and Introjective Identification and the Use of the Therapist's Self*. Northvale, NJ: Jason Aronson (also in Chinese).

Scharff, J. S. and Scharff, D. E. (1994) *Object Relations Therapy of Physical and Sexual Trauma*. Lanham, MD: Jason Aronson (Reprinted 2008).

Scharff, J. S. and Scharff, D. E. (2005) *The Primer of Object Relations*, 2nd edn. Northvale, NJ: Jason Aronson (also in Chinese).

Scharff, J. S. and Scharff, D. E. (2011b) The impact of Chinese cultures on a marital relationship. *Special Issue: Psychoanalysis in China. International Journal of Applied Psychoanalytic Studies*. 8(3):249–260. In D. E. Scharff and S. Varvin eds (2014) *Psychoanalysis in China*. London: Karnac Books. pp. 277–287.

Scharff, K. and Herrick, L. (2010) *Navigating Emotional Currents in Collaborative Divorce*. Chicago, IL: American Bar Association Press.

Scharff, K. and Herrick, L. (2016) *Mastering Crucial Moments in Separation and Divorce*. Chicago, IL: American Bar Association Press.

Shi, Q. (2014) The development of psychoanalysis in China. In D. E. Scharff and S. Varvin eds (2014) *Psychoanalysis in China*. London: Karnac. pp. 157–165.

Shi, Q. and Scharff, D. E. (2011) Cultural factors and projective identification in understanding a Chinese couple. *International Journal of Applied Psychoanalytic Studies* 8(3):207–217. In D. E. Scharff and S. Varvin eds (2014) *Psychoanalysis in China*. London: Karnac Books. pp. 288–297.

Shi, Q. and Scharff, J. S. (2008) Social change, intercultural conflict, and marital dynamics in a Chinese marriage in brief concurrent individual and couple therapy. *International Journal of Applied Psychoanalytic Studies* 5(4):302–321.

Sijie, Dai (2001) *Balzac and the Little Chinese Seamstress*. New York: Alfred A. Knopf. Film directed by Dai Sijie, 2003.

Solomon, R. H. (1971) *Mao's Revolution and the Chinese Political Culture*. Berkeley, CA: University of California Press.

Solomon, R. H. (1999) *Chinese Negotiating Behavior: Pursuing Interests through 'Old Friends'*. Washington, DC: United States Institute of Peace Press.

Stadter, M. (1996) *Object Relations Brief Therapy: The Therapeutic Relationship in Short-Term Work*. Northvale, NJ: Jason Aronson.

Stadter, M. and Jun, G. (2020) Shame East and West: Similarities, difference, culture and self. *Psychoanalysis and Psychotherapy in China* 3(1):1–21.

Stadter, M. and Scharff, D. E. (2000) Object relations brief couple therapy. In J. Carlson and L. Sperry (eds) *Brief Therapy with Individuals and Couples*. Phoenx, AZ: Zeig, Tucker & Theisen. pp. 191–219.

Tang, Catherine So-Kum and Lai, Beatrice Pui-Yee (2008) A review of empirical literature on the prevalence and risk markers of male-on-female intimate partner violence in contemporary China, 1987–2006. *Aggression and Violent Behavior* 13(1):10–28.

Thomas, N. (2016) In China, calls for end to aggressive child custody tactics. *Reuters World News*, December 28.

Tong, J. (2016) Mother, infant and woman's identity. *Psychoanalysis and Psychotherapy in China* 2:97–104.

Van der Kolk, B. (2014) *The Body Keeps the Score*. New York: Penguin Random House.

Verdery, A. M. (2019) Modeling the future of China's changing family structure to 2100. In N. Eberstadt (ed.) *China's Changing Family Structure*. Washington, DC: American Enterprise Institute. pp. 23–78.

Wang, F., Shen, K. and Cai, Y. (2019) Household change and intergenerational transfers in China: What lies ahead? In N. Eberstadt (ed.) *China's Changing Family Structure*. Washington, DC: American Enterprise Institute. pp. 102–115.

Wang, H. (2020) Femininity and masculinity in Chinese culture. *Psychoanalysis and Psychotherapy in China* 3(1):30–49.

Wang, L., Ou, W.-X. and Cha, C. (2012) Analysis of mental health level of children and adolescents with school refusal. *Chinese Journal of Child Health Care* 1:29–31.

Wikipedia (2019) *Domestic violence in China*.

Winnicott, D. W. (1971a) *Playing and Reality*. London: Tavistock.

Winnicott, D. W. (1971b) *Therapeutic Consultations in Child Psychiatry*. London: The Hogarth Press and the Institute of Psychoanalysis.

Wolin, S. J. and Wolin, S. (2010) *The Resilient Self: How Survivors of Troubled Families Rise Above Adversity*. London: Random House Publishing Group.

Wong, E. (2012) Reports of forced abortions fuel push to end Chinese law. *New York Times*, July 22.

Xu, X. (1997) The prevalence and determination of wife abuse in urban China. *Journal of Comparative Family Studies* 28(3):280–303.

Yan Yunxiang (2010) Introduction: Conflicting images of the individual and contested process of individualization. In M. H. Hansen and R. Svarverud (eds) *iChina: The Rise of the Individual in Modern Chinese Society*. Copenhagen: Nordic Institute of Asian Studies. pp. 1–38.

Yan Yunxiang (2013) Parent-driven divorce and individualisation among urban Chinese youth. *International Social Science Journal* 64(213/214):317–330.

Yang Jisheng (2008) *Tombstone: The Great Chinese Famine 1958–1962*. New York: Farrar, Straus and Giroux.

Yang Xiao, Jiang Lingpeng, Li Qihong and Li Huazhu (2017) Investigation and intervention study of school refusal in children and adolescents. *Journal of Clinical Psychosomatic Diseases* 1:59–65.

Yang Yunping (2011) The challenge of professional identity for Chinese clinicians in the process of learning and practicing psychoanalytic psychotherapy: Discussion on the frame of Chinese culture. *International Journal of Psychoanalysis* 92(3):733–743.

Yang Yunping (2014) The impact of psychic trauma on individuation and self-identity: How the psychic trauma of poverty affects individuation and self-identity in the context of the Chinese family. In D. E. Scharff and S. Varvin eds (2014) *Psychoanalysis in China*. London and New York: Karnac Books. pp. 137–149.

Yates, T. M., Egeland, B. and Sroufe, L. A. (2003) Rethinking resilience: A developmental process perspective. In S. S. Luthar (ed.) *Resilience and Vulnerability: Adaptation in the Context of Childhood Adversities*. New York: Cambridge University Press. pp. 234–256.

Ye Xiaoyan and Feng Xiaotian. (2000) Fertility status and fertility desire of urban and rural residents. *Society* (3):12–13.

Ye Yuan (2012) Tragic figures. *News China*, November, pp. 30–33.

Yen Duong (2018) From Vietnam, without love: The child brides of China. *This Week in Asia*, June 17.

Yi, Z. T. (1998) *Chinese Men and Women*. Beijing: China Federation of Literary & Art Circles Publishing Corp. Quoted in Wang, H. (2020) Femininity and masculinity in Chinese culture. In *Psychoanalysis and Psychotherapy in China*, volume 3:1.

Yuan Ye (2012) Orphan parents, tragic figures. *News China*, November 1, pp. 30–33.

Zhang, E. Y. (2011) China's sexual revolution. In A. Kleinman, Y. Yan, J. Jun, S. Lee, E. Zhang, T. Pan, F. Wu and J. Guo (eds) *Deep China: The Moral Life of the Person*. Berkeley, CA: University of California Press. pp.106–151.

Zhang, Lijia (2009) Domestic violence network in China: Translating the transnational concept of violence against women into local action. *Women's Studies International Forum* 32(3):227–239.

Zhang, L. (2019) China's divorce rate is spiking because women no longer have to accept unsatisfying marriages. *South China Morning Post*, November 27.

Zhong Jie (2011) Working with Chinese patients: Are there conflicts between Chinese culture and psychoanalysis? *Special Issue: Psychoanalysis in China. International Journal of Applied Psychoanalytic Studies*. 8(3):218–226. In D. E. Scharff and S. Varvin eds (2014) *Psychoanalysis in China*. London: Karnac. pp. 150–156.

Index

rural families and families of poverty 196–197

saving face: clinical material 22; see also loss of face

Scharff, Jill Savege 6, 16; background 7; clinical work 12, 16–26, 28, 30, 57–58, 111, 114–117, 125, 133, 145, 146, 182, 184–186, 189, 190, 199–206, 204f 209–211, 213, 215–223, 233–246, 250; countertransference 189; couple and family therapy and 8; Gao Jun and 16–17, 111, 125, 189, 199, 218, 239; Li Mengchao and 6, 8; as observer 125; projective identification and 8; teaching 14, 182, 190; Tong Jun and 11, 12; visiting China 6, 14, 228; writings 33, 37, 57–58, 67

Scharff, Kate 184

school dropout 73, 230–232, 249–250

school refusal 230–231

self 34

self-cutting 233, 235, 236, 250–252, 256

self-experience 9

separation, early childhood 225–226; see also grandparents, children sent to live with their

sexual abuse and trauma 67, 120

sexual behavior 123; age of first intercourse 121; family living arrangements and 123–124; marriage and 87, 90, 119, 124; One Child Policy and 41, 120–122; refusing sex 143, 155, 162, 276, 281; see also extramarital sex and affairs; see also sexuality

sexual desire 26, 121, 139, 256

sexual development 37, 248, 249

sexual difficulty, couple 124, 137; an example of 124–137

sexual health of unmarried women 123

sexuality 60, 120–123; adolescent 229, 249; clinical material 26, 73, 117, 124, 139, 140, 143, 155, 162–164, 166, 221, 223–224, 247, 248, 256, 262, 281, 282, 285; see also impotence; in college students and young adults 121–122; Communist Party (CCP) and 40, 119, 121;

gender roles, gender differences, and 39, 40, 58–60, 119, 120; see also Oedipal conflicts; sexual behavior

sexualization of youth culture 122

sexual pleasure 59, 60, 119–121, 282

Sexual Relationship, The (Scharff), 37, 124

sexual revolution 39–41, 119–121

shame: clinical material 13, 233, 236–237, 239, 247; guilt and 61–62; loss of face and 44, 61–63, 233, 239, 247; over divorce 29, 179; psychotherapy and 62; suicidality and 237, 249–250; terminology 62–63, 247; see also humiliation

Shi Qijia 6–9, 11, 14, 16, 138; clinical work 12, 57–58; psychoanalysis and 8, 9; as translator 11, 12

sibling relationships 269

six pocket child 48

slips of the tongue see mistranslation

social trauma 5, 68–71; see also cases, Nicole's family; see also Cultural Revolution, traumatic effects

social unconscious 144–145

splitting 34

spousal abuse see domestic violence and abuse

Spring Festival 49

squiggle game 203–205

Stadter, Michael 61–62, 94, 107, 234, 250

suicidality: adolescent 72, 230, 231, 233, 234, 236, 249–250, 253–255; child 232–233; clinical material 13, 72, 145–146, 178, 233, 234, 236, 237, 243–245, 247, 250, 253–255; criminal justice system and 178; shame and 237, 249–250

teachers 13; therapists as 54; Western 54, 270

teaching in China 9, 10, 13, 16, 52, 54

therapists see psychotherapists

third wheel 281–282

Tong Jun 7, 11, 12, 39, 56

transference: defined 37–38; see also cases, Fei Yang and Fong Jie

transitional objects 36

transitional phenomena 36

translation: challenges of 11, 64; see also mistranslation